Publications of the Algonquian Text Society
Collection de la Société d'édition de textes algonquiens

H.C. Wolfart, *General Editor*

wâskahikaniwiyiniw-âcimowina / Stories of the House People. Told by Peter Vandall and Joe Douquette. Edited, translated and with a glossary by Freda Ahenakew, 1987.

The Dog's Children: Anishinaabe Texts Told by Angeline Williams. Edited and translated by Leonard Bloomfield, newly edited and with a glossary by John D. Nichols, 1991.

kinêhiyâwiwininaw nêhiyawêwin / The Cree Language is Our Identity: The La Ronge Lectures of Sarah Whitecalf. Edited, translated and with a glossary by H.C. Wolfart & Freda Ahenakew, 1993.

âtalôhkâna nêsta tipâcimôwina / Cree Legends and Narratives from the West Coast of James Bay. Told by Simeon Scott *et al.* Text and translation, edited and with a glossary by C. Douglas Ellis, 1995.

ana kâ-pimwêwêhahk okakêskihkêmowina / The Counselling Speeches of Jim Kâ-Nîpitêhtêw. Edited, translated and with a glossary by Freda Ahenakew & H.C. Wolfart, 1998.

âh-âyîtaw isi ê-kî-kiskêyihtahkik maskihkiy / They Knew Both Sides of Medicine: Cree Tales of Curing and Cursing Told by Alice Ahenakew. Edited, translated and with a glossary by H.C. Wolfart & Freda Ahenakew, 2000.

Hinóno'éinoo3ítoono / Arapaho Historical Traditions, Told by Paul Moss. Edited, translated and with a glossary by Andrew Cowell & Alonzo Moss, Sr., 2005.

Sarah Whitecalf (bottom row, centre) at five or six years of age. The boy to her right is Smith Atimoyoo, born 1915.

mitoni niya nêhiyaw – nêhiyaw-iskwêw mitoni niya

Cree is who I truly am – me, I am truly a Cree woman

A life told by Sarah Whitecalf

Edited and translated by H.C. Wolfart and Freda Ahenakew, with a preface and photographs by Ted Whitecalf

UNIVERSITY OF MANITOBA PRESS

mitoni niya nêhiyaw: nêhiyaw-iskwêw mitoni niya/
Cree is who I truly am: Me, I am truly a Cree woman

25 24 23 22 21 1 2 3 4 5

All royalties from the sale of this book revert to the Algonquian Text Society's Publication Fund.

University of Manitoba Press
Winnipeg, Manitoba, Canada
Treaty 1 Territory
uofmpress.ca

Cataloguing data available from Library and Archives Canada
Publications of the Algonquian Text Society, ISSN 0829-755X
ISBN 978-0-88755-942-6 (PAPER)
ISBN 978-0-88755-946-4 (PDF)
ISBN 978-0-88755-944-0 (EPUB)
ISBN 978-0-88755-948-8 (BOUND)

Photographs by Ted Whitecalf

Printed in Canada

This book has been published with the help of a grant from the Federation for the Humanities and Social Sciences, through the Awards to Scholarly Publications Program, using funds provided by the Social Sciences and Humanities Research Council of Canada.

The publication of this volume was made through the support of the Cree Language Project at the University of Manitoba and financial assistance from the Saskatchewan Indian Cultural College in Saskatoon and the Saskatchewan Cree Language Retention Committee.

The University of Manitoba Press acknowledges the financial support for its publication program provided by the Government of Canada through the Canada Book Fund, the Canada Council for the Arts, the Manitoba Department of Sport, Culture, and Heritage, the Manitoba Arts Council, and the Manitoba Book Publishing Tax Credit.

Funded by the Government of Canada | Canada

CONTENTS

Preface

Ted Whitecalf

This book is the work of my late mother, Sarah Whitecalf, who recorded her reminiscences for two friends she made late in life: Freda Ahenakew and Chris Wolfart.

The recordings on which the present volume is based are highly personal. They were made on various occasions over the course of almost three years, beginning in March 1988 and ending in December 1990, less than a year before her death on 1 October 1991. Some of these recordings were made at my mom's in Saskatoon or at the late Freda Ahenakew's home at Muskeg Lake. Other interviews were done in the recording studio of the Linguistics Department at the University of Manitoba or during one of the many other trips on which my mom went with Freda. She was often in the company of her friends, including for example Cecilia Masuskapoe, Rosa Longneck and Grace Ahenakew, but sometimes also younger Cree speakers such as her grandsons Ricky and Donny Gladue.

My mother and Freda Ahenakew (also known as Freda Greyeyes) had met only a few years earlier – it was the late Smith Atimoyoo who introduced them when Freda was looking for a truly fluent Cree speaker. She wanted him to help with her *Nêhiyaw-waciscwanis,* where young children would be looked after in an exclusively Cree-speaking setting. My mom was a great role-model for the children, speaking nothing but Cree!

The language my mother speaks in these stories is the classical form of Plains Cree, or 'High Cree' as it is often called. Her choice of words and the way she constructs her sentences beautifully match the literary form of traditional Cree *âcimowina*. Since the chapters were recorded over the course of three years, some topics come up more than once; this increases the effect of repetition which is typical of spoken literature.

The chapters of this book are truly personal stories of my late mother's life, they provide sharp insights into her own experiences and, especially, her own views and memories and her own thoughts and perspectives. At the same time, to be sure, they may also be read as a representative account of the lives lived by Plains Cree women on the Saskatchewan prairies over much of the twentieth century. Chris and Freda's interpretation of my mother's words add another flavour to what might be heard by those wanting to learn from her teachings.

Family photographs have been used in this book to be more telling of her life at home. I also took a few additional pictures to illustrate the locales at Sweetgrass First Nation where some of the scenes in this book are set.

Introduction

H.C. Wolfart

These memoirs present a Cree woman's view of her world. It is a highly personal document based on the spoken word of the late Sarah Whitecalf (1919-1991), whose reminiscences are here printed in Cree exactly as she recorded them (and without any reference to the English translation on the opposite page). At the same time, her experiences and reactions are also representative of the lives lived by Plains Cree women on the Canadian prairies over much of the twentieth century. Taken together, these chapters constitute an autobiography of great personal authority and rare authenticity.

This book gives absolute priority to the spoken record, preserving the original Cree choice of words and sentence structures and, of course, Cree narrative strategies as faithfully as permitted by the printed page. The translation also follows the original Cree text as closely as possible, even if this sometimes results in awkward turns of phrase in English. But the English translation is at all times strictly secondary to the Cree original, retaining not only all repetitions – both within the individual texts and across the chapters recorded on separate occasions – but also all interrupted sentences and false starts of the kind that are typically smoothed over in a standard translation. If the English style of these translations should on occasion seem strange to readers expecting conventional English prose, we hope that it will in its close rendition of the Cree text prove engaging to those reading the texts for their literary or linguistic, historical or ethnological interest. Primary documents by any standard, the integrally preserved texts which make up this book are here printed as they were spoken.

THE AUTHOR

Sarah Whitecalf was born on 12 May 1919 at *Môsômininâhk*, literally 'amongst the Moosomins'. At that time, *Môsômin*'s band had only recently been moved to *Kinosêwi-sâkahikanihik* 'at Fish Lake' (officially referred to as "Jackfish Lake" and often also subsumed under the regional term "at Cochin") from its earlier site between the Battle River and the North Saskatchewan, where his reserve had originally been adjacent to those of *Kâ-pitikow* / Thunderchild and *Wîhkasko-kisêyin* / Sweetgrass not far west of Battleford.

The forced relocation to a site about 35 km away from their former reserve did not, apparently, sever the close ties between *Môsômin*'s people and those of *Wîhkasko-kisêyin,* who had remained at *Nakiwacîhk* (*lit.* 'at the abrupt edge of the hill'). When Sarah Whitecalf was about four years old, her widowed mother married a man from Sweetgrass, and she herself went to live there about ten years later and, after another three or four years, married into the Sweetgrass band. In the intervening years, between the ages of four and (roughly) fourteen, Sarah Whitecalf frequently went back and forth between her grandparents' house at Moosomin, where she had remained, and her mother's at Sweetgrass.

Most of her childhood, thus, was spent with her maternal grandparents, *Kâ-pêtwêwêmât* and *Osâkikwanêwisk* (who are introduced more fully, along with their colonial names Louis Applegarth and Catherine, in chapters 1 and 3). Their formative influence must have been all the stronger as the household consisted only of these three, and Sarah was not sent to school. The traumatic experience of losing one daughter, already practically an adult, at the Thunderchild Residential School at Delmas without even being told of her illness by the nuns, had caused Sarah's mother to resist the pleas of the local priest (Albert Lacombe's nephew Ernest Lacombe), leaving her daughter a monolingual Cree speaker.

As a consequence, Sarah Whitecalf remained for her entire life what she put most succinctly (though, characteristically, in the rhetorical form of a chiastic reversal) as follows:

> *..., êwako ohci mitoni niya nêhiyaw,*
> *nêhiyaw-iskwêw mitoni niya;*
> '..., and because of that, I am definitely a Cree,
> as for me, I am definitely a Cree woman;'

Even when she moved to Saskatoon, where she spent the better part of her last twenty years, she essentially spoke no English. She died on 1 October 1991.

Sarah Whitecalf's literary gifts are manifest in the substantial body of texts – many of them the fruit of their travels together – which she recorded for Freda Ahenakew over the course of her last few years.[1]

THE FIRST FOUR CHAPTERS: BECOMING A CREE WOMAN

The book begins with Sarah Whitecalf reviewing her life history, giving special prominence to the rôles played by her grandparents and her mother. While the four chapters, representing texts recorded on different occasions, all deal in one way or another with the exigencies of a subsistence economy, they vary in emphasis.

Chapter 1 tells of a nine-year old child being introduced to the domestic chores that will be an inescapable preoccupation for

---

1 The first volume of her texts to be published was a set of brief lectures given on one of their trips to a group of Freda Ahenakew's students: *kinêhiyâwiwininaw nêhiyawêwin / The Cree Language is Our Identity: The La Ronge Lectures of Sarah Whitecalf* (edited, translated and with a glossary by H.C. Wolfart & Freda Ahenakew, Publications of the Algonquian Text Society, Winnipeg: University of Manitoba Press, 1993).

the rest of her life. The most remarkable passage in this text is the author's laconic report of her marriage:

> *êkosi, piyisk nikî-miskamâson nâpêw, nikî-miskotâtonân, ...*
> 'and so, finally, I found a man for myself, we found each other, ...'

The form of words used in this account suggests that, contrary to common practice, the choice of husband was hers.

Chapter 2 touches on the ravages of the Spanish influenza epidemic of 1918-20, ending in a brief but compelling account of her older sister's death at residential school. As a consequence of these disasters, Sarah Whitecalf in effect grew up, as she stresses repeatedly, as an only child.

In chapter 3, she contrasts her childhood and youth among the Moosomins, *môsômininâhk*, and her adult life at *Nakiwacîhk* / Sweetgrass. While all Cree narrative tends to be punctuated by interjections from the audience, indicating responses ranging from mere attentiveness or recognition to approval or astonishment, this chapter over large stretches takes the form of a dialogue between Sarah Whitecalf and Freda Ahenakew (and, to a much lesser extent, H.C. Wolfart). The early part of the chapter concentrates on the author's grandparents; later she is asked about various sets of siblings and cousins, and her responses show a constant emphasis on having been brought up as an only child. Finally, she recalls a number of the Sweetgrass figures who had dictated their reminiscences to Leonard Bloomfield in 1925 and, in particular, her step-grandfather *Kâ-miyokîsihkwêw* / Fineday, the primary authority for David G. Mandelbaum's ethnography of 1936.[2]

2 See Leonard Bloomfield, *Sacred Stories of the Sweet Grass Cree* (National Museum of Canada Bulletin 60, Ottawa, 1930) and *Plains Cree Texts* (American Ethnological Society Publication 16, New York); Mandelbaum's thesis was published as *The Plains Cree* in 1940 and reissued in 1979 (Canadian Plains Research Centre, University of Regina); for a full biography of *Kâ-miyokîsihkwêw* see now also Garry Radison, *Fine Day: Plains Cree Warrior, Shaman and Elder* (Calgary, Smoke Ridge Books, 2013).

Chapter 4 goes into more detail on many of the domestic chores entrusted to the young woman. It also includes another account of her mother's refusal to send her to residential school. In her recollections of the first year of her married life, she once more pays special attention to the duties of a wife as they had been impressed upon her by her grandmother.

THE SECOND FOUR CHAPTERS: BEING A CREE WOMAN

The four texts constituting the second part of this book deal with specific events manifesting a life-changing force. They range from a distressing marriage to murder committed in a jealous rage, and they are altogether exceptional in portraying the personal feelings of a Cree woman forced to deal with a husband's alcoholism and the immense loneliness she suffered while tending a relative's children in a place far away from home – and, apparently just as debilitating, away from the company of other women.

In chapter 5 the author retells her mother's account of her arranged marriage at eighteen to a widower seen as much older than herself (probably in his thirties):

> *«êêkwa ê-pakwâtak awa kêhtê-nâpêw,» itwêw;*
> *«wahwâ, nikî-pakwâtên mâna mistah,» îtwêw;*
> '«now I hated this old man,» she said;
> «oh my, I used to hate it utterly,» she said;'

This text thus constitutes a valuable addition to the small set of documents recording an unguarded statement of a woman's view of what was essentially a forced marriage. The practicalities of life, to be sure, take up the major part of the text: the camp moved south into Flathead country to join the lucrative bounty hunt for coyotes, with a plentiful supply of illicit beef a welcome bonus, but a great deal of worry and trouble is caused by the riding escapades of her husband's eight-year-old son. A counterpoint is provided by the relative peace of their winter quarters in apple country, but the travails of the return journey come to a sad climax when she at last reaches home only to find that her older sister had died in her absence.

Chapter 6 is a horrible tale of wife-beating as a prelude to murder and suicide. It illuminates some of the structures and stresses of Plains Cree society as it functioned on the North Saskatchewan River half a century into the reserve period. Speaking as a witness, Sarah Whitecalf masterfully captures the helpless agony of the victim's parents in the face of their daughter's suffering, the deference shown to the headman, the importance of forebodings and portents, and not least the care for the dying, the dead and the infirm survivors – and her account is all the more revealing as these issues are quite incidental to the subject and the plot.

An autobiographical account or *âcimisowin* in the narrowest sense, chapter 7 stands out amongst the recorded instances of the genre. In carefully relating the author's emotional state, it offers a glimpse into the inner world of Cree existence that is extremely rare. With respect to Cree historical and literary norms, moreover, this text demonstrates that the factual character of an *âcimisowin* or *âcimowin* is not compromised, as readers used to classical European literatures might expect, by the presence within it of supernatural phenomena. On a more mundane level, the detailed account of Sarah Whitecalf's journey back from Montana is remarkable for the ingenuity and tenacity with which she makes her way while travelling alone for the first time in her life – and without English.

Chapter 8 is the deeply moving portrait of a Cree woman determined to protect her grandchildren even if this requires the unprecedented step of leaving husband and reserve and having to establish herself in town. It is a testament to her extraordinary courage and strength that she rose to break the rules governing a woman's conduct which she had been taught by her grandmother and respected all along to take charge of her own life.

THE THIRD FOUR CHAPTERS: THE SPIRITUAL LIFE

The contemplative essay on mourning practices which opens the first chapter, 9, of the third part leads up to a dramatic scene in which the recently departed son implores his inconsolable father and mother to cease of their grief so that he too might be released. The discussion then turns to the consolations offered by both Cree religion and Roman Catholicism.

The three historical reports or *âcimowina* in chapters 10, 11 and 12 relate a supernatural event that took place at *Nakiwacîhk* within living memory. While the wider significance of the case remains to be explored, even a superficial reading of the text illuminates the interplay of secular, indeed mundane, matters with religious issues and their ritual implementation.

From the perspective of linguistic analysis and philological scholarship, these three versions of "the same text," told on three different occasions and to distinct audiences over a period of almost three years (August 1988 to May 1990), yield a tantalising case study of the structures and processes of oral transmission.

As literary works, these three narratives of a single event splendidly illustrate their genre, which readily includes supernatural figures and their actions in a factual account, established as such by the familiar and carefully identified locale in which both the externally observable and the arcane events are said to have taken place and reconfirmed by the personal authority of named witnesses – in this case one of her step-grandmothers and, most important, the speaker herself.

THE ROLE OF THE EDITORS

The reminiscences and historical accounts which Sarah Whitecalf gave to Freda Ahenakew were spoken Cree texts recorded on a number of occasions between 1989 and 1990.

As shown in the chapter openings and the several kinds of dialogue, the audience addressed by Sarah Whitecalf [SW] in this book from time to time also included Cecilia Masuskapoe [CM],

Rosa Longneck [RL], Grace Ahenakew [GA], Chris Wolfart [HC] and an unidentified Cree speaker [NN] in addition, always, to Freda Ahenakew [FA].

The text of chapter 2 in fact was part of a much longer storytelling session shared by *Kêkêk* / Cecilia Masuskapoe and Sarah Whitecalf and originally published in Cree only.[3]

The careful transcription and presentation of these audio-recordings, including the insertion of punctuation marks to show the boundaries of clauses and sentences; of double and single quotation marks to indicate direct speech and other cited words and passages; and the division of the text into paragraphs and larger discourse units (identified in print by roman numerals), are the work of the editors. In its initial phase, from 1989 to 1996, this work was carried out jointly by the late Freda Ahenakew and H.C. Wolfart.[4] Continuing over another two decades, the later stages of linguistic analysis, editorial preparation and translation with their seemingly endless cycles of review and revision (and the errors and infelicities which inevitably remain) are the sole responsibility of the latter.

All editorial additions (mainly of word- or preverb-final vowels elided before a word- or stem-initial vowel in connected speech, or of the occasional word interrupted in the course of narration), including chapter and paragraph numbers, are typographically set off by square brackets to keep them distinct from the text itself. The special symbol -~ is attached to fragmentary words, and –~ marks interrupted sentences.

---

3 This text was originally published as chapter 3, section IV of an entire volume exclusively printed in Cree: *piko kîkway ê-nakacihtât: kêkêk otâcimowina ê-nêhiyawastêki*, mitoni ê-âh-itwêt mâna Cecilia Masuskapoe, itasinahamiyiwa ôhi nîso, H.C. Wolfart êkwa Freda Ahenakew [*There's Nothing She Can't Do: Kêkêk's Autobiography Published in Cree,* Exactly as told by Cecilia Masuskapoe, in a critical edition by H.C. Wolfart & Freda Ahenakew] (Algonquian and Iroquoian Linguistics, Memoir 21, 2010).

4 (with the gratefully acknowledged support of the Social Sciences and Humanities Research Council of Canada)

The Cree title of the book itself and the Cree chapter titles are taken from Sarah Whitecalf's texts.

Given the wealth of issues raised by these texts, detailed commentaries would have gone beyond the scope of this book. Studies of the texts as literary, historical and ethnological documents and a detailed treatment of the philological problems encountered and their editorial resolution are scheduled to appear separately.

In presenting the text unaltered, in a form that reflects the *viva voce* performance as closely as print permits, we respect the speaker's prerogative to keep her own history; in leaving the protagonists undisguised, we acknowledge the fact that, in small communities, pseudonyms offer a thin veil at most; against the paternalistic impulse to maintain an unbridgeable divide between participant and observer narratives, the Cree texts we have been publishing are an attempt to document an autonomous representation of what actually happened.

EDITORIAL CONVENTIONS AND SPECIAL SYMBOLS

xxxx	[text in roman type] primary language (Cree in the text, English in the translation)
xxxx	[text in italic type] secondary language (English in the text, Cree in the translation)
«xxxx»	[guillemets] quoted speech
‘xxxx’	[single quotation marks] [1] quoted speech (if embedded within quoted speech) [2] cited word
″xxxx″	[double quotation marks] quoted speech embedded within two outer layers of quoted speech
–	[long hyphen] syntactic or rhetorical break (usually sharper than those marked by comma or semicolon) within a sentence
( )	[parentheses] parenthetical insertion (usually spoken at lower pitch or volume)
-~-	[wave-hyphen within the word] fragmentary word, resumed
-~	[wave-hyphen at the end of the word] fragmentary word
–~	[long hyphen and wave-hyphen following the word] fragmentary sentence

[a]	[roman type enclosed in square brackets] editorially supplied word-final vowel (elided under the rules of vowel combination and restored on the basis of vocalic, prosodic or syntactic evidence)
[*xxxx*]	[italic type enclosed in square brackets] editorial comment (including such standard comments as [*laughs*], [*laughter*], [*gesture*], [*clap*], etc.)
[*sic*]	['indeed'] confirmation that the preceding word is correctly printed (usually in the case of an uncommon or otherwise remarkable form, e.g., minor idiosyncracies, dialect discrepancies, slips of the tongue)
[*sc.*]	['that is'] proposed emendation or completion of a fragment; explication or elaboration; omitted where an editorial insertion, marked by square brackets, simply blends into an English sentence
[*?sic*]	['really?'] caution that the identification of the preceding word remains in doubt
[*lit.*]	['literally'] literal translation of a technical term or geographical name

mitoni niya nêhiyaw
– nêhiyaw-iskwêw mitoni niya

Cree is who I truly am
– me, I am truly a Cree woman

I

Becoming a Cree woman

Sarah Whitecalf and Freda Ahenakew with children at the *Nêhiyaw-Waciscwanis*, c. 1988.

1

êkosi nikî-pê-ay-itâcihonân

This has been our way of life

êkosi nikî-pê-ay-itâcihonân

[FA:] *Sarah Whitecalf* awa, nakiwacîhk ohci kâ-wî-pîkiskwâtikoyahk anohc, *sixty-eight* êkwa ê-wî-ati-nâtahk. mêkwâc ôma ê-ây-~ ê-~ ôt[a] ê-wâh-wîcihikoyahk ôma kâ-kakwê-sipwêpayihtâyahk kanawêyimâwasowin; wîst êkota ê-wâh-wîtapimât ê-pa-pâh-pîkiskwâtât ôh âwâsisa, mâk ê-wî-wiy-âcimostâkoyahk [*sic*] tânisi wiyawâw ê-kî-ay-is-ôhpikinâwasocik, tânisi –~, êkwa mîna tânisi ê-kî-pê-is-ôhpikiniht wiya, ~-ohpikihiht, tânis ê-kî-isi-pimâcihocik. êkosi.

[SW:] mhm!

[1] â, ayihk, mistahi nitatamihik aw ôta iskwêw, ôma kâ-wî-isîhcikâsit, môy konita ôm ôta kâ-wî-pîkiskwêhit, nim-~ nikîskisamâk, êkwa mîna sôniyâwa nimiyik. êkosi, tâpwê anima kwayask ê-tôtahk êwako, ê-tâpiyinîhkâhtahk, nêhiyawi-kîkway ê-nôhtê-kiskêyihtahk, ê-nôhtê-pêhtahk. êkosi, êyiwêhk ê-isi-kaskihtâyân nika-kakwê-tôtên t-êsi-pîkiskwêyân. tâpiskôt mîna, otâkosihk, êkotowahk, kêht-~ osk-âyak nikî-pê-nâtikwak, mitâtahto-tipahikan ê-ispayik, êkotê nikî-nitawi-pîkiskwân, âta wiya namôy ê-pêyakoyân, kotak iskwêw nikî-wîcihik mâna, têpiyâhk mâna ê-nâh-nâtamawit wîst îta âskaw ta-pîkiskwêt. êkosi, tâpwê ê-isi-kaskihtâyân nikî-kakwê-kitotâwak êkota osk-âyak, kîkwây

This has been our way of life

[FA:] This is Sarah Whitecalf from *Nakiwacîhk* [Sweetgrass] who is going to speak to us today, she is approaching the age of sixty-eight. At the present time she is helping us here as we try to get a day-care running; she is there with the children herself and speaking to them but [now] she is going to tell us how they themselves used to raise their children and also how she herself came to be raised and how they used to make their living. That is it.

[SW:] mhm.

[Prologue]

[1] Well, I am very grateful to this woman here for the way she is treating me, it is not for nothing that she is asking me to speak here, she has formally presented me with tobacco and she has also given me money. Thus she is truly doing the proper thing and performing the fitting ritual since she wants to know about Cree matters and wants to hear about them. And so, to the extent of my ability I will try to do that and speak. Yesterday also, for example, that kind, some young people, had come fetch me, I had gone to speak there at ten o'clock, although I was not alone, another woman had come with me, she was only there to help me out from time to time when she too would sometimes speak. Thus it is true, I tried to the best of my ability to talk to the young people

tahto ê-nôhtê-pê-kiskêyihtahkik, êkosi kî-nôhtê-kiskêyihtamwak, tânis ê-kî-pê-isi-awâsisîwiyân, tânis ê-kî-pê-is-ôhpikihikawiyân. êkosi, iyikohk ê-kaskihtâyân, êwako nipê-âcimostawâwak, tânisi ê-kî-pê-isi-paminikawiyân kâ-kî-pê-awâsisîwiyân, môy kîkway nikâtâtotên, mîna namôy ninêpêwimon; ninakayâskên, tânitahtwâw êkwa êkota, êkosi nikî-pê-isi-mamisîwâtikwak, êkosi mîna mihcêtiwak, êkota kâ-kî-apicik, anima kâ-kî-wîtapimakik ôk ôsk-âyak, ê-ati-masinahahkik tânis ê-itwêyân.

[I]

[2] êkos êkwa, kik-âcimostâtinâwâw, nêhiyawi-kîkway kâ-nôhtê-kiskêyihtamêk, tânisi k-êtâcimostawakik anik ânita, namôy ômatowihk [*points to audio-recorder*] otinamwak nipîkiskwêwin, mâka masinahikêwak osk-âyak, kahkiyaw ê-têtipêwêpicik, ati-masinahikêwak ê-pîkiskwêyân. êkos êkwa, nipê-âcimostawâwak tânis ê-kî-pê-is-ôhpikihikawiyân, ê-pê-awâsisîwiyân, ôtê 'môsômininâhk' k-êsiyîhkâtêk askiy, êkotê nitaskîhkâninân, kâ-kî-ayâyân, êkot[ê] ê-kî-tas-ôhpikihikawiyân ê-pê-awâsisîwiyân. êkosi mîna, nikî-pê-pêyakôsâniwin, namôy âta miton ê-ohci-pêyakoyân, mâka nîtisânak kahkiyaw ê-kî-mêsci-pôni-pimâtisicik, niya piko ê-kî-iskwahpinêyân; êkos êkwa, mistahi nikî-sâkihik –~ nikî-sâkihikwak kêhtê-ayak, nôhkom nimosôm. êkwa nikâwiy (ê-nêwopiponêyân êsa kâ-kî-pê-onâpêmit ôta *Sweetgrass*, êwako 'nakiwacîhk' k-êsiyîhkâtêk askîhkân, nitaskîhkâninân), êkosi niya nêtê ê-~ nikî-kisâtinikawin môsôminêw-âskîhkânihk, êkotê nikî-tasi-kanawêyimikawin. mê-mîskoc [*sic*] âta wiya nikî-pimohtahikawin, kâ-kas-~ êkâ ta-kaskêyihtamân, nikâwiy ê-kî-pê-itohtahikawiyân, êkwa mîna nikâwiy êkotê ê-kî-pê-nitawâpamit.

there about as many things as they wanted to know, and in this way they wanted to know how it had been when I was a child and how I had been brought up. Thus I told them as much as I could about how I had been treated when I was a child, I do not hide anything in telling about that and I am not shy in speaking; I am used to it, having spoken there many times, and thus they have long relied on me for this, and so there were many who were sitting there when I sat with these young people, and they took notes on what I said.

[**I**] [Childhood and Youth, Marriage and Motherhood]

[2] Now then I will tell you about the Cree things which you want to know about, what I told them at that place, they did not record my speech on that kind [*points to audio-recorder*] but the young people took notes, all of them sitting in a circle, they took notes as I spoke. Now then I told them how it was when I was being brought up as a child over there at *Môsômininâhk* [Moosomin], as our reserve is called, that was the place where I used to live, that was where I was being brought up as a child. And I also was an only child, although I had not really been the only child, but all my siblings had died, without exception, I had been the only one to survive; now then she really loved me –~ the old people loved me, my grandmother and my grandfather. And my mother (I was four years old reportedly when she had come and married a man here at Sweetgrass, that reserve which is called *Nakiwacîhk* [Sweetgrass], our reserve), and thus I had been kept back at *Môsôminêw-âskîhkânihk* [Moosomin Reserve] and continued to be taken care of there. They did take me back and forth so I would not be lonesome, bringing me back to my mother, and my mother would also come to see me over there.

[3] êkos êkotê nikî-tas-ôy-ohpikihikawin, â, kî-kitimâkisiwak kêhtê-ayak, mitoni kî-kêhtê-ayiwiwak kâ-kî-kanawêyimicik – nôhkom, mitoni kî-nôtikwêwiw, êkwa mîna nimosôm, miton êtikwê têpakohp tahtomitanaw ayiwâk kî-itahtopiponêw nimosôm. êkos êkwa, êwako nitâtotên, nama kîkway sôniyâhkêwin ohci-pê-ayâw nimosôm, osâm ê-kî-kêhtê-ayiwit. kîkwây [*sic*] piko kâ-pipohk, kîkway sôniyâhkêwin ê-kî-kaskihtamâsot nimosôm, ê-kî-pakitahwât ê-nôcikinosêwêt, êkota ohci ê-kî-atâwâkêt kinosêwa kâ-piponiyik, êwako piko ê-kî-wâpahtamân kinos-~ ê-kî-sôniyâhkâkêt êkotowahk nimosôm. êkwa niya, nôhkom mâna nikî-wa-wîtapimâw, nikî-ka-kanawêyimik.

[4] êkwa kâ-nîpihk, nayêstaw kîkwây [*sic*], maskihkiy kî-mônahamwak ayisiyiniwak êkospîhk, 'omînisîhkês' [*sic*] kî-isiyîhkâtamwak ê-nêhiyawêhk, mâka ê-kî-atâwâkêhk anima maskihkiy. êkotowahk piko ê-kî-sôniyâhkâkêcik kêhcê-ayak, ahpô nîsta mâna nikî-osîhtamâkawin kîkway ta-mônahaskwâkêyân. êkota mâna, k-âti-nîpihk ôma, kâ-sâkikihk anima maskihkiy, nikiskisin mâna ê-kî-sipwêpiciyâhk, konit îtê pâtot-âyihk [*sic*] ê-papâ-wîkisiyâhk, êkwa mâna ê-kî-mônahikêt nôhkom, niya mîna, nimosôm. êkwa, cikêmâ nama kîkway kaskihcikêwin, nititwân, nimosôm ê-kî-tôtahk, êwako pikw ânim ê-kî-kakwê-isi-sôniyâhkêsicik mâna, t-ôh-pîhtwâcik, êtikwê kîkway êkos îsi t-âyâcik, cikêmâ kayâs kî-wêhtakihcikâniwiw, namôy tâpiskôc anohc; iyikohk kahkiyaw kîkway kâ-sôhkakihtêk.

[5] êkos êkwa, tânis ê-kî-pê-isi-~, êwakw ânim ê-kî-pê-isi-kakwê-pimâcihocik wîstawâw kêhtê-ayak kâ-kî-ohpikihicik, ê-kî-~ kayâs kî-mihcêtiwak pihêwak, 'ê-kî-nîmihitocik' kî-itwâniwiw mâna k-ôski-nîpihk. êkotowahk mâcika mâna wiya nimosôm ê-kî-papâ-nôcihât, ê-kî-tâpakwamawât, itê ôma kâ-matwê-pâh-pêhtâkosiyit, êkotowahk

[3] In this way I had gone on being brought up over there, well, the old people were poor, they were very old when they took care of me – my grandmother was a very old woman and my grandfather also, my grandfather must in fact have been more than seventy years old. Now then, that I have already told about, that my grandfather did not have any way of earning money, he was too old. The only thing in the winter, the only means my grandfather had of earning some money for himself was to set nets and catch fish, and with that he used to sell fish in winter, that was the only thing I used to see with which my grandfather earned some money. Now as for me, I used to stay at home with my grandmother and she used to take care of me.

[4] Now in the summer, there was only one thing, in those days the people dug seneca-root, *omînisîhkês* they called it in Cree, but this seneca-root used to be sold. That was the only way of earning money for the old people, and even for me they made something to dig seneca-root with. At that time, in early summer, when the seneca-root was coming out, I remember that we used to move camp, moving our little camp about somewhere into the wilds, then my grandmother would dig, and I too and also my grandfather. Now of course there wasn't any earning power, as I said, my grandfather used to do that, that was the only way for them to earn a little money to use for smoking and to have things like that, I guess, of course things were cheap in the old days, not like today; when everything is so expensive.

[5] Now then, that was how they tried to make a living, the old people who raised me, in the old days prairie chickens used to be plentiful, 'they are dancing' one used to say of them at the beginning of summer. That kind for instance my grandfather used to go about and pursue, he used to set snares for them wherever

kî-mâh-misi-nipahêw, êkwa pêskis ê-kî-tâpakwêt mâna nimosôm. hâw, êkoni mîciwin êkosi ê-kî-kakwê-isi-pihkohtâcik, êkwa anim ê-kakwê-sôniyâhkêsicik. êkosi, êkos ê-kî-pê-isi-pimâcihikawiyân. êkwa, kîkwây anima askîhkânîwi-sôniyâw, kat-~ tahtwâw kâ-miyoskamik, anohc kêyâpic êwako kipimipayihikonânaw, niyânanwâpisk kâ-miyitohk. êkospîhk ê-kî-wêhtakihcikêhk, kispêw mâna kahkiyaw ôtênâhk ê-kî-pê-itâwahitohk, niyânanwâpisk an[a] [*sic*] ê-pê-ohci-pimohcêhk nâh-niyânanwâpisk, ôki kâ-mâh-mihcêticik, êyiwêhk mâna kî-osôniyâmisiwak, mâka wiya niyanân tâpiskôc ê-kî-nistiyâhk piko, êko-~ niyânanosâp tahtwâpisk mâna, âhci piko mâna nîstanân ê-kî-pê-ispiciyâhk ôta, ôtênâhk, êwako '*North Battleford*' k-êsiyîhkâtamihk.

[6] êkosi, îh, êkot[a] ân[i] êkon ânihi piko niy ê-kî-pê-wâpahtamân sôniyâhkêwin, êkwa nôhkom, kwayask nikî-pê-kakwê-kiskinohamâk êtikwê mâna kîkway, mîna namôya nôh-pakitinikawin niya, ta-papâ-kâh-kiyokêpahtâyân konit ômis îsi, ta-papâ-mêtawêyân ayahtikamik [*sic*], ta-papâ-ay-ispahtâyân, mitoni tâpwê piko pêyakwanohk nikî-ka-kanawêyimikawin. nôhkom ê-kakwê-~ kwayask êtikwê ê-kî-kakwê-is-ôhpikihit, êkâ ta-papâmi-môhcowiyân ayahtokamik [*sic*]; êkosi nikî-kaskihik.

[7] êkwa, êkwa mîna, nayêstaw k-~ ê-kî-asamihcik kêhtê-ayak kayâs, kîkwây anim âstamispîhk êkwa, mistahi kîkway kî-asamâwak, asahtowikamikohk ê-kî-isitâpâsocik mâna; kôhkôsowiyin, êkwa pahkwêsikan, êkwa 'wâpayôminak' nitisiyîhkâtânânak ê-nêhiyawêyâhk, êkwa nihtiy. hâw, êkon ânihi pêyakwâw pêyak-pîsim ê-kî-ohci-mîcisocik mîna; êkosi.

[8] êkwa nimosôm –~ êkwa, kêkâ-mitâtaht ê-itahtopiponêyân piyisk, êwako mâna nikiskisin mîna, êkwa êkota ê-kî-kakwê-mâc-âtoskahit mitoni nôhkom, ê-kî-kakwê-kiskinohamawit kîkway. nikî-kaskihtân, kêkâ-mitâtaht ê-itahtopiponêyân niya, ê-kî-kakwê-kisîpêkinamâsoyân

they could be heard, he killed lots of that kind, and at the same time my grandfather also used to set snares [*sc.* for rabbits]. Well, these are the things they did to try and obtain food, and trying to earn a little money. In this way they were making a living for me. Now, what is the point of that Treaty payment each spring that still goes on for us today when the amount given is five dollars. At that time everything used to be cheap, everybody still would gather in town, travelling on the five dollars, the five dollars per person, and those that had many in their families had a little more money, but we for our part were only three, for example, and we received fifteen dollars, but we still would move here too, to the town of North Battleford as it is called.

[6] And so, look, these were the only ways I saw of earning money, now my grandmother must have tried to teach me things properly, and I also was not allowed to run around visiting just like that, without purpose, nor to go about playing in other people's houses, to run about there, sure enough, I was very much taken care of in one place only. My grandmother must have tried to raise me properly so that I would not fool around in other houses; in short, she used to be in charge of me.

[7] Now, now also, the old people used to be given only rations in the old days, in more recent times now they were provided with lots of food when they used to drive to the ration-house; bacon, and flour, and rice, *wâpayominak* we called that in Cree, and tea. Well, they also subsisted on these provisions handed out once a month; that was it.

[8] Now my grandfather –~ now when I was nine years old at last, that I remember also, now at that point my grandmother tried to begin to put me to work, she tried to teach me things. As for me, when I was nine years old I was able to try to wash my own clothes and my grandmother taught me how; my grandmother

nicayiwinisisa, nôhkom ê-kiskinohamawit; ê-kî-sîkinamawit mahkahkohk nôhkom, kâ-wî-~ kâh-kisâkamisahki nipiy, êkwa êkota nicayiwinisisa, niya ê-kisîpêkinikêstamâsoyân; êkwa, piyisk pâhkohkwêhona, kâsîhiyâkanâkana [*sic*], aspiskwêsimonêkinwa, êkoni ê-yâhkasiki, t-êsi-miyo-kaskihtâyân t-êsi-miyo-kisîpêkinamân; êkosi mân ê-kî-~, êkota êkos ê-kî-isi-kisî-~-isi-kiskinohamawit êwako nîkân nôhkom. piyisk, ê-kî-wiyascikêyân mâna, ê-wiyascikêtisahot nôhkom, piyisk ê-kâsîhiyâkanêyân; êkoni acoskêwinis[a] ê-kî-tôtamân, piyisk ê-kî-wêpâhtakahikêyân mâna, piyisk nipêwin ê-kanâtascamâsosiyân [*sic*], it[a] ê-ohci-waniskâyân. êkos êkwa, misakâmê êkosi nikî-ati-ay-isi-papâmihisosin, êyiwêhk ê-is-~, tâpitawi, tâpitawi nôhkom tahto-kîsikâw êkos ê-kî-isi-kiskinohamawit; piyisk nikî-kîsi-oskinîkiskwêwin, piyisk nikî-kîs-ôhpikihikwak ôki kêhtê-ayak.

[9] tânitahto êtikwê ê-itahtopiponêt nimosôm, miton êkwa ê-kisêyinîwit, kâ-kî-mâtahpinêt ê-âhkosit. êkos êkwa, piyisk niwanihânân nimosôm, pôni-pimâtisiw. êkot[ê] âta wiya kahkiyaw êkwa kî-mihcêtinâniwiw.

[10] êkos êkwa, êkota êcik ânim êkwa ê-kî-kisipipayik, ôma môsôminêw-âskîhkân ta-pê-nakatamân, cikêm[â] êkwa, mitoni ta-kî-kitimâkisiyâhk nôhkom, nam âwiyak êkwa ta-pamihikoyâhk, nam âwiyak ta-wîc-âyâmâyâhk. êkos êkwa, êkot[a] êkwa nikâwiy kâ-kî-pê-otinikoyâhk êkwa, ê-pê-kîwêhtahikoyâhk ôta, nakiwacîw-~-askîhkânihk, êkot[a] êkwa nôhkom nikî-pê-isi-kîwêhtahikawinân. nêm êkwa nîkinân nikî-nakatênân, nêtê. mâk âh-~, âhci piko pêyak-pipon êkotê nikî-isi-kîwêhtahikawinân, nôhkom ê-pê-~ ê-kâh-kaskêyihtahk, pêyak-pipon nikî-nitawi-piponisinân, mâka namôy ê-nîsiyâhk nôhkom, nikâwiy nikî-pê-wîc-âyâmikonânak, pêskis ê-pê-pakitahwâcik. êkos êkota ohc êkwa ê-miyoskamik

poured water in the tub for me, having first heated the water, and then I washed my own clothes, and later I washed towels and dish-towels and pillow cases, as these were light so that I could readily manage to wash them; and this my grandmother taught me first. In due course I would set the table when my grandmother sent me to do it, and then I would wash the dishes; those were the chores I performed, and next I would sweep the floors, and finally I made my own little bed from which I had gotten up. Now in this way I gradually came to look after myself in all things for my grand-mother kept teaching me all the time, all the time, every day; at last I was fully a young woman, at last these old people had fully brought me up to be a young woman.

[9] I wonder how old my grandfather must have been, now he was a very old man when he began to ail and became sick. So now in due course we lost my grandfather, he died. To be sure, everybody was there now [*sc.* at the wake and funeral].

[10] With that now, as it turned out, our life there had come to an end so that I was to leave *Môsôminêw-âskîhkân* [Moosomin Reserve] behind and that now of course my grandmother and I would be terribly poor, not having anyone to take care of us, no one with whom we might live. So now, at that point now my mother came to get us, she brought us back here, to *Nakiwacîw-âskîhkânihk* [Sweetgrass Reserve], now my grandmother and I had been brought back here. Now we had left our home behind over there. But we were still taken back there for another winter since my grandmother was so lonesome, we went and spent one more winter there, but my grandmother and I were not alone, my mother had come to live with us, besides she had come to fish with nets. So now we came back from there in the spring, and now my

ê-pê-kîwêyâhk, ay-âskaw[i] êkwa êkotê nôhkom otâpacihcikana kî-pê-kâh-kîwêhtatâniwiw *Sweetgrass* isi.

[11] êkosi, piyisk (êkot[a] êkwa, kâ-~ nikâwiy êkwa kâ-kî-kanawêyimikoyâhk); êkosi, piyisk nikî-miskamâson nâpêw, nikî-miskotâtonân, ê-wîc-âyâmak, êkot[a] êkwa, êkos êko-~, êkos êkota kâ-kî-isi-mêcimwâc-âyâyân êkwa nîsta, ôma nakiwacîw-âskîhkânihk. êkosi, êkos êkwa nikî-~, êkota kâ-kî-mêcimwâc-âyâyân, êkwa nâpêw ê-miskamâsoyân; namôy nôh-~ namôy, namôy kinwês nôh-papâ-kakwâtaki-wîkihkêmonân nikêhtê-ayiminânak, ta-wî-~ ta-wîc-âyâmâyâhkok, ta-pakosi-~ ta-pakosihâyâhkok. nikî-kakwê-pamihik nâpêw, ê-wîc-âyâmak oskinîkiw; êkos êkwa, kî-kaskihtâw sêmâk wâskahikan, êwakw ê-pipohk, wâskahikan ê-~ ê-ayâyâhk, wîsta misatimokamik ê-~ ê-osîhtamâsot, ita ê-ay-~ ê-~ misatimwa kwayask kî-wiyahpicikêw, kahkiyaw kîkway kî-âpacihtâw, sôskwâc ê-papâmitâpâsoyâhk.

[12] êkosi, piyisk nitôtawâsimisinân, êkota tasi. êkota nikî-tasi-wa-ohpikihânânak [*sic*] nicawâsimisak, âta wiya namôy mihcêtwâw nôh-pê-taw-~ nôh-pê-otawâsimisin, êkota nikî-tasi-mâyipayin nîswâw nitô-~ nitân-~ ninistamôsânak, t-êtwêyân. êkosi, êkota ohc êkwa, kotakak ê-ayâwakik êkonik êkwa, pikw êkwa, nikî-oy-~ k-ôy-ohpikihakik [*sic*], piyisk nikîs-ôhpikihâwak êkonik, nitawâsimisak; êkoni nipê-ay-itâcihowina [*sic*].

[13] namôy mistahi nânitaw nôh-pê-isi-kakwâtakihikwak nitawâsimisak, mîn ân-~, kî-iyinîsisiwak êkoyikohk, môy nânitaw mistahi nôh-pê-isi-kakwâtakihikwak. tânis ânima kâ-kî-pê-is-ôhpikihikawiyân, êkosi nikî-kakwê-is-ôhpikihâwak nitawâsimisak, êkâ mistahi ayahci-~ ayahtokamikohk [*sic*] ta-papâmi-mwêstâtahkamikisicik nitawâsimisak, pêyakwanohk ê-kî-mêtawêcik, ita ê-ihtatikawiyâhk, it[a] ê-wîkiyâhk.

grandmother's gear, a few things at a time, was brought back to Sweetgrass.

[11] And so, finally (at that point now it was my mother who looked after us); and so, finally, I found a man for myself, we found each other and I lived with him, and with that now it came about that I too remained at *Nakiwacîw-âskîhkânihk* [Sweetgrass Reserve] for good. So it was that I now remained there for good, now that I found a man for myself; we did not have to impose on our old people for long, to stay with them and to live off them. This man tried to take care of me, now I lived with this young man; now he was able to build a house at once, we had a house that winter and he also built himself a barn, there he kept a good team of horses, he had everything required [*sc.* harness, wagon, sleigh] and we could drive around right away.

[12] So in due course we had children while we lived there. We kept living there and brought up my children although I did not bear many children, while we lived there I twice suffered the loss of a child, my first-born ones as I might say. And so from then on, as I had the others, now I had to bring them up, finally I finished bringing up my children; these are the things which I have done in my life.

[13] My children did not in any way give me much trouble, they were quite smart, they did not give me much trouble in any way. Just as I had been brought up, that is how I tried to bring up my own children, so that they would not go around and raise hell in other people's homes too much, they would play in one place wherever we had been put, where we lived.

[II]

[14] êkwa kotak kîkway mîna nôhtê-kiskêyihtam awa, awa nitôkimâskwêm, nêhiyawi-kîkway, êkwa êwako pahkêkinohkêwin. nôhkom kî-pê-kakâyawâtisiw êsa, mistahi pahkêkinohkêwin kî-pê-tasih-~ kî-pê-tasîhkam. êkos êkwa, mitoni êtikwê kî-pê-tâpi-~-sâpo-kiskêyihtam pahkêkinohkêwin, piyisk nikâwiy, nikâwiy êkotowahk mitoni kî-tasi-nôtikwêwihikow [*sic*] piyisk wîsta, pahkêkinohkêwin, mistah ê-kî-pê-tasîhkahk. mistah âtoskêwiniwiw ôma pahkêkin kâ-tasîhkamihk, wâwîs môswêkinwa – namôy âni ta-kî-nahi-mitoni-pêyakôhkamâtohk, môswêkin ê-osîhcikâtêk. piyisk nikî-ati-kiskinohamâk, nikî-itik mâna nikâwiy, «namôy kâkikê kika-wâpamin, kakwê-kiskêyihta ôma pahkêkin, tânis ê-isîhtâhk,» nikî-itik mâna nikâwiy; «tâpwê mistahi, namôy kîkway awa wînêyihtam, k-ôsîhtât ôma,» nikî-itêyimâw mâna, mâk êcik ân[i] ê-kî-patêyihtamân, anima mân êkosi kâ-kî-itêyihtamân, nîst ê-osk-âyiwiyân, anima mâna nikâwiy kâ-kî-itêyimak ê-isîhcikêt, piyisk tâpwê nikî-kaskihtân. «hâw, pikw ân[i] êkâ ta-wînêyihtaman, t-êsi-kaskihtâyan ôma pahkêkin t-ôsîhtâyan,» ê-kî-isit mâna nikâwiy. okwâskwêpayihôsowayâna [*sic*], êkotowahk nikî-kiskinohamâk nîkân nikâwiy, tânisi t-ât[i]-îsîhimak.

[15] êkosi, tâpwê, piyisk kahkiyaw kîkway nikî-kaskihtân. êkoni mîna môy kayâs pêyak ôta iskwêw, osk-îskwêw, nikî-pê-kâh-kakwêcimik, êkon ânihi pahkêkinohkêwin, tânis ê-pê-ay-isiyinîhkâhtamihk, mâka mistah ânim âtoskêwin, namôy piko, kîspin wêtinâhk [*sic*] ê-wî-tasîhkamihk pahkêkinwa, osâm an[i] êtikwê piko pêyak-pîsim, mitoni mihcêt-ôtinikanêyâw [*sic*] anima pahkêkin, kâ-wî-kakwê-mamêtonîhk, kâ-wî-kakwê-osîhtâhk, kîspin namôy mâmâsîs ê-nôhtê-osîhtâhk, êkoni anihi nikî-pê-~, nikî-pê-kaskihtân êkoni ê-pê-tôtamân, mâk êkwa ispîhk ê-mâci-kakwâtakihtâyân, êkâ kîkway ê-kî-pê-sôhkatoskâtamân,

[**II**] [Tanning Hides]

[14] Now she also wants to know about another thing, the woman who is my boss [*sc.* Freda Ahenakew], a Cree matter, the tanning of hides. My grandmother had been such a hard worker, it is reported, she had devoted a great deal of effort to the tanning of hides. And so she must have had a thorough knowledge of tanning hides, and later my mother too, my mother also carried on that kind of work until she was at last an old woman, she used to devote a great deal of effort to the tanning of hides. There is so much work involved in tanning hides, especially moose-hides – you really cannot do it right on your own, the preparation of a moose-hide. In due course my mother taught me the art, she used to say to me, «You will not always have me around, try to learn how one prepares the hide,» my mother used to say to me; «It is true, she really does not mind the dirty chores when she prepares hides,» I used to think of her, but evidently I was mistaken in what I thought of the task, for I was a young thing when I thought that of my mother doing that work, and finally, it is true, I was able to do it myself. «Well, you must not think of it as dirty if you are to succeed in preparing hides,» my mother used to say to me. My mother first taught me how to tan the hide of a jumping deer, how to prepare that kind.

[15] And so, it is true, finally I was able to do everything. About that too, not long ago a woman here [*sc.* in Saskatoon], a young woman, came and asked me questions about that, the tanning of hides, how one had traditionally done it, but it is a lot of work, not only, if you take your time working the hide, it would not only take at least one month, the hide takes very many steps when you are trying to make a good job of it when preparing the hide, if you do not want to do a sloppy job, I used to be able to do

êkos êkwa êkospîhk ohci, nikî-pôyon nîst êwakw ânima, pahkêkinohkêwin isi ê-itôtamân.

[III]

[SW:] êkwa, kîkwây?

[FA:] kikî-mâh-misi-mawisonâwâw cî mâna, êkwa tânis ê-kî-isi-nahastâhk?

[SW:] êkwa mîna, êha.

[16] êkwa mîna, nikâwiy awa, mistahi kî-pê-kakâyawâtisiw, nanâtohk isi, nitaka mistah ê-kî-kakâyawisît. kî-kitimâkisiyiwa anihi nâpêwa kâ-kî-wîc-âyâmât, itowahk ôki nâpêwak k-ây-âhkosicik, ê-kî-êkotowiwiyit; mitoni nama kîkway ana nôhcâwîs atoskêwin ê-ohci-pê-kaskihtât ta-tôtahk.

[17] hâw, êkwa nikâwiy, têpiyâhk mâna ê-kî-pîkopicikêstamâht nikâwiy, pîsi-kistikâna it[a] ê-wî-kistikêt. êkota mîna, nitaka mistahi ê-kî-pê-nihtâwâcihocik, âsay êkwa êkota wiy ê-oskinîkiskwêwiyân anima. nikî-wîcihâw mâna nikâwiy, pîsi-kistikâna, kwayask miton ê-kistikêyâhk, kâh-osîhtamâkawiyâhko [*sic*] pîsi-kistikân. êkos êkwa kâh-kapê-ayi, êkota nikâwiy mân ê-kî-tatahkamikisiyâhk.

[18] piyisk êkwa mînisa, nanâtohk ê-at-ît-~ êkw ê-ati-kîsatihtêki ê-ati-mâh-miywâsiki; mistahi êkotowahk mîna kî-pê-kakâyawisîtotam nikâwiy, mawisowin. kâh-kapê-ayi ê-kî-papâmi-nitâmisoyâhk, misâskwatômina, tânis ê-kî-isi-nahastât nikâwiy. kâh-misi-mawisot-~ kâh-misi-mawisoyâhko [*sic*] mînisa, ahpô nikî-papâmitâpâsonân wâh-wâhyaw itê ê-papâmi-nitonamâhk, ê-ayâki misâskwatômina. êkwa êk-~, nikâwiy awa tânisi ê-kî-isi-nahastât, kâh-misi-mawisoci ôhi misâskwatômina, êkwa kî-pâsiminêw, pikw îtowihk ê-kanâtahk apahkwâsonêkin, ahpô aspascikan, êkota mân êkwa ê-kî-sîhkastâyâhk ôhi, misâskwatômina, kwayask ê-itênamâhk, ê-pâsamâhk; tahto-kîsikâw, isko miton

those things but now that I have begun to be quite ill and I am no longer capable of hard work, so from now on I too quit that, the tanning of hides.

[**III**] [Preserving Berries]

[SW:] Now what?

[FA:] Did you use to do a great deal of berry-picking, and how did you preserve them?

[SW:] Now that too, yes.

[16] Now my mother also used to be a very hard worker, in different ways, it was a good thing she worked so hard. The man she lived with was poorly, the kind of man who is sickly, that was the kind he was; my step-father used to be quite incapable of doing any work.

[17] Well, my mother now, so long as someone ploughed up the land for her, my mother would plant her vegetable garden. And at that time it also was a good thing that they used to be very much able to fend for themselves, for at that time I was already a young woman. I used to help my mother with the vegetable garden, we really planted it properly once someone had worked the garden plot for us. And so my mother and I used to spend all our time there.

[18] Now finally there were berries, all kinds of them were ripening now, and they were nice; my mother also used to work hard at that, berry-picking. We used to go around looking for saskatoons all the time, how my mother used to preserve them. When she -- we had picked a lot of berries, we even used to drive around in faraway places looking for berries, looking where there were saskatoons. And how my mother used to preserve them when she had picked a lot of saskatoons, now she used to dry the berries, and on any kind of canvas which was clean or on a

ê-pâstêki anihi misâskwatômina. namôy piko pêyak-maskimot, êkwa kî-sîpâhkatotêwa mîna, miton êkon êkwa kâ-mosci-pâsamihk, êkwa, êkoni mâna ê-kî-~

[NN:] *the phone*

[*external break*]

[FA:] êkwa.

[19] êkoni anihi misâskwatômina, pâsiminêwin kâ-tas-~ kâ-tasihtamân, miton ânihi miscahîs nikâwiy, pêyako-maskimot [*sic*] osâm piko, iyikohk ahpô ayiwâk, ê-kî-pâsahk; êkoni ê-kî-katikoni-kanawêyihtahk kâ-pipohk. êkot[a] ôhc êkwa mîna takwahiminâna mâna, kâ-kî-ati-miywâsiki ê-takwâkik. êkoni êkwa mîna mistahi nikî-pê-atoskâtênân, nikî-wîcihâw, ê-pê-atoskâtamâhk ê-papâmi-mawisoyâhk mâna. pêyak-maskimot [*sic*] kâ-kîsi-~ kâ-kîsi-mawisoyâhk iyikohk, êkot[a] êkwa mâna kâ-kî-takwahiminêt ana. kî-mosti-takwahiminêwak kayâs iskwêwak, êkosi ê-kî-isi-osîhtâcik, êkwa ê-kî-sî-~ êkoni mîna ê-kî-pâsahkik, ê-kî-mosci-pâsahkik anihi takwahiminâna. êkoni kî-kiyipâhkatotêwa, mîna mistah êkoni kî-ispayinwa mâna mitoni. êkoni mâna kêyâpic anohc nikiskisin nikâwiy, iyikohk ê-kî-ay-iskwâhtât; âskaw anihi mâna nisto-maskimot, iyikohk takwahiminâna ê-kî-ayât; katawâhk mân ê-kî-kipo-~ ê-kî-kipokwâtahk maskimotihk kâh-astâci; êkoni anihi ê-kî-nîmâwinihkêt, kâ-wî-piponiyik.

[20] êkota ohci, nanâtohk nîpiminâna, ayôskana [*sic*], êkos îsi mân ê-kî-papâ-mawisoyâhk kâ-nîpihk. mâka, êkospîhk wiya namôy cêskwa 'môtêyâpisk' k-êsiyîhkâtêk, anohc kâ-kaskâpiskahikêcik êkwa; môy êkoni wiya, namôy mân êkosi kîkway wiya ohc-îsîhcikâtam nikâwiy, ta-kaskâpiskahikêt, nayêstaw ê-kî-mosci-mîciyâhk; mân êkoni anihi, êkotowahk kâ-kî-mawisoyâhk, nikî-kâh-kwâhtohtânân [*sic*] mâna mitoni.

tablecloth we would now spread out the saskatoons and turn them over evenly and dry them; every day until these saskatoons were really dry. Not just a single flour-sack, and they used to take a long time to dry when you really dried them just like that, and then we used to –~

[NN:] the phone

[*external break*]

[FA:] Now.

[19] Of these saskatoons, in the process of drying the berries that I was discussing, my mother used to have quite a lot, one sack usually, that much or even more she used to dry; those she kept as provisions for the winter. And after that now also the chokecherries, they used to be nice in the fall. Now we used to do a lot of work with them too, I used to help her in processing them and in going around and picking them. When we had finished picking one sack full, then she would pound them. The women simply pounded them in the old days, that is how they prepared them, and then they dried those too, they used to simply dry the chokecherries. They used to dry fast, and they also used to amount to a lot more. And to this day I still remember how many of them my mother used to have; sometimes she had a full three sacks of chokecherries; she used to sew the sacks closed very carefully when she put them away; these she used to prepare as provisions for the coming winter.

[20] After that we went around picking high-bush cranberries, raspberries and various other berries like that in the summer. But at that time there were no 'sealer-jars' yet, as they are called, which they use for canning today; my mother did not have these to use or anything like them to do the canning, we only ate them like that; but when we used to pick that kind, we used to walk really long distances.

[IV]

[21] êkwa, wiya nika-~ k-êtwêyân, nama kîkway wîhkâc wiya, êkos îsi ta-~, piko mân ê-kî-mosc-âsamikawiyâhk ôma, kâ-minahot awiyak okwâskwêpayihôsa [*sic*], kâ-ma-minahohk ôma, êkotowihk mâna mîna. êkwa mîna, kahkiyaw kîkway kî-osîhtâw nikâwiy, kâhkêwakwa, nânitaw wiyâs k-ôhtinamâhk, kâhkêwakwa ê-kî-osîhtât mâna nikâwiy. êkwa mîna, kîkwây ê-kî-miywâsik mâna, kâhkêwakwa kâ-kîsi-pâstêki, êkwa îwahikana ê-kî-osîhât mâna; nôhkom[a] ê-kî-kiskinawâpamât, okâwiya, tânis ê-kî-ay-isîhtâyit, êkwa êkota takwahiminâna ê-kikinahk, pimiy. êwakw ân[i] ânima 'pimîhkân' k-êsiyîhkâtêk, iyikohk ê-kî-miywâsik mîna, nêhiyawi-mîcisowin. êkwa, ê-kî-tâpakwêt, wâh-wâhyaw ê-kî-ay-itohtêt, kâ-tay-~ ê-kî-tâpakwêt, cikêmâ kâ-pipohk pêyakwan mîn êkosi ê-kî-itahkamikisit mâna nikâwiy, ê-kî-tâpakwêt. êkwa, cikêmâ nititwân nôhcâwîs, ê-kî-âhkosit sôskwâc, môy ê-ohci-kaskihtât mistahi ta-pimohtêt. nayêstaw mâna nikâwiy ê-kî-nâh-nâtwâhimihtêt kâ-piponiyik, êkwa mîna –~ nîsta mâna, êkospîhk wiy êkw ê-oy-oskinîkiskwêwiyân, nîsta mâna ê-kî-nâh-nâtwâhimihtêyân ê-pîhtikwacimihtêyân.

[22] êkosi, êkosi nikî-pê-ay-itâcihonân, êkosi kahkiyaw anim âyisiyiniwak êkosi ê-kî-pê-itâcihocik; tahto ê-kakâyawâtisicik iskwêwak, êkosi kahkiyaw kî-pê-itâcihowak. êkwa mîna, êyiwêhk kî-ayâwêw mâna nikâwiy – 'pâhpahâhkwânak' ôki kâ-isiyîhkâtâyâhkok, kôhkôsa; kî-ayâwêw mâna –~, kî-ayâwêwak mâna nikâwiy. êkos êyiwêhk nikîstê-~-takahki-pimâcihonân, mâka nikâwiy ohci kâ-kî-kwayask-itâcihoyâhk; cikêmâ ayisk, nayêstaw ê-kî-pamihâyâhk nôhcâwîs, osâm êkâ ê-ohci-ma-miyw-âyât. piyisk êkotowahk ê-kî-misiwanâcihikot anim ôtâhkosiwin. êwako 'ê-oskanahpinêt' kî-ît-~ kî-isiyîhkâtamwak mân ânima âhkosiwin, êkotow-âhkosiwin [*sic*] an[a] ê-kî-ayât nôhcâwîs.

[**IV**] [Preparing Dried Meat]

[21] Now, as I said, there was never anything like that [*sc.* meat] –~, we simply would have to be provided with it when someone killed a jumping deer, when they were hunting, on that occasion usually. And my mother also prepared everything, dried meat, on the occasions when we came into some meat my mother used to make dried meat. And also, another thing which was good, when the dried meat had been fully dried, then she used to make pounded meat; she had learned how to make it by watching my grandmother, her own mother, and then she mixed in the choke-cherries and the grease. That is what is called *pimihkân*, another Cree food that used to be so good. Now, she also used to set snares [*sc.* for rabbits], my mother used to walk long distances when she set her snares, of course she used to do the same thing in winter, setting her snares. Now of course my step-father obviously used to be sick, I already said that, so that he was not able to walk very much. Only my mother used to cut wood into stove-lengths during the winter, and also –~ I too, for by that time I was a young woman, I too used to cut wood into stove-lengths and haul it inside.

[22] This is how we used to live, and this is how all the people used to live; all the women who were hard workers, all of them used to live like that. And at least my mother also kept some – chickens, as we call them, and some pigs; she used to keep them –~, my mother [and her household] used to keep them. In that way at least we had a pretty good life, but it was because of my mother that we had a decent life; for my step-father of course only was looked after by us, because he was not well. At last that kind, the illness he had, finished him off. They used to call that illness 'arthritis', that is the kind of disease my step-father had.

[V]

[FA:] tânisi mâk ê-kî-isi-postayiwinisahisoyêk?

[23] â, nikî-otêminân; nikî-otêminân, kî-iskwâhêw nikâwiy misatimwa; nêma nêtê k-âyâyân môsômininâhk, êkotê nitêminânak mihcêt ê-kî-ayâwâyâhkok, nimosôm mâna ê-kî-kanawêyimât êkotê pîhci-mênikanihk; ay-âspîhcinâk mâna kî-sipwê-têhtapiw ê-mâwasakotisahwât misatimwa. êkwa mâna, êkota mîna mâna nikiskisin, «kwayâci-yôhtênamawîhkan iskwâhtêmihkân, nikî-~ pêtisâpamiyani,» ê-kî-isit mâna; êkosi, mistiko-mênikana mâna kî-ihtakonwa. êkwa kâ-pêtisâpamak nimosôm, kâ-pê-asitisahwât misatimwa ôhi, pikwatastimwa, êkwa mân ê-kî-ispahtâyân mênikanihk, ê-nitawi-yâh-yîkatêtâpêyân [*sic*] iskwâhtêm, mênikana ôhi, tâpiskôt mênikanâhtikwa.

[24] êkosi; êkwa, ispîhk êkwa ê-~ nêso-~, anim êkwa ê-nêsowahpinêt nimosôm, êkot[a] êkwa kâ-kî-itât nikâwiya, ta-kakwê-kanawêyihtamâht, ta-kakwê-pisiskêyihtamâht êkwa nakiwacîhk, nikâwiy anihi misatimwa. nîs ôskinîkiwak, nisto, êkot[a] êkwa kâ-kî-masinahikêhât nikâwiy, ê-nâtitisahohcik aniki nitêminânak; mihcêt, miton êtikwê nîstanaw, môy wiya cikawâsis piko, ahpô ayiwâk, ê-pê-asitisahwâcik oskinîkiwak, ôtê ê-pê-itisahohcik êkwa nakiwacîhk aniki nitêminânak.

[25] hâw, êkonik êkwa aniki nitêminânak, êkonik ê-kî-ohci-postayiwinisêyâhk. êspîhcinâk [*sic*] mâna nôhcâwîs, ê-~, pêyak ê-kî-sipwêyâpêkipahât, ê-nitaw-âtâwâkêt nitêminâna; êkot[a] ê-kî-ohci-postayiwinisêyâhk. nânitaw mayaw kâ-wî-itahkamikahk, kâ-wî-mêcawêsihk nânitaw, âsay pêyak nitêminâna ê-kî-sipwêyâpêkipahât nôhcâwîs, ahpô oskastimwa ê-nitaw-âtâwâkêt. êkot[a] ê-kî-ohc-ôsôniyâmiyâhk, cikêmâ mîna êwakw âna nama kîkway sôniyâhkêwin ê-ohc-âyât.

[**V**] [The Cash Economy]

[FA:] But how did you get clothes for yourselves?

[23] Well, we had horses; we had horses, my mother had many horses; when I lived over there at *Môsômininâhk* [Moosomin] we used to have lots of horses there, my grandfather used to keep them in a pasture over there; once in a while he would ride off to round up the horses. And then, I also remember that, «Be ready to open the gate for me when you see me coming,» he used to say to me; that was the way, they used to be wooden fences. Now when I saw my grandfather coming, when he came driving the horses, a herd of wild horses, then I would run to the fence and go and drag the rails to the side to open the gate, these fences were made from wooden rails.

[24] So it was; then, at the time my grandfather became weak with illness, it was then that he told my mother that she should get someone to keep the horses for her, that she should get someone from *Nakiwacîhk* [Sweetgrass] to tend them for her, the horses, for my mother. It was then that my mother hired two or three young men to send for our horses; they were numerous, there must have been at least twenty, not just a few, or perhaps more than twenty, as the young men were driving them all in a herd, as they were driving our horses over there to *Nakiwacîhk*.

[25] Well, these our horses now, with these we got our clothes. Once in a while my step-father would lead one of our horses off and go and sell it; with that we used to get our clothes. As soon as there was an event coming up somewhere, when there was going to be a Sports Day somewhere, right away my step-father would lead one of our horses off or he would go and sell a young horse. With that we obtained money, of course that one also had no way of earning money.

[26] êkwa, piyisk êkosi, ê-kî-ati-mêscipayicik aniki nitêminânak, ê-kî-ati-mosci-mêstatâwâkêt nôhcâwîs; êtataw nikî-otêminân, piyisk êkosi mîn êwakw ân[a] ê-kî-isi-nakatikoyâhk. ê-nakatikot nikâwiy onâpêma, êkos êkwa, nayêstaw nîsw êtikwê kî-ayâwêw misatimwa. mâk êkwa, niy êkwa êkota, nêwo nikî-~ nikî-ohc-âyâwâwak misatimwak, êkonik; êkonik aniki nikî-kikîn ê-onâpêmiyân misatimwak. nîsta kinwês êkonik kâsispô [*sic*] nikî-ay-ayâwâwak. êkosi piko ê-kî-pê-isi-postayiwinisêyâhk nikâwiy; êkos ê-kî-is-ôsôniyâmicik mâna piko.

[27] êkosi, êkota ohci êkwa nâpêw niy ê-wîcêwak, êkota ohc êkwa wiya mistahi sôniyâw nikî-wa-wâpamâw mâna, cikêmâ kî-kakâyawisîw, kwayask kî-atoskêw, kwayask nikî-pamihik.

[SW:] êkosi.

[VI]

[FA:] kikaskikwâsowina mâka? kayâs cî ôma ê-ohci-mîkisistahikêyêk ê-kaskikwâsoyêk?

[28] êwako mîna nôhkom ê-kî-kiskinohamâkoyâhk. namôy kakêtihk nôhkom ê-kî-miywêyihtahk ê-kî-mîkisistahikêt, iyikohk mâna nimosôma ê-kî-osîhtamawât mîkisayiwinisa. ôhi 'iyinito-pahkêkinwêw-âyiwinisa' k-êtwêhk, sistahikana [*sic; ?sc.* mîkisistahikana] kâ-kikamoki, êkotowahk mâna nôhkom nayêstaw ê-kî-kaskikwâsot. êkwa mân êkota, pimic-âyihk ê-kî-apiyân, ê-kakwê-kiskinawâpamak, âskaw mîkisisa ê-kî-miyit, konita nîst êkota ê-tâpisahiminêyân mâna. êwakw ânim ê-kî-kakwê-isi-kiskinohamawit nôhkom mîkisistahikêwin; êkos ânim ê-kî-ayiwâkêyihtahk, ê-mîkisistahikêt. tâspwâw okaskikwâsowina, pêyakw-âyiwinis, mîkisayiwinisa, êkotowahk kî-~ kî-kikiskam nimosôm ê-wî-nahiniht, ê-postiskahk; êkoni iskwêyâc okaskikwâsowina.

[26] And so, in the end, our horses were running out, my step-father simply sold them all. We barely had any horses left after all this when he finally died. When my mother's husband died, at that point she only had two horses, I guess. But now it was up to me, then, I had four horses from that herd; these horses I took with me when I got married. I for my part used to have horses from that line for a long time. That was the only way for my mother and me to get our clothes; that was the only way they used to obtain money.

[27] And so after that, once I was married, after that I used to have lots of money, of course my husband used to be a hard worker, he used to work properly, he used to look after me properly.

[SW:] That is it.

[VI] [Beadwork]

[FA:] What about your sewing? Have you been doing beadwork and sewing for a long time?

[28] My grandmother taught us that too. My grandmother had a great love for beadwork, she used to make such beautiful beaded clothes for my grandfather. These 'plain leather clothes', as they say, with beadwork on them, that was the only kind my grandmother used to sew. Now I used to sit there across from her, trying to learn by watching her, sometimes she gave me some beads and, as for me, I just threaded them up. In that way my grandmother tried to teach me beading; she valued beadwork above everything else. As a matter of fact it was her sewing, a suit of beaded clothes, that was the kind my grandfather had on when he was to be buried, he wore that; that was the last of her sewing.

[29] â, pêyakwan êkosi nikâwiy, mistahi mîna kî-nihtâwikwâsow nikâwiy, wîst ê-mîkisistahikêt. ahpô kî-kaskihtâw, 'kâkwa' awa k-êtâyâhk, anihi, anik êkota kâ-kikamocik, êkotowahk ayiw-~ ê-kî-âpacihât mâna nikâwiy, maskisina ê-osîhtât, nanâtohk ê-itatiswât anihi kâwiya. êwako mîna nikaskihtân nîsta. êkos âniskâc êkota ohci mîna piyisk nitati-kaskihtân nimîkis-~ ê-kî-pê-mîkisistahikêyân. kayâs ê-pê-ohci-mîkisistahikêyân ê-oskinîkiskwêwiyân, ê-kî-pê-ohci-kaskihtâyân. anohc kêyâpic êwako nita-tasîhkên mâna. âta wiy êkwa, namôy tâpwê nitati-nahâpin ta-kî-kaskikwâsoyân, mâk êyiwêhk namôy nipa-pôyon, kêyâpic ê-ka-kaskikwâsoyân, êwako mîna mistahi miywâsin pêyak, ê-pa-pâhpakwacîhkamihk, iyikohk wiya konita t-ây-apihk, niy ôti wiya mâna, êkâ ê-miyomahcihoyân, iyikohk konita t-ây-apiyân, nika-kas-~ ê-ka-kaskikwâsoyân mâna. nanâtohk kîkway nikî-pê-kiskinohamâk nikâwiy; kaskikwâsowipayihcikêwin, mîn êwako nimiywêyihtên, ê-kaskikwâsowipayihcikêyân, k-ây-apiyân.

[SW:] êkosi.

[FA:] *thank you.*

[29] Well, the same with my mother, my mother was very good at sewing, and she too did beadwork. She even was able, we call him the porcupine, those, those quills that are on the porcupine, my mother made use of that kind when she made moccasins, she dyed the quills in various colours. I am able to do that too. And so, from one generation to the next, I was at last able to do beadwork. I have been beading for a long time, ever since I was a young girl I have been able to do beadwork. I still busy myself with that today. To be sure, my eyesight is not really good enough for me to be able to sew, but in spite of that I am not quitting, I am still sewing, that is another very good thing, one is kept busy instead of just sitting around, at least for myself, since I do not feel well, instead of just sitting around I keep on sewing. My mother taught me many different things; sewing with a sewing machine, that too I like, sewing with a sewing machine when I am home.

[SW:] That is it.

[FA:] Thank you.

Betsy Fineday née Applegarth, Sarah Whitecalf's mother (second from left), c. 1948. The girl on her right is Doreen Favel, born 1944.

2

êkosi nikî-tâs-ôy-ohpikihikawin

This is the way I was raised

êkosi nikî-tas-ôy-ohpikihikawin

[FA:] *Cecilia Masuskapoe* êkwa *Sarah Whitecalf* kêyâpic ê-wî-âcimocik, pakâhkam [*laughter*].

kiya cî êkwa? kikiskisin kîkway?

[SW:] namôya! [...; *?record*]

[CM:] misawâc ka-nâh-naskwêwasimitin.

[I]

[1] êwakw âw âwa ôta awa nîci-nôtikwêw kâ-pêsîht k-ây-âtotahk, kinwês môy ê-ohci-kiskinohamâsot, kiskinohamâtowikamikohk môy ê-ohci-pakitiniht t-âyât, nîst êkosi ê-kî-ispayihikoyân, nika-kiskisomik êwak ôm ôma; nîst êwakw ânima nik-âtotên, miton ê-kî-pêyakôsâniwiyân, niyê-~ 'k-êskwâhpinêhk' k-êtwêhk mân ôm îspîhk,

[CM:] êha.

êkospîhk êsa nîcisânak kahkiyaw ê-kî-mêscinêcik. nikâwiy awa, kotak awa –~, mâka –~, kotaka ê-kî-onâpêmit.

[CM:] âha.

ayak – êkwa kotak nîst ê-kî-oyôhtâwîyân, êkwa awa nôhtâwiy kotaka iskwêwa kî-nitawi-wîwiw. êkot[a] êkw âwa nôhtâwiy kî-mihcêtôsêw mitoni, êkos êkwa niya, ôk êkwa nîtisânak

This is the way I was raised

[FA:] Cecilia Masuskapoe and Sarah Whitecalf are still going to tell stories, I think [*laughter*].

Is it your turn now? Have you thought of anything?

[SW:] No! [*...; ?record*]

[CM:] I will keep responding to you in any case.

[**I**] [Parents and Siblings]

[1] It is she, my fellow-old woman [*sc.* CM], who was brought here and has been telling about not going to school for a long time, about not being allowed to go to school, the same thing happened to me too, she reminded me of this; I too will tell about that, I was very much an only child at the time of the Great Sickness [*sc.* the influenza epidemic of 1918-20], as it is called,

[CM:] Yes.

at that time, it is reported, all my siblings [*sc.* maternal half-siblings] had died. My mother, this was another –~, but –~, she had taken another husband.

[CM:] Yes.

They – now I too had another father [*sc.* her second husband], and my [*sc.* biological] father had gone and married another woman. Now in that union my father had quite a large number

– nikâwiy awa kayâhtê ê-kî-onâpêmit ôhi, êkota ohci nikî-owîtisânin ôki, âpihtaw ôki; êkos êkwa, 'k-êskwâhpinêhk' kâ-kî-itwêhk anima mâna kayâs êtikwê, êkot[a] ê-kî-mêscinêcik aya nîtisânak. êkwâ [*sic*] mîn ôhi nikâwiy kâ-kî-wîcêwât, nistam anihi, êkoni anihi, êwakw ân[a] ân[a] ês ê-kî-kikahpinêt ana, nôhcâwîs an[a] ê-kî-kiki-nipit ana, êkos ôtawâsimisa, pâh-pêyak-pîsim êsa piko ê-kî-askôkot, êkospîhk k-êskwâhpinêhk [*sic:* -â-] anima. êkwa aya, êkos êkwa, niya pikw êkw ê-kî-iskwahpinêyân [*sic:* -a-], êkospîhk anima k-êskwâhpinêhk. êkos âni nikî-pa-pêyakôsâniwin; êkos êkwa anima nîst êkwa – nikâwiy aw ânim êkwa kâ-sîkâwit, niyânan-askiy mitoni kî-pêyakow, ahpô êtikwê nikotwâsik; kîtahtawê kâ-kî-ay-ispayik ôm ôtê nakiwacîhk ê-~, nikâwiy aw ê-~ ê-pê-nâh-nitomiskwêwâtikot pêyak êkotê môsâpêwa. ê-kî-pa-pêyakot, êkosi mitoni mîna ê-kî-~ kwayask ê-kî-pa-pamihisot awa nikâwiy, êkos ânima ê-kî-pa-pakitahwâcihot mâna, ê-pa-pakitahwâcik kâ-piponiyik, êkwa otêm[a] ê-kî-awihiwêt kâ-takwâkiniyik ôm êkos îsi, kayâs kâ-kî-mosci-papâ-pawahikêcik mâna nâpêwak.

[CM:] âha.

êkos ânima mân ês âwa nikâwiy, êkos ê-kî-is-ôsôniyâmit awa nikâwiy, ê-awihiwêt otâpâna, êkos îs ê-itahpisoyit sôskwâc otêma ôhi; miton ê-kî-sa-sôniyâhkêsit.

[II]

[2] îh, êkos êkwa niy ôma, kâ-kî-pê-wiy-ohpikihikawiyân [*sic; cf.* -oy-], piyisk êkwa nikâwiy awa kâ-pê-onâpêmit êkwa ôma nakiwacîhk êkwa, nikiskisin mîna mân êwako ê-nêwopiponêyân ês ânima,

of children, so now for me, my siblings [maternal half-siblings] – my mother had previously had a husband and I had these siblings from this union, these half-siblings; so now it must have been at the time of the Great Sickness, as that used to be called long ago, at that time my [maternal half-] siblings had all died. Now the one to whom my mother had first been married, that one had also taken sick along with them, it is reported, that step-father of mine had died along with them, and his children had one by one died after him, a month apart, at that time of the Great Sickness. Now, so now as for me, now I was the only one to survive at that time of the Great Sickness. In that way then I was an only child; in that way then I too – now my mother was widowed, she was completely alone for five years, perhaps even six; at one time it came to pass over there at *Nakiwacîhk* [Sweetgrass] that a certain widower from over there would come and keep asking to marry my mother. She had been living alone, in this way my mother had very much looked after herself properly, in this way she had been making her living by fishing, in winter they used to set nets and in the fall she had hired out her team of horses and things like that, in the old days when men used to go about threshing by hand.

[CM:] Yes.

It was in this way that my mother, it is reported, my mother used to have a cash income, by hiring out her wagon, in this way she hired out her team fully harnessed up; she used to make quite a bit of money.

[II] [Riches to Rags]

[2] Look, it this way I had been brought up when now finally my mother came to take a husband at *Nakiwacîhk* [Sweetgrass], I also remember that, at the time I was four years old,

[CM:] nah!

kâ-kî-pêsîkawiyâhk anim âyi, ôtê êk ôma nakiwacîhk, nikâwiy aw ê-pêsîht ê-pê-onâpêmit – âhêy, tâpwê êtikwê ê-kî-kicimâkisiyit nikâwiy – kîkwây êtikwê nêtê oski-wâskahikan ê-miyikawiyâhk, êkot[a] ânim ôhci napakihtakwa ê-kî-miy-~-atâwêt anima, êkwayât ta-piponiswâtamâhk anima wâskahikan, anim ê-oski-wâskahikanêyâhk; mistiko-wâskahikan, mâk êkwa ôhi napakihtakwa k-~, mân êkw âyisk yâhk îtâp kayâs ê-kî-miywapihk.

[CM:] êwakw ânim ê-kî-miywapihk tâpwê.

[SW:] mhi [*laughs*].

êkwa ayihk, îh, âhci pikw ânima kâ-têpêyimot ê-pê-itohtahikawiyâhk ê-pê-onâpêmit nakiwacîhk. wahwâ, ê-kiskisiyân, miton êtataw ê-kiskisiyân, micon ân[i] ê-apisâsik wâskahikanis, ê-câsawâsik ê-kinwâk ôma wâskahikan, êkw âsiskiy[a] ê-apahkwâtêk. âpihtaw iyikohk, iyikohk ômis îs [*gesture*] ê-kipahikâtêk anima wâskahikanis, wiy ê-kî-môsâpêwit, anihi kâ-pêsîkot. apahkwâsonêkin, papakiwayânikamik [*laughter*], âpihtaw ê-kipahikâtêk anima wâskahikan. ê-kiskisiyân mân ê-tahtawêkinamân, ê-pâh-paspâpiyân; pêhkikwahwân [*sic*] nêtê ê-apit, kwêsk-âyihk âh-âpihtaw ê-napwêkinikâsot êkotê ê-apit; îh, iyikohk ê-kî-kitimâkisiyit anihi ê-pê-onâpêmit. êkwa wiy ôma nêt-~ ôma kâ-kî-sîkâwit, kahkiyaw kîkway âpacihcikana ê-kî-ayât, ahpô ê-kî-iskwâhât misatimwa, kî-omostosomiw; êkwa iyikohk anih âpacihcikana kîkway ê-kî-ayât, kahkiyaw êkwa êkotê anihi. miton ê-kî-wêyôtisit awa nikâwiy mîna, kayâhtê mistah ê-kî-kakâyawi-pimâcihoyit miton ônâpêma.

[CM:] êha.

êkwa, êkos êkwa niy êkwa, kâ-kî-oy-ohpikihicik êkwa ôki nîsta nôhkom, kêhtê-ayak ôki nimosôm; wiy ê-pêyakôsâniwiyân, êkot[a] êkwa kâ-kî-tas-âya-~, môsôminінâhk anima kâ-kî-tas-ôy-ohpikiyân

[CM:] Oh no!

it is reported, when we were brought over there now, there to *Nakiwacîhk* [Sweetgrass], my mother was brought there to get married – oh my, he [*sc.* her new husband] must truly have been quite poor compared to my mother – where was the new house given to us over there, she had bought lumber for it there, we were to spend the first winter in that house, we had a new house; it was a log house but with squared lumber, and in the old days of course that had made it a pretty good place to live in.

[CM:] That used to be a good place to live in, it is true.

[ṢW:] Hm [*laughs*].

Now look, she was willing nevertheless for us to be moved there and for her to get married into *Nakiwacîhk* [Sweetgrass]. Oh my, I remember, I remember very faintly, it was a very small house, this house was narrow and long and it had a sod roof. It was partitioned off like this [*gesture*] at the half-point, this little house, for he was a widower, the one who brought her there, half that house was partitioned off with tent covering, with canvas [*laughter*]. I remember parting the canvas and peeking through; there was a sleigh sitting over there, it was folded in half [*sc.* with one set of runners on top] and stacked over there; look, so poor was the one she had come to marry. Now over there where she had been widowed she'd had all the equipment, she'd even had plenty of horses, she'd had cattle; and she'd had so much of every kind of equipment, now she'd had all these things over there. My mother had also been very well to do, her previous husband had been an extremely active provider.

[CM:] Yes.

Now then, as for me, I too was brought up by these old people, my grandmother and my grandfather; for I was an only child, and while I was growing up in *Môsômininâhk* [Moosomin], practically

mitoni sôskwâc, pêyak kâ-kî-âhkosit [...; *?record*], tâpwê kwêh-kwêkwask mân ômis îsi [*gesture*] nikî-itohtahikawin mân ôma nîsta, ê-nitawâpahtihikawiyân awa nikâwiy, ê-kiyokâht, ê-kiyokawâyâhk.

[III]

[3] piyisk anim êkwa ê-ati-ma-misikitiyân. môy nîst ê-kî-wî-pakitinit nikâwiy awa, kiskinohamâtowikamikohk t-âyâyân. îh, pêyak êsa êkota nimis, êkos ânima wîsta, «môy ê-kî-wî-wîhtamawicik ayamihêwiskwêwak êkwa pâhkw-âyamihêwiyiniw, môy ê-wî-wîhtamâkawiyân,» itwêw, «ês ôma nicânis mitoni, mistahi ê-ay-âhkosit», itwêw, «êkây ê-wî-wîhtamawicik maskihkîwiskwêwak [*sc.* ayamihêwiskwêwak]» – êwak ôma talimwâs kiskinohamâtowikamik kâ-kî-ayâk, êkota anima. «ispîhk êkwa,» itwêw, «ê-pêhtamân,» itwêw, «nitânis mistahi ê-âhkosit, ê-itwêhk,» itwêw (oskinîkiskwêw, âsay ê-kîs-ôskinîkiskwêwiyit), «kâ-pê-itohtêyâhk êkwa,» itwêw – ôhtâwiya, okâwiya êkos îsi ê-pê-wîcêwât, âsay ê-kî-sîkâwit. «êy, kâ-pê-itohtêyâhk, awîn âwa nitânis, âsay mitoni kêkâc ê-pisisokanakisit,» ê-itwêt. «wahwâ, iyikohk kâ-kî-pakwâtamân êkospîhk,» ê-itwêt. «êkos êkwa, ât[a] êkw ê-wayawîhtahâyâhk ê-wî-~ ê-kîwêhtahâyâhk êkwa,» itwêw, «êkw ê-âta-nâh-nêhiyawatoskêmoyâhk,» itwêw, «namwââc [*sic*],» kihkihk ê-kî-nakatikot otân-~ [*?record*], ê-mâyipayit anih ôtânisa.

[4] îh, êwakw ânima wîsta mân êkos ê-kî-itwêt nikâwiy, osâm anima ê-pêyakôsâniwiyân, kâh-kapê-ayi mâna pâhkw-âyamihêwiyiniwa, *'Lacombe'* kî-itâw mâna pâhkw-âyamihêwiyiniw, êkoni mâna, «kikitimahâw kicânis, nama kîkway ta-nisitohtam, kê-~, ôtê kê-nîkâniwik t-âkayâsîmow, kwayask mitoni kiskinohamâsoci,» ê-kî-pê-itikot mâna – nîsta

right away one of them had taken sick [...; *?record*], it is true, I too used to be taken back and forth like this [*gesture*], I was taken to see my mother, to visit her, we visited her.

[III] [Rejecting Residential School]

[3] Now finally I was getting to be big. In my case, too, my mother would not let me go to school. Look, my one older sister, it is reported, it was the same for her, «The nuns and the Catholic priest would not tell me, no one would tell me,» she said, «evidently my little daughter had been very sick, she was severely ill,» she said, «and yet the nurses [*sc.* the nuns] would not tell me» – it was that school that used to be at Delmas, it was there. «At one time now,» she said, «I heard,» she said, «that my daughter was seriously ill, it was said,» she said (she was a young woman, she had already grown up to be a young woman), «now when we got there,» she said – she went there with her father and her mother, like that, she had already been widowed. «Hey, when we got there, here my daughter was already almost nothing but bones,» she said. «Oh my, I hated that so much at that time,» she said. «And so, although we now took her out and took her home,» she said, «and although we now called in Cree healers,» she said, «nothing helped,» her daughter left her behind despite it all, she suffered the loss of her daughter.

[4] Look, that is what she, too, my mother, used to say, it was because I was her only child, and the Catholic priest, Lacombe [*sc.* Ernest Lacombe] was the name of that Catholic priest, that one used to come all the time, «You are saddling your little daughter with a disadavantage, she will not understand anything, in the future she will speak English if she goes to school properly,» he used to come and say to her – as for me, I had wanted to go

mân ê-kî-nôhtê-itohtêyân; wiya kahkiyaw êkwa nîci-~ nîci-~ nîc-âwâsisîmâkanak, wiyawâw kahkiyaw talimwâs ê-kî-pê-kiskinohamâsocik. êkwa niya pik ôhci, mitoni mâna nikâwiy aw ê-kî-sâkihit, êkos ânima mân ê-kî-itwêt, «môy wîhkâc kîhtwâm.» piyisk êkos ê-kî-itât anih âyamihêwiyiniwa, «nitânis pêyak êkota kî-tasi-misiwanâtisiw, namôy ê-kî-wî-wîhtamawicik ayamihêwiyiniwak, ayamihêwiskwêwak; êkos ê-pêyakot aw êkwa, aw ê-iskwahpinêt, môy wîhkâc kîhtwâm ninôhtê-pakitinâw êwako kiskinohamâtowikamikohk,» ê-kî-itât mâna. êkos ôm ê-ispayik ôma, wayêsi [*sic*] niy êkâ sôskwâc kâ-kî-pîhtikwêyân kiskinohamâtowikamikohk [*laughs*].

[*external break*]

[IV]

[5] kî-âyiman kayâs,

[CM:] mistahi.

mitoni.

[CM:] mâk ânima, mistah ânim ê-miywâsik ayisk ôm êkwa kiskinohamâtowin, cî?

[SW:] anohc êkwa miywâsin, êha.

[CM:] miywâsin êkwa kiskinohamâtowin.

[SW:] mitoni ayiwâk tahk ôm ây-iskôl [*sic*], kiyikaw êkwa anohc k-âti-kîsîhtamâsocik êkwa osk-âyak.

[CM:] nêhiyâsisak, mêton êkwa wîstawâw pêyakwan tâpiskôt môniyâwak êkwa is-îyinîsiwak ôki.

[SW:] âha.

waniyaw êkwa êkosi at-îs-îyinîsiwak, mistahi iyinîsihkahikwak aniki. mâk êkwa mâna niyanân kâ-mâmiskôcikêyâhk ôma, ahpô awa niwîcêwâkanis, osâm kîhawêma [*sic*] êkwa âtiht mîn ôma kâ-wî-kakwê-ayiwâkipitahkik, êkâ kâ-wî-nêhiyawêcik mistah ôk ôsk-âyak, kikiskêyihtên; nawac anim âh-âpihtaw iyikohk

there too; for all my fellow-children, they had all gone to the residential school at Delmas. Now it was only my lot that my mother firmly kept me back with her, and that is what she used to say, «Never again.» She finally said this to the priest, «One of my daughters was near death while she was there, and the priests and the nuns would not tell me about it; so she is the only one now, she is the lone survivor, never again, I will not ever let that one go to school,» she used to say to him. That is what happened, it was entirely by coincidence that I did not go straight into residential school [*laughs*].

[*external break*]

[IV] [Speaking Cree]

[5] It was difficult in the old days,

[CM:] Very much so.

very difficult.

[CM:] But of course education is very good now, isn't it?

[SW:] Today it is good now, yes.

[CM:] Education is good now.

[SW:] And today, along with other things, more and more young people are completing their high-school now.

[CM:] The young Crees, they are really just as smart as the Whites now.

[SW:] Yes.

Now anybody and everybody is becoming smart like that, they [*sc.* the Whites] have made them extremely smart. But usually when we two discuss things, or with my dear friend here [*sc.* Freda Ahenakew], some of the young people are also trying to go too far kî-âpacihtâcik [*sic*] onêhiyawêwiniwâw anim, êkâ ta-wanihtâcik ê-nêhiyâwicik;

[CM:] êha, tâpwê anima.

ka-nêhiyawêmototâkêcik. tâpiskôc ôma kâ-kêhtê-ayiwihk, ta-kitotâcik, â, ka-pîkiskwâtikocik nêhiyawa, nôcikwêsiw[a] âhpô kisêyiniwa. hâw, êkwa ta-nêhiyawêmototawâcik êkwa ta-kitotâcik oskinîkiwak, âsay awa nôtikwêsiw miyomahcihow, mîn âwa kisêyiniw mistahi miywêyihtam ê-takahkihtawât, kiyâm pikoyikohk ê-takahkâpêwiyit, kiyâm pikoyikohk ê-takahkisîhoyit oskinîkiwa, ê-nêhiyawêmototâkot. êwakw ân[i] ânim êkosi tâpwê ê-isi-miywâsik,

[CM:] êha.

êwakw ânima ta-kî-pimitisahahkik anima tâpwê anima, êwakw ânim âta kâ-kî-nâh-nôcihtâyâhk anima êkosi. tâpwê mâka mihcêt mîna mân ôma kâ-kî-mâmawôpihikoyâhkok, êwakw ân[i] ânima ê-kî-nitawêyihtahkik ta-nisitohtamôhâyâhkok anim êkos ânima ta-kakwê-~; êkosi mâna nititwânân, «wâh-wîcihtâyêko, wîcihtâyêkw ânima ta-kakwê-nêhiyawêyêk, ka-kaskihtânâwâw êkâ ta-nêpêwimoyêk,»

[CM:] mhi.

êkosi mâna nititânânak tâpwê anima.

[6] môy pô-~ môy ê-pakwâcikâtêk anima âkayâsîmowin nayêstaw, kikiskêyihtên, mâka wîstawâw nahiyikohk ta-kakwê-nêhiyawihtwâcik, ta-kakwê-~ nêhiyâwiwin ta-kakwê-kiskêyihtahkik.

[CM:] ka-pimitisahahkik onêhiyâwiwiniwâw.

namôy misawât wîhkâc nêhiyawayisiyiniw [*sic*], âsay ê-nêhiya-~ ê-nêhiyâwit, môy wîhkât ta-kî-kwêskinikowisiw ta-môniyâsiwit. êwakw ânim âhpô piko, îh! môy ê-pakwâtamâhcik ôma mitoni môniyâw-kîkway ôma ta-tôtahkik, mâka êwakw ân[i] ânima, êwakw ân[i] ânima kâ-itêyihtâkwahk anima, pikw âwiyak misawâc

since they are not going to speak Cree very much, you know; they should use their Cree at least half-and-half so that they might not lose their Creeness;

[CM:] Yes, that is true.

so that they would speak Cree to people. When people are old, for example, they should speak to them, well, so that the Crees, old women or old men, would speak to them in turn. Indeed, so that the young men would now talk to them in Cree and speak to them, already every old woman is pleased and every old man likes it greatly to hear their nice sounds, it does not matter how handsome a man is, it does not matter how well a young man is dressed, when he speaks to them in Cree. That is what is truly good in that respect,

[CM:] Yes.

they should truly keep up with that, that is certainly what we have been trying to accomplish in that respect. It is indeed also true when they have taken us to meetings that many want us to make them understand that, to try that –~; that is what we usually say, «Every time you make an effort at it, if you make an effort at trying to speak Cree, you will learn not to be self-conscious,»

[CM:] Hm.

it is true, that is what we usually say to them.

[6] It is not that speaking English is disliked as such, you know, but they should try to balance it by behaving like Crees as well, they should try to learn to be Cree.

[CM:] They should keep up with their Creeness.

In any case, a Cree person will never, being Cree already, he will never be able to have the Powers turn him into a Whiteman. That, for instance, look! it is not that one dislikes it for them to be doing these typical White things, it is that, to be sure, that is what people think about that, and everyone wants that now in any case. Some

êkos ânima êkwa ê-isi-nitawêyihtahk. âtiht saskahamâkêwak nêtê, osk-âyak mân ôma sâskwatôn, êkos ê-nôhtê-isi-wîhtamâkosicik kîkway, pâh-pahk[i] ôma tâpiskôc ôma kiyânaw kâ-nêhiyâwiyahk, kâ-kî-pê-is-ôhpikiyahk, tânisi kâ-kî-pê-isi-wâpahtamahk nêhiyaw-kîkway ôma, êwakw ânima mâna ê-nôhtê-kiskêyihtahkik.

[CM:] mhi, tâpwê anima êwako, miywâsin ta-kanawêyihtamihk ê-kî-nêhiyâwihk, nêhiyâwiwin.

[FA:] kinôhtê-mâmitonêyihtênâwâw?

[SW:] ahâw!

[external break]

[V]

[FA:] –~ kâh-nakinamâni [*laughter*]!

[7] ayâ, nôhkom awa miyâmâc ê-kî-owîc-~ ê-kî-omisimâwit, êkwa môy wîhkâc ê-ôh-~ kî-âyi-~ –~ kî-nayêhcâwan mâna kayâs, môy wîhkâc –~ kâ-nipâkwêsimohk piko mân ê-kî-wâpahtocik anihi wîcisâna. kîtahtawê pêyakwâw kâ-pê-sipwêhtêcik, ê-pê-kiyôtêhtahiht êkwa awa nôhkom, êkos îs ôm ê-at-~ ê-nîpihk ôma, kâ-pê-kiyôtêhtahikot êkwa ôh ê-pê-sa-sipwêpicicik, â. êkwa aya, êkwa niyanân ninakatikawinân nêtê môsômininâhk anima, nikâwiy awa, êkwa kotakak aya, aya, 'cimariy manitôhkân' ôta mâna kî-isiyîhkâsow, nânitaw iskwêw pêyak;

[CM:] âha, nikiskêyimâw ana, nikiskêyimâw.

êwakw ân[a] âna mân êkotê ê-kî-wîc-âyâmâyâhkok;

[CM:] âha.

êwakw âna niwa-wîc-âyâmânân êkota, ê-ma-môsiskwêwicik ôma nikâwiy awa.

[8] âspin [*sic*] ôki nôhkom, â, nâtakâm ê-kî-pê-ay-ispicicik – tâniyikohk êtikwê kâ-na-nôcihtâcik anima, ôm êkot[ê]

young people now light the pipe for elders over there in Saskatoon, wanting to be told about things in this way, for us it is a part of our Creeness, it is how we had grown up, what we have seen of Cree things, that is what they usually want to know.

[CM:] Hm, that is true, it is good to safeguard one's Cree identity, the Creeness.

[FA:] Do you two want a break to think?

[SW:] Well then!

[*external break*]

[**V**] [My Grandmother and her Siblings]

[FA:] – [*sc.* you always start telling] when I have stopped it [*sc.* the audio-recorder] [*laughter*]!

[7] Well, I believe my grandmother was the oldest in the family, and she never –~, it used to be quite difficult in the old days, she never –~, only when there was a Sundance did she and her siblings see one another. At one time when they left to return, my grandmother had been brought to visit, it was like this, it was in the summer when this one [*sc.* my grandfather] had taken her on a visit, they left to camp on the way back, well. Now as for my mother and me, we were left behind at *Môsôminināhk* [Moosomin] along with some others, one woman from somewhere else was called *Cimariy Manitôhkân*;

[CM:] Yes, I know that one, I know her.

we used to stay with that one over there;

[CM:] Yes.

we were staying with that one at that point, she and my mother were both on their own.

[8] Away went my grandmother with her camp, well, they were moving camp up north – I do not know how long they must

ê-pê-ka-kiyôtêcik, êkoni ôhi wîcisâna ôh ê-pê-kiyokawât ôhi – pâhpîwiyin wiy âwa mâna nikî-pê-âh-otihtikonân [*sic*], ayisk kî-okimâhkâniwiw, êkwa mâna kêtahtawê [*sic*] kâ-mâh-misi-mâmawôpicik ôm âya okimâhkânak, êkotê mân ê-kî-pê-takohtêt, nîkinâhk mâna kî-ayâw awa kisêyiniw. kîtahtawê [*sic*] aya, êhêy ê-ay-ihkihk, kîtahtawê kâ-takopicicik êkwa ôki nimosôm, ê-takohtêcik êkwa ôm êkotê ohci, êy, iyikohk kâ-kî-môcikêyihtamâhk kâhkêwakwa nôhkom ê-pêtât, ê-misi-pêtât, nîso maskimota, miton ê-mâh-mâmâkwaskinêki êkota ôhi kâ-~ môso-kâhkêwakwa miton ê-wâh-wiyinowiki! wahwâ, êkwa waskwayiwata mân ôhi, kikiskêyihtên, k-êti-~;

[CM:] êha, nikiskêyihtên, kî-osîhcikâtêwa mâna. êkotowahk. êkotowahk ôma iyinimina, iyikohk ê-pêtât êkwa mîn êtikwê wîsakîmina anihi. konit êkwa nîswayak, êwakw âwa cimariy (êkota môy kakêtihk kî-miywâpacihêw nimâmâ aw âyihk), ê-kâh-kîsisahk êkwa awa cimariy anih âya, anihi mînisa. âhêy, iyikohk nis[i] êkota mîn ê-~, mîn ê-kî-môcikêyihtamâhk anima, iyikohk ê-kî-pêcikêcik. êkosi mîna kî-pêcipahkêkinwêsiw nôhkom, tâniyikohk mâk êtikwê wiy êwako. wâ, ê-kî-pêcipahkêkinwêt, êkos ânima mâna kî-ka-~ ê-isko-kiskêyihtamân – mitoni wâh-wîhkât tipiyawê kâ-wâhkôhtohk ôm ê-kî-wa-wâpahtohk. ôtê mîna pêyak wîcisâna kî-ayâyiwa, môniyâwi-sâkahikanihk, mîn êkotê osîma pêyak.

[CM:] êkwa tâh-tâpwê wâhyaw, cî?

âha! âsôn[ê] êkoni, pêyakwâw miyâmâc piko ê-kî-wâpamât anihi wîcisâna, êkos ê-kî-~, êkos ê-kî-isi-nâh-nakataskêcik anih ôsîmisa.

[9] êkosi mân ânima, êkwa nikî-kâh-kakwêcihkêmon, awiyiwa [*sic*] mahti – ohci-kâsispôw, êkonik ôki kêhtê-ayak ta-kî-~ owâhkômâkaniwâwa êkota ohc âwiyak, ê-âh-itohtêyân ôm

have taken to get there, they were gone far over there to visit, she had gone to visit her siblings – *Pâhpîwiyin* [of Whitefish Lake] had often come to our place, for he had been a chief and sometimes when there were big chiefs' meetings he would arrive over there, this old man would stay at our house. All at once, hehey, it happened, all at once my grandfather arrived with his camp, arriving from over there and, hey, we were so excited since my grandmother brought dried meat, she brought lots of it, two bags full and they were tightly packed down, it was dried meat of a moose and really fat! Oh my, and then the birch-bark baskets, you know;

[CM:] Yes, I know, people used to make them.

that kind. Of that kind full of blueberries, she brought so many, and I guess cranberries too. They were in two pots, it was *Cimariy* (on that occasion my mom found her a very great help), now *Cimariy* was cooking them, these berries. Hahey, we were so very excited on that occasion, they obviously had brought home so much. And my grandmother had also brought home some tanned hides but I do not know how many. Well, she had brought home tanned hides, that is all I know about that – very rarely would you get to see your blood relatives. One of her siblings [*sc.* sisters] also lived over there at *Môniyâwi-sâkahikanihk* [Montreal Lake], and one of her younger siblings also over there [*sc.* at Whitefish Lake].

[CM:] And these places were truly far, weren't they?

Yes! especially that one [*sc.* at Montreal Lake], I believe she only saw that sibling [*sc.* sister] once, in that way they both left this earth behind, she and her younger sibling.

[9] And so it was, and I did ask around who it would have been – if someone was a descendant from there, from the old people's [*sc.* my grandparents'] relatives, and as I went to Sun-

ê-nipâkwêsimohk, nikî-âcimostâkawin anim âya, âta wiy âwiyak kâsispôw, ôsisimiwâwa kî-wâh-wîhêw ana pêyak iskwêw. êkot[a] ânim ês ê-pê-~ ê-kihci-wa-wâhkôhtamâhk.

[CM:] pitamâ êkwa nakina êkwa, pitamâ nika-mîcinân iyinimina [*laughter*]! pê-nakina pitamâ!

[SW:] tânitê êtikwê pâskac ê-mâkonamihk.

[FA:] mhm.

dances here and there I was told that, that somebody was a descendant, to be sure, that certain woman was naming off their grandchildren. So we did have proper relatives there.

[CM:] Turn it [*sc.* the audio-recorder] off for now, let us eat blueberries first [*laughter*]! Come and turn it off for now!

[SW:] Where do you press it, by the way, I wonder.

[FA:] Hm.

Sarah and David Whitecalf with their son Ted Whitecalf, c. 1958.

3

mêh-mêskoc nikî-pimohtahikawin

I was taken back and forth

mêh-mêskoc nikî-pimohtahikawin

[FA:] kinôhtê-âcimâwak cî, ma cî k-ô-~ kâ-kî-omosômiyan, kêhtê-ayak ê-kî-pê-ohpikihiskik, tânisi, tânis êkonik ê-kî-ay-isiyîhkâsocik?

[SW:] mhm.

[FA:] kikî-âcimostawin wiy âta wiya niy âsay.

[SW:] âha, âsay wiya kikî-âcimostawin –~ kikî-âcimostawin –~ kikî-âcimostâtin.

[I]

[1] âha, miton âya, âsay kikî-wîhtamâtin êwakw ân[i] ânima, tânis ê-kî-pê-ay-is-âyâcik nikêhtê-ayimak. nimosôm awa ê-nêhiyawiyîhkâsot, 'kâ-pêtwêwêmât' kî-isiyîhkâsow, onêhiyawi-wîhowin; êkwa nôhkom wiya, wîst ê-nêhiyawiyîhkâsot, 'osâkikwanêwisk', êwako ê-kî-ohci-wîhot aya, kik[i] [*sic*] ôki pisiskisîsak kâ-wî-mâci-sâkikiniyiki opîwâwâwa, kikiskêyihtên, êwakw ân[i] ânima onêhiyawi-wîhowin ohc ê-kî-ayât.

[FA:] tânisi ê-kî-~, tânisi?

'osâkikwanêwisk'.

[FA:] osâhkikonêwisk [*sic*]?

osâkikwanêwisk, tâpiskôc omîkwana ê-pê-sâkikiyit ana, kikiskêyihtên, osk-âya, osk-âyisis, êkos ê-kî-isi-~, êkosi ê-kî-isiyîhkâsot nôhkom wiya.

I was taken back and forth

[FA:] Do you want to tell about them, had not your late grandfather, had not the old people raised you all along, what, what were their names?

[SW:] mhm.

[FA:] As for me, of course, you had told me about that already.

[SW:] Yes, you had told me about that -~ you had told me about that -~, I had told you about that already.

[I] [My Grandparents at Moosomin]

[1] Yes, actually I had told you about that already, what my old people had been about. My grandfather had a Cree name, his name was *Kâ-pêtwêwêmât*, his Cree name; now as for my grandmother, she too had a Cree name, *Osâkikwanêwisk*, she used to have her name from that, when their down is about to emerge on the fledgling birds, you know, that is where she had her Cree name from.

[FA:] What was it -~, what?

Osâkikwanêwisk.

[FA:] *Osâhkikonêwisk* [*sic*]?

Osâkikwanêwisk, as when their wing feathers come to emerge, you know, on a young one, on a very young bird, that used to be my grandmother's name.

[FA:] ha! môy kikiskêyihtên ê-ohci-ay-is-âkâyâsîwiyîhkâtihcik?

nimosôm an[a] âya, *'Louis'*, *'Louis Applegarth'*, *'Louis Applegarth'*; môy ninisitohtên êwakw ânima – osâm ê-âyîm-~, ê-kî-âyimêyihtamiyit otasahkêwa anima, 'kâ-pêtwêwêmât', kikiskêyihtên, môy, môy ê-kî-itwêyit anima êwako. êkos ânim êkwa, êwako wîhowin ê-kî-miyikot anima –

[FA:] ê-kî-miyikot?

– âha, *Louis Applegarth*. êkwa, tâsipwâw [*sic*] ana nisis ana, 'sîsîkwêw' k-êtitân, *'John Applegarth'* kî-isiyîhkâtâw mân êwako.

[FA:] mhm.

êkwa nôhkom, ayahk, *'Catherine'* kî-isiyîhkâsow, êwako omôniyâwi-wîhowin.

[2] êkwa mîn ê-kî-ayamihâcik, nêhiyaw-~, nêhiyaw-kêhtê-ayak miton âniki, mâk êkwa kî-ayamihâwak, ê-kî-pâhkw-âyamihâcik; êkot[a] ânih êkon ânihi ohc ânih âya. môy wiy ê-pê-awâsisîwicik, nôhtaw êtikwê ê-kî-~ ayamihâwin ê-kî-otinahkik, kikiskêyihtên, êkota anim ôhci osîkahâhcikâsowi-wîhowiniwâwa anihi. môy wîhkât nôh-pa-pêhtawâwak, «niwîkihtonân» – tit-êtwêcik wîhkâc [*laughs*]!

[FA:] êha.

kî-takahki-kêhtê-ayiwiwak wiya, êwakw ânim âsay kâ-kî-âcimoyân, tânisi ê-kî-pê-ay-isi-pimâtisicik kêhtê-ayak êkonik aniki, nimosôm awa, ma kîkway miscahi sôniyâhkêwin ê-ohci-pê-ayâc, kî-kêhtê-ayiwiw âsay; mâka mistahi kî-kâ-~, kinwês ôki kêhtê-ayak kâ-kî-kakâyawâtisicik, êkos ê-kî-pê-itowiwit nimosôm. ahpô mân ê-kî-papâmi-têhtapit kêyâpic, misatimwa ê-kî-ayâ-~, mihcêt misatimwa ê-kî-ayâwât; ê-kî-sa-sipwê-têhtapit mâna kâ-nîpihk; aspapiwin, têhtapîwatimwa ê-kî-ayâwât.

[FA:] mhm.

[FA:] Ha! You wouldn't know what their English names used to be?

My grandfather's name was Louis, Louis Applegarth, Louis Applegarth; I do not understand that – the Indian agent found that *Kâ-pêtwêwêmât* too difficult, you know, he could not, he could not say it. And so he had given him that name –

[FA:] He had given it to him?

– yes, Louis Applegarth. Now as a matter of fact, my father's brother, whose name was *Sîsîkwêw* as I told you, that one had been given the name John Applegarth.

[FA:] mhm.

And my grandmother, now, her name was Catherine, that was her White name.

[2] Now they used to be Christians, they were Cree –~, they were very much old people of the Cree, but they used to be Christians, they used to be Roman Catholics; that is the source of those names. They had not been from their childhood, they must have taken the Christian religion up at some later time, you know, that is where they had their baptismal names from. I have never heard them say «We are married» – that they would ever say that [*laughs*]!

[FA:] Yes.

They were very good old people, that I have told about already, how these old people had lived their lives all along, as for my grandfather, he never had any way of making much money, he was already old; but he was one of those old people who are very active for a long time, that is the kind my grandfather used to be. He would even ride around on horseback still, he had horses, he used to have many horses; he would ride off on horse-back in the summer; on a saddle, he used to have a saddle-horse.

[FA:] mhm.

êkwa mâna ê-kî-sipwê-têhtapit mâna, misatimwa nânitaw ôm âya, ê-kî-papâmi-mâwasakotisahwât mân ê-kostahk aya, wayawîtim-âskîhkânihk t-êtohtêcik ôki misatimwak.

[3] êkwa, êwakw ânima kâ-kî-âcimostâtân, kâ-pipohk, kîkwây pik ôsôniyâhkêwinis nimosôm, ê-kî-pakitahwât, ê-nôcikinosêwêt; êkwa ê-âhkwatimâcik ayisiyiniwak – môy wiya piko, kahkiyaw ayisiyiniwak êwakw ânim ê-kî-osôniyâhkêwinicik kayâs; êwakw ânima ê-kî-pê-kaskihtât nimosôm, kâ-nîpiniyik –~, kâ-piponiyik ôm êkosi ê-kî-pê-itatoskêt. kî-kakâyawâtisiw, ahpô kâh-wiyahpicikêci, ê-kî-na-nâtaskosiwêt. wâhyaw mîn ê-kî-mân-~ ê-kî-is-ô-~-oy-otâpâsot, ê-na-nâtaskosiwêt, maskosiy[a] ê-pêtât. «nitohtawîhkan!» kî-itwêw mâna, mitoni kî-kisîwêyiwa sasêwêyâkanisa ê-âpacihât, «nitohtawîhkan! nitawi-yôhtênamawîhkan iskwâhtêmihkân, pêtâyâni maskosiya,» ê-kî-itwêt; êkwa man-~, môy êtikwê ê-misikitiyân, ê-kî-ispahtâyân mâna, piyêtwêwêhtawakwâwi sasêwêyâkanak, ê-nitawi-yôhtêpitamân iskwâhtêmihkân; ê-takotâpâsot nimosôm. îh, iyikohk ê-kî-kakâyawâtisit! anoht mân êkwa kâ-koskwêyihtamân, nêhiyaw-kisêyiniwak wîpac ê-pôn-âyihk-~ ê-pôn-~, ê-nêsowâtisicik êkwa anohc miconi, mâcayak ohci wîscawâw âtiht.

[4] êkwa kâ-nîpihk, kâ-nôhcê-sôniyâhkêcik, êwakw ânim êkwa maskihkiy kâ-kî-ititân kâ-kî-mônahahkik mâna, 'mînisîhkês' kâ-kî-isiyîhkâtêk, ê-kî-miywakihtêk kayâs, êwakw ânima piko mîna ê-kî-wêhcasik isi-sôniyâhkêwinis ê-kî-sîpwêt-~ ê-kî-sipwêtâpâsoyâhk mâna; ahpô mâna nânitaw ê-kî-~ ê-kî-itohtêyâhk, êkotê ê-kî-nitawi-wa-wîkiyâhk mâna, ê-papâ-ma-mônahikêcik. êkwa ê-~, êkwa –~, môy mîna mâna ê-ohci-pâsahkik anima, nipîhk mâna cîki kî-nitaw-âstâwak ahpô ê-ayahahkik, êkos îs ê-kî-kosikwahk anima maskihkiy, kikiskêyihtên, ê-atâwâkêcik.

[FA:] êha.

êwakw ânima sôniyâhkêwinis, piko mîna mâna ê-~, ê-kî-tôtahkik.

Now he used to ride off on horse-back, in various places would he round up the horses for he was concerned that the horses would stray beyond the bounds of the reserve.

[3] Now, that which I told you about, in winter the only source of cash income my grandfather had was to set nets and to catch fish; and people would freeze them – not him alone, all the people used to made money with that long ago; that my grandfather was able to do, in the summer –~, in the winter that was the work he did. He used to be very active, he would even go for a load of hay every time he had harnessed the team. He also used to go far with his team, going for a load of hay and bringing in the hay. «Listen for me later!» he would say, he used little bells [*sc.* on the harness] which were really loud, «Listen for me later! Go and open the gate for me later, when I bring in the hay,» he used to say; I could not have been very big, I used to run to the gate every time I could hear the bells approaching, I would go and open the gate; when my grandfather arrived with his team. Look, he used to be so active! Today now it always amazes me that the old Cree men stop so early, getting quite weak, and some well before their time.

[4] Now in the summer, when they wanted to make a little money, they would dig that medicinal root, as I told you, the 'seneca-root' as it was called, it used to fetch a good price in the old days, that used to be the only thing with which it was easy to make a little money, we used to drive off by team and wagon; or we would go somewhere and go and camp there, going about digging seneca-root. Now, they also did not use to dry it, they used to put it close to water or cover it with dirt, in that way that medicinal root was heavy, you know, when they sold it.

[FA:] Yes.

That was a way of making a little money, they also had to do that. Not they alone, all the old people must have done that, all the

môy wiyawâw piko, kahkiyaw kêhtê-ayak êkos êtikwê mâna, kahkiyaw ayisiyiniwak ahpô iskwêwak, waniyaw, êkos ê-kî-pê-isi-pa-pimâcihocik.

[5] êkwa mîna mâna, ôma kâ-pê-ma-mâmiskôtamân, kayâs iyikohk, misatimwak nayêstaw ê-kî-pê-âpatisicik, êêy, tâpwê ê-kî-ay-âyimihohk kayâs, nêpâkwêsimohki, tâniyikohk ê-âhkwâstêk, ê-pimipicihk, kâ-nipâkwêsimohk nânitaw ê-itohtêhk. anohc êkwa, sêhkêpayîs ê-âpatisit namôy kâh-kinwês, pôskw-âyihk ê-takopayihk, êwako mîna mân ê-kiskisiyân anima ê-kî-pa-pimitâpâsohk. ê-ayês-~ ê-isitâpâsohk itê, ôma kâ-~ kâ-~ k-~ wâh-nipâkwêsimohki, êkwa ê-kî-nahâpahtamihk, ita kâ-tawâk ôm ê-paskêtâpâsohk, mayaw ita iyihk-~ îhkacawâs ôma k-âyâk, sâkahikanisisa, êkoc[a] ê-paskêhk, êkoca ê-pim-âyiwêpihk, ahpô ê-kapêsihk, êkoc[a] ê-mânokêhk, êkosi ê-kî-pê-itâcihocik kayâs ayisiyiniwak êwakw ânima, êkwa ê-kî-miywêyihtamihk ê-papâ-nitawi-wâpahkêhk ôma, êkotowahk nipâkwêsimowina; ahpô kâ-kiyôtêcik êkos ânima, ê-pa-pimipicicik anima, wâhyaw ê-kî-miywêyihtahkik ê-papâmipic-~-papâmâcihocik, wâhyaw ôma akâmi-tipahaskân. îh, ê-kî-kaskihtâcik anima mân ôta ohc ôma akâmi-tipahaskân ê-ispicicik (tânitahtwâw mâna kâ-ati-kapêsiwâkwê anima ahpô piko), mîn êkotê ê-kakwê-takohtêcik, môy wiyawâw pik ôta ohc ôki *Saskatchewan*, nêki mîna pêyakwan, *States* mâna wîstawâw ôtê is ôma ê-kî-pê-~ ê-kî-âyimisicik kayâs kêhtê-ayak, wâh-wâhyaw owâhkômâkaniwâwa ê-kî-ayâyit, êkospîhk mîn ânima mâna. êkwa kâ-nôhcê-wâpahtocik, êkos ânima piko mâna, piko ê-kî-pimipicicik kâ-nôhtê-wâpahtocik. mâka, ma kîkway kayâs mistah âskihkohkân ohti-pê-âpatisiw; ahpô *bus*, nama kîkway êkospîhk kayâs, ohc-âpatisiw ayisiyiniw ta-kî-pôsit.

[SW:] êkwa, kîkwây mîn êtikwê k-ây-âtotênânaw, kika-papâ-pîkiskwêyahk.

people, even the women, simply everyone, that was how they used to make a living.

[5] And also this which I have been discussing, in the old days it was so that they only used horses, hey, it was truly difficult in the old days, whenever there was a Sundance, it would be so hot as you travelled on the way to a Sundance somewhere. Today now, with the use of a car it does not take long, you get there the same day, I also remember driving along with team and wagon. You drove to where the Sundance was to be held, and you were quick to see where there was an opening [*sc.* in the bush] and you turned off there with your team and wagon, as soon as there was a little slough, some little lakes, you turned off there a little and stopped to rest there a little, or even camped there overnight and pitched your little tent there, that was the way the people used to live in the old days with respect to that, and everyone liked going about looking at that kind, the Sundances; it was the same even for visitors, they moved along with their camps, they loved moving their camps around far away, far across the border [*sc.* with the US]. Look, they were able to go from here and move across the border (I wonder how many times they camped along the way, for instance), trying to get there, not only the ones from Saskatchewan here, they were the same over there, they also came here from the States too, the old people in the old days had a hard time, their relatives were scattered far and wide, it used to be like that in those days, too. And when they wanted to see one another, that was the only way, they had to move along with their camp when they wanted to see one another. But in the old days there were no motor vehicles at all that might be used; not even a bus, there was nothing to be used in those days of long ago which people might ride on.

[SW:] Now, I wonder what else we might tell about so that we might go about speaking.

[FA:] mihcêtin êtikw âta, kitâcimowina.

[*external break*]

[II]

[6] êkw ânima, *Fineday* ana,

[FA:] êha.

Fineday ana, â, nimosôm, niya nimosôm. â, êwakw âna kâ-kî-pê-miskâkot anihi, *States* ohc ânihi, ê-kî-pê-âcimôhikot anima, kikiskêyihtên,

[FA:] êha.

êkos êkwa, mâka mîna nêhiyawak, 'otâcimôhiwêw' kî-isiyîhkâtêwak anih êkoni, anihi, tâpwê anima, pikw îtê mân âna sakâhk, êkotê mân âwa *Fineday* ê-kî-itohtahiht, êkotê ê-âcimôhikot anihi môniyâsa, kikiskêyihtên; êkotê mân ê-kî-nitaw-ây-âcimocik. êkos îs ôma kîkway, nêhiyaw-kîkway ana ê-kî-kakwê-pê-kiskêyihtahk ana, mâka môy ôhc-âkayâsîmow ana kisêyiniw ana, *Fineday* ana. ê-nêhiyawêhk, 'kâ-miyokîsihkwêw' kî-isiyîhkâsow, nimosôminân ana. êkwa, piko mâna wîsta tâpiskôt niya, nama kîkway ê-âkayâsîmot, ê-nêhiyawêt piko. kî-ihtakoyiwa mâna nâpêwa ê-kî-itwêstamâkot, kikiskêyihtên, ê-ati-wîhtamâht ana môniyâs ana, tânis ê-itwêt awa nimosôm, ê-itâcimoscawâc [*sic*]; nikiskisin êwakw ân[i] ânima, ayisk ê-awâsisîwiyân, kwêh-kwêkwask ômis îsi [*gesture*] mâna

[FA:] kikî-~

nikî-pim-îtohtân,

[SW:] êhâ,

môsômininâhk nikî-ayân âskaw, nikâwiy aw ê-kî-onâpêmit êkota *Sweetgrass*, anima. êwakw âwa *Fineday*, anima, êkota ê-kî-wîcihiwêt awa nikâwiy, okosisiyiwa ôh êkon ê-kî-onâpêmit nikâwiy; êwak

[FA:] There must be plenty, to be sure, of your stories. [*external break*]

[**II**] [Sweetgrass Old Men: *Kâ-miyokîsihkwêw* / Fineday]

[6] Now about that one, that Fineday,

[FA:] Yes.

that Fineday, well, my grandfather, for me he was my grandfather [*sc.* at Sweetgrass]. Well, it was him that the one from the States [*sc.* David Mandelbaum] had come to find, it was that he had come to get him to tell stories, you know,

[FA:] Yes.

and so now of course the Crees called that one *Otâcimôhiwêw* [*lit.* 'makes people tell stories'], that one, it is true, Fineday used to be taken anywhere in the bush, there that Whiteman would have him tell stories, you know; there they would go and tell stories. Things like this, he had come to try to find out about Cree things, but that old man did not speak English, that Fineday. In Cree his name was *Kâ-miyokîsihkwêw*, that grandfather of ours. Now he too, just like me, could not speak any English, he had to speak Cree exclusively. There used to be a man who would interpret for him, you know, that Whiteman would be told step by step what my grandfather was saying, as he was telling him about things; I remember that, because I was a child

[FA:] You were –~

I used to go back and forth like this [*gesture*],

[SW:] yes,

sometimes I was in *Môsômininâhk* [Moosomin], but it was that my mother had married a man in Sweetgrass here. It was this Fineday, it was that, my mother had married into that family, my mother

ôhci nikâwiy awa *'Fineday'* kî-âpacihtâw,

[FA:] âha.

'Mrs Fineday', nikâwiy, êkosi kî-isiyîh-~, êwakw ânima *name* kî-âpacihtâw mâna. êkosi, nikiskisin anim êwakw ânima k-êtwêyan anim âna, nîsta mâna nikî-wâpamâw ana nâpêw ana, ayahk mâna tâpiskôc *van, bus* kisâstaw, êkotowahk ana mân ê-kî-papâmipicit ana nâpêw ana, kâ-pê-takohtêt, kikiskêyihtên – âstamispîhk, tânitahtw-âskiy êtik ôma, êkotê ôtê nânitaw *States* ê-itohtêt, â, *Ernest* côhcôsis (kikî-kiskêyimâw?

[FA:] mhm.

Ernest côhcôsis),

[HC:] hm.

êwakw ân[a] êkotê ê-itohtêt, êkoni anihi nâpêwa, êkotê êsa kâ-kî-wâpamât,

[FA:] hmhm.

kêyâpic ê-pimâtisit êwakw ân[a] âna, ana otâcimôhiwêw, sêmâk ês ê-wâpamikot ôma *Saskatchewan* ê-wîhtamawât ê-ohtohtêt, êko-~, sêmâk êsa kâ-kî-wîhtamâkot kisêyiniwa êkoni anihi, «niya mâna kâ-kî-nitawâpamak ana, *Fineday*,» k-êtikot êsa, «otâcimowina ôta kahkiyaw nikanawêyihtamwân,» kâ-kî-itwêt. êkwa êwakw âwa *Ernest* côhcôsis kâ-kî-wîhtamawit, «kikiskisin cî êwakw ânima, êwako mân âna, 'otâcimôhiwêw' ê-kî-isiyîhkâtiht mâna môniyâs, awa mâna *Fineday* kâ-kî-pê-pîkiskwêhikot, êwakw ân[a] ôtê ninitawâpamâw *States*, kêyâpic ê-pimâtisit,» ê-kî-itwêt. sêmâk, «nikiskisin,» nititâw, «nikî-wâpamâw mân âna môniyâs» – môy mîna kisêyiniw, nahiyikohk oskinîkiw ana, mâna kâ-kî-takohtêt, kî-osk-âyiwiw êkospîhk ana.

[HC:] kayâs!

[SW:] kayâs! êha.

had married that one's son; for that reason my mother used the name 'Fineday',

[FA:] Yes.

'Mrs Fineday', that was my mother's name --~, she used that name. And so I remember what you [*sc.* Chris Wolfart] said about that one [*sc.* Mandelbaum], I too used to see that man, in a van like, in a kind of bus, that man used to travel around in that kind when he came here, you know – more recently, I wonder how many years ago it was since he went over there to the States somewhere, well, Ernest Tootoosis (did you know him?

[FA:] mhm.

Ernest Tootoosis?),

[HC:] hm.

he had gone there and he reportedly saw that man there,

[FA:] hmhm.

that one was still alive, that *Otâcimôhiwêw*, he reportedly recognised him [*sc.* Ernest Tootoosis] right away when he told him he came from Saskatchewan, and that old man reportedly told him right away, «It was I who used to go see Fineday,» he reportedly said to him, «I have kept all his stories here,» is what he had said. And it was Ernest Tootoosis himself who told me that, «Do you remember that time, the Whiteman who used to be called *Otâcimôhiwêw*, the one who had come to have Fineday speak to him, I went and saw that man there in the States, he is still alive,» he had said. Right away, «I remember,» I said to him, «I used to see that Whiteman» – not an old man either, rather a young man when he had come here; he had been young at that time.

[HC:] It was long ago!

[SW:] It was long ago! Yes.

[III]

[...]

[7] [SW:] nîkis-~ nikiskêyimâw êwakw ana kisêyiniw an[a], âha, kâ-kîsikâw-pîhtikwêw.

[FA:] âha.

[SW:] âha; 'kâ-kîsikâw-pîhtikwêw' kî-isiyîhkâsow kisêyiniw,

[FA:] êha.

[SW:] îh tâpwê.

[HC:] kikî-kiskêyimâw cî?

[SW:] âha, nikis-~, âha, nikî-kiskêyimâw mîn êwako *Sweetgrass*. êwako mîna nikiskêyimâw, nakiwacîhk ana kisêyiniw, êwako mîn ohci, êkoni mîn ê-kî-papâ-âcimôhât êwakw ân[a] âna, nâpêw ana, môniyâs ana; 'kâ-kîsikâw-pîhtikwêw' kî-isiyîhkâsow kisêyiniw ana. êwako mîna kayâs kîkway êtikwê mâna ê-kî-âyimôtahk ana kisêyiniw. êkoni – êcik ân[a] êtikwê kâh-nipit [*sic*], êcik ân[a] êkwa êwako, iya, nikî-kiskêyimâw ana.

[8] [SW:] ayahk mîna mâna, ê-kî-kakwê-~ nêhiyaw-nikamona mân ê-kî-kakwê-kiskêyihtahk, nistês ana mâna, '*Archie Fineday*' isiyîhkâsow, êwakw âna mân ê-kî-kiskinohamawât ayihk, nêhiyawatâmowina. tâpwê ê-kî-kaskihtât mîn âna môniyâs ê-nêhiyawatâmot anim âyihk,

[HC:] mhm.

[SW:] nêhiyaw-nikamon anima, pêyak –

[FA:] nama kîkway ômatowahk [*points to audio-recorder*] wiy êkospî?

[SW:] ma kîkway kayâs!

[FA:] ê-kî-masinahikêt piko.

[III] [Sweetgrass Old Men: *Kâ-kîsikâw-pîhtikwêw* / Coming-Day]

[...]

[7] [SW:] I knew that old man, yes, *Kâ-kîsikâw-pîhtikwêw*,

[FA:] Yes.

[SW:] Yes; *Kâ-kîsikâw-pîhtikwêw* was the old man's name,

[FA:] Yes.

[SW:] look, truly.

[HC:] Did you use to know him?

[SW:] Yes, yes; I also used to know that one on Sweetgrass. I knew him, that old man was at *Nakiwacîhk* [Sweetgrass], that man also used to go around getting him to tell stories, that Whiteman; *Kâ-kîsikâw-pîhtikwêw* was that old man's name. He, too, must have been discussing things about the old days, this old man. That one – apparently he must have died [*?sc.* Leonard Bloomfield], now apparently he too, well now, I used to know him.

[8] [SW:] And he would also try –~, he would try to learn Cree songs with words, my older parallel cousin, Archie Fineday was his name, he would teach him songs in Cree. And indeed that Whiteman also learnt to sing that one in Cree,

[HC:] mhm.

[SW:] that Cree song with words, one –~

[FA:] There was nothing like this [*points to audio-recorder*] at that time?

[SW:] There was none in the old days!

[FA:] He just wrote everything down.

[SW:] ê-kî-mit-~

[external break]

[9] [HC:] êkwa awa kisêyiniw, kâ-kîsikâw-pîhtikwêw,

[SW:] âha.

[HC:] â, kikiskêyimâw cî êwakw âwa?

[SW:] âha, nikî-kiskêyi-~, nikî-pê-kiskêyimâw kisêyiniw, mâk âyisk, namôy ân[a] âya –~, môy ê-ohci-wâpit, ana kisêyiniw, kâ-kîsikâw-pîhtikwêw; môy ê-ohci-nahâpit, nayêstaw aya –~, ômatowihk [*points to her cane*] ê-kî-âpacihtât ê-kî-pimohtahiht.

[HC:] mhm.

[SW:] mâka wiya kî-kakâyawâtisiw, tâpwê êtikw ânima kwayask kî-âcimow wîst êkota. êwako cî mîn îhtakoniyiwa otâcimowina êtikwê, cî?

[FA:] hmhm.

[SW:] kî-kisêyinîwiw an[a] êwakw âna kâ-kîsikâw-pîhtikwêw, tânitahto êtikwê mâka ê-kî-itahtopiponêt?

[10] [SW:] *Fineday* ana mîna kî-kisêyinîwisiw mitoni, kâ-miyokîsihkwêw êwako, –

[FA:] kâ-miyokîsihkwêw.

[SW:] âha; tâpiskôc ê-miyw-~ ê-miywâsik kîsik,

[HC:] mhm.

[SW:] kikiskêyihtên, êkos îsi mîn êwakw ân[a] ê-isiyîhkâ-~ ê-wî-isiyîhkâsot anima, kâ-miyokîsihkwêw; êkos ê-itwêmakaniyik anim ôwîhowin [*sic*].

[SW:] He used to –~
[*external break*]

[9] [HC:] Now this old man, *Kâ-kîsikâw-pîhtikwêw,*
[SW:] Yes.
[HC:] well, did you know this one?
[SW:] Yes, I have known the old man all along, but of course he was blind, that old man, *Kâ-kîsikâw-pîhtikwêw;* he could not see much, only –~, he would use one of these [*points to her cane*] and he would be led.
[HC:] mhm.
[SW:] But he was very active, he truly must have been a proper story-teller at the time. Are his stories available too, I wonder?
[FA:] hmhm.
[SW:] That *Kâ-kîsikâw-pîhtikwêw* was an old man, but I wonder how old he was?

[10] [SW:] That Fineday was quite old too, that *Kâ-miyokîsihkwêw* –
[FA:] *Kâ-miyokîsihkwêw.*
[SW:] yes; like the sky is beautiful,
[HC:] mhm.
[SW:] you know, that is the name he was going to have, *Kâ-miyokîsihkwêw;* that is the meaning of his name.

[11] [SW:] â, kayâs kêhtê-ayak, wiyawâw mistahi kî-pê-miywâsiniyiw otâcimowiniwâw, mâk ânohc êkwa niyanân ayisk ôma nôhtaw kâ-pimipayi-~ kâ-wî-kakwê-~, êwakw ânima ê-kiskinowâsohtamâhk kîkway, tânis âti [*sic*] ê-kî-pê-isi-pa-pêhtamâhk kîkway ôh âcimowina. nôhtaw nîsta, namôy mistahi kîkway, îkamâ kayâs ohti-pê-êkos-îsi-na-nâkatôhkêyân [*sic*]. anohc êkwa, êtikwê nikâh-kiskêyihtên kîspin nîst êkos îs êwak ôma ta-papâ-nâh-nitôskamân kîkway nêhiyaw-pîkiskwêwina, nêhiyaw-âcimowina kîkway, êkos îsi.

[FA:] pêyakwan mâka kikâh-kî-âtotên ôma mâna, ê-ay-it-~ ê-ay-itahkamikahk,

[SW:] mhm.

[FA:] ê-kî-ay-itahkamikahk, ê-kî-ay-itahkamikisiyêk, ê-ay-ispayiyêk wawiyatâcimowina, pikw îtowahk mosc-âcimowinisa.

[IV]

[12] [FA:] âsay cî anima ê-pimipayik?

[SW:] êwako cî ê-wî-pîkiskwêt?

[FA:] kiya, kiya, k-âya-~

[SW:] wîhkasko-kisêyin, â,

[FA:] kiwî-ay-âcimâw cî ana wîhkasko-kisêyin?

[SW:] âhêy, êwako wiya ê-awâsisîwiyân, môy nôhtisâpamâw [*sic*] ahpô êwakw âna kisêyiniw, wiya,

[FA:] mhm.

[SW:] môy ân[a] êwako wiy ân[a] êwako, kayâs an[a] êtikwê ê-kî-~ ê-kî-nipit, kikiskêyihtên, êwako kisêyiniw, môy nikiskêyimâw êwakw âna

[11] [SW:] Well, in the old days there used to be a great treasure of the old people's stories but of course for us today it is too late –~ when we try –~ as we listen and learn things, how we have gradually come to hear these stories. For me, too, it came too late, it was not very much, I never paid much attention to things like that in the old days. Today now, I guess I would know these things if I too were to go about in that way searching for Cree texts, for Cree historical accounts, in that way.

[FA:] But at the same time you could simply tell about how things happen,

[SW:] mhm.

[FA:] about how things used to happen, about things you all used to do, about funny incidents which happened to you all, any kind of just-so stories.

[IV] [Sweetgrass Old Men: *Wîhkasko-kisêyin* / Sweetgrass]

[12] [FA:] Is it [*sc.* the audio-recorder] running already?

[SW:] Is HE [*sc.* Chris Wolfart] going to speak?

[FA:] It is YOUR turn, yours,

[SW:] *Wîhkasko-kisêyin*, well,

[FA:] are you going to tell about *Wîhkasko-kisêyin*?

[SW:] well then, that one, when I was a child I did not even live to see that old man, him,

[FA:] mhm.

[SW:] for it was not that one, he must have died long ago, you know, that old man, I did not know that *Wîhkasko-kisêyin* as he was called; in the old days 'wîhkasko-kisêyin' kâ-kî-isiyîhkâsot; kayâs êwako ês ânita nakiwacîhk êsa pêyak nîkân kisêyiniw. ahpô, môy –~ môy nânitaw wîhkât niwâpahtên êwako *picture*, omasinipayiwin ana, wîhkasko-kisêyin.

[FA:] kî-âcimêwak cî mâka mâna kayâs kêhtê-ayak êkon ânihi?

[SW:] môy mistah êwako kîkway nipêhtên otâcimowin, êha.

[FA:] mâk âya, kî-ay-âcimikâsow cî mâna, ê-kî-ay-isiyinîhkêt?

[13] [SW:] êha, wîhcik-~, wîhcikaniwiw wiya mitoni, «wîhkasko-kisêyin,» ê-itwêskihk, mâk êkwa, namôya âcimikâsow êtikwê tânis ê-kî-pê-ay-isiyinîhkêt êwakw âna wîhkasko-kisêyin, mâk êkwa, namôy niy êwako kîkway nikiskêyihtên,

[FA:] kipêhtên –~

[SW:] êha, môy kîkway nipêhtên êwakw ânima âcimowin anima, mastaw ayisk ôma kâ-isi-otiniyêk [*sic*] ôma, namôy nâh-nâkac ôtê kîkway na-~, nâway nôh-pê-na-nâkatôhkân êkoni ôhi kîkway ta-kakwê-kiskêyihtamân ômis îs âcimowina; mas-~ mâka wiy ânima nikâh-kiskisomik aw ânima kâ-itwêt anih âyihk, mitoni wiy êwako nitô-~ nitôcihcikiskisin anima. mitoni, môy êwako kîkway nikiskêyihtên ana wîhkasko-kisêyin, kîkway otay-isiyinîhkêwin mîn ô-~ opê-itâcimowin kîkway; êwako nikiskêyihtên. pêyakwan ôtê môsômin kisêyiniw, môsômininâhk k-êtwêhk,

he reportedly was one of the leading old men over here in *Nakiwacîhk* [Sweetgrass]. I have never even seen his picture anywhere, a picture of him, of *Wîhkasko-kisêyin*.

[FA:] But did the old people long ago talk about that one?

[SW:] I never heard much in the way of stories about him, yes.

[FA:] But would stories be told be about him, what kind of a person he had been?

[13] [SW:] Yes, his name was mentioned a great deal, they are forever saying «*Wîhkasko-kisêyin*», but then apparently there are no stories about him, what kind of a person that *Wîhkasko-kisêyin* had been, but now as for me, I do not know anything about that,

[FA:] Have you heard –~

[SW:] Yes, I have not heard any stories about him, for it is only recently that you two [*sc.* Freda Ahenakew and Chris Wolfart] chose me as an authority, on various occasions over there I had not been paying attention to these things, that I would try to to learn about historical accounts like these; but he [*sc.* Chris Wolfart] keeps reminding me of them by what he says about them, and then I really remember far back. I do not know much about that *Wîhkasko-kisêyin*, anything about his character or any traditional accounts of him; that I know. The same with old man *Môsômin* over there at *Môsôminināhk* [Moosomin] as they say,

êwako mîna nama kîkway nikiskêyihtên êkotê ohc âcimowin.

[14] [SW:] ana mîn âya, *Poundmaker*, ma kîkway mîn êwakw âna nikiskêyihtên.

[FA:] mhm.

[SW:] êwako wiya mâna *picture* niwâpahtên ana, kisêyiniw, mâka môy mîn êwako kîkway nikiskêyihtên, otâcimowin kîkway tânis ôtay-isiyinîhkêwin êwako kisêyiniw.

[V]

[15] mîna mâna nôhkom kâ-kî-âcimot, ê-kî-kakâyawâtisicik kayâs nôtikwêwak êsa mâna, «hêy, kâh-kîsi-mîcisoyâni,» ê-kî-itwêt mân nôhkom, «tâpiskôt mân îskwêwak ê-mawinêhotoyâhk,» ê-kî-itwêt mâna, ê-pahkêkinohkêcik kîkisêpâ. mos-~ wîpac kîkisêpâ, wayawîtimihk, kiyâm ê-pipohk, êsa mân ê-âhkwatik ôma pahkêkin, «ê-kakwâhyaki-miyopayik pahkêkin ê-âhkwatik êkos îsi, ê-mâtahamihk,» ê-kî-itwêt mâna. «ê-kî-pâhpihicik mân îskwêwak, wâh-wîpac niya nîkân kâ-mâc-îhtâyân ôma kâ-pahkêkinohkêyân ê-matw-~ ê-matwêyâtahikêyân,» ê-kî-~ ê-kî-itwêt mâna. êwakw ânim ê-kî-isi-kakâyawâtisicik iskwêwak ôma ê-kî-pê-isi-pahkêkinohkêcik wîstawâw mistahi, êwako ê-kî-sôhkaniyik otatoskêwiniwâw; ê-kî-pê-kakâyawisihkahtahkik. êkwa mîna, mîciwin, tânisi kâ-i-~ anima kâ-itwêyân kâ-pê-is-ôsîhtamâsocik, kâ-isi-mîcisocik kâhkêwakwa nayêstaw, êkotowahk ê-kî-pê-omîciwinicik êwako mîna.

[FA:] kinosêwa êtikwê mîna kî-kaskâpaswêwak?

[16] êhâ, kinosêwa mîna! êkota mîna kâhkêwakwa ê-osîhtâcik, kinosêwa. êwako nikî-pê-wâpahtên mîna nôhkom êkosi ê-kî-pê-isîhcikêt, êkwa kâhkê-~ kinosêwa ôhi kâ-osîhâcik kâhkêwakwa, êkwa îwahikana mîn êkota, êha; îwahikana mîn

I also do not know any stories from there either.

[14] [SW:] Poundmaker also, I also do not know anything about him either.

[FA:] mhm.

[SW:] Of that one I have seen pictures, that old man, but I also do not know anything about him, accounts of him or about that old man's character.

[V] [My Grandmother at Moosomin]

[15] My grandmother too, when she would tell stories, in the old days the old women reportedly were very active, «Hey, every time I was finished eating [*sc.* breakfast],» my grandmother used to say, «it was like we women were trying to outdo each other,» she used to say, they would be working the hides in the morning. Early in the morning, outdoors, even in winter, the hide would be frozen, it is reported, «A hide that is frozen like that is excellent for scraping,» she used to say. «The women would laugh at me when again and again I was first out and working the hides, and one could hear my scraping,» she used to say. That is how active the women were, they used to do all the work of preparing the hides, that was hard work they did; they toiled at it tirelessly. And also with food, as I have said, how they prepared their own food, how they only ate dried meat, they also used to have that kind as their food.

[FA:] They must have smoked fish too?

[16] Yes, fish too! They made dried meat from that too, from fish. That I also used to see my grandmother do that way, when they prepared the fish to make dried meat and then also pounded meat from that, yes; then she also made pounded meat from that.

êkota mân ê-kî-osîhât. êwako mîna nikî-pê-ocihci-wâpahtên; êkos ê-kî-pê-isîhcikêt mâna.

[VI]

[...]

[17] [SW:] –~ âcimowina.

[FA:] awîn ê-kî-âcimostâsk ôh âcimowina k-âcimostawiyâhk?

[SW:] â, nôhkom; nôhkom ê-kî-pêhtawak. êkwa, êwakw âna nimosôm, kâ-kî-ohpikihit, êwako 'kâ-pêtwêwêmât' kî-isiyîhkâsow, êkoni ôh ôtâcimowiniwâwa.

[HC:] ki-~ kimâmâ omâmâwa?

[SW:] âha, nimâmâ omâmâwa.

[FA:] tânis ê-kî-isiyîhkâsocik?

[SW:] â, êwakw âna k-~, omôniyâwi-wîhowin nôhkom, '*Catherine Applegarth*',

[FA:] hm.

[SW:] êha, êkwa êwakw ânima k-êtitân, onêhiyawi-wîhowin, mâka namôy, môy mistahi ohc-âpacihtâw êwako, 'katinîn' kî-isiyîhkâtâw ê-nêhiyawiyîhkâtiht, âha.

[FA:] êkwa, kî-nêhiyawiyîhkâsow mîna?

[SW:] êkw ânim ô-~, êha, êkwa êwakw ânim 'ôsâkikwanêwisk', êwak ônêhiyawi-wîhowin, êha; mâk ê-âyimaniyik anima, nawat mâna 'katinîn' kî-isiyîhkâtâw. êkwa nimosôm, kâ-pêtwêwêmât, tâpiskôc kîkway ê-pêcimât, kikiskêyihtên, êkosi.

I have also lived long enough to have seen that; the way she used to do this.

[VI] [My Grandparents at Moosomin (reprise)]

[...]

[17] [SW:] –~ stories.

[FA:] Who had told you these histories which you are telling us about?

[SW:] Well, my grandmother; I used to hear my grandmother tell them. And then my grandfather, the one who had raised me, that one was called *Kâ-pêtwêwêmât*, these are their stories.

[HC:] Your mom's mom?

[SW:] Yes, my mom's mom.

[FA:] What were their names?

[SW:] Well, that one's, my grandmother's White name was Catherine Applegarth,

[FA:] hm.

[SW:] yes, and I told you that, her Cree name, but she did not use it very much, she was called *Katinîn* when she was mentioned by name in Cree, yes.

[FA:] And did she also have a Cree name?

[SW:] It was that, yes, now it was that one, *Osâkikwanêwisk*, that was her Cree name, yes; but that was too difficult and she was called *Katinîn* instead. Now my grandfather, *Kâ-pêtwêwêmât*, as if he called some spirit in, you know, in that way.

[...]

[FA:] tânisi kani kimosôm
ê-kî-isi-ay-~-môniyâwiyîhkâsot?

[SW:] *'Louis', 'Louis Applegarth'.*

[FA:] *Louis.*

[HC:] êkwa ê-nêhiyawêhk?

[SW:] 'kâ-pêtwêwêmât', 'kâ-pêtwêwêmât'.

[HC:] kâ-pêtwêwêmât.

[SW:] âh[a] êkosi, êkosi, 'kâ-pêtwêwêmât', êkosi
kî-isiyîhkâsow nimosôm.

[VII]

[18] [FA:] êkwa ê-kî-pêyakoyan?

[SW:] êkwa ê-kî-pêyakoyân ê-kî-ohpikihicik, êha. êkotê
môsôminaskîhk, êkotê, êkotê niy ôhci, êkotê
ê-kî-ayâyâhk, êkwa, nimâmâ ê-onâpêmit êkota,
ê-kî-nipiyit nikâwiy onâpêma, êkosi *five years* êsa
kî-pêyakow nikâwiy, ê-kî-nipiyit onâpêma.

[FA:] êwako kiy-~-ohtâwiy [*sic*] kiya?

[SW:] êkwa –~ môya, môy nôhtâwiy êwako. êkwa, êkota
êkwa, kâ-kî-~ kî-onâpêmiw êkota, *Finedays* ôki,
êkot[a] êkwa nikâwiy kâ-kî-pê-onâpêmit, êkos
êkota ohc êkwa kâ-kî-ayâyâhk.
ê-kî-nêwopiponêyân ês êkospîhk, kâ-kî-pêsîht
nikâwiy êkota kâ-kî-pê-onâpêmit, nakiwacîhk.
êkos ê-kî-pê-isi-~ êkos êkwa niya, nêtê êkwa niya
kêhtê-ayak nikî-kanawêyimikwak, nikî-pêyakon;

[...]

[FA:] What was your grandfather's White name again?

[SW:] Louis, Louis Applegarth.

[FA:] Louis.

[HC:] And in Cree?

[SW:] *Kâ-pêtwêwêmât, Kâ-pêtwêwêmât.*

[HC:] *Kâ-pêtwêwêmât.*

[SW:] Yes, that's it, that's it, *Kâ-pêtwêwêmât*, that was my grandfather's name.

[VII] [Parents and Siblings]

[18] [FA:] And you had been raised as an only child?

[SW:] Now they had raised me as an only child, yes. Over there at *Môsôminaskîhk* [Moosomin Reserve], over there, I am from over there, we used to live over there, then, my mom was married here, my mother's husband had died, in this way my mother lived alone for five years, it is reported, after her husband had died.

[FA:] Was that your father?

[SW:] Then –~ no, that was not my father. Now, at that point now she had taken a husband over here, among the Finedays, now when my mother had come to take a husband over here [at Sweetgrass], now from that point on we lived in that way.
I had been four years old at that time, it is said, when my mother had been brought over here, having come to take a husband at *Nakiwacîhk* [Sweetgrass]. So she had come here –~ now as for me, I stayed over there [*sc.* at Moosomin] and the old people kept me, I was an only child; there

âta wiya nôhtâwiy, mâka môy nikâwiy êkon ôhci-wîc-âyâmêw, aciyaw êtikwê êkon ê-wîc-âyâmât, êwako nôhtâwiy, namôy mâk êwako nôh-~ nôhci-kanawêyimik, nôhk-~, kêhtê-ayak ôki nikî-kanawêyimikwak. êkos ê-kî-pê-is-ôhpikihikawiyân, piyisk nikî-ka-kîs-ôhpikihikwak.

[FA:] kîkway cî kikî-osîmisin mâka, kimâmâ êkwa ê-oh-~ kîhtwâm ê-onâpêmit?

[SW:] môya, môy kîkway.

[FA:] ma kîkway.

[SW:] âha, ma kîkway, ma kîkway, âsay kî-kêhtêyâtisiw kâ-pê-onâpêmit, osâm anita. mâka wiya kotakak (anih ôhci kâ-kî-mâyipayit â-~, nikâwiy onâpêma),

[FA:] êha.

[SW:] nisto, nisto nimisak, êkotê môsômininâhk pimisinwak,

[FA:] ôh.

[SW:] ês ê-kî-nipicik,

[FA:] ôh.

[SW:] êkot[a] ôhci niya.

[FA:] êkosi namôy âyiwâk kîkway.

[SW:] êkosi namôy ây-~, itowahk wâh-wîhkâc k-âyâwâcik

[FA:] hm.

[SW:] iskwêwak awâsisa âtiht, kikiskêyihtên, êkotowahk nikâwiy, êkos ê-kî-pê-itowiwit.

[FA:] hm.

was my [*sc.* biological] father, to be sure, but my mother had not lived with him, she must have lived with him only for a short time, he was my father but he did not keep me, my grandm-~ the old people had kept me. I had come to be raised that way, finally they had finished raising me.

[FA:] But did you have any younger siblings, after your mom married again?

[SW:] No, there were none.

[FA:] None.

[SW:] Yes, there were none, there were none, she had already been too old when she came to be married, at this point. But there were others (from the one who had died on her, my mother's [first] husband),

[FA:] Yes.

[SW:] three, three older sisters, they lie buried over there in *Môsômininâhk* [Moosomin],

[FA:] Oh.

[SW:] they had died, it is reported,

[FA:] Oh.

[SW:] after that came I.

[FA:] So there was no one else.

[SW:] So there was no one –~, the kind who have children far apart,

[FA:] hm.

[SW:] some women have children far apart, you know, my mother was of that kind, she had always been of that kind.

[FA:] hm.

[SW:] êkos ê-kî-pê-isi-~-isi-pimâtisiyân. mâka wiya nôhtâwiy ohci, m-~ ayahk, âpihtaw, *my half-sister*, nîs ôta ayâwak, pêyak *Regina*, ê-maskihkîwiskwêwit, maskihkîwiskwêw *hospital* ê-atoskêt, nisîmisinân, ôta *Regina*.

[FA:] tânis êwako ê-isiyîhkâsot?

[SW:] *'Lillian'*; *'Lillian'*, mâka *last name* môy nikiskêyihtên, môniyâsa ê-kî-onâpêmit, ôtê ohc âkâmaskîhk, ê-kî-onâpêmit anihi, mâk êkota ôt[a] ê-kî-ayâcik *Regina*. êkos êkospîhk ohc ânihi kâ-nipiyit onâpêma, *cancer* ê-kî-ayâyit anih ônâpêma, êkwa, êkos êkospîhk ôm ôhc êkota ay-ayâw, ôta *Regin*[*a*] ê-ma-maskihkîwiskwêwit kêyâpic. êkwa kotak nimis, êwako nimisinân mitoni, nêtê êwako *Sweetgrass* ayâw. êwako mîna pêyakow, tâpiskôt niya, wiy ônâpêm[a] ê-kî-nipiyit; nîsw-âskiy êtikw êkw âspin kâ-nipiyit onâpêma.

[FA:] hm.

[SW:] êkwa êkota ohci –~

[FA:] tânis êwako isiyîhkâsow?

[SW:] *'Martha Whitford'*; *'Martha Whitford'*. êwakw ân[a] ân[a] êkos îsiyîhkâsow. êkwa êkota ohci nîtisâninânak nâpêwak mîna,

[FA:] hm.

[SW:] êkonik mîn âpihtaw, nîtisânak

[FA:] hm.

[SW:] aniki nâpêwak. êkos âta nitihtasinân.

[FA:] tânima tahto?

[SW:] tânitahto? mahti – â, ostêsimâw êkw âna kotak, êkwa kotak, nisto; nistam *Solomon*, *Johnny*, *Alec* – êha, nisto. pêyak kî-nipiw, ostêsimâw êwakw âna.

[SW:] I had come to live that way. But from my father, ah well, half, my half-sister, two live here, one in Regina, she is a nurse, she works as a hospital nurse, our youngest sister, here in Regina.

[FA:] What is that one's name?

[SW:] Lillian, Lillian, but I don't know the last name, she had married a Whiteman from overseas, she married that one, but they lived over here in Regina. And since her husband died of cancer, her husband had cancer, now since then she has been living here, she is still nursing here in Regina. Now the other one of my older sisters, that one is our oldest sister, she lives over there on Sweetgrass. She also lives alone, just like me, for her husband has died; it must be two years now since her husband died.

[FA:] hm.

[SW:] Now from that point on –~

[FA:] What is that one's name?

[SW:] Martha Whitford; Martha Whitford. That is what she is called. Now from that point on also our male siblings,

[FA:] hm.

[SW:] they also are my half-siblings,

[FA:] hm.

[SW:] these men. That, for sure, is the number of us.

[FA:] How many?

[SW:] How many? Let's see – well, the oldest brother and that other one, and another, they were three; first came Solomon, Johnny, Alec – yes, three. One has died, that one had been the oldest.

[FA:] *Whitfords* cî êkonik?

[SW:] môya, *Alberts.*

[FA:] ôh!

[SW:] âha, *Alberts.*

[FA:] kôhtâwiy wiya *Albert.*

[SW:] âha, *Albert* âha, *'John Albert'* kî-isiyîhkâsow nôhtâwiy;

[FA:] ôh.

[SW:] nôhtâwînân, êkonik âpihtaw nîtisânak.

[FA:] hm. êkwa –~, aya mâka, tâpiskôc aya, mahti tânis ôma k-êtâhkômacik – *cousins*? kîtimwak êkos îsi, kicâhkosak?

[SW:] â, nicâhkosak – tipiyawê êwakw ân[a] âna, k-êtwêyân ana, êkoni tipiyawê, êkosi mîna nikâwiy ê-kî-isi-nîsicik wîtisâna,

[FA:] hm!

[SW:] êwakw âna 'sîsîkwêw' k-êtitân,

[FA:] ôh!

[SW:] kikiskêyihtên,

[FA:] â, nâpêw ana.

[SW:] nâpêw, êkoni piko wîtisâna ê-kî-ihtakoyit,

[FA:] âha.

[SW:] êha, êkos ê-kî-isi-nîsicik piko wîstawâw. êkota, êkonik mîn ânik êtataw kî-ayâwêwak, kî-pêyakow, tâpiskôc k-êsi-pêyakoyân, êkos ê-kî-isi-pêyakoyit ana nisis otânisa, kayâs kî-nakatik onôtikwêma.

[FA:] Are those Whitfords?

[SW:] No, Alberts.

[FA:] Oh!

[SW:] Yes, Alberts.

[FA:] Your father was an Albert.

[SW:] Yes, an Albert, yes, my father's name was John Albert;

[FA:] Oh.

[SW:] he was our father, those are my half-siblings.

[FA:] hm. Now – but what about, like, let's see how you are related to them – *cousins*? Your male cross-cousins, that way, your female cross-cousins?

[SW:] Well, my female cross-cousins – that one [*sc.* their father] is a direct relative, the one I mentioned, and with that one as a direct relative, too, in this way they were two of them, my mother and her sibling,

[FA:] hm!

[SW:] that *Sîsîkwêw* I told you about,

[FA:] Oh!

[SW:] you know,

[FA:] Well, he is a man.

[SW:] a man, that was her only sibling,

[FA:] Yes.

[SW:] yes, in this way they too were only two of them. In that family they too had barely any [*sc.* children], she [*sc.* their daughter] was an only child, just as I was an only child, in this way my mother's brother only had one daughter, his wife died long ago.

[FA:] hm.

[SW:] êkos êkwa, êkoni anihi piko wîstawâw ê-k-~, êkonik mîna ê-kî-pêyakôsêcik aniki piko.

[FA:] tânisi wiy âkayâsîwiyîhkâsow ana sîsîkwêw?

[SW:] *'John Applegarth'*; *'John Applegarth'*, âha. êwako k-ây-âcimostâtân ôtê istêts [*sic*], êha, kâ-kî-mân-âyât a-~, wâskahikan, êwako.

[19] [SW:] êkos êwakw ân[a] âna nicâhkos, wîst êkos ê-kî-isi-pêyakot, mâka wiya mihcêtôsêw – mahti nist ôtânisa, nîs ôkosisa, niyânan; êkosi kî-isi-nipiw ana nicâhkos,

[FA:] hm!

[SW:] êwakw ân[a] êkosi. êkwa kotak – nikiyâskin, kotak mîna; êwakw âna, âcênam ohci,

[FA:] hm.

[SW:] âcênam, '*Harry* âcênam' kâ-kî-itiht, *Maggie* âcênam ê-okosisit, '*Ben* âcênam' isiyîhkâsôyiwa, *Maggie* âcênam okosisa, ostêsimâwa, êkoni, êkoni anihi pêyak nicâhkos ana onâpêmiw.

[FA:] hm.

[SW:] mwêhci môniyâsak êkonik, iyikohk mis-~ ê-misâk kistikân, *farm* ê-ayâcik.

[FA:] misi-kistikêwak?

[SW:] iyâyêy, misi-kistikêwak mwêhci môniyâsak.

[FA:] hm.

[SW:] In this way now they only had that one –~, they too only had one child.

[FA:] What was the English name of that *Sîsîkwêw*?

[SW:] John Applegarth; John Applegarth, yes. That was the one I was telling you about, yes, that used to have a house in the States, that one.

[19] [SW:] In this way that female cross-cousin of mine, in this way she too was an only child, but she had many children – let's see, three daughters, two sons, she had five; with that number that female cross-cousin of mine died,

[FA:] hm!

[SW:] that was it for her. Now another – I slipped up, also another [*sc.* female cross-cousin]; it was from that one, from *Âcênam*,

[FA:] hm.

[SW:] *Âcênam*, Harry *Âcênam*, as he was called, he was Maggie *Âcênam*'s son; Ben *Âcênam* is his name, Maggie *Âcênam*'s son, the oldest parallel cousin, that one female cross-cousin of mine is married to that one.

[FA:] hm.

[SW:] They are just like White people, so big is the farm, they have a farm.

[FA:] They are big farmers?

[SW:] Oh my gosh, they are big farmers just like White people.

[VIII]

[...]

[20] [FA:] êkwa, tânisi?

[HC:] êkwa ôki kotakak kisêyiniwak, â, ê-nitopayi-~ onitopayiwak,

[SW:] âha.

[HC:] â, kispakitôn awa,

[SW:] âha.

[HC:] kikiskêyimâw awa?

[SW:] namwâc, namôy wîhkât nipêhtên êwako.

[HC:] ahpô tahkohc awa?

[SW:] tahkohc, âha, êwako wiya mâna nimosôm nikî-pêhtawâw, êkos ê-kî-isiyîhkâtât pêyak, 'tahkohc'.

[FA:] ayahciyiniw?

[SW:] namôya, nêhiyaw; nêhiyaw, âha, âha.

[HC:] nêhiyaw. â, *Hobbema* ohci? ahpô *Edmonton*?

[SW:] *No,* ôta; nânitaw ôtê is ôma *north* isi, *Onion Lake* êkotê, itêhkê isi nânitaw an[a] êwakw âna nâpêw ohci, kisêyiniw êsa. nikî-pêhtawâw mân êkos ê-kî-itwêt, 'tahkohc' kî-isiyîhkâ-~, ê-kî-isiyîhkâtât mâna nimosôm. mihcêt kêhtê-ayak kayâs, êwakw ânima kâ-k-~ kâ-kî-nitopayihk êsa mâna, ê-nitopayicik ayisiyiniwak. mistah âta nikî-pê-~ â, nikî-môhcowin, nikî-awâsisîwin osâm, kâ-kî-pê-pêhtawak nimosôm. iyikohk ê-kî-âcimot mâna, kîkway êkos îs ôma,

[FA:] mhm.

[SW:] ê-kî-âtotahk kîkway, tânis ê-kî-pê-ispayik kayâs kîkway ôma. â, niya mâna, nikî-mêtawân mân ôta awâsisîhkânisak [*laughs*].

[VIII] [More Plains Cree Old Men]

[...]

[20] [FA:] Now, what?

[HC:] Now these other old men, well, the ones who went on raids –~ the warriors,

[SW:] Yes.

[HC:] well, this *Kispakiton,*

[SW:] Yes.

[HC:] do you know him?

[SW:] Not at all, I have never heard that name.

[HC:] Or this one, *Tahkohc*?

[SW:] *Tahkohc,* yes, I used to hear my grandfather talk about him, he called one by that name, *Tahkohc*.

[FA:] A Blackfoot?

[SW:] No, a Cree; a Cree, yes, yes.

[HC:] A Cree. Well, from Hobbema? or Edmonton?

[SW:] No, from here; somewhere up north, over there at Onion Lake, towards that way, that man reportedly was from there, that old man. I used to hear him say that, *Tahkohc* my grandfather used to call him. Many old people in the old days, that was when one used to go on raids, it is reported, people went on raiding parties. To be sure, I used to hear a great deal –~ well, I was foolish, I was too young when I used to hear my grandfather. So much would he tell historical accounts, things like this,

[FA:] mhm.

[SW:] he told about how things had happened long ago. Well, as for me, here I was still playing with dolls [*laughs*].

[21] [SW:] ât[a] âsay ê-oskinîkiskwêwiyân, êkâ kâ-kî-pimâtisit nimosôm. mâka osâm nôhtaw âsay kî-~, nânitaw *eighty* êtikwê ayiwâkêsîs ê-itahtopiponêt kâ-kî-nipit, nimosôm.

[...]

[22] [HC:] êkwa, kikiskêyimâw cî awa sâkêwêw?

[SW:] êha, êha; êwako mîna nikî-kiskêyimâw kisêyiniw. êwako mîna nikî-ocihci-wâpamâw sâkêwêw, êwakw âna nakiwacîhk ohci pêyak kisêyiniw;

[HC:] mhm!

[SW:] nikî-kiskêyimâw êwako.

[23] [HC:] êkwa awa, nâh-nâmiskiskêkâpaw [*sic*], nâh-nâmis-~

[SW:] *oh yea!* nâh-nâmiskwêkâpaw. êkosi miyâmâc, nâh-nâmiskwêkâpaw. kisê-~, môy mitoni kisêyiniw êwako; êwako, â, mâka namôy ê-ohci-wâpit, mâka pêyakwan êwako nêhiyawi-kisêyiniw tâpiskôc, kikiskêyihtên; mistahi kîkway wîst ê-kî-kiskêyihtahk âcimowina, nâh-nâmiskwêkâpaw. tâpiskôc ê-nîpawit êkwa [*gesture: nodding*]

[FA:] mhm.

[SW:] – êkos îs ânima, êwakw ânima *name*.

[...]

[21] [SW:] I was already a young woman, to be sure, when my grandfather died. But it was too early for me to pay attention –~, my grandfather must have been about eighty or a bit older when he died.

[...]

[22] [HC:] Now, do you know *Sâkêwêw*?

[SW:] Yes, yes; I also used to know that old man. I have also lived to see that *Sâkêwêw*, he was also one of the old men from *Nakiwacîhk* [Sweetgrass];

[HC:] mhm!

[SW:] I used to know him.

[23] [HC:] Now this one, *Nâh-nâmiskwêkâpaw* –~

[SW:] Oh yea! *Nâh-nâmiskwêkâpaw*. This is the right way, I do believe, *Nâh-nâmiskwêkâpaw*. That one was not really an old man; that one, well, but he was blind, but he was the same, much like an old man of the Cree, you know; he too used to know many histories, *Nâh-nâmiskwêkâpaw*. As if he is standing [*gesture: nodding*]

[FA:] mhm.

[SW:] – it is like that, that name.

[...]

Sarah Whitecalf, 1975.

4

miton ê-kî-pê-na-nêhiyaw-ôhpikihikawiyân

I was truly raised as a Cree woman

miton ê-kî-pê-na-nêhiyaw-ôhpikihikawiyân

[FA:] êkosi cî?

[RL:] hâw, kiy êkwa.

[SW:] mitoni kiwî-nâh-nipêmin, ê-takahkihtâtân [*laughter*].

[RL:] namôy wîhkâc nikâh-kîs-âcimon.

[SW:] âha, êkwa!

ka-wîhtên mâka nîsta –~

[FA:] hâw, êwakw âwa aya niwîcêwâkanis, *Sarah Whitecalf* ê-wî-âcimot êkwa, kîkwây êtikwê piko ê-wî-âtotahk.

[SW:] mhm [*laughs*].

[RL:] mêkwâc kâ-nâh-nitopayit [*laughs*].

[1] â, nîsta nik-âcimon tânis ê-kî-pê-isi-pa-pamihisoyâhk, ê-oskinîkiskwêwiyân mâcika nik-âcimon. âsay nikî-pê-âtotên, â, ê-kî-pê-awâsisîwiyân, tânis ê-kî-pê-isi-pa-pamihikawiyân ê-kî-pê-isi-ohpikihikawiyân, miton ê-kî-pê-na-nêhiyaw-ôhpikihikawiyân, kahkiyaw êwakw âsay nikî-pê-ay-âcimon; êkwa ôm êkwa, ispî êkwa ê-kîs-ôskinîkiskwêwiyân, êkota ôm ôta, 'kinosêwi-sâkahikan' isiyîhkâtêw, êkwa 'môsômininâhk' ('môsômin' ês ê-kî-isiyîhkâsot okimâhkânipan kayâs, êwakw ânim[a] ôhci 'môsômininâhk' k-êsiyîhkâtêk êwakw âskîhkân, êkonik ôk âyisiyiniwak

I was truly raised as a Cree woman

[FA:] Are you ready?

[RL:] Well, now it is your turn.

[SW:] You were truly about to put me to sleep gradually, I enjoyed listening to you [*laughter*].

[RL:] I would never come to an end in telling stories.

[SW:] Yes, now!

But you had better record an introduction for me too –~

[FA:] Well, this one is my dear partner Sarah Whitecalf who is going to tell stories now, I wonder what she is going to tell about.

[SW:] Yes [*laughs*].

[RL:] About the times she went on the warpath [*laughs*].

[Prologue]

[1] Well, I too will tell how we used to make a living for ourselves, for instance I will tell about myself as a young woman. I have already told about this, well, when I was a child, how I used to be looked after and how I used to be brought up and that I used to be brought up very much in the Cree way, all that I have already told earlier; now then, when I had fully grown up to be a young woman, it was there, it is called *Kinosewi-sâkahikan* [(Jack-)Fish Lake] and also *Môsôminināhk* [Moosomin] (*Môsômin* having been

kâ-kî-atâwâkêcik ôta ôma talimwâs ôm âskîhkân, mîn âwa 'kâ-pitikow' kâ-kî-itiht, ê-kî-nîswastêki êkon âskîhkâna êsa, kâ-kî-atâwâkêcik ôki, êkonik ayisiyiniwak); êkos êkwa, êêkotê [*sic*] ôma ê-kî-pê-oy-ohpikihikawiyân ê-pê-awâsisîwiyân.

[2] hâ, misakâmê, piyisk êkwa, ê-kîs-ôskinîkiskwêwiyân mitoni, âhci pik ôki kêhtê-ayak ê-kî-pa-pamihi-~ ê-kî-wa-wîc-âyâmakik nôhkom nimosôm, êkwa mîna nikî-pêyakon, nîcisânak ê-kî-mêstahpinêcik. êkwa ê-kî-wîc-ôyôhtâwîmakik oti, kotaka nikâwiy ê-kî-onâpêmit. êkwa ispîhk, nôhtâwiy wiy âwa, kotaka iskwêw[a] ê-kî-wîcêwât sêmâk, êkot[a] êkwa wiya kî-mihcêtiwak âpihtaw-nîtisânak [*sic*]; kêyâpic âtiht pimâtisiwak âpihtaw-nîtisânak, mâk êkwa ninistinân pikw îskwêwak. nimis êkwa pêyak nisîmisinân *Regina* ê-maskihkîwiskwêwit kayâs ohci, môn-~ môniyâs[a] ê-kî-onâpêmit. êkwa, êkos êkwa niyanân piko, êkwa nimis ôm êkwa, niyanân êkwa ê-na-nêhiyawâtisiyâhk, *Sweetgrass* wiy ây-âyâw, ê-kî-sîkâwit, onâpêma môy kayâs êkâ ê-pimâtisiyit.

[I]

[3] êkota ohc êk ôma kâ-wî-âcimoyân êkwa, ê-oskinîkiskwêwiyân. kîtahtawê nimosôm kâ-nakatikoyâhk, êkw êkâ ê-pimâtisit, tânis êkwa? nam âwiyak êkwa tita-pamihikoyâhk nôhkom awa, ka-nîsiyâhk pikw êkwa êkotê môsôminêw-âskîhkânihk. êkota êkwa, nikâwiy kâ-kî-otinikoyâhk êkwa, ta-pê-ayâyâhk êk ôt[a] ôma, 'nakiwacîhk' isiyîhkâtêw nitaskînân ê-nêhiyawiyîhkâtêk, êkot[a] êkwa kâ-kî-pê-itohtêyâhk êkwa, ê-pê-kîwêhtahikoyâhk êkwa nikâwiy, nam âwiyak ayisk êkwa nêtê ta-pamihikoyâhk, âta mitoni nikî-~ miyo-pamihisowak

the name of the late band chief long ago, that is the reason why that reserve is called *Môsômininâhk*, these were the people who had sold that reserve at Delmas, and also this one who had been called *Kâ-pitikow* [*sc.* Thunderchild], the two reserves having been adjacent to each other, these were the people who had sold them); now it was over there that I had been brought up as a child.

[2] Well, having lived there all along, now at last when I had fully grown up to be a young woman, I nevertheless was still living with these old people, my grandmother and my grandfather, and I also used to be an only child, all my siblings [*sc.* maternal half-siblings] having succumbed to disease. Now there were some with whom I had the father in common, my mother had married another man. Now my father too had right away taken another woman, and from that union my half-siblings were many; some of my half-siblings are still alive but there are only only three of us women left now. My older sister and I and our younger sister who has been a nurse in Regina from way back, she had married a Whiteman. Thus now we two are the only ones, my older sister and I now, we are the only ones living the Cree way, she lives at Sweetgrass, she is a widow, her husband having died not long ago.

[**I**] [A Young Woman's Life]

[3] Now I am going to tell about that time, when I was a young woman. After a time my grandfather had left us behind, now that he had died, what now? My grandmother and I did not have anyone to look after us, we would be just the two of us now over there, at *Môsôminêw-âskîhkânihk* [Moosomin Reserve]. It was then that my mother took us in, for us to come and live here now, our reserve is called *Nakiwacîhk* [Sweetgrass] in Cree, we went over here then, my mother brought us home with her now for there was no one over there to look after us, although the old people had

kêhtê-ayak, kî-miywâsiniyiw wâskahikan mân ê-kî-ayâcik, êkwa mîn ê-kî-otêmicik, mitoni mîn ê-kî-otêmicik. êkwa mîn âwa nikâwiy, miton ê-kî-ayâwât êkotê misatimwa. kîtahtawê êkwa, êwakw âw êkwa ê-mâtahpinêt êkw ânima nimosôm, «hâw êkwa, kika-pamihtamâkawin êkwa kitêmak, môy êkwa ayiwâk kikî-pamihtamâtin,» ê-itikot ôhtâwiya nikâwiy. êkos êkwa nitêminânak aniki ê-kî-pê-~, oskinîkiwa ê-masinahikêhâcik nistw ê-têhtapiyit, ê-pê-kîwêtisahohcik ê-pôni-nipâkwêsimohk nitêminânak. nakiwacîhk êkwa ê-pê-ihtatât êkwa awa nikâwiy otêma, êkot[a] êkwa ê-pamihtamâht êkwa.

[4] êkosi, êkot[a] êkwa, kâ-kî-mâci-wîc-âyâmâyâhk êkwa awa nikâwiy, ê-wîc-âyâmâyâhkok. âta wiy ê-kî-na-nîsicik piko, môy kotaka kîkway otawâsimisa awa nôhcâwîs; wîst ê-kî-kîwâtinamât nisto, nôhcâwîs ana, otawâsimisa, mâka wiyawâw, aniki wîstawâw anik ôhkomiwâwa, omosômiwâwa ê-kî-ohpikihikocik. êkos êkwa, êkot[a] êkwa niyanân nôhkom awa kâ-kî-pamihikoyâhk. êkwa awa nôhcâwîs – kî-kitimâkisiw wîsta nikâwiy (tâpiskôc ôma, awa nîc-ôtâcimow aw ôma kâ-itâcimisot ôma, mwêhc êkosi nîstanân ê-kî-pê-ispayihikoyâhk), nôhcâwîs ana, 'oskanahpinêw' kâ-itwêhk, êkosi ê-kî-is-âyât; mâka wîst ê-kî-minihkwêskit mistah âna nôhcâwîs, piyisk ê-kî-nanamipayit ê-kî-cîhcîpipayit, iyikohk ominihkwêwin anim ê-kî-tôtâkot, iyikohk ê-kî-sâkihtât. mâka wiy êwakw âta wiya, môy êkoyikohk miton îyikohk, mâka mistahi kî-wêhcihtâw mayaw ôcênâsihk k-êtohtêt, kispêw mân ê-kî-minihkwêc, tâpwê ayisk anima kayâs ê-kî-âyimahk, mâka mêskoc [*sic*] ê-kî-wêhtakihtêk kahkiyaw kîkway êkos îsi, mîciwin ôma.

[5] êkwa, êkwa êkos êkw ânohc awa nipê-na-nômakê-âh-âcimostawâw êwako k-ôskinîkiskwêwiyân, môy âhpô ohci-kaskihtâw mamiyê [*?sic*] nôht-~ awa nôhcâwîs

looked after themselves really well, the house where they had used to live had been a good house, and they also used to have horses, they also used to have lots of horses. And my mother also used to keep horses over there. After a time now it came to pass that my grandfather took sick, «Well now, you will have someone look after your horses for you, I can no longer look after them for you,» my mother was told by her father. Thus now these horses of ours came –~, they hired three young men on horseback and these horses of ours were driven back [*sc.* to Sweetgrass] after a Sun-dance. Now my mother moved her horses back to *Nakiwacîhk* [Sweetgrass] and had someone look after them for her there.

[4] Thus it was there now that we began to live with my mother, we lived with them. To be sure, they were only the two of them living there, my step-father had no more children with my mother; he too had three motherless children, they were my step-father's children but they too were raised by their grandmother and grandfather. Thus now my grandmother and I were looked after by her. And my step-father – my mother too used to be poor (it was like what this my fellow story-teller told about herself, that was exactly what happened to us too); my step-father had arthritis, as they say, he was suffering from that; but he also was a heavy drinker, that step-father of mine, and finally he would shake and he would jerk, so much had his drinking affected him, so much had he loved it. But for that one himself, on the other hand, it was not that much, despite his condition he used to find it very easy as soon as he got to town, and he would still drink, for it is true that times were difficult in the old days but on the other hand everything was cheap, food and the like.

[5] Now, thus now, I was telling her [*sc.* Rosa Longneck] about that one at the start today, when I was a young woman, my step-father was not even able to cut wood for us, when they

ta-nikohtâkoyâhk, kâ-wî-nikohtêcik, piko nikâwiy ê-kî-wîcihiwêt, êkos ânima, pâstêwi-mihta ôhi, piko mâna nikâwiy ê-kî-wîcihiwêt; nitaka wîsta nikâwiy ê-kî-kakâyawisît mistahi, ê-wîcihiwêt mihta ê-astâcik kâ-takwâkik ôma, ê-ay-astâcik mihta. êkwa niy âsay ê-oskinîkiskwêwiyân, nikî-pa-pamihtâson mâna, nôhkom mâna ê-wa-wîtapimak ê-ka-kwayâci-piminawasoyân êkos îsi, êkwa ôki nikâwiy ê-ay-âwatâcik mihta. kîkwây kayâs kîskipocimihtêwin êkospîhk, êkwa, êkwa mâna kâ-pipohk, êkos ânima mâna, ê-kî-mosci-nâh-nâtwâhimihtêt nikâwiy; ê-mosci-nâh-nâtwâhimihtêt piko. êkwa ê-wîcihak niy ê-pîhtikwêyâwatâyân, êwako kîsâc kâ-wî-tipiskâk mâna, ê-kî-misi-nâh-nâtwâhimihtêhk ayisk mâna kâ-wî-tipiskâk, ê-kwayâtastamâsohk mihta; êkwa mâna niy êkoca, ê-kî-pîhtikwêyâwacimihtêyân mâna nikâwiy ê-wîcihak.

[6] kîtahtawê âskaw, nikâwiy k-ôtamiyot, pîhc-âyihk kîkway mistahi kâ-tasîhkahk, niy êkwa mân êkot[a] ê-kî-na-nâh-nâtwâhimihtêyân, ê-nâh-nâtwâhimihtêyân, niya miht[a] ê-ta-tasîhkamân. êkosi –~ êkosi; êkosi nîstanân ê-kî-itatoskêyâhk. êkwa nama kîkway kayâs mônahipân, mistahi kî-kakwâhyaki-miywâsin nipiy, sîpîsis, ê-kî-~, êkot[a] ê-kî-pimihtik, êkwa nâh-nâway ôk âyisiyiniwak êkot-~, êwak ôm ê-kano-wîkicik ôma sîpîsis, êwak-~, kahkiyaw êwako ê-ohtahipâtamihk – môy wîhkâc ê-ohc-âhkwatik anima n-~, anima sîpîsis, ê-kî-itwêcik mâna m-~ aya, iyikohk mân ê-kî-wâsêciwahk ôma, nama kî-~, môy wîhkâc ê-ohc-âhkwatik anima sîpîsis. mâka kî-itwêwak mâna nâh-nâway môhkiciwanipêkwa ê-ayâki, êkwa mistah âyisk miywâsin ôma môhkiciwanipêkwâpoy mitoni; êkosi, îh, êwakw ânima nâh-nâway ê-kî-ohtahipâtamihk anima, môy wîhkâc ê-ohc-âhkwatik. ê-kî-mosci-ka-kwâpikêyâhk ê-nîsonikêyâhk, êêy, kâ-wî-tipiskâk ê-kwâpikêtisahokawiyân, kîsâc ê-astâyâhk nipiy. ma kîkway kayâs mônahipân, wiya niyanân ôm êkotê isi.

were going to chop wood my mother would have to go along, in that way, for the deadwood my mother would have to go along; it was a good thing my mother worked so very hard, she would go along to put up firewood in the fall, they were putting up firewood. And I was a young woman already, I used to look after everyone, I used to stay with my grandmother and prepare the meals and things like that, and my mother and the others would haul firewood. What was there long ago for sawing firewood at that time of year now, now in winter, it used to be like that, my mother would chop wood into stove-lengths with nothing but an axe; she had nothing else to chop wood into stove-lengths. And I helped her haul firewood indoors, we used to do this before it got dark for there used to be lots of wood-cutting as it was about to get dark, one used to get the firewood ready; and then I too used to help my mother haul firewood inside.

[6] At times when my mother was busy with something, when she had lots to do inside, then I too would be chopping the firewood into stove-lengths, I would chop the firewood into stove-lengths and I would put up the wood. That was the way –~ that was the way; that was the way we too used to work. Now there was no well in the old days; the water was extremely good, a creek ran along there and people lived all along it, they lived along this creek, all the people got their water from it – that creek never froze, they used to say, it used to flow so clear, not –~ that creek never froze. But they used to say there were springs all along it, and of course spring water is very good indeed; in that way, look, people all along it used to get their water from it, it never froze. We simply used to get water by pails, two pails at a time, hey, when it was about to get dark I would be sent for water, we were putting water by in advance. For there were no wells in the old days for us over there.

[7] êkosi, miton êkos ânim âwa nikâwiy, êêy, kahkiyaw kîkway kî-kakâyawisîtotam mîciwin ohci, ê-kî-tâpakwêwi-pimâcihot, kâh-ka-kîsowahpisoci kâ-pipohk ôma, êkos ê-sipwêhtêt ê-nâtitâpakwânêt. êêy, tâniyikohk êtikwê mâna wâh-âpihtâ-kîsikâki ê-kî-ta-takohtêt, ê-pa-~ ê-pa-pêsiwât wâposwa. êkospîhk anim êkwa mâcika k-ôcihcipayik anima tâpwê wâposwayânak kâ-kî-atâwâkêhk, êy, kî-cîhkîstam êkwa êkota nikâwiy, môy wîhkâc sôniyâw ê-ohci-wâpamâyâhk, ayisk nama kîkway awa nôhcâwîs atoskêwin tôtam. êkwa, ê-kî-cîhkîstahk nikâwiy, êkos anima kâh-pahkonâci wâposwa, êê-misi-pahkonikêt, âskaw mêton ê-papêtikwâskaciyit ê-pêtowatêt wâposwa, êkwa pitamâ êkoni ê-ta-tihkahât nikâwiy, kâh-tihkapitwâw[i] ôki wâposwak êkwa ê-kî-mâci-pahkonikêt, êkwa ê-sâ-sîpahwât. ê-kî-misi-mâh-mâwacihât mâna wâposwayâna, êkwa ispîhk ê-atâwâkêhk aniki wâposwayânak.

[8] êkwa, êkos êkwa aya, îh, êkos ânim ê-kî-itâcihoyâhk, êkwa, kâ-~ kî-asamâwak êkospîhk kêhtê-ayak, nitaka môy kakêtihk ê-kî-ma-miyopayik ê-kî-isi-ma-miyo-pimâcihoyâhk, nayêstaw awa nôhcâwîs ê-kî-apit pîhc-âyihk, ê-kî-apit pîhc-âyihk mâna. ê-kî-kwâs-~, mâka wiya kî-kaskihtâw ê-kî-masinahikêhiwêt mân ôma kâ-takwâkik, kâ-maskosîhkêhk ôma kâ-nîpihk, kâkikê kî-otôskinîkîmiw, êkwa mân ôma kâ-wî-maskosîhkêhk, êkwa êkota mâna ê-kî-mis-ôsîhtâcik ôk âyi, k-ôtôskinîkîmit ôm âyi, maskosiya; êkw êsa mân êkoca ayihk, ê-wîcêwât oskinîkiwa, ôh ê-nât-~ ê-âwatâcik.

[9] êkwa, tâpwê wiya misi-misatimokamik mân ê-kî-ayât, nîswâw ê-kipahikâtêk. mitoni wiy ê-kî-miyonâkohcikêyâhk, napakihtako-wâskahikan – ayihk oti, mistiko-wâskahikan, mâka kî-apahkwâtêwa ayisk mâna napakihtakwa; êwakw ânima kayâs ê-kî-takahki-wâskahikanêhk, êkosi nikî-itapinân mâna. êkwa, misatimokamikohk ôma, kâ-takwâkik, êêy, nikâwiy

[7] In this way my mother was, hey, she was a very hard worker at whatever she did with respect to food, she made her livelihood by snaring rabbits, in winter when she had wrapped herself up, with that she would go off and check her snares to bring back rabbits. Hey, I do not know at what time she used to get back, perhaps about mid-day, carrying rabbits. It was at that time, for instance, that the news got around that one could in fact sell rabbit-skins, hey, now my mother was all excited about that, we never got to see money for my step-father did not do any work. Now my mother was all excited about it, and thus, when she had skinned the rabbits, my mother would skin lots of them, sometimes bringing in doubled-up frozen rabbits on her back and first putting them to thaw out, and when these rabbits had thawed out, then she would begin the skinning and stretch them. She used to collect a great many rabbit-skins, and at that point those rabbit-skins were sold.

[8] Now, in that way, look, that was how we made our living, and then the old people used to get rations at that time, it was a good thing that circumstances worked out very well indeed for us and we had a good livelihood, with my step-father only sitting in the house, he used to sit in the house. But he used to be able to hire people in the fall, in the summer at haying time, he forever had hired hands, and now as haying time came around, now they used to put up lots of hay when he hired them; and at that time he would go with the young men to haul in the hay.

[9] Now it was true he had a big barn, it was divided into two sections. We did have a very good-looking place, a house built of lumber – no, it was a log house but of course the roof was made of lumber; that used to be a good house in the old days, and in that way we used to be set up. Now the barn, hey, in the fall my mother would do the mudding, when it began to get cold, my mother used

ê-sisocêskiwakinikêc, kâ-mâci-kâh-kisinâk, ê-kî-sisoskiwakinikêt mâna nikâwiy, nîkinân ôma; mîn ôma misatimokamik, iyikohk ê-ka-kîsôcêskiwakinahk; mitoni wêhtitaw ê-kî-ma-miyonâkohcikêsit, tâpiskôc wiy âta wiya ayisiyiniw; êkota mân êkwa misatimo-maskosiya, wîstihkân miton ê-kinwâpêkastêk, êkota ê-kî-ayâk. êkotowahk ôma wîsta nikâwiy mân ê-kî-ohpikihât, êkotowahk mîn ê-kî-ohtâcihoyâhk nitaka, ôki êkotowahk k-êtwêt awa misihêwa [*sic*], â, sîsîpihkânak, êkw âniki (tânisi êtikw âniki mâna, kakwâhyaki-kisîwêwak mâna, 'niskihkânak' nikî-itwânân mâna niyanân, kî-nahâsiwak, kî-mâh-misikitiwak mâna), êkotowahk mîna mâna nikâwiy ê-kî-ohpikihât mâna. êkwa êkoni piskis [*sic*] aniki nîstanân mân ê-kî-kanawêyimâyâhkik. îh, ahpô pikw êkota k-âti-miyoskamik, âsay wâwa nikî-ohtâcihonân, ê-mîciyâhk; êkwa êkos ânima, kâ-mîcihk ôma mîna, kâ-kôt-~ kâ-kôta-kîkway-~ âkwâskam mîciwin ôma k-êspayik, pêyak mân ê-kî-ka-kîsiskwêtahwât mâna nikâwiy. êwako ê-mowâyâhk awa, pâhpahâhkwân awa, êkwa, êkwa ôma, kî-kaskihcâw wiy âwa mâna nôhcâwîs awa, ê-kî-pa-pamihât misatimwa, kîkisêpâ. êwako wiya namôy nôh-tôtênân, ta-pamihâyâhkik, kâh-wawêyici, kâh-pa-postayiwinisêci êkwa ê-saskahosot, kîkisêpâ êkwa ê-nitawi-pa-pamihât êkwa misatimwa ôhi, ê-pakit-~ têpiyâhk kâh-pakiciwêpinâci, êkos ê-minihkwêpahtâcik ôki misatimwak; kâ-pê-pîhc-~ kâ-pê-ay-âmaciwêyit, kâw ê-pîhtikwahât. êwako pikw âtoskêwin, êwako kî-kaskihtâw êkos ê-tôtahk.

[10] êkwa ôm êkwa, êkwa mân ôma, kâ-pipohk ôma, mistah êkospîhk kayâs kî-mâci-miyopayiw, kêhtê-ayak ôk ê-asamihcik, ayahk, iyikohk ê-kî-mis-âsamihcik, nôhkom awa êkwa nikâwiy êkwa wiy âwa nôhcâwîs, ê-nisticik ê-asamihcik, namôy kakêtihk iyikohk mâna ê-kî-asamihcik êkospîhk (âsay êkospîhk mostoso-wiyâs, â nakacâ, tâh-tâniyikohk êtikwê mostoso-wiyâs mân ôma ê-kî-kîskatahikâtêk, kâ-nâsiwêcik), nistwayak êwakw

to do the mudding, on our house; and also the barn, she insulated it by mudding; she had quite a good-looking place, it seemed like for people; and there now was the hay for the horses, it was a long stack piled up there. My mother also used to raise that kind, it was a good thing that we also had that kind to live on, that kind which she [*sc.* my fellow story-teller] talked about, chickens, well, domestic ducks, and those (what are those, they always are terribly noisy, domestic geese we used to call them, they used to be very watchful and big), that kind, too, my mother used to raise. And we also used to keep those separately for ourselves. Look, even when it was only getting to be spring, we already used to live on eggs, we ate them; and in that way, when you ate them too, when it happened that there was not much food, my mother would chop one chicken's head off. We would eat that, this chicken, now, and my step-father did manage to look after the horses in the morning. We [*sc.* my mother and I] did not do that, to look after them, when he had got ready, when he had got dressed, then he would use a cane, then he would go and look after the horses in the morning, so long as he had let them out the horses would simply run down to the water; when they came back up the hill, he would put them inside. That was all the work he did, that he used to be able to do.

[10] Now it was this, in winter, at that time it began to get much better in the old days; the old people used to get rations, they used to get so much in the way of rations, my grandmother and my mother and my step-father, there were three who got rations, they used to get such a substantial amount of rations at that time (at that time they already received beef, well, a great deal, I wonder how big a cut of beef each of them used to have apportioned to them when they went to fetch things), there were three shares of that meat, they used to get so much. Everything,

ânima wiyâs, iyikohk ê-kî-asamihcik. kahkiyaw kîkway, êkota ohci namôy mistahi kîkway ê-ohti-nôhtêpayiyâhk, askîwi-pimiy êtikwê piko êkwa cistêmâw, êkos îsi. kahkiyaw kîkway, wiyâs, pahkwêsikan, sîwinikan, sîwihtâkan, kîkisêpâ-mîciwin, wâpayôminak, êkwa ôki pînisak, êkwa, ayahk, wâpiski-pimiya, pîswêhkasikan, êkwa kocawâkanisa, êkwa 'kîkisêpâ-mîciwin' k-êsiyîhkâtâyâhk awa kâ-nêhiyawêhk awa, êkotowahk. mitoni mistahi kîkway, iyikohk ê-kî-~, iyikohk ê-kî-asamihcik, pêyak ayisiyiniw – êkosi ê-itasamihcik, tâh-tâni-~ nikotwâw cî nâh-nîso mâna pimîsa ê-kî-asam-~; êkos ânima ê-kî-~, iyikohk ê-kî-miyo-pimâcihoyâhk wiy âta wiya. môy wîhkâc ohc-îtohtêwak mistah âtâwêwikamikohk, kâ-manêhpwâcik pik ôma, êkwa êkos ânima k-êtwêyan anima, kâ-tâpakwêt ôma, ê-kî-kâh-kimotamâkot mâna sihkosa awa nikâwiy; êkos ê-pa-pêsiwât mîn êkotowahk. êkwa êko-~, êkoni êkwa ê-kî-ohci-pîhtwâcik anihi mâna; anima kêhciwâk anita ôcênâsihk, 'talimwâs' isiyîhkâtêw anima, êkotê mân êkwa ê-kî-itoh-~-isp-~ -ay-isitâpâsocik mâna, ê-nitawi-nâcicistêmâwêcik êkos îsi kîkway, askîwi-pimiy, êkos îsi ê-kî-~, ê-kî-ayi-~-nitaw-âtâwêcik mâna kîkwâs ôm êkos îs ê-na-nôhtêpayihk.

[11] êkwa ôki, têpahamâtohki kîkway piko ê-kî-wâpamâyâhk sôniyâs. êkwa ôk êkwa k-âcimoyân, nitêminânak, mostoswa mîna kî-ayâwêw nikâwiy. nôhtâwiy aw ê-~, ê-kî-miyikoyâhk mostoswa anihi, êkos êkwa, êkota ohci mostoswa êkwa kî-ayâwêw nikâwiy, kî-omostosomiw. êkwa awa nôhcâwîs, ê-kî-pakwâtât mân ânihi mostoswa, ê-kâhkwêyimât. môya, ê-kî-~, môy mân ê-kî-wî-pamihtamawât anihi nikâwiya mostoswa [*sic*], ê-kî-papâ-mâm-~, ê-kî-pakitinihcik mân âniki mostoswak ê-kî-papâmâcihocik. êkwa awa pêyak onîcâniw, êkon ôhi kihc âwa nôhtâwiy kâ-kî-miyikoyâhk ôhi onîcâniwa (kâ-misikiticik ôki pîtoso-mostoswak, mitoni kâ-kakânowotêcik, 'masinâsowi-mostos'

so from that point on we did not lack for much, only coal-oil and tobacco I guess, things like that. Everything, meat, flour, sugar, salt, oatmeal, rice, and these beans and lard, baking powder and matches, and what we call *kîkisêpâ-mîciwin* [*sc.* oatmeal] in speaking Cree, that kind. There was lots and lots, they used to get so much, each person – that is what they received as rations, so much each, or was not each person given two pails of lard; that is the way it used to be, at least we lived so well. They hardly ever went to the store, only when they were out of smokes, and it was just as you [*sc.* Rosa Longneck] said, when my mother snared rabbits the weasels used to steal them from her; thus she would bring that kind home too. And on the strength of these they used to have smokes; it was close to the little town, Delmas it is called, there they used to drive and go to get tobacco and things like that, coal-oil, they used to go and buy things like that and other little things like that when one ran short.

[11] Now these, we did not get to see any money except on the annual Treaty Days. Now these I have been telling about, our horses, my mother also had cows. My father had given us these cows, and in that way my mother had more cattle from there, she had cattle. Now my step-father used to dislike these cows, he was jealous of them. He would not look after them for her, my mother's cattle, they went about, these cattle used to be left to wander about. Now this one cow, this cow above all the others my father had given to us (these cows of a different breed which are big and have very long horns, 'pinto cows' they used to call them), this cow used to be detestable; that cow used to go about everywhere eating the felt liners of horse collars, she used

kî-isiyîhkâtêwak mâna), kî-wînêyihtâkosiw mostos; pikw îta aspikwayawêhikana ê-kî-papâmi-mîcit mân âna mostos, ê-kî-kâh-kitimahât iskwêwa, okisîpêkinikêwiniyiwa ê-kî-papâ-misîhtahk mâna. êêy, kî-pakwâtikosiw mostos êkos ê-kî-tôtahk. mâk âyisk namôy wî-kanawêyimêw mênikanihk awa nôhcâwîs. êkosi; êkon ôh êkwa mostoswa ôhi, êkwa ôki misatimwak, piyisk anihi nikâwiy ê-kî-mêsci-~ ê-kî-mêsc-âcâwâkêt anihi omoscosoma; êkota ê-kî-ohci-wâh-osôniyâmit pikw âwa nôht-~ nikâwiy mâna.

[12] êkwa nitêminânak ôki, mayaw nânitaw kâ-wî-itahkamikahk ôma kâ-nîpihk, âsay nôhcâwîs awa pêyak kâh-tâpakwêwêpinâtwâw[i] ôhi misatimwa oskastimwa, âsay kî-atimitâpâsow nôhcâwîs, ê-nitaw-âtâwâkêt anihi mostos-~ anihi misatimwa oskastimwa. nânitaw kâ-wî-itahkamikahk ôma kâ-kî-mâh-mêcawêsihk mâna kayâs, kâ-kî-nâh-nipâkwêsimohk, kâ-kî-misi-mêtawêhk *North Battleford*; êkota piko ê-kî-ohc-ôsôniyâm-~ – piyisk anik êkonik nisihkâc ê-kî-ati-ma-mêst-~-ma-mêstinât anihi, âha; êkos âyisk piko kî-ohc-ôsôniyâmiwak mâna, nânitaw kâ-wî-itahkamikahk.

[13] êkwa ayi, êkwa, êkos ânima mîna, napatâkwa, ê-kî-têhtapit mâna nôhcâwîs, misatimwa, pîkopicikana, pîkopicikan ôm âyi ê-pimi-pîko-~ ê-pa-pîkopicikêt nôhcâwîs, pîsi-kistikân êkwa êkota nikâwiy aw ê-osîhtamâht, pîsi-kiscikânis. êêê, wiy âta wiya mâna mitoni ê-kî-kwât-~-takahkisîhtâhk mân ôma pîsi-kiscikânis. êkwa mân ê-kî-isinâkosiyâhk nikâwiy ê-kistikêyâhk ôma, ê-kî-kâh-kihtimiwihit mâna nikâwiy. êêy, kâh-kapê-ayi ê-kî-at-~-ayâyâhk mâna pîsi-kistikânihk, ê-kistikêyâhk nîkân ôma. êkwa mân âyi, namôy kakêtihk ê-kî-ma-miyokihcikêyâhk kâ-takwâkik, nikiskisin mân îyikohk ê-kî-wî-nipahi-ma-miyokihcikêyâhk mân ôhi kistikâna. wahwâ, êkwa kâ-takwâkik ê-kî-mônahikêhk mâna, ê-mônahikêhk, êkwa

to cause grief for the women by going about and chewing up their laundry. Hey, this cow was hated for doing these things. But that was because my step-father would not keep her inside the fence. Thus; now this cow, and also these horses, finally my mother sold all her cows; only from that source did my mother have some cash income from time to time.

[12] Now our horses, as soon as some event or other would come up in the summer, already my step-father, when they had lassoed a horse, a young horse, already my step-father used to drive away, going to sell that cow –~ that horse, that young horse. When some event or other would come up, when they used to have sports days in the old days, when they used to hold Sun-dances, when they used to have the fair at North Battleford; only from that did he use to have cash income –~ in the end they, one by one he had sold them all, yes; for only in this way did they have cash income, when some event or other would come up.

[13] Now, now for that too, for potatoes, my step-father used to ride horseback, with ploughs, with this plough my step-father used to plough along, and there my mother had a garden prepared for her, a small garden. Heeey, did one ever make a nice job of that small garden. Now my mother and I would be seen planting it, over and over my mother used to tire me out. Heey, all day long we used to be in the garden, first planting it. Then we used to have a most beautiful garden in the fall, I remember how we used to grow such exceptionally beautiful vegetables. Oh my, now in the fall there used to be the digging, digging the vegetables and hauling them in. My mother used to plant a great many potatoes and all kinds of turnips and carrots; and finally, as she watched others do with various kinds, in that

êkoni ê-pîhtikwêyâwatâhk. namôy kâh-kakêtihk napatâkwa mâna ê-kî-isi-kistikêt awa nikâwiy, nanâtohk otisihkâna, oskâtâskwa; piyisk ê-isi-ka-kiskinawâpamât nanâtohk kîkway ôhi, êkos îsi mâna ê-kî-ka-kiscikêsit awa nikâwiy. îh, mitoni nikî-miy-ôhtâcihonân. anohc êkwa mâna nipê-~ nipa-pâhpinân ôma, wîsta mân âwa niwîcêwâkan ê-kî-pa-pêhtawât mâna nôhcâwîsa. mistah ê-kî-mamihcimoskit, ohtitaw payinitêwak ôki êkos îs-âyâwak, mistahi mamihcimoskiwak.

[FA:] awîniki?

payinitêwak ôki, *Finedays* ôk ôtê k-âyâcik, ohcitaw kêhtê-ayisiyiniwak ôk êkos ê-kî-pê-is-âyâcik, ê-kî-mamihcimoskicik mistahi. îh, namôy âwa nôhcâwîs ê-ohc-ôtatoskêwinit; â, kîtahtawê mâna wîci-nâpêwa kâ-kiyokâkot ôma, (namôy kakêtihk mîn ê-kî-pîhtikwâkawiyâhk, wahwâ, nânitaw k-ôhti-takopayicik kâ-wî-nîmihitohk kâ-pipohk, âsay iyâyaw okiyôtêwak nîkinâhk, ê-kî-~, osâm êtikwê cikêmâ ôhi wîstihkâna, iyikohk kâkikê ê-kî-iskwâhtâcik ôm âyi misatimwa, êkota ôk ôkiyôtêwak mân ê-kî-pê-mani-nakîcik); â, êkwa mân âwa nôhcâwîs, kâ-kiyokêt –~, tâpiskôt nâpêw kâ-kiyokâht ôma, «â, nikistikân niya, êkosi ta-kî-tôtahkik ayisiyiniwak, pîsi-kistikâna, napatâkwa nikistikân, êkoni kapê-pipon ê-âpacihtâyân,» êkosi mâna! – anohc mân êkwa nipâhpinân, ê-kî-mamihcimot, niyanân ôma mân ê-kî-kakwâtakihoyâhk. kîtahtawê ê-isi-môhcowiyân; âsay mâka mîn êkosi k-êt[i]-îtwêt awa, «îh,» nititâw (môy mâk âwiyak ê-nitohtawit, mâk ôkiyo-~, ôk-~ s-~ okiyokêwak oti, niyanân pik ôm ê-na-nayêstawapiyâhk; mâka mîn êwak ôma kâ-wî-mâh-mamihcimot ôm îyikohk, kistikân[a] ê-~ ê-kî-mân[a]-ôyosîmihtômakahki ôh âyi, nikistikâninâna, napatâkwa, âniskâc mîn êkoca mân ê-kî-ac[i]-ôhci-ka-kiscikêyâhk

way my mother planted some other vegetables. Look, we used to live very well off these. Today we often laugh about it, and my husband too used to hear my step-father brag. He was a great braggart, the *Payinitêwak* are like that by their very nature, they are great braggarts.

[FA:] Who?

The *Payinitêwak*, the Finedays that live over here, these old people have always been like that by their very nature, they used to be great braggarts. Look, my step-father was not a worker; well, at times when his fellow men came to visit him (we used to have a great many visitors too, oh my, when people drove in from elsewhere ahead of a dance in winter, already the visitors from afar headed for our house as their first stop, for they [*sc.* my mother and step-father] of course used to have so many stacks of hay at all times for the horses, and the visitors from afar used to stop there as their first choice); well, then my step-father, when he had visitors –~, he acted the man when someone visited him, «Well, as for me, I have a garden, that's what people should do, have a vegetable garden, I plant potatoes and use them all winter long,» so it went! – today we laugh about it, he used to brag while it was us who used to do the hard work. At one time, as stupid as I am; already as usual he was talking like that, «Look,» I said to him (but no one else was listening to me, at least not the visitors, it was only us and we were alone; as usual he kept bragging about that so much, these vegetables, our vegetables would usually last until there were new ones, potatoes, and we also used them as seed potatoes to plant more from year to year). «I did the planting,» and that was the way it

ôhi napatâkwa). «nikistikân,» êkos îs ôma, «îh,» nititâw, nipâh-~ nipa-pâhpipayin ôma, «îh,» nititâw, «tânispîhk êtikwê wîhkâc aw ê-kistikêt, niyanân ôma nikâwiy kâ-kakwâtakîyâhk mân ê-kistikêyâhk,» ê-kî-itak mâna.

[II]

[14] êkos ânima nîstanân ê-kî-pê-ay-ispayihikoyâhk, kahkiyaw kîkway nikâwiy, mistah ê-kî-kakâyawisîtotahk mâka pêskis anima ê-kî-wîcihak. mâk êcik ân[i] ê-kî-miyo-tôtawit, iyikohk ê-~ ê-kî-atoskahit ôm êkos îsi, ê-kiskinohamawit atoskêwin. anohc êkwa, namôy mistah ôskinîkiskwêw êkosi t-êtatoskêt kîkway, ta-wîcihtâsot ôma, ta-wîcihâcik. cikêmâ mîna niya, âta wiy ânohc ayisk ôki –~ ôki k-ôhpikihihcik mistahi okiskinohamâsowiniwâw otamihikwak, mâka niya nama kîkway kiskinohamâsowin, mitoni tâpwê piko nikî-pê-nêhiyawi-ohpikihikawin, môy âhpô kiskinohamâtowikamikohk nôh-pê-ayân. êkwa ât[a] ê-kî-miywâsik, akâmi-sîpîhk piko itêyihtâkwan ôma talimwâs kâ-kî-ihtakohk, êkota ôma kâ-kî-mêcimwâc-âyâcik okiskinohamâsowak ôki. êkwa, îh, ât[a] ânima kî-nahipayiw êkota anima ta-kî-kiskinohamâsoyân, mâk êkwa nikâwiy mân ê-kî-sâkihit; osâm ê-pêyakôsâniwiyân, itêyihtâkwan ôma, êkâ kâ-kî-ohci-pakitinit ta-kiskinohamâsoyân êkota niya. pêyak êsa nimis êkota kî-kiskinohamâsow, êwakw ânima mân ê-kî-pakwâtahk, âsay ê-kîs-ôskinîkiskwêwit nimis ana, «iyikohk miton ê-kî-pâhkatahpinêt nitânis,» ê-kî-itât mân âyamihêwiyiniwa, '*Lacombe*' kî-isiyîhkâsow ayamihêwiyiniw, pâhkw-âyamihêwiyiniw. «kikitimahâw, ôtê kê-nîkânîwik, môy t-âkayâsîmow kitânis; nawat ta-pakitinat, ta-kiskinohamâsot,» ê-kî-itikot mâna. êkwa mân êkwa ê-kî-wîhtamawât, «osâm, âsay kî-pâhkatahpinêw êkota oskinîkiskwêw ê-ayâwak, namôy sêmâk nôh-wîhtamâkwak ayamihêwiskwêwak, pâtos iyikohk ê-pêhtamâhk

was, «Look,» I said to him, and I broke up laughing about it, «Look,» I said to him, «since when did this one ever do the planting, I wonder, it is my mother and I who do the hard work of planting,» I said to him.

[**II**] [Rejecting Residential School]

[14] That has been our experience too, my mother used to do everything, she used to work very hard at it but at the same time I did help her. But actually, I guess, she did me a favour by making me work so much like that and teaching me to work. Today there are not many young girls who work like that on something, to help with things, to help someone. For me also, as might be expected, of course in the case of those being brought up today their schooling keeps them very busy, but for me there was no schooling, from the outset I was very much brought up as a Cree, I never even was in a school. Now, to be sure there was a good school right across the river at Delmas, it may be thought, it was where the students were in residence permanently. And, look, to be sure it was convenient that I should have gone to school there, but my mother kept me back with her; because I was an only child, it may be thought, may have been the reason in my case why she would not let me go to school there. My older sister had, it is reported, gone to school there, and she [*sc.* my mother] hated what happened, my older sister had already been a young woman, «To such an extent had my daughter been ill unattended [*sc.* without notice to her mother],» she had told the priest, Lacombe was the priest's name [*sc.* Ernest Lacombe], a Catholic priest. «You are saddling her with a disadvantage, in the future your daughter will not speak English; it would be better for you to let her to go to school,» he used to tell her. Then she explained it to him, «This is the reason, already a young woman of my family had been ill there

ê-âhkosit nitânis, âsay êkwa mêton ê-kawâhkatosot ê-kawahpinêt, ê-nit-~ ê-nitawi-wayawîhtahâyâhk; îh, namôy ânim ê-ohci-wîhtamâkawiyân êkospîhk. nikî-wanihâw êwakw âna nitânis, êkospîhk ohc âwa kâ-pêyakot; namôy êkwa êwako,» ê-kî-itât mâna nikâwiy aw âyamihêwiyiniwa, êwak ôhc anim êkâ kâ-kî-kiskinohamâsoyân.

[III]

[15] êkosi, piyisk aniyê, piyisk aniyê, nistw-âskiy mâka piko nikâwiy awa nikî-wîc-âyâmâw. êkos êkwa kâ-kî-ati-wîcêwak êkwa nâpêw, kâ-kî-wîc-âyâmak. tâpwê êkwa, êwakw êkwa, nikî-~, mitoni mîna kî-kakâyawisîw awa ê-wîc-âyâmak aw ôskinîkiw, pêh-pêyakwan ê-kî-pê-~, iyikohk, âta wiy âyiwâk nawac kî-kêhtê-oskinîkiw.

[16] êkwa ani, ê-pipohk êkwa ôm êkwa, â, êtikwê mân ê-kî-pê-isi-ka-kakêskimiht wîst ôm ê-pê-oskinîkit, kâ-mâci-kîskatahwât ê-ati-misi-~ ê-ati-miyoskamik mistikwa, ê-nâh-nâtâwahât, mêtoni kî-takahkahpicikêw awa, cîpêhcakwawêsa mâna ê-kî-otâpahât. mitoni wiya ê-takahkinâkohcikêt ôma nistam anima êkwa ê-onâpêmiyân. ê-ay-âwahât, êkwa pêyak kisêyiniw kî-ihtakow, êkot[ê] ê-kî-nihtâ-pasahwât mistikwa, êkoni mîn êkwa k-êtikot, «hâ, mitoni mâh-miyosiwak ôki mistikwak,» itik ês ôma, «nawat ta-pasahohcik, mitoni ta-miywâsin wâskahikan.» êkosi tâpwê, mîna kî-atoskêmow ê-pasahohcik ôki mistikwak kwayask. êkosi; ê-ati-~ ê-ati-ka-kîsi-nîpihk êkwa, tahkohtaciwêyâwahêw êkwa, itê êk ôma ta-wîkiyâhk, êkotê. îh, pêya-~ pêyak-pipon pikw ê-kî-wîkihkêmoyâhk ninîkihikonânak ôki, âsay êwakw ânim ê-nîpihk mîn êkwa nisikos êkwa awa kâ-wî-kakwê-piskihci-wihiko-~-wîkihikoyâhk. êkosi; tâpwê ê-kîsi-miyoskamik, miton ôma kâ-kâh-kîsi-nîpihk, âsay

unattended, and the nuns did not inform me in time, not until later did we hear that my daughter was ill, and by then she was already terribly wasted away and sick in bed and we went and took her out; look, we were not informed about this at that time. I lost that daughter of mine, since that time this one has been the only one; not that one now,» my mother used to tell the priest, that was the reason why I was never able to go to school.

[III] [Married Life]

[15] Thus, in the end, in the end I had only lived with my mother for three years. Then I had gone on to marry a man and had lived with him. And indeed he also was a very good worker, this young man with whom I lived, we were both the same age but he was slightly older as a young man.

[16] Now then, as it was winter now, well, he too must have been counselled about this as he grew up to be a young man, towards spring he began to cut logs and hauled them in one by one, he had a very good team, he used to drive a team of greys. He really made a good showing when I first took a husband. As he was hauling logs, there was a certain old man who was good at trimming them, and now that one said to him, «Well, these logs are really nice,» he said to him, «It would be better if they were trimmed for the house to be really nice.» Thus, indeed, he also hired someone for these logs to be properly trimmed. So it was; as it was getting to be fully summer now, he hauled them up to the top of the hill now, to where we would live over there. Look, we only lived with our parents one winter, and already that following summer my mother-in-law tried to make us live in a separate place. So it was; when it was fully spring, when it was gradually getting to be fully summer, already she wanted us to buy some canvas, and so it was that my old man was all the time cutting these posts, only that

papakiwânikamikwêkin ninitawêyimikonân ta-kâhcitinamâhk, êkwa êkos ânima cimacikana ôhi, êkotowahk piko ê-kî-~ tâpitawi mâna ê-kî-kîskatahahk awa nikisêyinîm, êêy, ê-kîskatahikêt. êkwa ê-ati-~, êkos êkwa ê-ma-mawi-~-mâwacisôniyâwêt êkwa, êkota ohc ôski-macêkinwêyâhk [*sic*], êkw ê-cipahamâcohk ôm ê-aci-~, êkwa an[i] êkwa kâ-~ k-âtâwêhikawiyâhk êkwa mîkiwâhpêkin êkwa, (kîkwây niy êkospîhk ê-osk-âyiwiyân, nayêstaw ê-piminawasowêyân êkwa, môy âyisk âkwâskam nôh-nihtâwikwâson), êy, nisikos awa kahkiyaw kîkway ê-kî-nihtâwihtât, mîkiwâhp ê-wiyisahk, êkwa êkota iskwêwak nîso ê-pê-ta-takohtêcik. êwako ê-wîhkwêpicik êkwa wâsakâm ê-otihtinamâtocik ôm âyi, papakiwânikamik ôm ê-~ ê-osîhtamâkawiyân, ê-nêwokwâtêk.

[17] êkos ê-kîsikwâtahkik êkwa ôma mîkiwâhp êkwa, êkwa an[i] êkwa kâ-~, êkwa ê-kotaskitâhk ôma mîkiwâhp êkwa, êê, ê-nipahi-takahkêyihtamân, mîkiwâhp êkw ê-oski-macêkinwêyân. îh, sêmâk êkot[a] ê-kî-ati-mosci-wîkiyâhk anima, ê-pa-pêyako-pamihisoyâhk, kî-kaskihtâw ê-pamihit kwayask mitoni. ê-ay-âh-itohtacikêt ôma êkos îsi, mêtoni nikî-ma-miywâcihik, kwayask ê-pa-pamihisoyâhk, êkwa –~. îh, êwakw êkw ê-ati-takwâkik, êkwa nêh[i] êkwa mistikwa êkwa, êkot[a] êkwa k-ôyastamâkoyâhk mîna pêyak awa kisêyiniw, atoskêmow mîna, wâskahikan êkwa ê-osîhtamâkawiyâhk êkwa êkota. êkota êk ôki, ita ôma kâ-nahâhkapiyân, mitoni mîn êkw êkota mâmawôhkamâtonâniwiw ayihk ê-sisocêskiwakinikêhk, ê-sisocêskiwakinamihk ôma nîkinân. wahwâ, nitakahkêyihtên niya, mân[i] âwêskâ [*sic*] miywâsisinôpan [*sic*] ôma wâskahikan ita ê-ayâyâhk. êkwa ayihk, êkwa mîn êkwa ati-papâ-pawahikêw êkwa, ôma kayâs kâ-kî-mosci-pawahikêhk ôma mâna, êkos îsi, ê-papâ-pawahikêt êkwa, ê-wî-kakwê-kaskihtât êkwa napakihtakwa

kind, heey, he kept chopping. In this way now he was saving up money, and with that we now had new canvas for a tipi, when they made us buy tipi canvas at the Treaty Days (as for me, what did I know in those days, I was young and only did the cooking then for I was not that good at sewing), hey, my mother-in-law was good at doing everything, she cut out the tipi, and two women came there. They all sat in a circle around it and each grabbed a part, they were making a tent for me of four pieces sewn together.

[17] Thus they finished sewing the tipi, and as they now set up the tipi, hey, I was terribly happy, now I had a tipi made of new canvas. Look, we simply lived there right away, we were alone and looking after ourselves, he managed to look after me really well. He was taking posts to town and things like that, he was making a very good life for me, we looked after ourselves properly, and –~. Look, it was that fall, now those logs, at that point now this one old man also set them up for us, and he [*sc.* my husband] had also hired someone for the house to be built for us at that point. Now at that point it was these, the family I had married into, now at that point there also was a general get-together for the mudding, they were mudding our house. Oh my, as for me, I was happy, it really seemed the house was so nice where we lived. And now, now he used to go around harvesting, in the old days you would do the harvesting by hand, like that, he went out harvesting, trying to earn lumber to make the floor, things like that. And we were indeed able to get the lumber for the flooring, and the roof was put on that house; it was really the right size for us from the outset. So it was; hey, just as I had always

t-ânâskêhk ôma, êkos îsi. tâpwê mîn ê-kî-kaskihtâyâhk, napakihtakw[a] ânihi, ê-anâskâhcikâtêk, êk ôt[ê] ê-apahkwêhk anima wâskahikan; nahiyikohk miton ê-ispîhcâk tâpwê piko niyanân ohci. êkosi; êy, mitoni mân ânima kâ-kî-is-ây-akâwâtamân, êkosi nikî-kakwê-isi-pa-pamihison, pêyak mâna nisikos ê-kî-pê-ocihci-wâpamak, namôy kakêtihk ê-kî-kanâci-pamihot! ahpô onipêwin, môy wîhkâc awiyak ê-ohci-pimisihk nipêwinihk, iyikohk mân ê-kî-~ wâpiskanâskân ê-ay-astât ôhi, iyikohk ê-kî-wî-kanâci-pamihot; pîhtaw âpihtawikosisâniskwêw-âya. hâyêy, nîst êkota, môy kakêt-~, êkosi, mitoni mân êkosi nîst ê-kî-kakwê-isi-pamihisoyân, êkwa mitoni mîna, ôh êkwa nitâpacihcikaninâna êkos ês kinosêwi-sâkahikanihk iyikohk, êkota êkwa nikî-ohtinênân kîkway mîna, nikâwiy aw ê-miyit, mîcisowinâhtik, akocikan, têhtapiwina; êkotow-âya, itowahk ôma k-âyâyan anihi nêhiyawi-têhtapiwina tâpiskôc, êkotowahk ayisk kayâs. îh, mitoni sôskwâc, sêmâk niya nikî-miyo-pamihison mitoni sôskwâc, kayâs ôki kotawânâpiskwak kâ-kî-~ ê-âspatapicik, kâ-kî-itwêhk mâna, êkotowahk nikâwiy, ê-kî-wî-nipahi-miyosiyit, mostoswa ê-atâwâkêt, ê-kî-atâwêt, êkoni nikî-âsônamâk. êkwa ôk ôtê kinosêwi-sâkahikanihk itê kâ-kî-ohci-pic-~-picihtatâhk ôhi nicayânisinâna, êkota wiya kotawânâpiskwa, kayâs ôk âsinîwi-kotawânâpiskwak mâna, êkoni wiya mîskot nikâwiy kî-ayâwêw. êkos ânima mitoni nikî-ma-miyo-pamihison mitoni sôskwâc. êkw ê-ati-takwâkik êkwa –~

[*external break*]

[FA:] tânita kani kâ-ihtâyan aspin?

[18] ayâ, aspin anim êkwa kâ-t-~ kâ-nôhtêpayiyâhk anim êkwa ê-mâci-kâh-kisinâk, namôy êkwa misatimokamik kî-osîhtamâsow awa ni-~ niwîkimâkan; kayâs ê-kî-isi-wêhcasik, tâpiskôt mênikan ê-isîhtât êkwa, 'sîkwaskan-~ sîkwaskatahikani-misatimokamik' kî-isiyîhkâtamwak mâna,

wished to do it, that is the way I tried to look after myself, there was one of my aunts that I had lived to see still, she was an extraordinarily clean housekeeper! Even her bed, no one ever even lay on the bed, she put such a white blanket over it, she was intent on being such a clean housekeeper; of course she was a Halfbreed woman. Hayey, I too was terribly –~, I too very much tried to look after my own like that, and we also really, we got so much of our household things from there at *Kinosêwi-sâkahikanihk* [(Jack-)Fish Lake], my mother gave them to me, a table, a cupboard, chairs; things like that, like the kind you [*sc.* Freda Ahenakew] have, like that traditional Cree bench [*sc.* without a back], for that was the kind long ago. Look, from the start, right away I looked after myself really well from the start, these stoves of long ago had a back on them, as they used to say, my mother used to have an especially beautiful stove of that kind, she had bought it when she sold a cow, she turned that over to me. And as for them, there was a stove amongst our things that had been brought over from *Kinosêwi-sâkahikanihk*, these castiron stoves of long ago, my mother had that one in exchange. Thus I looked after myself really well from the start. Now it was getting to be fall –~

[*external break*]

[FA:] Where was it, I forgot, you were when you left off?

[18] Well, when I left off it was when we were running short of things at the time when it gradually began to get cold, and then my husband was unable to construct a barn for himself, in the old days it used to be simple, he made it like a fence, they used to call it a 'horsebarn of logs-and-straw', that kind my husband made

êkotowahk êkwa k-ôsîhtamâ-~ k-ôsîhtât êkwa wiya nim-~ awa niwîkimâkan, misatimwa ita t-âsiwahât. êkw ân[i] êkotowahk êkwa, hêy, êkwa ê-âwatât êkwa ê-mâh-miyiht ôhi, sa-~ sîkwatahikana êkwa. tâpwê, mîn êkon ânih ê-kî-kîsowâki, sîkwaskatahikani-misatimokamik ê-oy-osîhtamâsot, ita otêma ê-osîhât [*sc.* ê-asiwahât]. êkosi; îh, êkos ânima nikî-kîsi-wiyapinân. âsay êwakw ânim ê-at[i]-âkwâ-nîpihk âsay nikî-pîmakâmênâwason ê-nôhâwasoyân [*laughter*]! ê-~ [*laughter*] – awas, kêkât nânitaw nititwân [*laughter*].

[19] tâpwê anima êkos ê-kî-pê-ispayik nîsta, mâk âyisk kêhtê-ayak nikî-ohpikihikwak, namôy kakêtihk nikî-pê-kitotik mân âwa nôhkom, ta-kakwê-isi-~-kîkway-isi-pamihisoyân ôma, ispîhk nâpêw wîc-âyâmaki, ahpô mâna nikî-itik, «â, onâpêmiyani, ê-kwayâci-paminawatiht [*sic*] ana nâpêw k-âtoskêt, cikêmâ nâpêw môsihtâw k-âtoskêt, nôhtêhkatêw; kîspin ê-mac-âyiwit nâpêw mistahi, â, kâ-nêstosit k-âtoskêt, kisiwâhkatosow ani kâ-takohtêt, êkâ kîkway kâ-kwayâtastamâht,» ê-kî-isit ahpô mâna nôhkom, «pê-kisiwâhkatosow ana, tânêhk ôhci êkâ ê-kwayâci-paminawatat [*sic*].» kahkiyaw kîkway nikî-pê-sa-sêkimik mân âwa nôhkom, êkos êkos ânima mwêhc ê-kî-wî-kakwê-tôtamân anima nôhkom awa, tânisi kâ-kî-isi-kitosit; aspin ê-nitaw-~ kîkway k-ôsîhtât awa niwîkimâkan, êkos êkwa niy ê-kî-isinâkohcikêyân, ê-kî-kakwê-kwayâci-piminawasoyân [*sic*] mâna, ê-paminawatak [*sic*] awa niwîkimâkan ôma kâ-~ kâ-sipwêhtêt kâ-nitaw-âtoskêt, sôskwâc ê-~ kâ-takosihk, âsay nikîsi-kahkiyaw-kîkway-ka-kwayâcihtân, nikîsi-paminawatâw [*sic*], sôskwâc ê-ma-mîcisot. êkosi nîst ânim ê-kî-pê-isi-pa-pamihisoyân, mîn ê-miyoskamik (êkos ânima nîstanân êkwa mîn âyisk nikî-pê-is-ôhpikihik nikâwiy), nîst êkwa mân ê-kî-kakwê-kistikêyân; mîn êkota kî-kaskihtâw awa, ê-pîkopicikêstamâkawiyân ita pîsi-kiscikânisa ê-ka-kistikêyân. ê-kî-ka-kiscikêwi-pimâcihosiyân, îh, êkota mîna nîst êkot[a]

in which to keep the horses. Now it was that kind, hey, now he was hauling the straw bales he had been given. It is true, they used to be warm, and he constructed a horsebarn of logs-and-straw for himself and kept his horses in there. So it was; look, with that we were all done getting set up. As the summer reached its peak [in August], I already held a baby in my arms, I was nursing a baby [*laughter*]! – go on, I just about said something [*laughter*].

[19] It is true, this is the way it had come to happen for me too, for the old people had raised me, my grandmother had always spoken to me of a great many things, how to try to look after myself with respect to things once I was married to a man, and she even used to tell me, «Well, when you have a husband, that man who is working has a meal prepared and cooked, of course a man feels it when he is working, he is hungry; if a man is of a really mean disposition, well, when he is tired from work, he will definitely be hungry and in a foul mood when he gets home and nothing has been prepared for him,» my grandmother even used to tell me, «He will come home hungry and in a foul mood because you do not have a meal prepared and cooked.» My grandmother had always been cautioning me in all things, and thus I used to try to do this exactly as she had used to speak to me; when my husband went off to do something, then I too used to make things look right, I used to try to make ready and do the cooking, cooking for my husband when he set off and went to work, and when he got back I right away already had everything finished and ready, I had finished cooking for him and he had his meal right away. That way I too had come to look after myself, and in the spring also (we too, for that way also my mother had raised me), I too used to try to plant a garden, and at that time he used to manage it, I had a garden ploughed for me where I planted vegetables. I used to live off the

ê-takwâkik, môy kakêtihk ê-kî-ma-miyokihcikêyâhk mîna, kis-~ ê-ohc-~, kistikâna ôhi napatâkwa ê-isi-~ nanâtohk kîkway.

[20] êkwa mîna, nikî-pê-mâwasako-wîcihikawin mîna, cikêmô êkwa nitôcamôsêsin [*sic*] êkota, ê-wî-mônahikêhk êkwa, mîn êkota nikî-pê-wîcihikawin, nikâwiy ê-pê-wîcihit êkwa kotaka, ostima, ê-pê-mônahikêstamâkawiyân. wahwâ, mitoni mâna t-ây-âtotamihk ôma kayâs ât[a] ê-kî-pê-âyimahk, mâka mîna miton ê-kî-wêhcasik ê-kî-isi-pê-takahki-pimâcihohk mitoni. nîst êkos ânima misakâmê kahkiyaw ê-kî-pê-isi-kakwê-tôtamân ê-kî-pê-pimâcihoyân.

[21] mâka niyanân ôma, nikâwiy êkwa niya, namôy îtowa-~, itowahk kay-~ k-ây-âwatôsêcik, êkos ê-kî-pêt-~, êkos ohc-~ êkos ê-kî-pê-is-âyâyân; nikâwiy awa namôy ohci-~ kâ-sakôsêcik ôk îskwêwak, môy êkos ôhci-pê-is-âyâw, êkwa mîna niya, âniskâc anim êkos ê-kî-pê-is-ôtawâsimisiyân nîsta, môy mihcêtwâw ê-ohci-pê-ayâwakik awâsisak. êkos ê-kî-isi-~-at[i]-îsi-pa-pôn-ôtawâsimisiyân, tâspwâw ê-nîsicik ôma piko nâpêwak ê-iskwahpinêcik êkwa nitânis, êkonik pikw ê-pimâtisicik nitawâsimisak.

garden quite a bit, look, I for my part also lived off that in the fall, we also used to have a plentiful crop of all kinds of vegetables and potatoes.

[20] Now I also used to have a lot of help from everybody, for of course my time was taken up by my baby, and when it was time for harvesting the potatoes, I had help, my mother came to help me and also another, her niece [*sc.* her brother's daughter], I had them come to dig my potatoes for me. Oh my, one should really be telling about how difficult it used to be in the old days, for sure, but it also used to be really easy and one used to make a very nice living. That way I too used to try to do everything all along as I used to make my living.

[21] But it was the case that we, my mother and I, were not of the kind, of the kind that have lots of children, that is how I used to be; my mother had not been like those women who have one child after another, and, as for me, I as well, from one generation to the next, in having children like that, I also did not give birth to children often. In that way, consequently, as I reached the end of my childbearing years, there are only two boys that survive and then my daughter, these are my only children that are living.

II

Being a Cree woman

Sarah Whitecalf (right) and friends at Sweetgrass Sundance, 1981.

5

êwak ôm ê-kî-ay-itâcimisot awa nikâwiy

This is my mother's own story

êwak ôm ê-kî-ay-itâcimisot awa nikâwiy

[1] âsay mîna niwi-~ niwî-âcimâw ôta nikâwiy, namôy nik-ôh-kisipâcimâw nikâwiy ê-kî-pê-isi-~ mâna, wiy êwak ôm ê-kî-ay-itâcimisot mân ê-kî-ay-âtotahk.

[2] kayâs ôma, kîkwây êtikwê ayisiyinîhkipanak ôki, ê-kî-papâ-nitawi-picîstahkik mâna, ê-kî-âcimot mâna nikâwiy, ê-kî-ayihk, ôtê wâhyaw akâmi-tipahaskân, 'awasâpisk' ê-kî-isiyîhkâtahk mâna, «tânitê êtikwê piko,» nikî-itêyihtên mâna, «awasâpisk.» ê-kî-ma-mosci-pa-pimipicicik [*sic*] ês êkotê ê-itâwahitocik, tânitahto êtik ôm ê-itahtotâpânêcik ê-nêwotâpânêcik miyâmâ nânitaw, ês êkotê ê-kî-ispicicik, ê-ay-itohtêcik â, akâmi-tipahaskân ôtê 'awasâpisk' kî-isiyîhkâtam mâna piyisk – êcik ânima misi-wâhyawêskamik anima, ahpô niya, nikî-~ nikî-nitawi-wâpahtên anim êkotê is ânim îtêhkê kâ-kî-âcimot mân ê-kî-ay-ispicicik, ôta ê-ohti-sipwêpicicik ôma *North Battleford* ôma kayâs-âskîhkân –~, ôma kayâs-ôtênaw, êkota ês ê-kî-ohci-sa-sipwêpicicik, êê-ma-mosci-pimipicicik [*sic*]! ê-na-~ êkotê ôma paskwâhk ôma tahk ê-ay-ispicicik ôm ê-mam-~ ê-na-nimitâsipicicik akâmi-tipahaskân ê-~, nistam ê-onâpêmit, ayinânêwosâp kî-itwêw mân[a] êkospîhk ê-itahtopiponwêt, nikâwiy awa.

This is my mother's own story

[1] As usual I am going to tell about my mother on here [*sc.* on the audio-recorder], I will never have reached the end of all there is to tell about my mother, how she used to –~, for this one she used to tell about in speaking of herself.

[2] In the old days, what may it have been that made the people who are now dead go moving about with their camps, my mother used to tell, it was over there far across the border [*sc.* with the United States], they used to call it 'Beyond the Rocky Mountains', «Wherever that may be,» I used to think, «Beyond the Rocky Mountains.» They reportedly used to move along by team over there with their camps, moving as a group, I wonder how many teams they were, I believe they were about four teams, reportedly they were moving over there with their camps, they went there, well, over there across the border, they called it 'Beyond the Rocky Mountains', finally – as it turns out, it was extremely far away, even I have gone to see it over there in that direction, where she used to tell that they were headed with their camps, departing from the old reserve here at North Battleford with their camps –~, from the Old Town [*sc.* Battleford, on the south side of the river], reportedly departing from there with their camps, moving along by team with their camps! They kept moving over there to the prairie with their camps, moving out onto the open prairie with their camps and across the border, she was newly married, she was eighteen years old at that time, my mother used to say.

[3] êkwa, êwako k-êtwêyân, namôy ê-ohci-pê-tipêyimisohk, kayâs anim êkos ê-kî-pê-ispayik ohci, namôy ê-ohci-pê-tipêyimisohk. «âyêy!» ê-itwêt nikâwiy, «nikî-pakwâtên mâna,» ê-itwêt, nistam ê-oskinîkiskwêwit êkoni onâpêma, katâc mîna owîwiwa [*sic*] ê-kî-mêkiskwêwamimiht [*sic*] êsa, ê-sîkâwit awa nâpêw; êkon ês ê-mêkiskwêwamimiht ê-oskinîkiskwêwit awa nikâwiy. «wahwâ, êkwa ê-nîsiyit otawâsimisa,» itwêw, «ê-mâh-misikitiyit âsay,» itwêw. «miton ê-mâh-misikitiyit âsay ôh ôtânisa, pêyak aw ê-oskinîkiskwêsisiwit,» itwêw, «mitoni, êkwa pêyak ôhi nâpêsisa,» itwêw, «âsay mâk ê-kakâyawâtisit mîn âwa nâpêsis mitoni, ôh ôkosisa,» itwêw, «êkoni –~ êwakw âwa kâ-miyiht ômạ niy,» îtwêw, «ta-~ t-ônâpêmiyân aw,» îtwêw, «êêkwa [*sic*] ê-pakwâtak awa kêhtê-nâpêw,» itwêw; «wahwâ, nikî-pakwâtên mâna mistah,» îtwêw; «êkwa ôm,» îtwêw, «ayahk,» itwêw, –~

[*external break*]

êwakw ân[i] ânima, k-âcimak nikâwiy awa, ôhi kêhtê-nâpêwa mâna kâ-kî-âcimât ê-kî-pakwâtât âta, mâk ê-kî-tôtamôhiht sôskwâc, ta-wîkimât anihi nâpêwa.

[4] êkwa mâna, êkwa, k-ât-~ kâ-sipwêhtêcik ês êkwa anim ôta ohci ê-picicik (kayâs ayisk ôk âyisiyiniwak ê-kî-kitimâkahk âta, mistah ê-kî-papâmâcihocik, ê-kî-papâmipicicik wâh-wâhyaw, ê-kî-ay-ispicicik mâna), nanâtohk kispêw êcikwê mâna kîkway wîstawâw ê-kî-kakwê-isi-pa-pimâcihocik. mâcik ânim êkota nikâwiy mân âwa k-êtwêt, anihi nâpêwa kâ-kî-wîc-âyâmât, «môy wîhkâc ê-ohci-pimi-wa-wîtapimak ka-pa-pim-~ ê-pa-pimipicihk, ê-kî-ay-askôkêyân mân[a],» îtwêw, «nâway niy ê-pa-pimipiciyân,» itwêw. «êkwa wiy,» îtwêw, «ê-kî-têhtapit mân,» îtwêw, «awa kâ-kî-wîcêwak,» kî-itwêw mâna. «ê-kî-têhtapi-~ ê-pimi-têhtapit wiya, wâh-wâhyaw ê-pimi-pâh-paskêpayit, êkospîhk êsa,

[3] Now, as I said, one did not make one's own decisions [*sc.* as a woman], it used to be like that in the old days, one did not make one's own decisions. «Ah!» my mother used to say, «I hated it,» she said, she was a young woman and he was her first husband, and it had to be to a married man, too, to whom she had been given in marriage, it is reported, the man was a widower; to that one she was given in marriage, the young woman who was my mother. «Oh my, now there were his two children,» she said, «they were both big already,» she said. «They were really big already, his daughter, this one was developing into a young woman,» she said, «really, and one was a boy,» she said, «but this one was already capable of looking after himself, this son of his,» she said, «his –~ he was the one to whom I was given,» she said, «for me to have him as my husband,» she said, «now I hated this old man [*sc.* probably in his thirties],» she said; «oh my, I used to hate it utterly,» she said; «and this,» she said, «ah,» she said, –~

[*external break*]

It was that, what I was telling about my mother, although she hated this old man whom she used to tell about, she was simply made to marry that man.

[4] Now then, now when they departed from here, it is reported, with their camps (for in the old days it was poor but the people travelled about a great deal, moving about with their camps, moving to far away places), even though they too must have tried every possible way of making a living. For instance as my mother used to say about that man she had lived with, «I never sat beside him as one moved camp, I used to follow behind,» she said, «I used to drive behind with the camp,» she said. «Now he,» she said, «he used to ride a horse,» she said, «the one to whom I had been married,» she used to say. «He rode –~ he used to ride along, riding far off the trail here and there as we went along, at

ê-kî-nôcimahihkaniwêcik ayisiyiniwak waniyaw, êkotê ôm âkâmi-tipahaskân êkos ê-kî-isi-pimâcihocik; êwakw ânim êtikwê ohci, êkotê êsa k-ôh-kî-ispicicik ê-kî-nôcimahihkaniwêt. mahihkanisis-~, mahihkanisisak (ê-itahtôsêt awa mêscacâkanis, mêscacâkanis awa, mahihkanisisa kahkiyaw ta-mêscihât êwakw âw âyisiy-~, awa, pêyak awa ta-mêscihimiht otawâsimisa kiki wiya; «ê-kî-payipihtêhohcik» kî-itwêw mâna nikâwiy, tânis êtikw ânim îsi? «ê-kî-payipihtêhohcik ôki,» ê-kî-itwêt mâna nikâwiy, namôy –~, mis-~, ôk êsa miton ê-kî-mistakisocik kêhtê-ayak mâna kîspin –), êkos ês ânim ê-kî-pim-îtahkamikisiyit mâna, mêscacâkanisa ôhi ê-kî-pimi-nôcihât êsa mân âna, ê-pimi-nâh-nitonawât, wâh-wâhyaw ê-pim-îsi-pâh-paskêpayit ôma. êkwa itê ôma kâ-wî-kapêsihk êkwa, êkot[ê] êkw êsa mân êkotê ê-kî-takopayiyit êsa mâna, ê-pêsiwâyit ôhi mêscicâkanisa ôhi, ê-itahtôsêyit, «namôy kakêtihk iyikohk ê-kî-sôniyâhkêt, ê-~ k-~ âta wiya namôy wiya piko, tânitaht ôki êkos ê-kî-at-îtahkamikisicik nâpêwak, ê-at-~ ôma k-âti-pa-pimipicihk,» ê-kî-itwêt mâna nikâwiy awa.

[5] êkwa, êkwa ês ôma mân ôh ôtôsima ôhi oskinîk-~ ê-nâpêsisiwiyit – îh, tânitahtw êtik ôma k-êtwêt, matwân cî ôma namôy êyinânêw [*sic*] ê-itahtopiponêyit, «mitoni wiya ê-kî-kakêhtâwisît aw,» îtwêw anih ô-~, okosisiyiwa, «êkwa mân ê-kî-ta-têhtapit,» itwêw. êwak ôma mân ê-kî-pa-pim-âtotahk ôm ê-pim-ây-itâcihocik ôma, «êkw âwa mâna wiy ê-kî-têhtapit,» itwêw. «êkwa mân[a],» îtwêw, «môy kakêtihk ê-kî-ati-sâ-sasîhciwihikoyâhkok ôki, ôki niwîcêwâkaninânak,» itwêw, «ôma mâna kâ-pimipicihk,» itwêw, «kâ-pimi-kapêsihk ôm,» îtwêw. «âyêy, kîtahtawê mân,» îtwêw, «kîk-~ kiyîkisêpâyâk[i],» ê-itwêt, «awîn ôma mân îskwâhtêmihk kî-astêw, pîhc-âyihk ohci, wiyâs,» ê-kî-itwêt mâna nikâwiy, «iyây-iyikohk [*sic*] wiyâs mâna pîhc-âyihk ê-astêk, pîhc-âyihk ohci papakiwayânikamikohk, îh,

that time, it was reported, all kinds of people used to hunt wolves, in that way they made their living over there across the border; that must have been the reason that they had reportedly moved over there with their camps and he had taken up the wolf hunt. Cubs (as many offspring as this coyote had [*sc.* the whole litter], this coyote, in order for that man to kill every last one of the cubs, for every last one of the young to be killed along with her, «They used to have their ears tagged,» my mother used to say, I wonder how that was done? «They used to have their ears tagged,» my mother used to say, the old ones reportedly were really valuable if –), in that he reportedly used to be involved as he went along, that one reportedly used to hunt these coyotes as he went along, looking for them as he went along, riding far off the trail here and there as he went along. Now over there where one was going to make camp, over there he used to arrive, it is reported, bringing in these coyotes and as many cubs as they had, «He used to make an enormous amount of money, although it was not only him, a number of the men were involved in that while one was moving along with one's camp,» my mother used to say.

[5] Now, now her step-son reportedly was a boy – look, how old she must have said he was, wasn't it that he was eight years old? «He was very advanced for his age,» she said about that son of his, «and he used to ride along on horseback,» she said. This she would be telling about as they were travelling along, «Now this one used to ride on horseback,» she said. «And now,» she said, «our fellow travellers would often put us to shame,» she said, «when one used to move along with one's camp,» she said, «when one camped overnight on the way,» she said. «What on earth! at times,» she said, «early in the morning,» she said, «what was this? there would be meat placed inside the doorway,» my mother used

nîpâ-tipisk êtikwê nê-nipâyâhko ê-kî-pê-pîhtikwê-pakitinahkik mân ôk,» îtwêw; «ê-kî-ati-kâh-kîminasocik anima, ôki misakâmê, namôy ôhc-âti-na-nôhtêhkatâniwiw,» ê-kî-itwêt mâna nikâwiy, «mitoni wiy ê-kî-ati-ma-miyo-pimâcihohk anima,» ê-kî-itwêt mâna nikâwiy, «namôy k-~ ât[a] ôhci-na-nôhtêhkatâniwiw,» ê-itwêt. «wahwâ, ôki mâna niwîcêwâkaninânak, nî-~ ê-kî-ati-kâh-~-kîmôci-nâh-nipahâcik [*sic*] mostoswa mân ês ôma mân,» îtwêw, ayisk kayâs ês ôm êkotê akâmi-tipahaskânihk ôma, ê-kî-mâh-~ ê-kî-mâh-mis-âyâ-~ ê-kî-mâh-~-iskwâhâcik [*sic*] êsa mostoswa êtikwê mâna, êkwa namôy ôhci-ma-mênikanihkâtêki kayâs, namôy –~, mênikana namôy ê-ohc-âyâki, tâsipwâw [*sic*] êsa mâna pikw îta ê-kî-pimi-ka-kapêsicik, êkâ kîkway mênikana kayâs; êkotowihk ês ôki mâna ê-kî-pimi-kâh-kîmôtahpinasocik. êkos êsa mân êkwa ê-kî-tapasîpicicik kâ-kîkisêpâyâk, «tânitahtwâw anim êkos ê-kî-at-îtahkamikisicik ôki niwîcêwâkaninânak,» ê-itwêt.

[6] êkwa ayihk, «êkwa mân,» îtwêw, «awa mâna,» itwêw, «êw-~ nîswâw ê-kî-ati-sêkisiyân,» ê-kî-itwêt nikâwiy, «kîtahtawê,» itwêw, «ê-ati-pa-pimipicihk,» itwêw. «êy, wâhyaw mân âwa nâpêsis ê-pa-pêti-têhtapit [*sic*], piyisk mân ê-pê-~ têpiyâhk mân ê-pa-pêcisâpamak wâhyaw, êê-pa-pêci-têhtapit [*sic*] mân,» îtwêw, «êkwa wâhyaw ôma kâ-nakatiht,» itwêw, «êkota mân êkwa, êêkwayâc [*sic*] êkwa mân êkot[a] ôhci ê-pê-sipwêpayit,» itwêw, «ê-pê-nawaswêt êkwa mân,» îtwêw. «ê-kihtimêyihtahk êtikwê mân ôma, pêyâ-~ pêyakwanohk ê-pa-pimipiciwiht ôma, pêyâhcik ê-pa-pimipiciwiht,» itwêw, «êkwa ê-nôhtê-kisîpayit,» itwêw, «êwakw ânima mâna kâ-kî-tôtahk,» itwêw; «êêkota [*sic*] ohc êkwa mân ê-pê-kisîpayit ê-pê-nawaswêt,» itwêw. «wahwâ,» itwêw, «kîtahtawê ôma mâka mîna êkos,» îtwêw, «ââspin [*sic*] namôy ê-na-nôkosit,» itwêw, «ê-pê-~, – kîtahtawê kâ-pê-sâkêwêpayit awa

to say, «so much meat was placed inside, inside the tent, look, in the dark of the night while we were asleep, they must have come inside and put it down there,» she said; «they would make a kill on the sly as one went along, all along the way, one never went hungry as one went along,» my mother used to say, «one used to live very well as one went along,» my mother used to say, «one definitely did not go hungry,» she said. «Oh my, our fellow travellers reportedly used to kill cattle on the sly as one went along,» she said, for in the old days, it is reported, over there across the border, it is reported, they must have had large numbers of cattle, and no fences had been put up in the old days, there were no fences, as a matter of fact they used to be able to camp just anywhere, it is reported, as they went along since there were no fences in the old days; in these places, it is reported, they used to do their butchering secretly as they went along. In that way now, it is reported, they used to flee with their camps early in the morning, «A number of times did our fellow travellers do that on the way,» she said.

[6] Now then, «Now it was,» she said, «it was him,» she said, «twice I was frightened on our way,» my mother had said, «at one time,» she said, «as one was moving along with one's camp,» she said, «hey, that boy was riding far behind, finally I barely saw him coming in the distance, he came riding far behind,» she said, «now it was that he had been left far behind,» she said, «it was then, only then did he come riding from there,» she said, «now he was giving chase,» she said. «He must have got tired of them moving in one place with respect to him as they went along, of their slow pace in moving along,» she said, «now he wanted to ride fast,» she said, «that is what he used to do,» she said; «from there now he came racing and giving chase,» she said. «Oh my,» she said, «at one time it was like that again,» she said, «gone he was

misatim,» itwêw, «âyêy, awîn ôma nam âwiyak kî-pê-têhtapiw,» itwêw, «nayêstaw misatim awa ê-pê-sâkêwêpayit,» itwêw, «êkwa ê-ay-askôkêyân ôm ôki ê-pimipicicik, awîn âwa,» ê-itwêt, «kî-pê-acitakocin,» ê-itwêt, «ostikwân ôma, têpiyâhk êkâ ê-pê-pâh-pakamihtiniyik,» ê-itwêt, «ê-pê-ac-~ ê-pê-kosâwêkocihk,» ê-itwêt, «oskâcis ôma ê-micimopayiniyik tâpisikoskâcikanihk,» itwêw, «kî-pê-kosâwêkocin; êkos ê-isi-têh-têpwâtakik ôki nîkân k-âtimipicicik,» itwêw, «êkwa ê-nakîhk êkwa,» itwêw, «ê-têpwêyân, ê-pê-~, 'namôy pê-têhtapiw awa!' ê-~ ko-~ ê-pê-kosâwêkocihk ôhi misatimwa, ê-pê-na-nisihkêpayit awa misatim,» ê-itwêt nikâwiy. «êkwa wiy âwa, ê-pê-ay-acitakocihk aw,» ê-itwêt. «wahwâ, tâpiskôc êkâ ta-pimâtisit ê-itêyihtamân,» ê-itwêt. «êkos ê-pê-isi-nîhci-kwâskohticik ôki nâpêwak, ê-pê-ispahtâcik, ê-wî-kakwê-nakinâcik ôhi misatimwa,» itwêw, «tâpwê nakinêwak ôhi, miton âta mis-ôyôspisîwatim [*sic*] aw,» îtwêw, «ôhi mâna kâ-mani-têhtapit,» itwêw. «êêy, êkwa ê-tahtiniht, 'oskâcis aw ês ê-âcipayiniyik ôta, tâpisikoskâcikanihk,' ê-itwêcik,» itwêw. «wiy âta wiya namôy nânitaw ê-is-âyât,» itwêw, «'nêhiyaw awa' ê-itâcik,» itwêw.

[7] «êkos,» îtwêw, «ê-ay-âpahkawisît, tâpiskôt môy nânitaw ê-ohc-ây-is-âyât,» itwêw. «êkos ân[i],» îtwêw, «mitoni tânitahto-kîsikâw êtikwê, namôy êkwa ohci-têhtapiw ê-kî-sa-sakâpêkahpitim-~ [*sc.* -sakâpêkahpitimiht], ê-sakâpêkipahimak mân ôhi misatimwa ê-pimi-pa-pôsit,» itwêw. «êkwa wiyaskotam âskaw mân ê-kî-pimi-pa-pamihastimwêt,» itwêw.

[8] «kîtahtawê êkwa mîn,» îtwêw, «kâ-nôhtê-têhtapit êkwa mîn,» îtwêw; «êkwa mîn êkwa kâ-pakitiniht êkwa,» itwêw, «ta-têhtapit,» itwêw. «âsay êkwa mîn,» îtwêw, «nâway

and could not be seen,» she said, «then all of a sudden the horse came riding into view,» she said, «what on earth! what was this? no one had come riding it,» she said, «only the horse came moving into view,» she said, «now I was at the rear as the others moved along with their camps,» she said, «and here he came hanging upside down,» she said, «such that his head was just short of hitting the ground,» she said, «he came dangling in mid-air,» she said, «with his little leg stuck in the stirrup,» she said, «he came dangling in mid-air; so I called out over and over to those who were in the lead, with their wagons moving away,» she said, «and then one stopped,» she said, «as I called out, 'He has not come back on his horse!' as he came dangling from the horse in mid-air, and the horse coming back at a gallop,» my mother said. «Now as for him, he came hanging upside down,» she said. «Oh my, it seemed he would not be alive, I thought,» she said. With that the men came jumping down off their horses and running there, they were going to try to stop the horse,» she said, «and indeed they stopped it, it was a very gentle horse, to be sure,» she said, «the one it was the choice for him to ride,» she said. «Heey, now one untied him, 'His leg, it is reported, had been caught here on the stirrup,' they said,» she said. «At least he was not hurt,» she said, «'He is an Indian,' they said of him,» she said.

[7] «So it was,» she said, «when he came to, it seemed there was nothing wrong with him,» she said. «So indeed it was,» she said, «for quite a few days now he did not ride on horseback, the horse was tied –~ [*sc.* to the wagon], I led his horse while he was riding in the wagon,» she said. «Now he would sometimes take a turn at driving the team,» she said.

[8] «Another time again,» she said, «he wanted to ride on horseback again,» she said; «now he was allowed again,» she said, «to ride on horseback,» she said. «And already again,» she said,

ê-pa-pimipiciyân,» itwêw, «tâh-têp-îyikohk mân ê-kî-ati-kapêsiyâhk,» itwêw. «kîtahtawê,» itwêw – kinwês êtikw ânim ê-kî-nôcihtâcik, wâhyaw anima kâ-~, m-~ 'awasâpisk' kâ-kî-isiyîhkâtahk mâna, nêm ôtênaw nêtê, 'misôliy' [*sic*] isiyîhkâtêw, êkwa 'napakistikwânak', kî-isiyîhkâtam [*sic*] mân îta êkwa kâ-kî-nitawi-takohtêcik; 'misôliy' ôtênaw êkota isiyîhkâtêw, êkwa 'ispôkân', kêyâpic êkoni ôt-~ mis-ôtênawa ihtakonwa êkotê anima. êkwa, nôhtaw âstamita niya, mitâtahtomitanaw-tipahaskân nikî-itohtân âstamita êkota, êwakw ânim îta ispôkân k-âyâk ôtênaw, môy nôhti-nitawi-wâpahtên [*sic*], mâka mitoni kwayask nikî-kiskisin anima, ê-kî-ay-itâtotahk mâna nikâwiy, itê ê-kî-ay-ayâcik napakistikwâninâhk, êkota anima napakistikwâninâhk kâ-kî-itohtêyân. mâka niya wiy ê-misi-nîmihitohk, êkotê kâ-kî-nitawi-takosiniyân anima. êkwa ê-kâh-kakwêcihkêmoyân êkoni ôtênawa, «mitâtahtomitanaw-tipahaskân ôta ohci,» nikî-itikawin anima.

[9] êkwa awa nikâwiy k-âcimak anim êkwa mîna, «kîtahtawê mîn,» îtwêw, «êkos ânima mâka mîn ê-tôtahk,» itwêw, «âsay mîn,» îtwêw, «êy, mân ôm ê-pê-ay-iyâwinâkosit mân,» îtwêw, «ê-pa-pêti-têhtapit ôm,» îtwêw, «kîtahtawê,» itwêw, «aspin pik ôma kâ-kî-pê-iyâwinâkosit, awînipan kê-pê-sâkêwêpayit, iyât[a]-âpasâpiyân[i],» îtwêw, «awînipan kê-pê-sâkêwêpayit,» itwêw. «tânitê êkwa? wahwâ, piyisk êkwa mîn êkwa, ê-ayiwêpihk,» itwêw, «wahwâ, awînipan kê-takopayit,» itwêw. «êkwa ôhtâwiy[a] êkwa ê-pê-takopayiyit,» itwêw, «êkw ê-âsê-kîwêpayit êkwa aw,» îtwêw, «ê-papâ-nitonikêt,» itwêw. «ê-wani-~, mîn êkwa êkota ê-wani-mitimêpayit mêskanaw,» itwêw, «ê-wanisihk,» itwêw, «ê-wanisimiht ôm,« îtwêw.

[10] «wahwâ, êkot[a] êkwa mîn îyikohk ê-sêkihtâsot,» itwêw, «ê-sâ-sipwêpayiyit ôhtâwiya,» itwêw. «piyisk ê-pê-sipwêpicihk êkwa,» itwêw, «êkot[a] êkwa wêtinahk êkwa ê-kapêsihk êkwa,»

«I was following the wagons,» she said, «we used to camp for the night at regular intervals,» she said. «At one time,» she said – they must have been at it for a long time, it was far, the place they used to call 'Beyond the Rocky Mountains', that town over yonder is called Missoula, and Flatheads she always called the place for which they used to be headed; Missoula the town was called, and Spokane, these big towns still exist over there. Now as for me, I stayed short of there, on the hither side, I went to a place a hundred miles on the hither side, that place where the town of Spokane is situated I did not go to see, but I very clearly remember what my mother used to tell about it, where they were staying in Flathead country, it was there in Flathead country that I had gone. But as for me, there was a big pow-wow, it was there that I had been headed for. Now when I asked people about those towns, «It is a hundred miles from here,» I was told.

[9] Now it is my mother again that I am telling about, «At one time also,» she said, «he was doing the same thing again, to be sure,» she said, «again already,» she said, «hey, he was barely visible as he came,» she said, «he was coming on horseback,» she said, «all of a sudden,» she said, «the last I had seen was that he was barely visible as he came, no rider would come into view, even though I looked back,» she said, «no rider would come into view,» she said. «Where is he now? Oh my, finally now again one came to a stop,» she said, «oh my, no rider would turn up,» she said. «Now his father came riding into camp,» she said, «now he turned around and rode back,» she said, «he went around looking,» she said. «Now he had taken the wrong trail there,» she said, «he was lost,» she said, «he had been led astray,» she said.

[10] «Oh my, at that point again he had everyone so scared,» she said, «his father kept riding off,» she said. «Finally they started moving camp now,» she said, «without haste setting

itwêw. «wahwâ, êkw ê-sâ-sipwêpayicik ôki nâpêwak, ê-âh-âsê-kîwêpayicik êkwa,» itwêw, «ê-papâ-nâh-nit-~ ê-nâh-nitonâht êkwa,» itwêw, «êkwa ôhtâwiya, ôcênâsihk êkwa,» itwêw, «êkotê ê-papâ-nâh-nitôskâkot,» itwêw. «kîtahtawê, ê-pâh-pîkiskwêmohcikêt awa, êtikw âwa kâ-kî-wîcêwak,» itwêw, «kîtahtawê nânitaw k-âcimiht, ê-miskâht, ê-nitawi-takosihk,» itwêw nikâwiy awa. «êwakw âw îtê ê-nitawi-takohtêt, ê-~, miton ê-misi-wanisihk,» itwêw, «itê môniyâsak ê-mônahisôniyâwêcik,» ê-kî-itwêt mâna nikâwiy, «êkotê ôm êsa kâ-nitawi-tako-têhtapit aw,» îtwêw. «êkotê kâ-pê-wîhcikâtêk, 'kîkwawâsis [*sic*] êtik ôta kâ-pê-takosihk ê-têhtapit?' – 'êwakw êtikwê,' ê-itwêwiht ês,» îtwêw, «'êwakw êtikw âwa kâ-wanihiht, êkos ôta nika-kanawêyimânân, namôy nika-pakitinânân, ôta tit-âyâw, ôta ta-pê-miskawâw,' ê-pê-isi-pîkiskwêmohcikêwiht,» itwêw.

[11] «êkos,» îtwêw, «tâpwê anim,» îtwêw, «êkotê êkwa ôhtâwiya ê-isi-môskîscikêyit ês êkwa,» itwêw. «itê ôk âsinîwacîhk ê-mônis-~ ê-mônahisôniyâwêcik môniyâsak,» itwêw, «êkotê anima nê-~ kî-~ ê-isi-wanisihk,» itwêw. «wahwâ, nikî-ati-kâh-kakwâtakêyihtên ani mitoni; êkos âni piyêsîht êkwa,» itwêw. «wahwâ, miton êkwa ê-âyîcimikot êkwa ôhtâwiya,» itwêw, «êkây êkwa êkosi ta-tôtahk,» itwêw, «êkây wâh-wâhyaw t-âskôkêt,» itwêw, «êkos ân[i] âta wiya kî-pônihtâw,» itwêw nikâwiy. «êkwa,» itwêw, «êkwa awa kâ-kî-wîcêwak,» itwêw, «êy, mitoni sôniyâhkâkêw ôhi,» itwêw, «ita êkwa ôhi mis-ôtênawa kâ-otihtamâhk, êkot[a] êkwa awa ê-atâw-~-atâwâkêt aw ôhi mêscacâkanisiwayân[a],» îtwêw, «ê-pakwanêhtawakêhikêhk,» itwêw nikâwiy.

up camp for the night there,» she said. «Oh my, now the men kept riding off, turning around and riding back where we had come from,» she said, «now they were out searching for him,» she said, «now his father also went to the little town,» she said, «he was looking around for him over there,» she said. «All of a sudden, as he was phoning around, it must have been the one to whom I had been married,» she said, «it was all of a sudden that someone told about him that he had been found and had turned up at some place,» my mother said. «It was this one, and where he had turned up, he had been thoroughly lost,» she said, «where the Whites mine for gold,» my mother used to say, «over there he had reportedly turned up on horseback,» she said. «It was from over there that it had been announced, 'What child can it be that has arrived here on horseback? It must be that one,' was said with reference to him,» she said, «'It must be the one who has been lost, so we will keep him here, we will not let him go, so that he will remain here and they can come and find him here,' someone who phoned here said with reference to him,» she said.

[11] «So it was,» she said, «that was indeed the case,» she said, «now his father raced out there, it is reported,» she said. «Where the Whites mine for gold in the Rocky Mountains,» she said, «it was over there that he had got lost,» she said. «Oh my, I was greatly worried all the way; as he was in that way brought back now,» she said. «Oh my, now his father really was insistent in telling him,» she said, «that he must not do that,» she said, «that he must not lag too far behind,» she said, «with that indeed he did stop,» my mother said. «Now,» she said, «now the one to whom I had been married,» she said, «hey, he made a lot of money with these,» she said, «now when we reached these big towns, there now he sold his coyote pelts,» she said, «with holes in their ears,» my mother said.

[12] «êkwa êkota,» itwêw, «pêyak êkwa mis-ôtênaw,» itwêw, «êkot[a] ânim ê-takohtêyâhk,» itwêw, «êkot[a] êkwa,» ê-itwêt, «pêyakwayak, môy wâhyaw êkota napakistikwânak ôk ês ôm ê-ayâcik,» itwêw, «pêyakwayak êkwa,» itwêw, «kâ-miskahkik, âpihtawikosisâ-~ môniyâ-~, môniyâs aw,» îtwêw, «mâk âw êkota, nikî-miyopayin êkota ôm ê-takohtêyâhk,» itwêw, «âpihtawikosisâniskwêw awa, ê-onâpêmit ôhi môniyâsa,» itwêw. «êkota êkwa,» itwêw, «miton êkwa ê-wî-~ ê-takwâkik,» itwêw, «êkota êkwa ê-wîkiyâhk êkwa,» itwêw, «ê-ayâyâhk,» itwêw. «êkwa aw îskwêw êkwa,» itwêw, «mitoni piy-~ mitoni nikitimâkêyimik aw îskwêw,» itwêw, «wiy ê-osk-âyiwiyân êkospîhk,» itwêw. «êkwa, êkwa aya, ôtênâhk êkwa ê-itohtêyâhk êkwa,» itwêw, «ê-isitâpâsoyâhk,» itwêw nikâwiy, «êêy, mitoni kîsâc êkwa ê-otinikêyâhk, pipon-âya kîkway ôh,» îtwêw, «ê-isi-sîhkimit aw,» îtwêw, «kâ-kî-wîcêwak aw,» îtwêw, «iyikohk ê-otinikêyâhk pipon-âya kîkway ôh,» îtwêw, «êkwa mîn ôhi papakiwayânêkinwa iyikohk ê-otinamân,» itwêw.

[13] «êkos,» îtwêw, «êkota anim êkwa ê-wî-piponisiyâhk êkwa,» itwêw. «êkwa ôm ê-takwâkik ôm,» îtwêw, «ê-mawisoyâhk mâna, picikwâsa ê-kistikêcik ôki, aw âpihtawikosisâniskwêw,» itwêw; «ê-mawisoyâhk, mêton ê-wîcihak ê-atoskahit aw îskwêw,» itwêw.

[14] «êkwa mân,» ê-itwêt, «êkot[a] ê-kî-kiskêyihtamân,» itwêw, «picikwâsak ôk ê-pî-~ ê-pîhtosamôhit,» itwêw, «ê-pîhtoswâyâhkok ôki picikwâsak,» ê-itwêt. «êkwa mân,» îtwêw, «êkoni êkwa ôh,» îtwêw, «ê-kî-sîhkahâyâhkok, wâhyaw tâpiskôc kâ-pâsiminêhk, êkos ê-isîhcikâtêki mis-~, wayawîtimihk ê-ayât ayihk,» itwêw, «mîcisowinâhtik,» itwêw, «êkota mân ôki misiwê ê-kî-sîhkahâyâhkok ôki picikwâsak,» ê-itwêt. «êkonik anik âyihk, ê-pâswâcik anihi picikwâsa, mwêhc ôki k-âtâwêhk ôki kâ-pâsocik picikwâsak,» ê-itwêt nikâwiy, «êkos ê-kî-ay-isîhât an[a] îskwêw

[12] «Now it was there,» she said, «now at a certain big town,» she said, «as we arrived there,» she said, «it was there now,» she said, «at a certain place now, not far from where the Flatheads live,» she said, «at a certain place now,» she said, «that they found it, a Halfbreed-~ this White person,» she said, «but this one there, I was fortunate when we arrived there,» she said, «she was a Halfbreed woman and had a Whiteman for her husband,» she said. «It was there now,» she said, «it was really fall now,» she said, «there we now lived,» she said, «and stayed,» she said. «Now this woman,» she said, «this woman really was kind to me,» she said, «for I was young at that time,» she said. «Now, now then, now we went to town,» she said, «we drove there,» my mother said, «heey, we bought a lot of stuff in preparation, winter things,» she said, «as he had urged me to do,» she said, «the one to whom I had been married,» she said, «we bought so much of these winter things,» she said, «and I also bought such a lot of yard goods,» she said.

[13] «So it was,» she said, «there now we were going to winter,» she said. «Now it was fall,» she said, «we picked berries, and these people had an apple orchard, this Halfbreed woman,» she said; «we picked berries, I really helped her and she put me to work,» she said.

[14] «Now I also,» she said, «gained knowledge there,» she said, «she had me peel the apples,» she said, «we were peeling the apples,» she said. «Now we also,» she said, «with respect to these,» she said, «we used to spread them out loosely, far apart as when you dry berries, that is how they are processed, she had a table,» she said, «outside,» she said, «there we used to spread the apples out loosely, all over this table,» she said. «These, ah, these apples they dried, exactly like the dried applies you buy,» my mother said, «that was how that woman processed them,» she said, «she simply

an[a] ânihi,» ê-itwêt, «ê-mosci-pâswât,» ê-itwêt; «êkoni anihi kapê-pipon ê-~ ê-kanawêyimât,» itwêw. «êkwa mîn,» îtwêw, «ê-kî-pê-~, êkwa mân,» îtwêw, «ê-pê-nitomit mân,» îtwêw, «kîkway êkwa mîn ôma kâ-nitawêyihtahk mâna, ki-~ ta-nitawi-wîcihak,» itwêw, «ta-nitawi-wîcôhkamawak. mitoni nikî-ohtâcihon êkota,» ê-itwêt, «iyikohk kîkway mân ê-kî-miyit mîna, kâh-kîsitêpoc[i] ôm,» îtwêw, «kâh-kîsisahki; ê-kîwêhtatâyân ôma kîkway mîciwin, kâh-kwayâtihkasahk[i],» îtwêw.

[15] «êkwa mîna mân,» îtwêw, «ê-kî-ka-kâh-kaskikwâtamawit niskotâkaya,» itwêw, «ê-ka-kâh-kaskikwâsôpayihtât, miton ê-kî-kitimâkêyimit an[a] âpihtawikosisâniskwêw,» ê-itwêt.

[16] «êkwa mân,» îtwêw, «mistah ê-kî-miywêyihtahkik napakistikwânak ôk âyihk,» itwêw, «ê-mêtawêcik ayihk,» itwêw, «misi-kâcikanihk,» ê-kî-itwêt mâna nikâwiy. «ê-kî-tâh-tako-têhtapicik mân êkota,» itwêw, «napakistikwânak ôk,» îtwêw, «ê-pê-mâh-mawinêhwâcik ôhi nêhiyawa ôh,» îtwêw, «misi-kâcikanihk ê-mâh-mêtawêcik,» itwêw. «wahwâ, namôy kakêtihk mân ê-kî-nipahi-mâh-miyosiyit akwanân[a] ê-pâh-paskitahâcik,» itwêw, «ayihk, kâ-têhtapicik ôki napakistikwânak,» ê-kî-ay-itâcimot mâna nikâwiy.

[17] «êkos êkwa,» itwêw, «êkwa ê-miyoskamik êkwa,» itwêw, «êkwa kâ-wî-pê-kîwêyâhk êkwa, ê-at-ôy-oski-nîpihk,» itwêw, «'êkwa ka-kîwânânaw êkwa,' ê-itwêt awa kâ-kî-wîcêwak,» itwêw. «êkos ânim êkwa,» itwêw, «ê-oski-nîpihk êkwa, ê-pê-ka-kîwêyâhk êkwa mîna, pêyâhtik ê-pê-~» (kîkwây anima misi-wâhyawêskamik anima! anohc êkwa pâh-pêyak-kîsikâw piko kâ-nôcihtâcik sîhkêpayîsak [*sic*] ôk âkâmi-tipahaskân, ahpô piko kayâs, êwakw ânima, îh, iyikohk wâhyawêskamik ê-ay-isi-pa-pimipicicik); êkwa pêyakw-âyi [*sic*] ayihk,» ê-kî-itwêt mîna mâna, «pêyakw-âyi ê-kî-aci-wîcêwâyâhkok osk-âyak,

dried them,» she said; «she kept them all through the winter,» she said. «And also,» she said, «and then,» she said, «she came and called on me,» she said, «when she wanted that I should help her with something,» she said, «that I should go and help her with her work. I profited a lot from there,» she said, «she also used to give me such a lot of things when she would do her cooking,» she said, «when she had cooked something; I took food home with me when she had cooked it ahead of time,» she said.

[15] «And then she also,» she said, «she used to sew my dresses for me,» she said, «she would sew them on a sewing machine, that Halfbreed woman really was kind to me,» she said.

[16] «Now the Flatheads also,» she said, «used to be very fond,» she said, «of playing,» she said, «the bone game,» my mother used to say. «They used to arrive there in groups on horseback,» she said, «the Flatheads,» she said, «coming to challenge the Crees,» she said, «they kept playing the bone game,» she said. «Oh my, the saddle-cloths they put over them [*sc.* their horses] were exceedingly beautiful,» she said, «when the Flatheads were mounted,» so my mother used to tell.

[17] «So it was now,» she said, «now in spring,» she said, «now when we were going to return home, as it was getting to be early summer [*sc.* April-May],» she said, «'Now we shall go home,' said the one to whom I had been married,» she said. «So that was it now,» she said, «it was early summer now and we were also returning home now, slowly –~» (what an enormous distance that was! Today the cars only take one day to get across the border when in the old days, it was, look, that they were moving such a huge distance by team); «now one couple,» she also used to say, «we went together with one young couple, they too were newly

wîscawâw ê-oski-wîkihtocik,» ê-icwêc, «wahwâ, mistahi ê-kî-kicimâkisicik,» ê-kî-icwêc mâna nikâwiy, «ê-pêyakwahpicikêsicik, iyinic-ôcâpânihk,» ê-kî-itwêt mâna. «êkonik ôk êkotê ê-wî-kakwê-tako-wîcihiwêcik akâmi-tipahaskân, êkotê onîkihikwa ê-ayâyit awa nâpêw,» itwêw, «êkotê ê-kakwê-takoht-~-wîcihiwêcik. nama – mistah ê-kî-kicimâkisicik, nama kîkway mîkiwâhpis ê-ayâcik,» ê-kî-itwêt mâna nikâwiy, «êkoca mâna sîpâ ocôcâpâniwâhk ê-kî-apahkwêsicik mân,» ê-itwêt, «êkocê sîpâ ê-nipâcik,» ê-kî-itwêt mâna nikâwiy, «misakâmê êkos,» îtwêw, «mâka wiya mitoni kî-wîcihâwak, omî-~ mîciwinihk is,» îtwêw, «wîstawâw mân ê-kî-at-âsamihcik ôma mîciwin kâ-minahowiht,» ê-kî-ay-itâcimât mâna. «mâk ân[i] êkwa nêtê akâmi-tipahaskân ê-takohtêcik, namôy kakêtihk an[i] êkwa kî-~ kî-miywêyihtamiyiwa an[a] ôskinîkiw, okêhtê-ayima ê-takosihk êkotê; êkota isko nikî-wîcêwânânak êkonik,» ê-kî-itwêt mâna. «êkwa anim êkwa kâ-~, mîn êkwa pêyâhtik ê-pê-ka-kîwêpiciyâhk,» itwêw, «ê-pê-ka-kîwêhk êkwa,» itwêw; «ê-pê-ka-kîwêpicihk êkwa,» itwêw. «êkwa êkota ayihk,» itwêw, «êkwa êtikwê, miton êkwa êtik ôki nikêhtê-ayimak êkwa ê-wanihicik ôm,» îtwêw, «kinwês êkwa, pêyak-askiy [*sic*] miton êkwa ê-sipwêhtahikawiyân, êkotê ôma akâmi-tipahaskân ôm,» îtwêw. êwakw ânima mân ê-kî-âtotahk, 'misôniy' [*sic*] ê-kî-isiyîhkâtahk anim ôtênaw, êkwa 'ispôkân', êkoni anihi, êkot[ê] ê-kî-ayât anim ôtênâhk anihi, êkon êsa mân êkot[ê] ê-kî-itohtêcik êkoni ôtênawa, napakistikwâninâhk.

[18] êkwa, «êkwa êwak ôm êkwa kâ-pê-ka-kîwêhtahikawiyân,» itwêw, «nama kîkway ê-ka-kiskêyihcikêyân,» itwêw, «ês ôma nimis êkây ê-kî-pimâtisit,» itwêw; «ê-omisimâwit,» itwêw; «êwako ê-kî-mwêsiskawak nimis, iyikohk kinwês ê-sipwêhtahikawiyân,» itwêw, «kinwês ê-nitaw-âyâyân,» itwêw.

married,» she said with kindness, «oh my, they were terribly poor,» my mother used to say with kindness, «they were on a plain little cart, driving a little one-horse rig,» she used to say. «They were going to try to get to that place across the border to join in, the man's parents were living over there,» she said, «and they were trying to get over there to join in. They were terribly poor, they had no tent,» my mother used to say, «there underneath their little cart they used to put a little cover,» she said, «and under there they slept,» my mother used to say, «it was like that the whole way,» she said, «but they had a lot of help when it came to food,» she said, «they too used to be given food to eat when there was a kill with respect to them,» so she used to tell about them. «But now as they arrived over yonder across the border, that young man's old people were extremely happy that he had arrived over there; we had them with us up to that place,» she used to say. «Now we were slowly moving back home with our camp,» she said, «now one was returning home,» she said, «now one was moving back home,» she said. «Now it was at that time,» she said, «it must have been then, now my old people really must have lost me [*sc.* not known where I was],» she said, «now it had been a long time, it had been a whole year since I was taken away to that place over there across the border,» she said. She used to tell about that, she called that town Missoula, and Spokane, those were the ones, over there in that town she had stayed, to those towns over there they had gone, it is reported, in Flathead country.

[18] Now, «Now when I was being taken back home,» she said, «I did not know anything about things,» she said, «that my older sister, it is reported, had died,» she said; «she was the oldest sister,» she said; «I came too late to see my older sister, I had been taken away for such a long time,» she said, «I had gone and stayed away for a long time,» she said.

[19] «êkwa êtikwê nikêhtê-ayimak êkwa ê-pîkiskâtisicik,» itwêw, «nimis awa ê-wanihiht ôm,» îtwêw, «ê-wanihâcik, ê-wanihâyâhk,» itwêw. «'â, êkwa kika-nitonawânaw kicânisinaw,' ê-itwêcik ês ôki, nikâwiy nôhtâwiy,» itwêw, «'kika-nitonawânaw kitânisinaw êkwa,' k-êtwêcik ês êkwa,» itwêw. «êkosi, têkohtêyâhk, ê-takwâkik nitakopicinân ôta,» itwêw; «môsôminêw-âskîhkânihk ôta,» itwêw. «êkota piyêhtamân nimis ê-kî-nakatikoyâhk,» itwêw, «ê-mwêsiskawak nimis,» itwêw, «nitâcimostâkawin,» itwêw.

[20] «âsay êkwa êkota ôki nikâwiy nôhtâwiy môy êkota ayâwak,» itwêw, «'ê-wî-nitopicîstâkawiyan ôma, ê-wî-nitonâkawiyan ôma, mistahi kaskêyihtamwak, ôma kâ-mâyipayicik,' nititikawin,» itwêw. «îh, iyikohk anim,» ê-itwêt, «âhci pikw ânima pêyak-askiy [*sic*] namôy ê-ohci-wâpamakik nikâwiy nôhtâwiy,» itwêw, «maskwacîsihk, êkotê wiyawâw ê-itohtêcik ôki nikâwiy, êkot[ê] ê-nitawi-piponisicik,» itwêw; «âhci piko pêyak-askiy [*sic*] nikâwiy, môy ê-ohci-wâpamakik anima, ât[a] ê-takohtahikawiyân ôta,» ê-kî-itât-~ ê-kî-ay-itâtotahk mâna nikâwiy; êkotê anih ê-o-~ ê-oy-ohtoht-~, êkotê ê-ohtohtêcik.

[21] êkosi wiy êwakw ânima mîna nikîsîhtân anim êwakw âcimowin ôta, nikâwiy awa kêyâpic ê-ay-âcimak, tânisi mân ê-kî-ay-isiyinîhkêt kayâs ê-osk-âyiwicik wîstawâw.

[*external break*]

[19] «Now my old people must have been grieving,» she said, «over the loss of my older sister,» she said, «they had lost her, we had lost her,» she said. «'Well, now we shall look for our little daughter,' they had reportedly said, my mother and my father,» she said, «'Now we shall look for our daughter,' is what they had reportedly said now,» she said. «So it was, when we arrived, we arrived here with our camp in the fall,» she said, «here at *Môsôminêw-âskîhkânihk* [Moosomin Reserve],» she said. «It was at that point that I heard that my older sister had left us,» she said, «I had come too late to see my older sister,» she said, «I was told about it,» she said.

[20] «Now already at that time my mother and my father were not there,» she said, «'The intent was to move camp in search of you, the intent was to look for you, they are grief-stricken over their loss,' I was told,» she said. «Look, it was so long,» she said, «it was still another year that I did not see my mother and my father,» she said, «at the Bear Hills, there they had gone, my mother and her family, there they had gone to winter,» she said; «it was still another year that I did not see my mother and her family, even though I had been taken back here,» so my mother used to tell about it; from over there, they came from over there.

[21] With that I have also completed that story on here [*sc.* on the audio-recorder], I am still telling about my mother, how she had led her life in the old days when they themselves were young.

[*external break*]

Sarah Whitecalf, c. 1989.

6

iyikohk ê-kî-sôhkêpayik anima nipahtâkêwin

So horrible was that murder

iyikohk ê-kî-sôhkêpayik anima nipahtâkêwin

[1] tânispîhk êtikw ânim êwako pâskac, tânitahto-askiy êtikw ânima, tâniyikohk anim âspin [*?record*] –

[FA:] cêskwa, sipwêkotêw ês ân[i] âsay. âsay mîn âwa niwîcêwâkan *Sarah* ê-wî-âcimot.

– êwakw ânim êkâ kâ-kiskêyihtamân, tâniyikohk ê-kî-masinahikâtêk êkospîhk anim âskiy, kâ-kî-ispayik, ôtê ôm ê-~ ê-kiskisiyân, mitoni mân ê-kiskisiyân ê-awâsisîwiyân, mîna tâniyikohk êtikw ânim ê-kî-itahtopiponêyân êkospîhk, *Sweetgrass* ôta, misiwê kî-pêhtâkwan êtikw ânim êkospîhk. ayisiyi-~, pêyak awa nâpêw, êkotê *Sweetgrass* ê-kî-nipahât owîkimâkana. kayâsês anima, mitoni wiy âsay ê-misikitiyân, osâm mitoni nikiskêyihtên anim ê-~ kâ-kî-ay-ispayik; miton ê-kî-kitimahât ana nâpêw mân ôwîkimâkana – kâ-nôtiniskwêwêskicik ôki, êkos ê-kî-is-âyât ana nâpêw; ê-nêhiyawiyîhkâsot, 'kâ-piyêsiwakohpêw' kî-isiyîhkâsow ana nâpêw.

[2] êkwa, kîtahtawê, êkot[a] ôm ê-ay-ayâyân, nikâwiy aw ê-wa-wîc-âyâmak *Sweetgrass* ôta, ê-takwâkik anima, anim âsay ôma kâ-mâci-mâh-mawisohk mâna takwahiminâna k-âtihtêki, ê-ihkihk. tânis êtikwê mân âwa nimosôminân, 'payinitêy' kî-isiyîhkâsow, ê-kî-kiskêyihtahk anima, kîkway nânitaw ê-wî-ispayik, iyikohk ê-kî-iyinîsicik kayâs kisêyiniwak, ayahk; môy ê-ôh-cîhkêyihtahk aya, nanânis ta-wîkihk, ês ânim ê-isi-wâhkôhtahk anima tâpiskôc, ayisk owiyasiwêhkân [*sic*] ana nimosôminân ana 'payinitêy' kâ-kî-itiht.

So horrible was that murder

[1] I wonder when that was, how many years ago it must have been, how many –

[FA:] Wait, it started running already, it shows. My partner Sarah is going to tell a story again.

– that is what I don't know, what year it was at the time when that happened, I remember it was over there, I clearly remember that I was a child, I also don't know how old I must have been then, it happened here at Sweetgrass but it must have been heard about all over the place at that time. Over there in Sweetgrass, a man had killed his wife. It must have been quite a long time ago, I was really big already because I fully understood what was happening; that man had been treating his wife most brutally – that man was of the kind that are always beating their women; that man's Cree name was *Kâ-piyêsiwakohpêw*.

[2] Now at one time I was over there, living with my mother here at Sweetgrass, it was fall and people were already beginning to pick chokecherries as they ripened, it was that time of the year. I don't know how our grandfather, Fineday was his name, knew that something was going to happen, the old men were so perceptive in the old days, eh; he did not like to have his family, as it were, living spread out, it is reported, for he was a councillor, our grandfather Fineday as he was called.

[3] êkwa ayihk, kîtahtaw âna pêyak ê-nîpihk, miton êtikwê kapê-ayi ê-kî-kostâcit ana mâna nimosôm ana, ê-kî-astâhikot kîkway. êkwa kêhtinâc ôma nânitaw ê-kî-niyânanokam-~niyânanokamik, kayâs ayis îkamâ wîhkâc –~, osâm piko mân ê-kî-wayawîpicihk ôma, papakiwayânikamikohk ê-kî-miywêyihtamihk ê-papâ-ma-mosci-wîkihk. êkwa, êkos ôma ê-ispayik, kîtahtawê mân ê-kî-âhtokêyâhk, êkwa ita ôma k-âhto-~ k-âhtokêyâhk ôma, êkos îs ânima nanânis, ômis îs [*gesture*] ê-isi-ma-miywâsik mân îta, ê-kî-wâ-~, ê-kî-wîkiyâhk mâna, mâka ê-asas-~ ê-asaskitêki ôhi nawat piko nîkinâna. êkwa ayihk, êkos ânima mâka mîn ê-papâ-ay-âhc-âhtokêyâhk anima, «êkotê êkwa,» ê-kî-itwêt mân âna kisêyiniw; êkos ê-kî-nitohtâht mîna kahkiyaw ôh ôs-~, êkos îs ôh ôtayisiyinîma, ta-kî-itwêhk.

[4] kîtahtawê kâ-pê-pîhtikwêt kîkisêpâ nawac, kâ-pê-pîhtikwêt, «ayihk ôma,» kâ-pê-itwêt, ot-~ ôh ôkosis[a] ê-pê-wîhtamawât, nimâmâ kâ-kî-onâpêmit, «ayihk ôm,» îtwêw, «miton ôma, kîkway nitastâhikon,» k-êtwêt awa kisêyiniw, «âsay ôki kahkiyaw ôki nipê-wâh-wîhtamawâwak ôki kâ-pê-isi-wîkicik,» itwêw, ê-niyânanokamikisiyâhk anim êkota, «nipê-wâh-wîhtamawâwak ôk,» îtwêw, «âsay,» itwêw, «êkos ôm,» îtwêw, «ê-wî-pâh-~ [*sc.* -pâh-picicik], ê-wî-~ tit-âhtokêyahk, ta-piciyahk,» itwêw; «miton âni nitastâhikon ôma kîkway,» k-êtwêt awa kisêyiniw. «mitoni wani-tipiskâw misiwê,» itwêw, «ôtê isi pik ôma,» itwêw, «ôma sêkwah-âyihk, manitow kâ-matwêhikêt k-âyâk âstamita, êkota ê-wâsêyâk, ê-itêyihtamân,» kâ-pê-itwêt awa kisêyiniw. «êkota, maht êkotê tit-êspiciyahk, t-âhtokêyahk kahkiyaw,» itêw ôhi ôcowâm-~ ôh ôkosisa, «miton ê-astâhikoyân ôma kîkway,» itwêw. êkosi kâ-itwêt [*sic*], «êha,» itêw awa nôhcâwîs, «êha,» itêw; «mâk îyikohk niyanân kî-ma-mîcisoyâhko, nik-âhtokânân, ic[i],» îtêw awa nôhcâwîs. «ôki wiy âsay, wiy-ô-~

[3] Now at one time that one, my grandfather, must have had a foreboding all summer long, something had him worried. Now, there actually were about five camps, for in the old days you never –~ as a rule everyone used to move out and people liked simply to live in tents here and there. Now this is the way it was, sometimes we would move our camp elsewhere, and in the place to which we moved our camp we used to live in a spread-out pattern where it was good like this [*gesture*] but our tents were more or less together. Now we were again moving our camp from place to place in this way, «Over there now,» that old man would say; and everyone would listen to his directions, all his people, one might say.

[4] Suddenly he came into our tent a bit later in the morning, «It is,» he had come to say, coming to tell his son who was my mom's husband, «It is,» he said, «something has me greatly worried,» is what the old man said, «I have already come and told all of them who have come to live here,» he said, we had five camps at that place, «I have come and told each of them,» he said, «already,» he said, «it is like this,» he said, «we are to move our camps to another place, we are to move camp,» he said; «something has me worried greatly indeed,» is what the old man said. «It is really dark everywhere,» he said, «only over here,» he said, «in the sheltered place this side of where *Manitow kâ-matwêhikêt* lies, there it seems bright to me,» is what the old man had come to say. «That place, let us move camp over there, let us all move our camps to that place,» he said to his son, «something has me greatly worried,» he said. That is what he had said, «Yes,» my step-father said to him, «yes,» he said to him; «but as for us, we will only move our camp there after we have finished eating, later,» my step-father said to him. «I have already told each of these others, they are already getting

nipê-wâh-wîhtamawâwak, âsay wî-wawêyîwak, sapik ôti nîsta êkos ôm,» îtwêw, itwêw awa nôhcâwîs –~ itwêw awa nimosôm.

[5] êkosi; kî-âh-atimitâpâsowak ôki mayaw ê-kîsi-pâh-pôsihcikêcik, êkot[ê] ê-âh-atimipicicik ôk îsi; kê-~ mâka mis-îyôtin [*sic*], êkwa niyanân ôma nîkinân, ê-~ miton ê-nahimaskitêk ôma papakiwayânikamik, mitoni kwayask awa ca-cîstêkahokâtêw [*sic*] ôma nîkinân ôm ê-sîpwêkahikâtêk, êkwa awa nikâwiy êkos âti-kisâkamisikêw, wiy ôma k-êtwêhk ôma, k-êtwêt awa nôhcâwîs, kî-kîsi-mîcisoyâhko, niyanân iyikohk anima tit-âhtokêyâhk.

[6] êkosi; nikâwiy aw êkwa ê-ati-kisâkamisikêt sôskwâc ôma, êkosi ê-kîsi-kisâkamisikêt nikâwiy awa, êkos âti-wiyascikêsiw; êkota ohci [*?record*] wiy ê-nistiyâhk piko, niya pikw âwâsis êkota, nikâwiy êkwa nôhcâwîs.

[7] êkosi; ôki wiya kahkiyaw âsay ê-ay-âhtokêcik âsay, ê-picicik kahkiyaw. kîtahtawê, mwêhc ê-wî-mâci-mîcisoyâhk ôma, îh, kâ-pê-yôhtêpayik ôm ômis [*gesture*] ê-ispicikâtêk ôma papakiwayânikamik, êkota êkwa, âhêy, awîn âwa nôcikwêsiw, miconi nôcikwêsiw, kâ-pê-pîhtikwê-kwâskohtit. êkos îs ânima, papakiwayânikamikwâhtik ôma kâ-cimatêk, êkotê, êkotê ê-nahapipayihot, mistik ôm ê-micimît. wahwâ, konita k-êtakocihk awa nôtikwêw, mitoni ê-wî-nipahatâhtahk, mêton ôskîsikwa iyây-iyikohk [*sic*]; êkosi, «ayahk,» k-êtwêt, «ay-api, nisikosê!» icêw awa nikâwiy ê-kî-osikosâhkômât, «ay-api, nisikosê!» icêw. «â, namôy kinwês, nistim! tâniwâ owiyasiwêhkân?» k-êtwêt, êwakw âwa kâ-picihtahiwêt awa nimosôminân, «tâniwâ owiyasiwêhkân? ê-pê-wîhtamawak ôm ôwiyasiwêhkân,» k-êtwêt, «ayahk, nipahêw! kâ-piyêsiwakohpêw wîwa,» k-êtwêt (êkos ê-kî-isiyîhkâsot ana nâpêw, 'kâ-piyêsiwakohpêw' kî-isiyîhkâsow). wahwâ, nôhcâwîs awa konit ê-~, konit ê-kitâpamât ôhi nôtikwêwa, «nipahêw!» konit

ready, and I myself too, as a matter of fact,» he said, my step-father said –~ my grandfather said.

[5] So it was; they had all driven away with their wagons as soon as they had finished loading up, they were all moving camp away over there; but a high wind came up, now as for us, our home was facing squarely into the wind, the tent was very securely pegged down, it was tautly stretched, and so my mother now went ahead to make tea, for as it had.been said, as my step-father had said, as for us, we would make the move of our camp only after we had finished eating.

[6] So it was; now my mother went ahead and made tea straight away, and so, having finished making the tea, my mother went ahead setting places to eat; for [*?record*] there were only three of us, I was the only child there, my mother and my step-father.

[7] So it was; all the others were already moving away with their camps, they all were moving camp. Suddenly, just as we were beginning to eat, look, the tent-flaps flew open, they were pulled back like this [*gesture*], and then, hey, what was this?! a little old woman, very much a little old woman, came jumping in. And with that, over there where the tent-pole stands, over there she came to crouch while holding on to the pole. Oh my, the old woman was just shaking, she was completely out of breath, her eyes were so big; and so, «Ah,» is what she said, «Sit down, my aunt!» my mother said to her, addressing her as her cross-aunt, «sit down, my aunt!» she said to her. «Well, not for long, my niece! where is the councillor?» is what she said, that was our grandfather who directed the camp move, «Where is the councillor? I have come to tell the councillor about it,» is what she said, «ah, *Kâ-piyêsiwakohpêw* has killed his wife!» is what she said (this was that man's name, *Kâ-piyêsiwakohpêw* was his name). Oh my, my step-father simply –~, he simply looked at that old woman,

ê-itwêt, «êha, nipahêw! ohtitaw pikw îspayiw owiyasiwêhkân nîkân êtikwê kîkway ta-wîhtamâht,» itwêw.

[8] ayîhtatahkamik êkwa mîn âwa nikâwiy, «nisikosê, mîcisosîhkan ôma nihtiy!» – «namôya, nistim! niwî-nipahatâhtên, pitamâ nik-âscêtâhtên [*sic*]; piko t-êspahtâyân, owiyasiwêhkân ta-nitawi-wîhtamawak.» êkwa itêw nikâwiy, «êwak ôm ôma k-âtimamok ôma sêkwah-âyihk ôm îsi mêskanaw, êkota nânitaw k-êtwêt, êkotê ê-wî-âhtokêcik, kahkiyaw ôm ê-wî-âhtokêyâhk êkotê is,» îtêw nikâwiy. ah, konic êkwa kêsiskaw awa nihciy êkwa awa nôcikwêsiw ê-minihkwêc êkwa, «âhêy, ahpô êtik ôm âsay nikisêyinîma ta-kîsahpinatêw,» itwêw awa nôcikwêsiw –

[to FA:] – êwakw âna nêtê kâ-kî-kakwêcimikoyahk ana, «kinisitawêyimâw cî, aya, kâ-pêyako-pîhtokwêw [*sic*] cî (tânisi kani ôma), kâ-kîsikâw-pîhtokwêw [*sic*]?»

[FA:] ôh, âha.

[SW:] êha; êwakw âw âw âwa kisêyiniw kâ-wî-âcimak, êkoni anihi ê-kî-otânisit anihi kâ-nipahimiht.

[FA:] ôh.

[SW:] êha; êkwa namôy ê-ohci-wâpit ana kisêyiniw, mitoni mamiwê nikî-wâpamâw ana kisêyiniw an[a] êwako, 'kâ-kîsikâw-pîhtokwêw' [*sic*] kâ-kî-itiht; môy ê-ohci-wâpit.

«êy, ê-kwâpikêyâhk, nistim,» itwêw, «êy, akâmihk k-ôh-pê-pâh-pâ-~ kâ-wi-~ k-ôh-matwêwêk,» itwêw, itwêw ana nôtikwêw ana, «êkos ê-pê-isi-tapasîyâhk, aspin ê-pê-kawahoht nitânis,» itwêw.

[FA:] ôh.

«êkwa awa kisêyiniw, 'ispahtâ! oyasiwêhkân [*sic*] nitawi-wîhtamaw!' ê-isit ôma,» itwêw, «'kiyâm wiya niya' –

«He killed her!» he merely said, «Yes, he killed her! It is right and fitting that the councillor should be first, I guess, to be told about it,» he said.

[8] Stalling for time, my mother again: «My aunt, eat a little, and here is some tea!» – «No, my niece! I am going to be out of breath, first let me catch my breath a bit; I must run there to go tell the councillor about it.» Now my mother said to her, «The trail that leads there to the sheltered place, it is in that direction that he said they were going to move their camps, we are all going to move our camps in that direction,» my mother said to her. Well, now the little old woman took a moment to drink some tea, «Hey, he may even have finished off my old man already,» the little old woman said –

[to FA:] – that one over yonder [*sc.* Chris Wolfart two years earlier in Winnipeg] had asked us about him, «Do you know him, ah, *Kâ-pêyako-pîhtikwêw* (what was it again?), *Kâ-kîsikâw-pîhtikwêw?*»

[FA:] Oh, yes.

[SW:] Yes, this is the old man about whom I am going to tell, the one who was killed was his daughter.

[FA:] Oh.

[SW:] Yes; and that old man was blind, I hardly ever used to see that old man, *Kâ-kîsikaw-pîhtikwêw* as he was called; he was blind.

«Hey, we were going for water, my niece,» she said, «hey, the shot we heard was from across the river,» she said, the old woman said, «we came fleeing this way and the last I saw, my daughter was felled by a shot,» she said.

[FA:] Oh.

«Now the old man: 'Run there! Go tell the councillor about it!' he said to me,» she said, «'Never mind about me' – ' "I will kill all of

' "kahkiyaw ani ka-mêscihitinâwâw," kititikonaw, kisêyiniw!' ê-itak ôm âspin nici-~ nîci-kîhkâw,» itwêw. «'kiyâm wiya niya, niyâ sipwêpahtâ! êkosi nitawi-wîhta! kiyâm wiya niya! ahpô ôma nitânisa nêpahtamawit, îkamâ misawâc kê-pêtisâpahtamâsoyân, wî-~ wi-~ wî-pê-nipahici,' aspin ê-itwêt nikisêyinîm,» itwêw awa nôcikwêsiw.

[9] êkosi; êkos ânima nîstanân ma kîkway mîcisowin, «êkos îsi niyâ!» itwêw awa nikâ-~ nôhcâwîs awa; aya, âsay ayisk aw êkwa nôcikwêsiw, aspin ê-ati-wayawîpayihot ôma.

[FA:] âha.

«êkos îsi,» k-êtiht awa nikâwiy, «niya nika-nahastân ôhi mîciwina, mîciwinisa ôhi nik-âsiwacikân; mîna nika-pâh-pôsihcikân itâp niya kwayask, êkotê nik-ât[i]-ây-ispicin,» itwêw awa nôhcâwîs, «sipwêhtah awa! niyâ tapasîk! nânitaw isi tâpwê wî-nipahikotwâw[i] ôki, ta-pê-sêkihâw awa, papâmi-nitonâkotwâwi, papâmi-nitonâhc[i] âwa nôtikwêw,» k-êtwêt awa nôhcâwîs. êkosi tâpwê – tâniyikohk êtikw ânima mân ê-itikitiyân. îh, êkos êkwa tâpwê êkwa, nisipwê-~ nikâwiy aw êkwa nisipwê-sakiniskêpahik, nisipwêpahtânân. ah, awîn âwa, wiy âca wiy âwa, aya, nôcikwêsiw awa, ay-âpihcaw-âyihk kî-aci-cîpacapiw, ê-ac-âcimâyâhk, miconi mîn ê-wawânatâhtahk êkota awa nôtikwêw. «êkosi, nistim!» konit ê-itwêt, «niyâ miyâskawik, nistim!» itwêw; «nitaw-îspîhci-wîhtamâhk wiyasiwêhkân [*sic*]!» itwêw.

[10] êkosi, tâpwê pikw ê-itwêt ôma wiy ê-itikoyâhk, ôm êkosi nikâwiy awa nitati-sipwêpahtânân.

[FA:] âha.

nêtê ê-takohtêyâhk, âsay wiyawâw kîsi-mâh-mânokêwak ôki kahkiyaw, k-âhtokêcik ôki,

[FA:] âha.

you," he said to us, old man!' was the last I said to my fellow-oldster,» she said. «'Never mind about me, go ahead, run on! Just go and tell about it! Never mind about me! Since he even killed my daughter on me, it is not that I will see it coming to me in any case [*sc.* being blind] if he comes to kill me,' was the last my old man was saying,» the old woman said.

[9] So it was; with that, there was no meal for us either, «Go ahead just like that!» my step-father said; ah, for the little old woman, the last I saw, had already rushed out.

[FA:] Indeed.

«Just like that,» was what my mother was told, «As for me, I will put the food away, I will pack up the left-over food; after that I too will also load up properly, then I will go ahead and move camp over there,» my step-father said, «Be off with this one [*sc.* the child Sarah]! Go ahead, you two flee! If he is truly going to kill them in one place or another, she will be frightened if he goes about looking for them, if he goes about looking for the old woman,» is what my step-father said. And indeed so it was – I wonder how old I might have been. Look, now so it was, it was true, now my mother was holding my hand as we left, we left at a run. Well, what was this?! ah, the little old woman was at least halfway, she sat upright as we caught up to her, at that point the old woman was having a very hard time breathing. «That is it, my niece!» she merely said, «Go on and run past me, my niece!» she said; «go ahead and tell the councillor about it!» she said.

[10] So as she said, as she said to us, my mother and I promptly ran off again.

[FA:] Indeed.

When we arrived over yonder, they had already finished putting up their tents, all those who had moved away with their camps,

[FA:] Indeed.

êkos îyâyaw awa nimosôm wîkihk awa, êkota ninitawi-nahikâpawinân; awînik ôki kî-~ kî-mêkwâ-âh-apiwak pîhc-âyihk, ê-mêkwâ-mîcisocik, pisinê êkwa ê-âpihtâ-kîsikani-mîcisocik

[FA:] mhm.

ôma wiyawâw. êkosi, nikâwiy êkw âwa kâ-wîhtamawât, «ôta nôcikwêsiw nipê-miyâskacipahânân, ê-papâ-wîhtahk, opê-wîhtamawâh ês ôhi kisêyiniwa, kâ-~ kâ-pê-mwêsiskawât, mâk âspin ôtê ê-pê-miyâskacipahâyâhk,» itêw awa nikâwiy. «ê-nipahât êsa kâ-piyêsiwakohpêw wîwa, ôta tasi, wâskahikanisihk, owâskahikanisiwâhk ôki kêhtê-ayak,» itwêw.

[11] êkosi; êkos ânima, namôy kîkway; takopiciw êkwa awa nôhcâ-~, awa nôhcâwîs awa, êkos âti-ma-mânokêwak; êkwa mân êkot[a] êkwa, ê-itâcimot ana nôcikwêsiw, «ayihk ôm,» îtwêw, ê-takohtêt anim êkwa, êkot[a] ê-takopahtât, «ayihk,» itwêw, «otâkosihk ôm,» îtwêw, «mitoni nahiyikohk ê-ispîhci-kîsikâk,» itwêw, «namôy wiya cêskw ê-âpihtâ-kîsikâk,» itwêw, «kâ-pimi-nakîcik êkotê, awa nitânisinân,» itwêw, «talimwâs ê-itohtêcik» (êkot[a] âyisk piko ê-kî-~, êwakw ânim ôcênâs piko, talimwâs ôma,

[FA:] mhm.

êwako pik ôcênâs nistam, êkota kâkikê nêhiyawak ê-kî-nitawi-otinikêcik,

[FA:] mhm.

êkwa mîn êkot[a] âyisk kâ-kî-misâk kiskinohamâtowikamik,

[FA:] âha.

pâhkw-âyamihêwi-kiskinohamâtowikamik, êêkotê [*sic*] ê-kî-pakitinihcik ôki kahkiyaw niyanân ohc âwâsisak, wâsakâm mîn ôhci).

[FA:] âha.

so the first thing we went to my grandfather's tent and stood there; what was this?! they were already in the midst of sitting inside their tent and eating, they were only now eating their dinner.

[FA:] mhm.

So now my mother told them about it, «We ran past a little old woman on our way here, she is going around to report it, she had as she said come to tell the old man about it but missed him, the last we saw we ran past her on our way,» my mother said to them. «*Kâ-piyêsiwakohpêw* has killed his wife, it is reported, it all happened here at the little house, at the old people's little house,» she said.

[11] So it was; that was it, there was nothing else; now my step-father arrived with his camp, and so they went ahead and put up the tent; and there now that little old woman made her report: «It was this,» she said, as she arrived now, arriving there at a run, «it was,» she said, «it was yesterday,» she said, «it was right before dinner-time,» she said, «it was not noon yet,» she said, «when they stopped over there on their way, our daughter,» she said, «they were going to Delmas» (for it was only there –~, that little town was the only one, this Delmas,

[FA:] mhm.

the first little town nearby, the Crees used to go there all the time to shop,

[FA:] mhm.

and it was there, also, that the big residential school used to be,

[FA:] Indeed.

the Roman Catholic residential school, all the children from our area used to be put in that school, from around here too).

[FA:] Indeed.

[12] êkosi; «êkotê ês ôki, kâ-pimi-nakîcik,» itwêw, «'â, nêkâ! ê-itohtêyâhk ôma akâmihk, tanimâs [*sic*], ê-nitaw-ôcinikêsiyâhk,' k-êtât –~ ê-isit awa nitânis,» itwêw, «'kîkwây nêtawêyihtaman?' – 'â, môy mistahi kîkway, kanakê ici wiyâsis pim-âsamisîhkan, pimi-kîwêyêko,' ê-itak nitânis,» itwêw awa nôtikwêw, «mwêhc ôm êkos ê-itwêyân,» itwêw, «'kanakê ici wiyâsis pêtamawîhkâhk, kôhtâwiy mîcimâpôs t-ôsîhtamawak,' ê-itak nitânis; êkos âspin, namôy kinwês, têpiyâhk ôm êkos ê-pim-îsit, êkosi kî-ati-sipwêhtêwak, tanimâs [*sic*] ê-is-~ ê-ispayicik,»

[FA:] mhm.

itwêw awa nôtikwêw. êkos êkwa, nêtê êtikw êkwa tanimâs [*sic*] ê-takohtêcik ê-takotâpâsocik, sa-sakahpitastimwêw êkwa awa nâpêw,

[FA:] âha.

pitamâ, «niyâ, nitaw-îspîhci-pîhtikwê! nitaw-is-~ nitaw-îspîhc-ôtinikê!» ê-itât ês ôh ôwîkimâkana. êkwa, awîn ês âwa, kâ-kêswân êkota kâ-kî-oyôhtâwîyân kî-ay-ayâw atâwêwikamikohk anita, ê-~ mêkwâc ê-oy-ocinikêsit, kâ-kî-oyôhtâwîyân awa, êkoni awa êtikwê mistahi mâna ê-kî-kâhkwêyimât awa kêswân awa nâpêw, nôhtâwiya ôhi.

[13] êkosi; aw êkwa ê-wâpamât ôhi nôhtâwiya ê-oy-ocinikêsiyit êkota, kâ-~ êkosi sôskwâc êsa kâ-wayawît. «êy, mâka mîna kê-kisiwâsit, âhci pikw êkota ayâyâni,» itêyihtam aw ês îskwêw – «'êkosi ê-itêyihtamân,' ê-itwêt awa nitânis,» itwêw, «'kâ-wayawîyân, pôti, ôm ê-ati-wayawîyân, kâw ê-at-ây-itohtêyân otâpânihk, "iyaw! tânisi, k-êspîhc-ôtinikâh ôma," k-êsit awa,' ê-itât onâpêma,» itwêw. «' "namôya, môy ninôhtê-otinikân êkos îsi, osâm,

[12] So it was; «On their way over there, it is reported, they had stopped,» she said, «'Well, mom! We are going across the river, we are going to Delmas to do some shopping,' is what she said to them –~ my daughter said to me,» she said, «'What do you want?' – 'Well, not very much, perhaps you could come by later and bring me a bit of meat to eat if you come by on your way home,' I said to my daughter,» the old woman said, «I was in the midst of saying that,» she said, «'Perhaps you could bring us back a bit of meat, so I can make some soup for your father,' I said to my daughter; with that they were gone, it wasn't long, she just came by to say this to me, and so they went ahead and left, they were driving to Delmas,»

[FA:] mhm.

the old woman said. So now, as they must have arrived at Delmas, arriving by team and wagon, now the man was tying up the horses,

[FA:] Indeed.

first, «Go on, go ahead inside! Go ahead with your shopping!» he reportedly said to his wife. Now what was this?! it just so happened, it is reported, that my late father was there, he was there in the store, he was in the midst of doing some shopping, my late father, and it was he, as it happened, of whom this man must have been so terribly jealous, of my father.

[13] So it was; now, seeing my father shopping there, she immediately, it is reported, went outside. «Hey, as usual he will be angry if I continue to stay there,» the woman thought, it is reported – «'That is what I thought,' my daughter said,» she said, «'when I went outside, lo and behold, as I was going outside on my way back to the wagon, "Ho! what is the matter, I thought you were getting on with your shopping," is what he said to me,' she said about her husband,» she said. «' "No, I did not want to shop like

êkota an[a] âyâw, ana mâna kâ-pakwâtat mistahi," ê-itak,' itwêw ês ônapêma an[a] îskwêw,

[FA:] âha.

êkos ê-itwêt nitânis,» itwêw, «êkos îtwêw.» îh, tânis êtokwê êkota, namôy nânitaw êkota itwêw, kîspin âhci piko ta-kî-pîhtikwêcik, atâwêwikamikohk anima;

[FA:] âha.

êkos êkwa pê-kîwêwak, pê-kîwêpayiwak sôskwâc. kîtah-~ môy wâhyaw êtokwê [*sic*] ê-pê-miyâskahkik, ôtên-~ anima talimwâs, anim ôcênâs êtikw ânim ê-ati-miyâskahkik, êkota ês êkwa âsay kâ-pê-mâci-nôtiniskwêwêt ana nâpêw. êkwa awa nôhtâwiy ê-kî-~, êkosi wîst êkwa ati-na-nâwayôtis-~ [*sc.* -nâwayôtisahikêw] ka-kîwêtâpâsow awa nôhtâwiy,

[FA:] mhm.

pêyakow mâka wiya.

[FA:] mhm.

êkosi, ay, kîtahtaw ês ôm ê-ati-mêkwâ-pimitâpâsot ôma (kîkwây kayâs *highway*, nama kîkway

[FA:] mhm.

êkospîhk kî-~, konit êyinito-mêskanaw [*sic*] mân ê-kî-âpatahk), ê-ati-sâkêwêtâpâsot ês âwa nôhtâwiy, awîn ês ôta, ôhi kî-ati-nôcihimâwa iskwêwa, ê-ati-misi-pakamahomiht matwê. wê-osâm-sâkêwêpicikêt [*sic*] ôma, êkosi, nakîw êsa, namôy âhci piko wî-~ sâkêwê-ayihk wî-ispicikêw, ayisk mêkwâ-pakamahomâwa matwê nêh îskwêwa. kapê-ay ês ânim êkosi, siyâkêwêtâpâsoc[i], âwîn ês ôma mâna kî-at-~ kî-ati-pakamahomâwa anih îskwêwa, êkos êsa mân ê-nakît.

that, because that one is there, the one you always hate so much," I said to him,' that woman said, it is reported, of her husband,

[FA:] Indeed.

that is what my daughter said,» she said, «that is what she said.» Look, I don't know what happened then, she [*sc.* the old woman] did not say anything about that, if they had gone inside the store again;

[FA:] Indeed.

so now they came back, they drove straight back. They could not have passed far beyond Delmas, passing through that little town, at that point already, it is reported, that man began to beat his wife. Now my father was following behind –~ my father, too, was driving back home,

[FA:] mhm.

but he was alone.

[FA:] mhm.

So, hey, suddenly, it is reported, while he came driving along (there was no such thing as a highway in the old days, there was none of that at the time,

[FA:] mhm.

it was simply a dirt track that was used), as my father gradually came driving into view, it is reported, here what was this?! reportedly the woman was being beaten as they went, he could see that she was being hit severely as they went along. Having accidentally driven into view, he now stopped, it is reported, he would not drive further into view for he could see that woman in the distance was still being hit. It went like that all along, it is reported, every time he would drive into view, what was this?! that woman was being hit as they went along, it was reported, so he would stop, it is reported.

[14] êkosi; piyis êk ôm êkwa, ôm êkwa sîpiy ê-otihtahkik, âsowahonân, 'nôtinitowi-sîpiy' ê-kî-isiyîhkâtêk, ê-kî-mosc-âsowahamihk mâna, êkosi, êkot[a] êkwa mîna kinwês, pêhow ês êkwa êkota nôhtâwiy, iyikohk aw êkwa, t-âsowahahkik ôki.

[FA:] mhm.

kiyîs-âsowahahkik ôki matwê, êkwayâc êkwa, «wâhyaw ayâwak,» ê-itêyihtahk êtikwê mîn êkwa, kâw êkwa mîna kâ-sipwêtâpâsot êsa nôhtâwiy.

[15] êkosi; êkwa êtikwê ayi, êkota ohc êkwa ê-kîs-âsowahaman, ômis [*gesture*] îtamonwa, pêyak ôm ôtê is âskîhkânihk, êkwa ôm âwa nôhtâwiy omêskanaw wiya, wâhyaw konit îtê wiy ê-kî-wîkicik mâna nôhtâwiy; êwak ôm êkwa wiy ôm ômêskanaw êkwa, êkota iskohk awa –~, êkota iskohk kiskêyihtam ôh âspin k-âti-pâh-pakamahomiht. êkosi kîwêtâpâsow nôhtâwiy.

[16] êkw êkwa nêtê êkwa, «iyaw, miton êkwa nikôtawi-pêhâwak,» itwêw, «'awînipan ôki, tâpwê mitoni wî-nîpâhtêwak,' nititwân,» itwêw, «âsay êkwa ê-ati-wawâninâkwahk,» itwêw, «ê-at-ôtâkosik miton,» îtwêw; «'â, ahpw êtikwê nêtê kî-pa-pimitâpâsowak âsay,' nititik awa kisêyiniw,» itwêw, «'ahpw êtik ôma kî-pa-pimitâpâsowak,' nititik awa kisêyiniw,» itwêw.

[17] «êkos,» îtwêw, «iyaw, miton ê-ati-kîsi-wani-tipiskâk,» ê-itwêt, «âsay,» itwêw, «miton ê-ati-kîsi-wani-tipiskâk,» itwêw; «kîtahtawê kâ-pâh-pêhtamân kîkway,» itwêw (p-~ ayisk papakiwayânikamikosihk ê-wîkicik),

[FA:] mhm.

«ê-wîkiyâhk ôma papakiwayânikamikosihk,» itwêw; «kâ-pâh-pêhtamân kîkway, ôta akâmahcâhk, kotak mêskanaw ômis [*gesture*] ê-pim-î-~ ê-pim-îtamok, êkotê ôm âkâmi-mêskanâhk ôma, akâmahcâsihk,» itwêw, «êkotê kâ-pâh-pêhtamân ê-tâh-têpwêhk,»

[14] So it was; now at last it was that they reached the river, the crossing, it is called *Nôtinitowi-sîpiy* [Battle River], you simply used to drive across a ford, so it was, and they were there again for a long time, at that point again my father waited, it is reported, until they had crossed the river.

[FA:] mhm.

When one could see that they had crossed the river, «They are a long ways off,» he must have thought then, only then, it is reported, did my father drive off again.

[15] So it was; now it must have been, from the point where you are done fording the river, the roads fork like this [*gesture*], one runs over here towards the reserve, and the other was my father's road, my father and his household used to live way out there; that was his road now, up to this point, up to this point he witnessed it, the last he saw was the woman getting hit over and over as they went along. So my father drove home with his wagon.

[16] Now over yonder now, «Ho, now I gave up waiting for them,» she said, «'They are gone, they are truly going to get into the dark of night,' I said,» she said, «Now it was already getting dusk,» she said, «it was really getting to be evening,» she said; «'Well, they may well have driven by over yonder already,' the old man said to me,» she said, «'they may well have driven by,' the old man said to me,» she said.

[17] «So it was,» she said, «ho, it was getting to be quite dark,» she said, «already,» she said, «it was getting to be quite dark,» she said; «suddenly I kept hearing something,» she said (for they were living in a little tent),

[FA:] mhm.

«we were living in a little tent,» she said; «I kept hearing something here across the hill, another road runs along like this [*gesture*] over there, it was on this road across the creek, across the little hill,» she itwêw. «'îh, kisêyiniw! matwê-tâh-têpwâniwiw ôta, nama cî wiya kicânisinaw, êkotê ê-pimi-nakîcik; aspin wiyâsis niwî-asamikoh,' k-êtwêyân,»

[FA:] mhm.

itwêw awa nôcikwêsiw (mitoni mân ôm êkosi ê-kî-~ ê-isi-ta-tâpâtotamân, ê-kî-isi-nitohtawak ana nôcikwêsiw),

[FA:] mhm.

«êkos,» îtwêw, «kâ-wayawîyân, 'mahti nik-êspahtân,' kâ-wayawîyân,» itwêw, «nitati-pinasiwêpahtân ôm ê-pasaskamikâk, anita piko nakahcâsihk, êkot[a] ê-pimamok ôma mêskanaw. tânisi mîn ê-itâpisiniyân, awîn âwa kî-mêkwâ-nôcihâw aw êkota nitânis,» ê-itwêt. «namôya ê-kîskwêpêyit anih ônâpêma,» ê-itwêt, «awîn âwa kî-mêkwâ-nôcihâw êkota nitânis,» itwêw, «îîh [*sic*], kakwâhyakahkamik, tâpwê mân âwa ê-ka-kitimahât nitânisa, 'nica-cîsihikwak ôki, "êtikw ê-tâh-têpwâtikawiyân," ê-itêyihtamân, mâka mîn êcik âwa ê-pakamahwât,' nititwân, nitit-~, êkosi piko ê-itwêyân,» itwêw ana nôtikwêw. «êkos,» îtwêw, «pôs-~, êkos âta wiya pônahpinatêw,» itwêw. êkosi, «piyôsipayihot ôh ôtâpânâskwa,» itwêw, «otôtâpâniwâwa,» itwêw; «mîn êkwa êkota ê-nakacipahât, ê-ati-~ kî-atimitâpâsow,» itwêw. «êkos êkwa awa nicânis pê-pa-pasikôw,» itwêw. «êkos ân[i],» îtwêw, «nipê-ka-kîwê-wîcêk, nipê-na-nîhtaciwânân,» itwêw, «âspin [*sic*] k-âtimwêwêsihk aw ôtâpân,» itwêw, «wiy âsay anim ê-ati-takwâkinow-âyâk [*sic*], êkosi nipîhtikwânân,» itwêw. «'iyaw, tânisi?' nititik awa kisêyiniw,» itwêw; «'iyaw, mâka mîn ês âwa ê-pimi-misi-nôcihiht kicânisinaw, nica-cîsihikwak, "êtikwê wiyâs ê-pim-âsamikoyahk," ê-itêyimak, mâka mîn ês âwa ê-pimi-misi-nôcihiht awa, ita ôma, êkos ôm âspin ê-sipwêtâpâsoyit, mâka mîna ê-ati-~ ê-nakacipahiht,' nititâw awa kisêyiniw,» itwêw.

said, «it was over there that I kept hearing someone call out over and over,» she said. «'Look, old man! You can hear it, someone is calling out over and over here, perhaps it is our daughter, they may have stopped over there on the way; the last I knew, she was going to bring me a bit of meat,' is what I was saying,»

[FA:] mhm.

the little old woman said (and I relate this account exactly as I had heard it from that little old woman),

[FA:] mhm.

«and so,» she said, «I went outside, 'Let me run over there,' I went outside,» she said, «I went on to run down this ravine, only there against a steep hill does that road run along. And what did I see, here my daughter was in the midst of being beaten up,» she said. «Her husband was not drunk,» she said, «but here my daughter was in the midst of being beaten up,» she said, «Look, what was going on?! he was truly treating my daughter brutally, 'They had raised my hopes, "Someone must be calling me [*sc.* to bring me some meat]," I thought, but, as it turned out, as usual it is this one hitting her,' I said, that is all I said,» that old woman said. «And so,» she said, «at least he let off battering her,» she said. And so, «Leaping unto his wagon,» she said, «their wagon,» she said; «now he took off and left her behind there, he drove on,» she said. «So now my daughter got up,» she said. «And with that,» she said, «she came back home with me, we came back down the hill,» she said, «the last we knew, one could hear the wagon going off,» she said, «and as it was already getting to be fall, we went inside,» she said. «'Ho, what happened?' the old man said to me,» she said; «'Ho, as usual evidently our daughter was severely beaten up again as they went along, they had raised my hopes, "Perhaps she is bringing us some meat on their way," I thought of her, but as usual evidently it was her being severely beaten up on the way over here, and then

«êkos,» îtwêw, «îkamâ mâka kê-pîkiskwêt awa kisêyiniw; êkos,» îtwêw, «nitay-apinân êkwa,» itwêw, «êkwa êwako ôma nicânis, êkos ôma kâ-itâtotahk,» itwêw, «ê-wâpamâcik êkotê ôh,» îtwêw, «ôhi kâ-pakwâtâyit êkosi k-~, êkotê anim ôhc êkwa, misakâmê ê-pê-nôcihiht tâh-têp-îyikohk, ê-ay-itwê-~ ê-ay-itâcimot awa nitânis,» itwêw. «kîtahtawê mêkwâc ôma k-âpiyâhk, ayisk ôma pimîwi-wâsaskocênikanis ôm ê-kî-saskahamân,» icwêw, «wâs-~ wa-wâsaskotêw pîhc-âyihk, nêtê isi nawac akâm-âyihk awa nitânis apiw,» itwêw, «êkwa niyanân ôta cîki kocawânâpiskosihk awa nîci-kîhkâw nitapinân,» itwêw. «kîtahtawê awa nicêmisisinân,» ê-itwêt, «tâpiskôc ôma k-êt-~ [*?record*], mêton ê-mâh-mikisimot,» ê-itwêt, «acimosis aw,»

[FA:] mhm.

îtwêw; «tâpiskôt mân âwiya ê-wî-otihtinât,» itwêw, «kîhawêma [*sic*] mîna mâna, tâpiskôc ê-pêtâmot,» itwêw, «ê-tôtahk aw âcimosis,» itwêw; «êkosi, âhci piko nitay-apinân,» itwêw; «â, ê-pa-pîkiskwêyâhk ôm,» îtwêw. «êy, tânisi mîna kîtahtawê,» ê-itwêt, «ê-mêkwâ-apiyâhk ôm,» îtwêw, «kâ-pê-tawi-~, îh, aspin ôma kâ-kî-atimitâpâsot,» itwêw, «kâ-pê-tawihtêpayik pa-~ ôma papakiwayânikamikos,» ê-itwêt, «êwak ôma papakiwayânikamikwâhtik ê-cimatêk, êkota kâ-pê-kwâskohtapit awa ninahâhkisîm, awîn âwa pâskisikanis kî-tahkonam,» ê-itwêt, «ômis [*gesture*] ê-itascêyik [*sic*] ôta ohcikwanihk, pakitinam, êkwa ôtê nitânis is ê-apit,» itwêw. «'tânisi?' k-êtât,» itwêw, «'tânisi? kiwî-misimin cî ôma kâ-t-~ k-ây-ihtôtâtân [*sic*] ôma?' k-êtât ôhi nitânisa,» itwêw. «êkosi, êkwa awa nitânis kâ-pîkiskwêt, 'namôya, namôy ka-kî-misimitin, napêc cî kikâh-misimitin, êkwayâc cî an[i] êkosi kitay-itâspinasin, ta-ma-misimitân nânapâwisk?' k-êtât awa nitânis,» itwêw. «êkos,» îtwêw, «'kah!' k-êtwêt awa ninahâhkisîm,»

he was gone and driving away, and she was left behind again,' I told the old man,» she said. «So it was,» she said, «of course the old man wouldn't say anything; so it was,» she said, «now we sat there,» she said, «now this is the account my daughter gave,» she said, «they saw this one over there,» she said, «the one whom he hated, so from there on now, she was beaten all along the way, off and on, my daughter reported,» she said. «Suddenly as we sat there, for I had lit a little oil lamp,» she said, «there was light inside, my daughter sat a little further over there across the tent,» she said, «and my fellow-oldster and I sat here close by the stove,» she said. «Suddenly our little dog,» she said, «as if –~ [*?record*] he was really barking,» she said, «this little dog,»

[FA:] mhm.

she said; «as if he was going to grab at someone,» she said, «and sometimes also the other way, as if he was fleeing towards the tent,» she said, «that is what the little dog did,» she said; «so we kept sitting there,» she said, «well, we were talking,» she said. «Hey, what was this all of a sudden?!» she said, «while we were sitting,» she said, «–~, look, the last we saw he had driven the other way,» she said, «the tent-flaps flew open,» she said, «and there where the tent-pole stood, there my son-in-law came leaping in, into a crouching position, what was this?! he was carrying a gun,» she said, «it was placed here across his knees like this [*gesture*], he lowered it towards where my daughter was sitting over there,» she said. « 'How is it?' is what he said to her,» she said, «'How is it? Are you going to report me for what I did to you?' is what he said to my daughter,» she said. «So now it was my daughter who spoke, 'No, I will not be able to report you, why should I report you now, is it the first time you have battered me like that, that I should report you now?' is what my daughter said to him,» she said. «And so,» she said, «'That's it!' is what my son-in-law said,» she said,

itwêw, «'kah! êwako kâ-pê-~ kâ-wî-kiskêyihtamân,' k-êtwêt awa nitân-~ awa ninahâhkisîm,» itwêw, «aspin êkos ê-at-îs[i]-âsê-wayawît,» itwêw, «ôm âsic ôpâskisikanis,» itwêw. «êkos,» îtwêw, «mâninakisk êkwa,» ê-itwêt, «kapê-ayi ê-mikisimot aw âcimosis, tâh-têp-îyikohk ê-mikisimopayit aw âcimosis,» itwêw, «êkwa êkota êkwa, niy êkwa mâka mîna niwî-nipahi-kostâcin, nikî-kostâw ninahâhkisîm, ê-kî-kiskêyimak ê-kî-~ iyikohk ê-kî-macisit mân,» îtwêw, «'îh!' nititâw awa nicânis,» itwêw, «'awas, âstawênêtân ôma wâsaskocênikanis, êkos îsi wa-wani-tipiskapitân, nâh-nahastâsotân pêskis,' nititâw awa nicânis,» itwêw, «'mistah ôma mâna wiya niy ê-kostak kinâpêm; cikâstêpâhkwêpiyahk[i] ôma, ka-pâh-pawinê-pâskisokonaw ana kinâ-~ kinâpêm,' nititâw awa nicânis,» itwêw. «êkos,» îtwêw, «ninâh-nahastâsimonihkânân, nikôkîyâskwahên ôma wâsaskocênikanis,» itwêw. «êkosi; êkosi nitisi-kawisimonân,» itwêw; «piyisk ninipânân, wiy âta wiya nimiyo-nipânân,» itwêw, «wiyâpahk, ê-ati-~ wiyâpahk, wîpac ôma nawac,» itwêw, «ê-kî-ma-mîcisoyâhk,» itwêw; «kîtahtawê,» itwêw, «êy, ômis [*gesture*] îtihkowiw aw ôskotâkaya nitânis,» itwêw, «iyikohk ê-pakamahoht ôm,» îtwêw, «miton-~ miton ômis [*gesture*] îsi-mihkowiniyiwa oskotâkaya,» itwêw. «'ayi mahti,' k-êsit,» itwêw, «'kwâpikêtân!' k-êsit,» itwêw, «'ta-kî-kwâpikêyahk ôma, ta-kî-kisî-~ nika-kisîpêkinikêsin, miton ôma niwînêyimison niskotâkaya k-êsinâkwahki, nika-kisîpêkinên,' k-êsit,» itwêw, «'pêskis nôhtâwiy opapakiwayânisa nika-kisîpêkinamwân,' k-êsit –~ k-êtwêt,» itwêw. «'îh, wâcistak, awas! miton ôma mâna wiya niya kinâpêm ê-kostak,' nititâw,» itwêw, «'miton ôma mâna wiya niya kinâpêm ê-kostak; nânitaw is ôma, êkâ kâh-kîwêkwê, ahpô êtik ôm ôta nânitaw ta-papâ-osâhtâw, ta-papâ-osâpamisk,' nititâw awa nitânis,» itwêw. «'iyâ,' k-êsit awa nitânis, 'awas, miton ôma kitôsâmi-mahpinân mâna, maninâk [*sic*] êtikwê,' k-êsit awa nitânis,» itwêw. «êkos,»

«'That's it! That is what I wanted to know,' is what my son-in-law said,» she said, «and so, the last we knew he was gone back outside,» she said, «with his gun» she said. «So it was,» she said, «now it kept on,» she said, «the little dog kept barking, he would start barking off and on,» she said, «now at that point, as for me, now as usual I was getting extremely scared, I was scared of my son-in-law, I knew him for the evil person he used to be,» she said, «'Look!' I said to my daughter,» she said, «'go on, let us put the lamp out, let us sit in the dark like that and let us make up our beds besides,' I said to my daughter,» she said, «'I am terribly scared of your husband; if our silhouettes are visible as we sit, your husband will be shooting us through the tent,' I said to my daughter,» she said. «And so,» she said, «we made up the beds, I pushed the wick down to douse the lamp,» she said. «So it was; in that way we went to bed,» she said; «finally we slept, in fact we did have a good sleep,» she said, «in the morning, when it was getting morning,» she said, «we had eaten rather early,» she said; «at one point,» she said, «hey, my daughter had blood on her dress like this [*gesture*],» she said, «she had been hit so badly,» she said, «there were large bloodstains on her dress like this [*gesture*],» she said. «'Let us go,' is what she said to me, 'Let us fetch water,' is what she said to me,» she said, «'we should fetch water, I will wash some clothes, I feel so dirty with the way my dress looks, I will wash it,' is what she said to me,» she said, 'I will wash my father's shirts, too,' is what she said to me –~ is what she said,» she said. «'Look, oh my, go away! As for me, I am terribly scared of your husband,' I said to her,» she said, «'as for me, I am terribly scared of your husband; somewhere, if he didn't go home, he may still be hanging around here to watch from somewhere, to hang around and watch you,' I said to my daughter,» she said. «'Oh you,' is what my daughter said to me, 'go on, you are always such a coward, surely he wouldn't,' is what

îtwêw, «âsay mîna kîhtwâm,» itwêw, «'êkwa, kwâpikêtân, nâh-nîsonikêtân, êkosi pêyakwâw piko, îh, êkoyikohk ôma nika-têpipayin, nâh-nîswêskihk tahkonamahko nipiy,' nititik nitânis,» itwêw, «êkot[a] êkwa kiyâm kâ-tâpwêhtawak,» itwêw. «'kiyipa ê-nôhtê-mîskocayiwinisêsiyân ôma,' nititik,» itwêw.

[18] «êkos êkwa,» itwêw, «'kisêyiniw! ê-wî-kwâpikêyâhk, ê-wî-kisîpêkinikêt kicânisinaw,' nititâw awa kisêyiniw,» itwêw. «êkos êkw âskihkwak nitâh-otinânânak,» itwêw, «ninîhtaciwânân» (wâhyawêsîs anima mâna ê-kî-ohtahipêcik mitoni, ê-ohtahip-~ itê anim ê-isi-kwâpikêcik

[FA:] mhm.

ôma sîpîsis itê ê-pimihtik, wâhyawêsîs); kîtahtawê, «êkos,» îtwêw, «ninâh-nîhtaciwânân ôm ê-~,» (pêyakwâw êkot[a] ômis [*gesture*] ê-at-îtahcâk, âsay mîn ômis îsi [*gesture*], êkota ohc êkwa wâhyawêsîs ê-isi-tahtakwahcamâ-~, êkota êkwa sîpîsis ê-pimihtik, nîstanân mân êwako nikî-ohtahipânân anima sîpîsis). êkwa, êkwa ayihk, «êkos,» îtwêw, «nika-kwâ-~, kâ-pinasiwêyâhk ê-kwâpikêyâhk; êkos,» îtwêw, «nikâh-kwâpahênân [*sic*] êk ôma, ê-kâh-kêhciwê-kwâpahikêyâhk ôma, ita mâna, ê-timîk ôm,» îtwêw, «ê-cimîsik,» itwêw, «ê-kospahâyâhkik ôki nitaskihkonânak,» itwêw; «iskwayâc ôma nîst ê-kwâpahamân askihk ê-wî-pê-kwêskîyân, [*clap*] tâni mîn âkâmihk k-ôh-matwêwêk,» ê-itwêt; «akâmi-sîpîsisihk [*clap*] k-ôh-matwêwêk,» itwêw. «'îh! îh, êkosi k-êtitân,' nititâw sêmâk nitânis,» itwêw, «mêton ôta [*gesture*], nânitaw, 'côô!' tâpiskôc ê-itwêhk,» itwêw, «'îh, êkosi k-êtitân,' nititâw awa nitânis,» itwêw. «êkos ânim,» îtwêw, «nitaskihkonânak êkotê ê-isi-nakatâmototawâyâhkok,» itwêw (êkwa ani ê-kî-ispahcâsik anima mâna,

[FA:] mhm.

my daughter said to me,» she said. «So,» she said, «once more already,» she said, «'Now let us fetch water, let us each get two pails of water, so we will only go once, look, with that I will have enough, if we carry two pails of water each,' my daughter said to me,» she said, «so it was then that I agreed at last,» she said. «'Hurry, I want to change my clothes,' she said to me,» she said.

[18] «So now,» she said, «'Old man! We are going to fetch water, our daughter is going to wash clothes,' I said to the old man,» she said. «So now we each took pails,» she said, «we went down the hill» (it was really quite a ways where they used to fetch their water, where they went for their water

[FA:] mhm.

where that creek flows along, quite a ways); suddenly, «And so,» she said, «we went down the hills (one hill is shaped like this [*gesture*] and again one like this [*gesture*], and from that point on the terrain is flat for quite a ways, that is where the creek flows along, we too [*sc.* Sarah and her mother and step-father] used to get our water from that creek). Now, now then, «And then,» she said, «we went down the hill and got water; then,» she said, «we scooped the water up into our pails, we scooped it right out of the river into our pails, where it is deep,» she said, «it is quite deep,» she said, «and we put our pails to the side,» she said; «I too had scooped up my last pail of water and was about to turn around back this way, [*clap*] here there was the sound of a shot from across the water,» she said; «[*clap*] the sound of a shot from across the creek,» she said. «'Look! look, that's what I told you,' I said to my daughter right away,» she said, «it was right here [*gesture*], roughly as if someone said '*côô!*',» she said, «'Look! that's what I told you,' I said to my daughter,» she said. «So it was,» she said, «we left our pails and fled over there,» she said (now the little hill was quite steep

[FA:] mhm.

ta-pê-âmaciwêyâmohk; otâpânâsko-mêskanaw ômis [*gesture*] ê-ati-~, êkwa ôc[a] ât[a] ânima ê-caskamamosik.)

[FA:] âha.

«êkos îs ê-pê-âmaciwêpahtâyâhk,» ê-itwêt, «konit ôta ôma nayawatatâwahk,» ê-itwêt, «'côô!' tâpiskôc mân ê-itwêhk,» itwêw; «nama kîkway âpasâpâmowin,» ê-itwêt, «iyâyaw, êwakw ânima mân ê-ohpwêyâwahkihtik môswasinîs» (ôm êkwa ê-kîsi-tahkohtaciwêpahtâcik, êkot[a] êkwa k-êtwêyân, wâhyawêsîs k-êsi-tahtakwâk); «miton êtikwê ay-âpihtaw-âyihk ât[a] ê-ayâyâhk ôma paskwâs,» itwêw, «mêskanâs ôm ê-mitimêyâmoyâhk,» itwêw, «ôh, kîtahtawê,» itwêw, «âsay mîn,» ê-itwêt, «âsay mîna [*clap*] kâ-mâh-matwêwêk,» ê-itwêt; «nit-~ êkot[a] êkwa k-âpasâpâmoyâhk,» ê-itwêt, «ê-ay-âpasâpipayihoyân, awîn âw ôma, ita kâ-pê-tahkohtaciwêyâhk ôm,» îtwêw, «awîn âw êkota kî-nahapi-~, âsay ês ê-kî-nahapipayihot, êkotê ohc êkwa [*clap*] ê-pâh-pâskisokoyâhk,» ê-itwêt. «êkos,» îtwêw, «hây, nitânis awa kâ-ma-mawimot êkwa,» itwêw, «wiy âyisk êtikwê tahk[i] ôma,

[FA:] mhm.

iyikohk kâ-pâskisokot onâpêma, 'êkâya, ninâp-~ niwîkimâkan, ka-kitimahin!' ê-itwêt aspin piko nitânis,» ê-itwêt, «ômis ê-is-~ ômis [*gesture*] ê-ihtôtahk [*sic*] ê-ay-âpasâpâmot,» ê-itwêt (ê-kî-itwêhk mân ômatowihk nîkân ê-kî-sâ-sâpopayihtâyit anih ônâpêma, anim ômisi kâ-tôtahk). «êkos îsi âhci piko, nama kîkway nakîwin, sôskwâc ê-ispîhcipahcâyân nîsc,» ê-itwêt, «ê-kakwê-pê-amaciwê-~» (âsay mîn êkota ta-tahkohtaciwêpahtâcik).

[19] «êkos êtikwê pê-sipwêpahtâw, ê-pê-nawaswâtikoyâhk,» itwêw, «âh, katisk êkot[a] ânim ê-pê-kîsi-tahkohtaciwêpahtâyâhk,» ê-itwêt, «êêkos [*sic*] âhci piko nitapasîn, âh, ê-âpasâpipayihoyân, âs-~

for someone fleeing back uphill; it was a cart track that went like this [*gesture*], though here there was a little shortcut.)

[FA:] Indeed.

«In this way we ran back up the hill,» she said, «it was about here, midway up the river bank,» she said, «as if someone said *'côô!'*,» she said; «there was no turning back to look,» she said, «instead, it was a case of the bullets raising the dirt as they hit» (now they had raced all the way to the top of the hill, it was there that I said that it was flat for quite a ways); «we must have been halfway across this little prairie,» she said, «fleeing along this trail,» she said, «oh, all of a sudden,» she said, «again,» she said, «again [*clap*] the sound of shots,» she said; «at that point we turned back to look,» she said, «and as I glanced back, what was this?! there where we had reached the top of the hill,» she said, «what was this?! evidently he had already achieved a crouching position there, and now [*clap*] he kept shooting at us from over there,» she said. «And then,» she said, «oh no, now my daughter let out a cry,» she said, «it must have been her all along

[FA:] mhm.

that her husband was aiming at, «'Don't be cruel to me, my husband!' was the last my daughter said,» she said, «she made this gesture [*gesture*] as she was turning back to look,» she said (it was said that her husband's shots first went through in this place, when she did this). «And still, despite it all, there was no stopping, I too ran as hard as I could,» she said, «trying to get back up the hill (at that point they already had to run up another hill).

[19] «And so she must have run on as he came in pursuit of us,» she said, «Well, we had barely raced all the way to the top of the hill,» she said, «I was still fleeing in that way, well, and

êkota nitânis kâ-pê-kawahoht,» ê-itwêt. «aspin piko ê-kawahoht nitânis,» ê-itwêt; «nama kîkway nakikwâskohtiwin,» ê-itwêt, «âhci pikw ê-pê-tapasîyân niy,» îtwêw, «âsay mîn êkwa êkota ê-at-âmaciwêmosik ôma, môy mâk ât[a] ê-~ ê-ispahcâk wiya, êy, êkota êkw ê-pê-nâh-nôsô-pâskisot awa ninahâhkisîm,» itwêw, «nîswâw wiya kêhtinât, mêtoni mân ôta, 'côô!' ê-itihtâkwahk,» itwêw; «kiyîsi-tahkohtaciwêpahtâyân,» itwêw, «awîn âwa, kâ-pêhtawak ê-matwê-pîkiskwêt,» itwêw, «ê-matwê-têpwêt,» itwêw. «'êhêhahay, nisâkihâh niwîkimâkan, êkos êcik âwa tâpwê ê-nipahak,' ê-matwê-itwêt êkwa mîna kîhawêma [*sic*],» itwêw, «nip-~ ê-âpasâpâmoyân, awîn âwa kî-wîcikâpawistawêw, êkota aw âsay nitânis ê-matwê-pimisihk,» ê-itwêt, «'êkos êcik âw ê-nipahak niwîkimâkan, êkos êtikwê piko ta-wîcêwak,' ê-itwêt. êkos êkwa nitakopahtân êkwa, nipîhtikwê-kwâskohtin nîkisinâhk,» itwêw. «îh, êkot[a] êkwa kâ-wîhtamawak aw,» îtwêw, «'kisêyiniw! nipahâw ôma kitânisinaw, aspin ôta ê-pê-kawahoht,' ê-itwêyân,» itwêw. «'niyâ mâka, sipwêpahtâ êkosi! owiyasiwêhkân nitawi-wîhtamaw! pikw êwako nîkân ta-kiskêyihtahk,' ê-isit ôma» – ê-kî-itâcimot mân âna nôcikwêsiw, îh, êkos ânima kâ-pê-sipwêpahtât. (nayawac-âyihk êkota nôhtaw, êkoca kêhcê-ayak mâna kî-wîkiwak nôcikwêsiw, câpiskôc awa kâ-icâcihot, ê-kî-pa-pêyakokêt ana mâna

[FA:] mhm.

nôcikwêsiw); «êwako, êwakw âw êkwa kâ-pê-ispahtâyân awa nôtikwêw,» itwêw, «'êy,' nititâw,» itwêw, «'ê-pimi-wîhtamâtân ôma,' nititâw,» itwêw, «'nipahêw ôm êkwa! wêsâmihk êkwa, kâ-piyêsiwakohpêw wîwa; maht ôtê kîsta mâmihk ispahtâ, nitawi-wîhta, nitawi-wîhtamawik ôki mâmihk kâ-wîkicik!' nititâw,»

glancing back to look, it was at that point that my daughter was being felled by a shot,» she said. «The last I saw was my daughter being felled by a shot,» she said; «there wasn't a moment's stopping,» she said, «as for me, I was still fleeing back,» she said, «again now at this point there was another little rise in the trail but it was not steep, hey, there my son-in-law was shooting at me now as I came running,» she said, «twice for sure it sounded *'côô'* right here,» she said; «as I reached the top of the hill running,» she said, «what was this?! I heard him, he could be heard talking,» she said, «he could be heard yelling,» she said. «'Woe betide me! I did love my wife, and so it turns out that I have truly killed her,' he could be heard saying now in an ironic reversal,» she said, «as I turned back to look, here he was standing beside her, at that point my daughter could already be seen lying there,» she said, «'So it turns out that I have killed my wife, so now I guess I will have to go with her,' he said. So now I ran up to our little place and jumped inside,» she said. «Look, it was then that I told him about it,» she said, «'Old man! Our daughter has been killed, the last I saw she was felled by a shot on the way here,' I said,» she said. «'Go on though, run off like this! Go and tell the councillor about it! He must be the first to know about it,' he said to me,» – having made her report this way, look, that little old woman ran off like this. (It was not quite midway, another old couple used to live there, a little old woman, just like this one lived, that little old woman

[FA:] mhm.

used to live alone); «It was this one, it was this old woman to whom I came running,» she said, «'Hey,' I said to her,» she said, «'I am coming by to tell you about it,' I said to her,» she said, «'now he has killed her! at last *Kâ-piyêsiwakohpêw* has killed his wife; you, too, please run downstream, go and tell about it, go and tell the people who live downstream about it!' I said to her,» she said,

itwêw, «'êkâya wiya êwak ôma kâ-wîkiyâhk ati-pimipahtâ! ôtê isi nakahcâhk ôma, nakâskwêyâhk, êwakw îsi-têtipêwêpahtâ, têpiyâhk nêki nitawi-wîhtamawatwâwi, asahkêwikamikohk tit-êspayiwak nikotwâw ta-nitawi-wîhtahkik,' nititâw awa nôtikwêw,» itwêw (êkwa kî-kakâyawi-kîhkâw ana nôtikwêw ana wîst âna), «'êha,' nititik,» itwêw, «'mêyâkwâm, miton âni mêkwâ-mêskanâhk nitânis pimisin,' nititâw,» itwêw.

[20] êkosi tâpwê, îh, êkos ânim êkwa kâ-pê-sipwêpahtât êkwa kâ-pê-wîhtahk êkwa nîkinâhk. êkos êkwa êwakw âwa nôtikwêw êtikwê, sôskwâc ês êkwa âpihtâ-kîsikâhk wîst ê-isi-kîmôc-sipwêpahtât, êkota ohci ômis [*gesture*] ê-is-âyi-têtipêwêpahtât nêma, mâmihk pêyakokamik mân ê-kî-wîkicik wîstawâw, môy wîhkâc ê-ohci-nakatahkik (niyanân ôma piko mân êkos îsi, kahkiyaw mân âyisiyiniwak ôk ôkistikêwiyiniwak, ê-kî-âmaciwê-âhtokêcik ôma k-ôski-nîpihk; êkwayâc ôma kâ-takwâkik mân êkotê ê-kî-pê-nâh-nîhtaciwêpicicik), îh, miton ânim âspîs, nistokamik anima pikw êkotê ê-pimi-wîkicik anim ôki kêhcê-ayak, nêki mâmihk, êkwa êkonik ôki kâ-nipahimiht oko-~

[*external break*]

[FA:] êwakw âwa niwîcêwâkan *Sarah* ê-wî-kîs-âcimot ôma kâ-mâc-âcimot. êkosi.

[SW:] (êkwa ayi, ayîhtatahkamik anim êkwa, îh, ôki kêhtê-ayak êkwa, namôy ânima sêmâk awa wiyasiwêhkân [*sic*] ê-itohtêt, anima kâ-pê-wîhtamâht.)

[21] êkosi wiy âw êtikwê awa, nôtikwêw awa mâmihk kâ-nitawi-wîhtahk, sêmâk sipwêpayiw ana nâpêw, asahkêwikamikohk ê-pê-ispayit, ê-pê-wîhtahk, otasahkêw[a] ê-pê-wîhtamawât, simâkanisak ka-nâtitisahohcik. êkwa êkota,

«'Don't run past where we live! Run along the side hill, against the steep cut in the land, run right around that, as long as you go and tell those yonder about it so that one of them might ride to the agency to go and tell about it,' I said to this old woman,» she said (that old woman, too, was a very agile old person), «'Yes,' she said to me,» she said, «'Take care, my daughter is lying right on the trail,' I said to her,» she said.

[20] And truly, look, it was then that she came running to come and tell about it at our place. And so this other old woman must have left straight towards the south, it is reported, hiding as she ran off, and from there ran around that place yonder in this way [*gesture*], there was a single house downstream and these people used to live by themselves, they never left there (we were the only ones like that, all the people, the farmers all used to move up the hill with their camps in the early summer; only in the fall would they come moving camp back down the hill), look, they were very few, there were only three houses over there with old people, those who lived downstream, including the ones whose daughter had been killed –~.

[*external break*]

[FA:] It is my partner Sarah who is going to complete the story she has begun to tell. That's it.

[SW:] (Now he took his time about it, look, these old people now, the councillor did not go there right away after one had come and he had been told about that.)

[21] So this one, the old woman having gone and told about it downstream, that man must have set off on horseback right away, he came riding up to the agency, he came to tell about it, he came to tell the farm instructor about it so the police would be sent

oskinîkiw mîn êkota pê-takopayiw (okosisiwâwa âsay, êkonik ôki kâ-nitawi-wîhtamâmiht), wîst ât[a] ê-pê-wîhtahk êwakw ân[a] ôskinîkiw, mâk âyisk âsay kîsi-kiskêyihtam awa wiyasiwêhkân [*sic*]. ayîhtatahkamik êkwa awa owiyasiwêhkân [*sic*] mîn êkwa, kahkiyaw ôki niyânan nâpêwak, êkonik, «piko ta-wîcêwiyêk,» k-êtwêt awa nimosôm, «ta-kitâpamiyêk kwayask, tânisi maht âwa nâpêw awa, ka-nitawâpênawâyahk,» itwêw, kî-at[i]-âsohtêwak êk ôki nâpêwak ôki, ê-nitaw-wâpamâ-~ ê-wîcêht awa kisêyiniw ôm îtê k-êtohtêt.

[22] êkosi, «pôt ôm,» ê-kî-itwêt mâna nôhcâwîs, nôhcâwîsak ôk ê-isi-nîsicik, «pôt âwa kis-~, awa nâpêw, ômis [*gesture*] ês ê-itapit ana, nâpêwak ôki k-êtap-~

[FA:] âha.

ômisi k-êtapicik, ôta pâskisikanis anim ê-astêyik, êk ôta wîwa ê-pimisiniyit, an[a] îskwêw êsa, ê-kakwê-âh-ispayihot, môy cêskw ê-nipit.»

[FA:] môy!

[SW:] êha, ê-kakwê-âh-ispayihoc ês ôhi, ê-yâh-yâwipitât onâpêma –

[FA:] onâpêma?

[SW:] êha, ita ôma kâ-pimisiniyit.

[FA:] ê-kî-nipahisot cî ana nâpêw?

ê-~ âsay awa nâpêw ê-kîsi-nipahisot, «miton ês ômatowihk [*gesture*],» ê-itâcik, «ômis [*gesture*] ê-isi-mihkowit,» ê-kî-itâcik mâna. êkwa êtikw âwa nô-~ nimosôm awa, pâskisikanis anim ê-otinamwât, êkwa ês ê-nitawi-pahkahôhât, «tâpiskôc kêyâpic ê-yêhêsit [*sic*],» ê-itât, «mâka miton ômis [*gesture*] ê-itapit,» ê-itâ-~ ê-kî-itâcik mâna,

[FA:] hm.

for. Now at that point a young man arrived there on horseback (he was the son of the people who had already been told about it), although that young man, too, had come to report it, but in fact the councillor already knew all about it. Now the councillor took his time, speaking to all five of these men [*sc.* his sons], «You have to come with me,» is what my grandfather said, «you have to observe me properly, how this man is found, we have to check on him,» he said, now these men went off together, they were going to see, they were going with the old man when he went there.

[22] So, «Behold,» my step-father used to say, both my step-father and his brother, «behold this man, he sat like this [*gesture*], it is reported, the way men

[FA:] Indeed.

usually sit, here was the gun and here lay his wife, that woman, it is reported, was trying to move towards him bit by bit, she was not dead yet.»

[FA:] No!

[SW:] Yes, she was trying bit by bit to move towards him, it is reported, bit by bit reaching for her husband –

[FA:] Her husband?

[SW:] Yes, where he lay.

[FA:] That man had killed himself?

The man had already killed himself, «It was right here [*gesture*], it is reported,» they said about him, «he was bloody in this place [*gesture*],» they used to say about him. And my grandfather must have taken the gun from him, then he went and checked his pulse, it is reported, «It seems he is still breathing a little,» he said about him, «but he really sat like this [*gesture*],» they used to say about him,

[FA:] hm.

«miton ômis [*gesture*] ê-itapit,» ê-itâcik; êkos ôma pâskisikanis êsa k-ôtinamwâc. êkwa ês ân[a] îskwêw ana (wiya ciyêkwac ana nâpêw sêmâk ê-kî-nipit), êkwa âw îskwêw êkwa, konic ês ê-yâh-yâwipicâc ôhi.

[23] êkosi; pê-kîwêwak – môya, môy pê-kîwêwak, pêhowak êkwa êkotê, tâpwê wîpac êtikwê nawac, otasahkêw takopayiw êkota, êkwa simâkanisak mîna. nâh-nâway takopayiwak, maskihkîwiyiniw mîna. piyisk êkwa nikâwiy wîsta, otâpâs-~ sipwêtâpâsowak êkwa nikâwiy asici. êkwa êwako nêki mâmihk kâ-nitawi-wîhtamâhcik, êkonik mîna kahkiyaw pê-itohtêwak, iskwêw kan-~, kik[i] ây[a] âna. êkwa êkota, iskwêw an[a] êkwa pimâcisisiw, êkw êkwa ê-nâtiht, êkwa an[a] îskwêw papakiwayânikamikohk anit[a] ê-pê-pîhtikwahiht, êk ôk êsa nikâwiy ê-nânapâcihâcik anih ê-mîskotayiwinisahâcik kwayask, ê-pêtât nâha mâmihk êtikw ân[a] îskwêw otayiwinisa, êkoni êkwa ê-postiskamôhiht awa. êkosi êwakw ân[a] ê-pê-sipwêpahiht ana, âhkosîwikamikohk ê-pê-itohtahiht aw îskwêw.

[FA:] mhm.

[24] êkwa aya, êkwa wiy âwa nâpêw awa, êkosi nipahisow. êkwa êtikwê êkota, nôhcâwîs ana kotak, êkota ês ê-nitomikot simâkanisa, êkota cîk ê-nitaw-îspicikêt, ita ôhi ê-pimisiniyit, «wahwâ, nama kîkway kitimâkih-~ kitimâkinamwak simâkanisak,» itwêw ('nicihkwacim' ê-kî-itâhkômâcik mân ânihi kâ-nipahisoyit nâpêwa);

[FA:] âha.

«sôskwâc oskâtiyîhk ê-kî-itinâcik, êkwa pêyak ôtê wiyawi-~ [*sc.* wiyawiyîhk], sôskwâc miscikowacîhkânisihk anita, ê-pôsiwêpinâcik ê-kî-miscikwaskisinêsit awa nicihkwacim,» itwêw. «êkos,» îtwêw, «akâmi-sîpîsisihk ohci, itê anima kâ-pê-~ k-âskamâcikêt anima» (êkot[a] âkâmi-sîpîsisihk otânisiwâwa ê-kî-wîkiyit an[a] îskwêw

«he really sat like this [*gesture*],» they said about him; so he took this gun from him, it is reported. Now that woman, it is reported (that man by contrast had died right away), now this woman, it is reported, she was simply trying bit by bit to reach him.

[23] So it was; they came home – no, they did not come home, now they waited over there, truly they cannot have waited long, the farm instructor arrived there and also the police. They arrived one after the other, and also the doctor. Finally now my mother too, now they drove off together with my mother. And those people from yonder downstream who had been told about it, they all came too, along with that woman. Now at that point that woman still had a little life left in her, now she was brought and taken into that tent, that woman, and my mother and the others tended to her, it is reported, and changed her clothes properly, that woman from yonder downstream must have brought some of her clothes, those they put on her now. And then they took her away, they took this woman to the hospital.

[FA:] mhm.

[24] So now, now this man, so he killed himself. And at this point, I guess, this other one, my step-father's brother, it is reported, at this point was called upon by the police, and he went and drove close there where this one was lying, «Oh my, the police had no respect for anything to do with him,» he said (they used to call him by the kin-term 'my cross-nephew', that man who had killed himself);

[FA:] Indeed.

«they just picked him up by his legs, one held his upper body, they just threw my cross-nephew there into the wagon-box and you could hear his boots as they hit the wood,» he said. «So it was,» he said, «from across the creek, from where he had lain in ambush» (their daughter had lived across the creek, it was their house, –~ it ana, owâskahikaniwâw –~ owâskahikaniyiw, mâka namôy âwiyak ê-apit), «êkota ês âwa nâpêw awa sôskwâc, sôskwât mîna êkos ânima nêwayak ê-kî-itinâcik ê-pîhtikwê-wêp-~, konita kâ-matwêskisinêsihk tâwihtak an[a] êkota,» itwêw. «êkw ê-nâh-nitonikêcik,» itwêw, «simâkanisak ôk,» îtwêw, «ê-nitonikâtâcik,» itwêw, «ômayikohk [*gesture*] êtikwê,» ê-kî-itwêt mâna nôhcâwîs ana, «kâsîyiyâkanâkanisihk [*sic*] ê-wêwêkinikâsoyic iyinico-pahkwêsikanisa, ôtê êsa ê-kî-asiwahât,» itwêw, «êkon êcikwê ê-kî-papâ-nîmâsit,» itwêw, «êkoni anihi kâ-miskawâcik simâkanisak,» itwêw; «ê-kî-wâh-wâpamâcik,» itwêw, «kâw ê-titipêkinâcik, aspin êkota kâw êkot[a] ê-sêkonimâcik,» ê-itwêt.

[FA:] hm!

[25] êkos ê-pîhtikwê-wêpiniht an[a] êkota, nîso-tipiskâw ana nâpêw êkota ê-kî-pimisihk,

[FA:] hm!

ê-pêyakosihk, êkosi ê-kî-isi-~ ê-isi-kipahwâcik simâkanisak. ê-kî-nîso-tipiskâk, êkot[a] êkwa êkwayâc êkwa kâ-pê-~ kâ-wî-nahiniht ana nâpêw. êkot[a] êkwa, namôy mîn ê-ohti-nitawêyihtahkik ahpô akohp kîkway ta-~ t-âkwanahimiht êkos îsi ta-wêwêkinimiht. sôskwâc ê-isîhoyit, êkos îsi, mosci-mistikowat (kayâs kî-kitimâkan,

[FA:] mhm.

môy kîkway ohc-âtâwâniwiw mistikowata, piko ê-kî-mosc-ôsîhtâhk mistikowata); îh, têpiyâhk ê-mosc-ôsîhcikâtêyik ana omistikowat, môy âhpô ê-wêwêkinikâtêyik nânitaw isi, êkot[a] ân[a] âspin ana nâpêw ês ê-asiwaci-wêpiniht, êkos ê-isi-kipi-sakahoht; êwakw ân[a] êkosi ê-kî-isi-nitawi-nahiniht, ôhi mîna ita kitimâkisiwina tit-âstêki, môy pîhc-âyihk ê-ohti-nahiniht ana (nikî-wâpahtên mâna, ê-kî-nîswastêk[i] ê-~ aniki, anik ê-nipahisocik), êkota wîst ê-kî-nahiniht ana nâpêw, môy pîhto-~, môy pîhci-mênikan.

was their daughter's house, but there was no one home), «there this man was simply, they simply picked him up at four ends and threw him inside –~, you could hear his boots hitting the floor there,» he said. «Now they made their searches,» he said, «the police,» he said, «they searched him,» he said, «to this degree [*gesture*] apparently,» that brother of my step-father always said, «there was a little bannock wrapped up in a tea towel, he had put it in here, it is reported,» he said, «he must have taken it for the road,» he said, «that was what the police found,» he said; «they all looked at it,» he said, «they wrapped it up again, and with that they put it back there into his shirt,» he said.

[FA:] hm!

[25] So they threw him in there, that man lay there for two nights,

[FA:] hm!

he lay there alone, and in this way did the police lock him in there. Not until two nights had passed was that man buried. At that point they did not even want a blanket or something for him to be covered like that, for him to be wrapped up. Just as he was dressed, like that, a plain box (it was hard in the old days,

[FA:] mhm.

no one used to buy coffins, one had to make plain boxes); look, no more than this plain box for him, there was not even a covering of any kind, that man was just thrown in, it is reported, and nailed up like that; this way he was taken and buried where the bodies of the miserables are buried, he was not buried inside the cemetery (I used to see it, there used to be two graves of those who had killed themselves), there that man, too, was buried, not inside the cemetery fence.

[26] ê-kî-nîso-tipiskâk anima wîsta, ana kâ-pêtâhk ana iskwêw ana wiyaw anima, wîst êkwa môy ê-pimâtisit. pôt êkw ânima môswasinîs ostikwânihk êkwa wîtihpihk êtikw âwa, kikiskêyihtên,

[FA:] âha.

ê-isi-pisci-pô-~-pohciwêpahamihk [*sic*] (kîkwây wiya [*sc.* kayâs], anohc wiya tâh-mas-~ tâh-maniswêwak, môy-~, maskihkîwiyiniwak ê-ma-miyôcik anohc kahkiyaw kîkway). êkwa mîn êkoca nikâwiy ê-icohcêcik êkwa, ê-wî-nîpêpiwiht êkwa. «ômis [*gesture*] ê-âh-itahpitêyiki ocihciya, ê-wâh-wêwêkahpitêyiki,» ê-itwêt, «êkwa mîn ôstikwân,» ê-itwêt, «kwayask,» itwêw. ê-nîpêpiwiht êkwa êkota anim êkwa, êkosi mîn êwakw âna mwêscas ê-kî-ati-na-nahiniht.

[27] êkosi; wahwâ, namô-~, îh, êkospîhk anima, môy wîhkât mistahi ê-ohc-îsp-~, nân-~, êkos ê-ohci-pê-ispayik ôma sôhkahât,

[FA:] mhm.

ta-pê-na-nipahitocik, namôy kakêtihk anim êkospîhk ay-~, «mistahi ê-kî-ay-itinikêt,» ê-kî-itêyimiht ana nâpêw, anim ê-itahkamikisit.

[28] êkosi; êy, ê-kî-koskwêyihtâkwahk, êkos âniki kêhcê-ayak ê-kî-nâcipicîhihcik, nikî-ka-kanawêyimânânak aniki nîkinâhk, nikî-wa-wîkimânânak aniki kêhtê-ayak.

[FA:] hm!

êkwa otânisa, kî-pêyakoyiwa an[a] îskwêw an[a] ê-kî-~, êkoni piko ê-kî-iskwahpinêyit otânisa. êkoni êkwa awa nikâwiy, kâ-miyikoc anihi nôcikwêwa, ôsisimiyiwa ôhi, ta-tâpâhkômât awa, nikâwiy anihi t-ôtânisit, kikiskêyihtên?

[FA:] âha.

êkosi tâpwê, miyâw ayisk, êkosi tâpwê kî-otânisîhkâw anihi,

[FA:] mhm.

anihi wêyokâwîyit. êkwa êwakw ân[a] âna nimis, mîna nikî-wa-wîkimânânak mîn êkwa anim êkwa ê-ati-kwêski-takwâkik. ê-kî-wî-kîskwêyêyihtahk, ê-kî-wâh-waniskâskwêyit mân ês

[26] After two nights had passed they brought the woman's body too, now she had died too. Behold, that bullet was in her head, it must have lodged in her brain, you know

[FA:] Indeed.

(what was there [*sc.* in the old days]? today they would have operated her, the doctors are good today in everything). And now my mother and the others went there, they were going to have a wake for her. «Her hands were both tied like this [*gesture*], they were all bandaged up,» she said, «and also her head,» she said, «properly,» she said. So now a wake was held for her there, and shortly after that she was buried.

[27] So it was; oh my, no –~ look, that was at the time, never had anything so violent taken place,

[FA:] mhm.

for people to be killing each other, at that time there was not a great deal –~ «He committed an awful crime,» it was thought of that man, about what he did.

[28] So it was; hey, everyone found it shocking, and so those old people and their belongings were fetched, we kept them at our house, we had those old people live with us.

[FA:] hm!

And her daughter, she had been the only one that woman had, that was her only surviving daughter. So now that old woman gave her grandchild to my mother to adopt and have her as her daughter, you know?

[FA:] Indeed.

And truly so it was, for she was given to her, and so she truly had her for an adopted daughter,

[FA:] mhm.

the one whose mother it was [*sc.* that was killed]. And it was that one, my older sister, we were also living with them when it turned

ê-kitâpamikoyâhk, ômis [*gesture*] ê-isisiniyâhk papakiwayânikamikohk, «mwêhci pisiskiwak ê-isinâko-~ ê-isinawakik,» ê-kî-itikoyâhk êsa mâna.

[FA:] hm!

kî-mâh-manitôhkâsôtotawâw ana, êwakw âwa kêhciwâk nimosôm kî-saskahamawâw ê-nanâtawihât, ê-pâh-pisiskîwinâkêt an[a] îskwêw.

[FA:] hm.

iyikohk ê-kî-kitimâkisit êkwa. îh, êkwa ôm êkwa êwako k-ây-âtotamân.

[29] kîtahtawê êwakw âwa nâpêw, êkonik ôki mâmihk, k-êtwêyân, kâ-kî-nitawi-wîhtamâhcik,

[FA:] mhm.

kîtahtawê – nîsw-âyamihêwi-kîsikâw ê-kî-ispayik, ê-kî-~ ê-kî-isi-kîsahkamikisit awa nâpêw,

[FA:] âha.

kâ-nipahisot, nîsw-âyamihêwi-kîsikâw ê-kî-ispayik, wâh-wanihastimwêw awa nâpêw, êtikwê awa,

[FA:] âha.

papâ-na-nâh-nitawastimwêw êkwa, mîna mâna sêpwêhtêt, êtikwê ê-papâ-na-nâh-nitawastimwêt; êkwa, «ê-sêskâmocik, sakâhk êtikwê ê-ayâcik,» ê-kî-~ ê-kî-itwêt ês ôh ôtêma, êkây ê-kî-miskawât. kîtahtawê ôm ê-pimi-pimohtêt ôma, sêkwah-âyihk ôma k-êtwêyân, âstamahcâhk

[FA:] âha.

(nakiwaciy ayisk anima, tâh-tâpwê anima nakiwaciy), êkot[a] ânima, kîtahtawê ês êkota kâ-pêhtawât sakâhk misatimwa ê-kâh-kitoyit (êtikwê kîkway awa misatim têpiyâhk ê-pêhtahk), kâ-pêhtahk ês êkota misatimw[a] ê-matwê-kitoyit, «hâ, êwako, êkonik kâ-wanihakik,» itêyihtam.

to fall. She was going mad, she would raise her head and watch us, it is reported, looking at us like this [*gesture*] as we lay sleeping in the tent, «They look just like animals to me,» she used to say about us, it is reported.

[FA:] hm!

She was doctored repeatedly, my grandfather himself had a pipe lit for him as he doctored her, that woman used to have people look like animals to her.

[FA:] hm.

She used to be so pitiful now. Look, this now is my account.

[29] Suddenly this man, one of those I said were living downstream, whom someone had gone and told,

[FA:] mhm.

suddenly – two weeks had passed since this man had done his terrible deed, that he killed himself,

[FA:] Indeed.

two weeks had passed, this man must have lost his horses,

[FA:] Indeed.

he went about looking for his horses and he would leave again, he must have been going about looking for his horses; then, «They fled into the bush, they must be in the bush,» he said about his horses, it is reported, since he could not find them. Suddenly as he was walking along in that sheltered place, as I said, facing the edge of the hill

[FA:] Indeed.

(for it was *nakiwaciy*, that abrupt edge of the hill, it truly was *nakiwaciy*, that abrupt edge of the hill), it was there, there suddenly, it is reported, he heard a horse whinnying in the bush (the horse at any rate must have heard something), he distinctly heard a horse whinnying there, it is reported, «Well, it is the one, the ones I have lost,» he thought.

[FA:] mhm.

kâ-sa-sêskisit êsa, ôm êkwa ê-ati-pimohtêt ôma tahk âw êtikwê misatim ê-pêhtahk ôma, mîna mâna êsa mêtwê-kitot. piyisk, âhêy, awîn ês âwa, k-ôtihtât têhtapîwatimwa. îh, ês âw êtikw âwa ê-kî-pê-têhtapit aw êkwa anima kîkisêpâ, mêtoni, mistik aw ê-cimasot, ita aw ê-sakahpisot misatim, mêton êkos îsi wâsakâm ê-paskwatâwahkihtât awa misatim, iyikohk ê-~

[FA:] ê-nôhtêhkatêt?

ê-nôhtêhkatêt, ê-nôhtêyâpâkwêt, aspapiwin ês ânima ciyêkwac ôtê watâhk ê-itamoniyik, misatim ana.

[30] êkosi; kâh-otinât [*sic*] awa nâpêw, âsay mîn êkota mistahi koskwêyihtam awa nâpêw, kâh-ay-âpihkonât [*sic*] ôhi misatimwa, pê-ma-matâwi-sâpêkinêw [*sic*]. êkosi kîwêhtahêw wîkiwâhk isi. wîhtam, ê-miskawât ôhi misatimwa, «êkoni êtik ôh ôtêht-~, êkon ôh ôtêhtapiwina ôhi, êcik ân[i] êtikwê ê-kî-pê-têhtapit awa naspi-kîkisêpâ,» itwêw ês âna nâpêw.

[FA:] âha.

êkos ânima, mîn ês êkwa kâ-pê-âmaciwêpayit ês êkwa, ê-pê-âmaciwêhtahât anihi misatimwa, asahkêwikamikohk ê-pê-itohtahât, êkota ta-wâpamiht ana misatim. îh, êwakw ânima namôy kakêtihk ê-kî-koskwêyihtâkwahk ana nâpêw ê-kî-ay-isîhcikêt, anima kâ-itahkamikisit. ah, âhêy, êkwa owâskahikaniwâw, anim ôwâskahikanisiwâw, konit ês ê-ay-itakotêyik[i] ê-wêwêpâstaniyiki an[a] ôkisîpêkinikêwina wayawîtimihk, êkwa opâsiminêwina mînisa, takwahiminâna, êkos ê-isi-sîhkastêyiki; êkos ê-ay-itastêyiki anih ôpâsiminêwina an[a] îskwêw.

[FA:] hm.

[31] êkosi; îh, êkos ânima kî-is-âyâ-~, kî-~, tânitahto-kîsikâw êtikw ê-kî-ay-ispayik anim êkw âya, pêhtâkwan mâka mîna

[FA:] mhm.

So he walked into the bush, it is reported, and now as he walked ahead closer the horse must have heard that, it could be heard whinnying again, it is reported. At last, hey, what was this?!, it is reported, he walked up to a saddle horse. Look, he must have come riding a horse that morning, it is reported, very early, there stood a tree where this horse was tied up, and in this way the horse had grazed the ground bare right around, it was so -~.

[FA:] It was hungry?

It was hungry, it was thirsty, that horse, and the saddle, it is reported, had turned around, it was over here under the belly.

[30] So it was; when the man had taken it, at that point the man was already greatly shocked about it [*sc.* the murder-suicide], when he had untied the horse, he led it back out into the open. So he took it back to their place. He reported that he had found the horse, «This must be his, his saddle horse, evidently he must have been riding it early in the morning,» that man said, it is reported.

[FA:] Indeed.

And so he rode back up the hill, it is reported, he took that horse back up the hill, he brought it back to the agency so they would see the horse there. Look, everyone was extremely shocked at the deed that man had committed, at what he had done. Well, hey, now their house, that little house of theirs, her washing, it is reported, was still hanging outside and blowing in the wind, and her berries which she was drying, chokecherries, were spread out to dry; that woman's berries were still out drying.

[FA:] hm!

[31] So it was; look, they were like that, I don't know how many days it may have been, it was heard that of course the Indian

sôniyâwikimâw, ê-wî-pê-ispayicik êkota simâkanisak, êkwa ê-wî-atâwâkêwiht anih ôcayânisiwâwa.

[FA:] mhm.

êkwa, nikâwiy ôki mâka mîna kî-itohtêwak anima wîstawâw, kî-âh-itohtêwak iskwêwak tahtw-~ ê-kî-nisitawêyihtâkosicik ayis, ê-nicawi-nîhtinamwâcik [*sic*] okisîpêkinikêwina, mîn ânihi omînisimiyiwa ê-nitawi-mâwasakonahkik. êkota iskohk kâ-kiskêyihtamân.

[32] êwakw âna mîna, îh, êkospî iyikohk ê-kî-sôhkêpayik anima nipahtâkêwin, kinwês anima mitoni namôy ê-ohci-pô-~-pônipayik êwakw ân[i] ânima, iyikohk ê-kî-koskwêyihtâkwahk. anohc êkwa kapê-kîsikâw ka-pêhtamahk, awiyak ka-ma-mâyinikêt, tâpiskôc êkwa konita, iyikohk mistah ê-ma-mâyinikêcik anohc ayisiyiniwak.

[FA:] mhm.

miton ânima mosci tâpiskôc ê-ay-âtayôhkêhk, ê-ay-itihtâkwahk êwak ôm âcimowin, miton ôm êkosi ê-isi-ta-tâpâcimoyân anima, ê-kî-isi-ka-kiskêyimak-~ ê-kî-isi-ka-kiskêyihtamân anima, kêswân êkota ê-ayâyân. êkosi mîna kî-wâh-wiyasiwâniwiw, kî-pâh-pîkiskwêhâw ana nôtikwêw, tânis ânima kêhtinâc anima;

[FA:] âha.

êkwa mân ê-kî-pê-~ ê-kicocihc mâna, ê-kî-kitotâcik ôki nikâwiy, anima kâ-itâcimot, êkâ ta-kakwê-patâcimot

[FA:] âha.

nêtê pîkiskwêhihci, êkosi mân ê-kî-isi-kakêskimâcik anihi nôcikwêsiwa.

[FA:] hm.

wahwâ, kî-koskwêyihtâkwan, nikiskisin anima mâna.

agent, that the police were going to ride there and that their clothes were going to be sold.

[FA:] mhm.

Now my mother and the others had gone there again themselves, the women had gone there, for they were well known, they went and took down her washing, and picked up her berries. That is as far as I know it.

[32] It also was that man, look, at that time, the murder had been so violent, it really did not cease being talked about for a long time, it was found so shocking. Today now we will hear about it all day long that someone has committed a crime, it seems like nothing now, people are committing so many serious crimes today.

[FA:] mhm.

It very much seems as if one were simply telling a made-up story, as if this account sounded like that, I am reporting it exactly the way it took place, the way I knew-~ the way I knew it step by step, it so happened that I was there. Now they also held court proceedings, that old woman was questioned about how it actually happened;

[FA:] Indeed.

in the meantime she'd had some tutoring, my mother and the others had tutored her about her account, the intention being that she would not swerve from her account

[FA:] Indeed.

when she was questioned over yonder, in this way they had counselled that little old woman.

[FA:] hm.

Oh my, it was found shocking, I always remember that.

[33] êkos êkwa kî-ati-ta-takwâkin, êkwa anim êkwa miton ânim êkwa ê-~, êkos âni kî-~ kî-ay-âstêpayiw an[a] êtikwê kisêyiniw ana kâ-kî-~, êwak ôm êcik ôma êtik ôma kâ-kî-kostahk ôma,

[FA:] âha.

îh, anima pisisik kâ-kî-kakwê-papâ-ay-âhtokêyâhk, mîn ânima, «wani-tipiskâw,» k-êtwêt. êkos âyis mâna itwâniwiw, tâpiskôc ê-wani-tipiskâk, ita maci-kîkway kâ-wî-ispayik, kikiskêyihtên.

[FA:] êha.

êkos ê-kî-isinahkik ôki kayâs ôki kêhtê-ayak, kîkway kâ-kiskêyihtahkik; êkwa wâsêyâw, êkota ê-kanâtahk, êwakw ân[i] ânima, kâ-wâsêk-îsinahkik [*?sic*] nânitaw.

[FA:] mhm.

êkos ânima kayâs ê-kî-pê-ispayik; kî-koskwêyihtâkwan anim, êkospî ê-kî-itahkamikisit ana nâpêw.

[34] êkwa anima mîna nîkân, êcik ânima êkâ katawâhk ê-wî-ispayik. kâ-kî-omosômiyân, êwakw âwa pêyakwan aw ôwiyasiwêhkân, asahkêwikamikohk ê-isitâpâsot. êkot[ê] êtikw ê-otami-pâh-pîkiskwêcik ôki nâpêwak, êkota anim êcik âni mîna êkâ kwayask an[a] ê-tôtahk ana. ê-ati-sipwêhtêt êkwa ê-wî-pê-sipwêtâpâsot ês ôm êkwa, ita ê-kî-sakahpitât awa wêtêmit, awîn âwa kî-apiyiwa ôhi pêyak otêma, mitoni misi-takahkatimwa, kî-mostapiyiwa êsa, êkw âwa pêyak ê-na-nîpawiyit otôtâpahâkana. atimwa anihi, otêmiwâw[a] ê-kî-ca-cîpacihtawakêyit mâna, tâpiskôc simâkanisîwatim,

[FA:] mhm.

kiki-pimâtis anihi misatimwa ê-kî-kîs-kîskihtawakêmât.

[FA:] hm.

îh, êwakw ânim êcik ânima sê-~, ana, atim anima sêmâk môy kwayask ê-ohci-tôtahk.

[33] So now it was becoming fall, and it was really –~, so it was getting better, what that old man evidently must have been fearing,

[FA:] Indeed.

look, we had been trying to move somewhere else with our camps all the time, and, «It is dark,» is what he said. For that used to be said, it seems dark where something bad is going to happen, you know.

[FA:] Indeed.

In the old days it looked like that to the old people, the ones who had knowledge of things; and it is light, at that point it is clean, it is that where it looks bright to them.

[FA:] mhm.

That did happen in the old days; it was found shocking at the time when that man committed that crime.

[34] Now there is also the portent beforehand when, as it turns out, something awful is going to happen. My late grandfather, that same councillor, was driving to the agency with his wagon. The men must have been preoccupied with talking over there, and at that point that one, as it turns out, did something which was not right. As he was leaving and about to drive away with his wagon, it is reported, where the owner of the horses had tied them up, what was this?! one of the horses was down, a really nice horse, it was simply down there on the ground, it is reported, and one of his team was standing up. That dog, their dog, with pointed ears just like a police dog,

[FA:] mhm.

had bitten off both its ears, of the live horse.

[FA:] hm.

Look, that was something, as it turns out, that dog straight away did something that was not right.

[35] êkosi; kî-pâskisw-~ sêmâk êkota kî-pâskiswêwak anihi, nitawi-wîhtam ayisk awa kisêyiniw. otasahkêw ôm ê-kî-opâskisikanit, «môy âwa kwayask ê-tôtahk awa, awa kâ-tôtahk,» nitaw-îtwêw ês âwa wiyasiwêhkân, «kîkway awa, ê-wîh-~, ê-at-~ ê-wî-kakwê-kiskêyihtamôhiwêt aw âtim kâ-tôtahk,» k-êtât êsa, «namôy nitêma awa niwî-nipahimâwa, wiya ta-nipiw,» ê-itwêt ês âna wiyasiwêhkân.

[FA:] hm!

êkosi pâskiswêwak nâpêwak anih âtimwa.

[36] îh, êwakw ânima nîkân ê-kî-ispayik; êwakw ânim êkwa nawac ê-ati-takwâkik, anima kâ-kî-tôta-~-itahkamikisit ana nâpêw.

[FA:] hm.

mâmaskâc, ê-koskwêyihtâkwahk êwakw ânim ê-kî-~, êkospîhk ê-kî-ispayik, îh. êkos ânima môy sêmâk anim ôhci-kiskêyihtâkwan anima, mwêstas êkwa mâna kî-pa-pêhtâkwan ana nôhtâwiy, wiy ânima nôhtâwiy ê-kî-kâhkwêyimikot anihi nâp-~, anihi nâpêwa.

[FA:] mhm.

êkos ânima.

[35] So it was; straight away they shot –~, at that point they shot that one, for the old man went to tell about it. The farm instructor had a gun, «It is doing something that is not right, the one who has done this,» the councillor went and said, it is reported, «the dog did it for a reason, it was going to try and provide a sign for people by doing that,» is what he said to them, it is reported, «I am not going to kill my horse but this one, it is to die,» that councillor said, it is reported.

[FA:] hm.

So the men shot that dog.

[36] Look, that happened beforehand; that was earlier that fall when that man had committed that crime.

[FA:] hm.

It was strange, it was found shocking at the time when that happened, look. And that was not known straight away but later on it was heard that it was my father, for it was my father of whom that man had been jealous.

[FA:] mhm.

That is all.

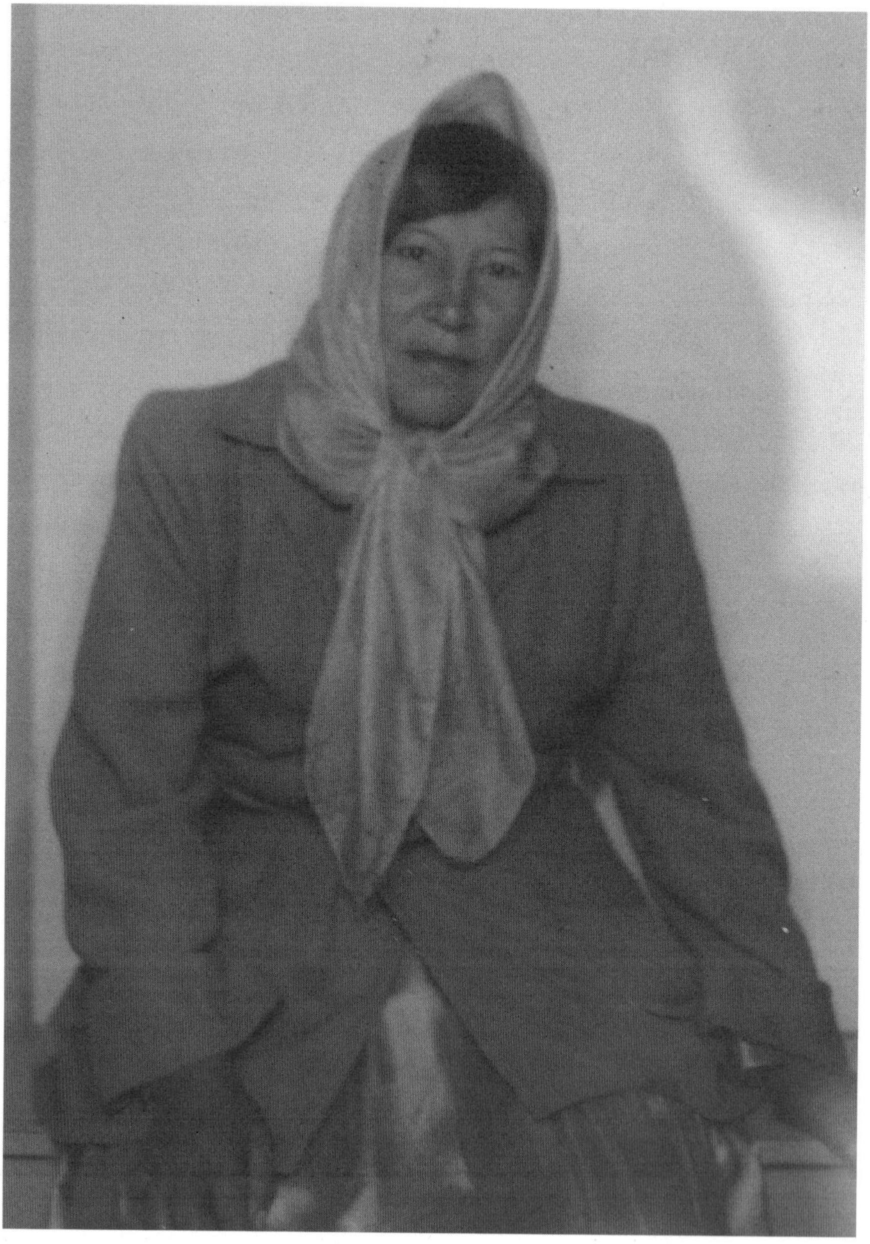

Sarah Whitecalf, c. 1952.

7

ê-nipahi-kâh-kaskêyihtamân

I was desperately lonesome

ê-nipahi-kâh-kaskêyihtamân

[1] â, âsay mîn ôta niwî-pîkiskwân anohc; anohc êkwa, iskwayâc ôta kit-âyâyâhk, niya *Mrs Whitecalf* kâ-papâmohtêyâhk awa niwîcêwâkan; êkos êkwa iskwayât ôta, niwî-âcimoscawâsiw isko ta-wîcêwak. mitoni nitakahkêyihtên ôta kâ-pê-itohtêyân, miywâsin, êkoyikohk miywâsin. pêyakwan mâka isi-mâh-mâyi-kîsikâw tâpiskôt ôtê, itê k-ôhtohtêyâhk ôma sâskwatôn, pêyakwan isi-~ môy miyo-kîsikâw, wâwîs cî ôta sa-~ wâwîs cî ôm ôtê nâtakâm, mitoni wâhyaw k-âyâyâhk.

[2] êkos êkwa, pêyak niwî-âtotên kêyâpic âcimowinis, ê-kî-pakwâtamân mistahi, ê-kî-misi-pâhkacipayihoyân mitoni. kîtahtawê ôtê nipê-nâtikawinân, akâmi-tipahaskân pêyak ê-ohci-takopayit nikosis, pê-nîsiwak nâpêwak, pêyak owîcêwâkana. kâ-pê-takopayicik, mitoni namôy ê-ay-aswêyihtamân, kayâs ê-kî-sipwêhtêt, akâmi-tipahaskân ê-kî-isi-sipwêhtêt ê-oskinîkit; êkos êkotê kî-nitawi-ma-mêcimwâcîw ê-nitaw-âtoskêt, nama wîhkâc ohci-pê-kîwêw, piyisk êkotê nikî-pa-pêhtênân, «ê-wîwit,» ê-itiht, «pîkaniwiyinîwiskwêsa.»

[3] êkwa, kîtahtaw êkwa kâ-takohtêt anim êkwa, wahwâ, wêsk âniyê êkwa ê-pê-nâtikoyâhk, niy êkwa nikisêyinîma kahkiyaw sôskwâc, ê-wî-kakwê-sipwêhtahikoyâhk êkotê is âkâmi-tipahaskân – pôti mâk êkwa, nikisêyinîm awa, miton ê-atoskêt sôskwâc sôhki môniyâsinâhk, tahto-kîsikâw sôskwâc ê-itohtêt môniyâsinâhk, okistikêwiyiniwa ê-atoskawât. êkos êkwa wiya sôskwât mitoni môy cîhkêyihtam kit-êtohtêt, êkwa mîn âwa nikosisinân osîmimâs,

I was desperately lonesome

[1] Well, as usual I am going to speak on here [*sc.* on the audio-recorder] today; today is our last day here [*sc.* at Lac La Ronge], I am Mrs Whitecalf and I am travelling around with my partner; this is the last day now, I am going to tell her a little story so long as I am with her. I am very happy that I have come here, it is nice, it is so nice. But the weather is just as cold as over there in Saskatoon where we have come from, it is the same bad weather, especially –~ especially since we are a long way north over here.

[2] Now then I am still going to tell another little story, I thoroughly hated the experience, I had very much got myself into a terrible predicament. At one time a nephew of mine arrived over here to fetch us, he drove up from the States, there were two of them, both men, he and a friend of his. They came driving up when I was least expecting them, he had left long ago, he had left for the States as a young man; so he had gone to stay over there for good and gone to work, he had never come back home, and finally we had been hearing from over there, «He is married,» it was said of him, «to some Piegan woman.»

[3] Now, it was all of a sudden now that he arrived, oh my, out of the blue now he had come to fetch us, me and my old man all in one fell swoop, he was going to try and take us over there to the States – but what was this, at that time my old man was very much committed to work amongst the Whites, he went to a Whiteman's place every day, he was working for a farmer.

ê-kiskinohamâkot, nawac êkoni nôhtê-kisâtêw, namôy nôhtê-sipwêhtahêw. wahwâ, niy êkwa, niy êkwa niwâh-wîsâmik, ês ôma ê-wêpiniht, ê-wêpinikot owîkimâkana, nikotwâsik ocawâsimis[a] ê-kiki-wêpinikot, kâhtap ê-ispîhtisiyit, omisimâsa kêkâ-mitâtaht ê-itahtopiponêyit, êkwa êkota ohci, nâpêsisa matwân cî ê-pêyakopiponêyit, katisk ê-papâ-~-wî-papâmohcêsiyit, êkoni ôhi ê-kiki-wêpiniht kahkiyaw ocawâsimisa. «namôy kinwês, kanakê ahpô pêyak-pîsim, ê-atoskêyân ôma pîwâpisko-mêskanâhk nîsta,» nititikonân. mitoni kwayask nitasotamâk, ta-pê-isi-pê-kîwêwak wî-pê-kîwêyâni, ta-pê-kîwêhtahit ahpw ê-p-~, ahpô ta-pê-nômohtahit, awê-~ ta-pê-pôsiyân pwasihk, êkosi nitis-âsotamâk.

[4] yoh, âta nawac piko niwî-âyimêyihtên, mâk êkwa mîna, pêyak-pîsim ta-kakwê-kaskihtâyân, ta-nitaw-âyâyân êkotê. wahwâ, kiyâm kâ-~, «wiya k-~ têpêyimoci kikâwîs,» itik ôhcâwîsa, «wiya têpêyimoci, wiya kika-wîcêwâw; wiya ka-kîwêhtahâw,» itik, «niy êkwa niy ôta awâsisak nika-kanawêyimâwak,» itwêw, âta wiya nitânis ô-~, awa nitânis awa, êkwa ôh ôtawâsimisa, êkwa niy âwa pikw âw ôskinîkîs awa, êwako piko niya ta-nakatak âta wiya; êkosi. wahwâ, tiyêpêyimoyân êkwa niya, ê-wâh-wawêyîyân êkwa. ê-kîsi-wawêyîyân êkwa, wâpahk[i] êkwa t-êsi-sipwêhtêyân. wahwâ, mistahi nimâh-mâmitonêyihtên ât[a] ôma; tânisi? êkwa êkospîhk, mitoni namôy nôh-~, namôy nôh-na-nihtâ-âkayâsîmon, mîna namôy nôh-nihtâ-papâmâcihon. kâ-têpêyimoyân êkwa kiyâm, wiyâpahk, tâpwê ê-pimi-takopayicik – mitoni wiya takahkitâpânêw, miton ôskitâpâna ê-âpacihât.

So now he was not very keen in the first place to go over there, and then also our youngest son was in school and he [my husband] wanted rather to stay with him, he did not want to take him out. Oh my, as for me now, now he kept asking me to go with him since he had evidently been left on his own, his wife had left him, she had left him with his six children, with their ages at regular intervals one after the other, from the eldest girl who was nine years old on down to a little boy who was, I think, about one year old and just beginning to walk, he had been left with all these children of his. «Not for long, for no more than one month, I for my part am working on the railroad,» he said to us. He earnestly promised me that he would have a way for me to come back home when I was going to come back home, that he would even bring me back home or bring me part of the way home and I would come home on the bus, this he promised me.

[4] Ho, although I was kind of hesitant, now I also was to try and manage it for one month, to go and stay over there. Oh my, alright, «If your auntie agrees,» his paternal uncle told him, «if she agrees she is to go with you; you are to take her home,» he said to him, «then I for my part will look after the children here,» he said, though of course there was my daughter, this daughter of mine and her children, and as for me there was only this adolescent boy now, as for me, on the other hand, I would only leave that one behind; that was it. Oh my, as for me now, as I came to agree, now I made my preparations. Having completed my preparations, now I was to leave the next morning. Oh my, my thoughts were greatly troubled, however; what was I doing? Now at that time I did not speak any English at all, and I had no experience of travelling around. Now that I had agreed, alright, the next morning they duly drove up – he did have a very nice car, he was driving a brand-new car.

[5] êkosi; kâ-~ êkwa kâ-sipwê-wîcihiwêyân [?*sic*], êy, aspin piko nitawâsisimak ê-mawîhkâsicik nikosis ê-mawîhkâsit, nôsisi-~ kahkiyaw nitânis mîna, ê-mawîhkâsicik êkwa ê-wî-sipwêpayiyâhk. êkosi, tâ-~ mêtoni sôskwâc ôtê isi, nimitâw âpihtâ-kîsikâhk isi ê-isi-sipwêpayiyâhk, tânitê êtikwê piko nama wîhkâc êkotê ê-papâ-wâpahtamân. êy, mâninakisk nipimipayihtâh, nimisi-~ nimisi-nîpâpayinân, niwâpani-pimipayinân sôskwât, nama kîkway nipimi-wâpahtên, ê-kîsikâk ê-misi-wâpani-pimipayiyâhk, tânitê êtikwê ôcênâs pêyak. êkw êkota, nitat-ôtihtênân ê-kîkisêpâyâk, êkot[a] ân[i] êkwa nitati-nîhtakosînân, êkota ê-ati-kîkisêpâ-mîcisoyâhk. «môy wâhyaw ôta ohci,» nititik, «kêkâ-mitâtahtosâp-tipahaskân piko, ôta ohci, *Lethbridge*,» itwêw awa nikosis, «êwako 'kaskaskisêhkânihk' k-êsiyîhkâtahkik nêhiyawak,» itwêw. êkosi, âsay mîna sêpwêpayiyâhk ê-kî-kîsi-mîcisoyâhk, tâpwê namôy nitâhtêyihtên, namôy îspi-kîsikâw, êkotê ê-takopayiyâhk, ôm ôtênâw, 'kaskaskisêhkânihk' k-êsiyîhkâtahk.

[6] êkosi; êkwa niy êkwa, êkot[a] êkwa kêsiskaw mîna nitasamikwak; êkwa wiyawâw kêsiskaw ê-papâmipahtâcik ôtênâhk, nêhiyawa ê-kakwê-wâpamâcik, awiya *Saskatchewan* ohci; nayawâs pê-takohtêwak, mitoni nam âwiya wa-wâpamêwak. êkota anim êsa mâc[i] ôhci [*sic*], ôki mâna kâ-kî-nitawi-tâh-tasîhkahkik kistikâna, kâ-kî-pê-misi-nâh-nâtihcik, êkotow[a] [*sic*] ânim ê-ihtatêyimâcik, êkota nânitaw t-âyâyit, «êkoni ôh âskiya mâna kâ-pê-atoskâtahkik ôki, *Saskatchewan* ohci,» nititik. êkos ân[i] êkwa mîna sêpwêpayiyâhk.

[7] mîn êkota namôy nitâhtêyihtên, «âsay ôm êkota,» k-êtwêt, «mâcikôcican, nikâwîs! êkota ôm ê-mâc-âyâcik ôki pîtos-âyisiyiniwak,» itwêw. mîn êkot[a] ânima môy ê-âhtêyihtamân,

[5] So it was; when I left with them now, hey, the last I saw of my children was that they were crying for me, my son was crying for me, my grandchi-~ my daughter too and all her children were crying for me now as we were going to drive off. That was it, we drove straight in that direction over there, out onto the open prairie towards the south, wherever we were going I had never before seen any of the land over there. Hey, we drove and drove, we drove deep into the night, we drove right until dawn, I could not see anything, day broke and we had travelled all the way until the dawn, I don't know where but there was a little town. That place now we came to at daybreak, there now we got out of the car, there we had breakfast. «It is not far from here,» he said to me, «only nineteen miles from here to Lethbridge,» my nephew said, «that *Kaskaskisêhkânihk* as the Crees call it,» he said. In due course, then, as we were driving off again after we had finished our breakfast, it was true, I did not think it was far, it was not late in the morning as we drove into this town he had called *Kaskaskisêhkânihk*.

[6] So it was; as for me now, there now they fed me again, quite soon; as for them now, they took a little time to run around the town trying to see some Crees, someone from Saskatchewan; they had no luck and came back, they did not see anyone at all. It was evidently from there initially that they used to come and always fetch them in great numbers, those who used to go and work the [sugarbeet] farms, they were expecting that kind to be about there, «These are the fields in which they usually come to work, from Saskatchewan,» he said to me. With that now we were driving off again.

[7] There also I did not think it was far when he said, «Here it is already,» he said, «Just watch, my auntie! This is where these different people start to live,» he said. There also

iyikohk âsay ê-otihtamâhk pîtos-âyisiyiniwak, êkonik anik âya, 'mihkoyiniwak' k-êtâcik, êkonik nîkân otaskîhkâniwâw, êkota nitat-ôtihtênân, êwakw ê-ati-miyâ-~, êwako ê-kisipiskamâhk êtikw ânim âskîhkân, êy, âsay êkota mâh-miyakinâkwan, iyikohk ê-âh-ispâki asinîwaciya, mitoni wiya nitati-takahkêyihtên, êkota wiy ê-at-ây-itâpiyân. mâk ôhcitaw pik ôma ê-pê-asêkotêk nimâmitonêyihcikan mitoni tânis êtik-~, aspin ôki kâ-môskwaskatakik, ohtitaw tânis êtikwê nitat[i]-âh-itêyihtên; nitasi-miywêyihtên ôma kotak askiy ê-nitawâpahtamân. âsay mîn êkota nitat-ôtihtênân, êwakw ês ôm êkwa, pîkaniwiyiniwak otaskîhkâniwâw êkwa, 'prâwiniy' [*sic*] isiyîhkâtêw ôcênâs, êkota (miton âyisk aniki ê-ôtênâwihtâcik ês âniki, mêkwâ-ôcênâsihk ê-wâh-wîkicik ôki, pîkaniwiyiniwak), êkota mîna nitati-nakînân, êkotê ês ôma, ocawâsimisa nîsw ê-kî-pê-astahcikot, ocânis[a] êkw ânih ôpêpîma, êkonik êkwa ê-ati-naskwênâyâhkok anik âwâsisak. â, mâmâsîs ani nitas-~ nitasamikonân awa pîkaniwiyinîwiskwêw, mitoni nama kîkway cacîhk, ê-itasamikoyâhk awa pîkaniwiyinîwiskwêw awa. êkota ohc êkwa nisipwêpayinân. mwêhci nîso ôcênâsa ê-~ ê-otihtamâhk, êkota nitakopayinân, môy ôtâkosin, êkw êkwa, tahkâ-~, êkota ês ôma êkwa k-âyât, k-âtoskêt awa nikosis; 'selpiy' isiyîhkâtêw êwak ôcênâs anima; êyiwêhk êwak ôma miton êwako miywâsin.

[8] êkosi; êy, nipim-~ tânitê êtikwê piko ê-pimipayiyâhk, wîkihk êkwa. tâpwê nitôtihtênân, wîki anim îta ê-ayât. êy, ocawâsimisa ôhi, n-~ niyânan (niyânan ahpô cî nêwo) ê-nakatât nâpêsisa, êkonik, pêyak oskinîkiwa ê-kî-kanawêyimâwasôhât êkota êkon ê-wîtapimâyit, kiskinohamâtowikamikohk ê-itohtêcik aniki nôsisimak. nitakohtânân êkota. îhaw [*sic*], âsay êkwa ê-wî-tipiskâk, âsay êwako mistahi nimâmitonêyihtên êkota, «ê-pâhkacipayihoyân,» ê-itêyihtamân; mitoni nam âwiyak iskwêw,

I did not think it was long before we already came up to where these different people are, the 'Blood people' as they called them, it is their reserve first, we were coming up to that, and as we reached the end of that reserve, I guess, hey, it already looked strange here and there, so high were the Rocky Mountains, I was very happy to look out as we went past them. But it was unavoidable that my mind turned right back, to how things might be, the last I had seen of them was that I had left them behind crying, I had to keep thinking of how things might be [*sc.* back home]; at the same time I was glad to be seeing another country. In due course now we were coming up to that place now, evidently the reserve of the Piegans now, Browning the little town is called, there (for they really make a town evidently, the Piegan people live right in the little town), there we also stopped, over there he had evidently left two of his children to be looked after when he came, his little daughter and that baby, now we came by on our way and picked those children up. Well, that Piegan woman gave us a very perfunctory lunch, that Piegan woman gave us nothing especially good to eat. Now we drove off from there. Afterwards we came up to two little towns, there we arrived and drove in, it wasn't evening yet, evidently it was there now that he lived, it was where my nephew worked; Shelby that little town is called; all in all, it was quite a nice little town.

[8] So it was; hey, wherever we must have been driving, now we were at his house. Truly we came up to his house where he lived. Hey, his children, five (five or four), he had left these little boys behind, he had engaged a young man to look after the children and he was staying there with them, these grandnieces and grandnephews of mine went to school. There we drove up. Well now, it was already getting dark now, already I was seriously having second thoughts there, «I've got myself into a quite a

nam âwiyak ê-nisitawêyimak, wiyawâw piko *Saskatchewan* ohci. êy, êkwa ani, «matwân cî ôma nika-kaskihtân, pêyak-pîsim ôta kit-âyâyân,» nititêyihtên, âta miywâsiniyiw ôma wâskahikan, miyo-pamihisow mitoni pîhc-âyihk, ma kîkway wiya ta-kôtaw-ôtinamân, kisîpêkinikêpayîs ahpô pikw âyâw, wîh-kisîpêkinamawakwâwi.

[9] êkosi; kinwêsîs êkota nitayân, nitayânân, nitay-ayân, kîtahtaw êkwa, wahwâ, âsay êkwa ê-wâpahk, êkota nimâci-mâton, miton ôhcitaw piko nipîtotêyihtên, «mêtoni nimisi-pâhkacipayihon ôma,» nititêyihtên, ni-~ âsay êkota niwî-mâh-môskwêyihtên ê-wâpahk, konita mân ê-kiyohtêyân pîhc-âyihk wâskahikanihk, namôy nikî-wayawîn mîn âyisk mêkwâ-ôtênâhk, konita mân ê-kiyohtêyân pîhc-âyihk. ê-at[i]-ôt-~ ê-at-ôtâkosik mitoni, k-âp-~ pêyak kâ-pê-takwakocihk êkota iskwêw, êcik âw ôtê ohc ân[a] îskwêw, yêkawiskâwikamâhk, nêhiyawak wiy âta wiya, «â, ê-pêhtamân ôma, kiya cî ôma *Saskatchewan* k-ôhtohtêyan?» nititik aw îskwêw; «êha,» nititâw; «wahwâ,» itwêw, «namôy kakêtihk mân ê-miywêyihtamân, awiyak êkotê *Saskatchewan* k-ôhtohtêt,» itwêw, «pikw âni mâna ta-kakwê-nitawi-nakiskawak awiyak,» itwêw. «kayââs [*sic*] ôm ôta ê-ohc-âyâyâhk niyanân,» itwêw, «ê-at-~ ê-papâ-âh-atoskêt awa niwîkimâkan,» itwêw, aw îskwêw, «êkotê ôm ê-ohtoh-~, êkotê ôm ôhci niyanân, yêkawiskâwikamâhk,» itwêw aw îskwêw. êêkw [*sic*] ês ân[a] êkwa, êyiwêhk êkwa êwako, «ka-pê-kâh-kiyokâtin, an-~ môy wâhyaw ôta niwîkin,» nititik.

[10] êkosi; ohcitaw piko mistahi nikâh-kaskêyihtên, môy kakêtihk iyikohk nikâh-kaskêyihtên. mitoni mâna tâpwê ê-kî-pakwâtamân, piyisk an[i] êkwa cîkâhtaw, môy kakêtihk êkwa iyikohk tahk êkwa ninôhtê-pê-kîwân. êkwa nama kîkway mistah ê-osôniyâmisiyân, ta-kî-pê-têpinêhikêyân, wâhyaw ôm

predicament,» I was thinking; there was no woman at all, I did not know anyone, they were the only ones from Saskatchewan. Hey, and then, «I wonder if I'll manage to stay here for one month,» I thought, although it was a nice house, he had it very nice inside, I would not lack anything, he even had a washer if I was to do the laundry for them.

[9] So it was; I stayed there for quite a while, we stayed there, I was staying there, and then at one time, oh my, it was already morning now, there I began to cry, of course I still found it very strange, «I have really got myself into a terrible predicament,» I thought, in the morning already I was crying despondently there, I was aimlessly pacing about inside the house, I also could not go outside because it was right in town, I was aimlessly pacing about indoors. It was getting to be evening when a woman came rushing up there in her vehicle, lo and behold, that woman was from over there at *Yêkawiskâwikamâhk* [Sandy Lake], at least they were Crees, «Well, I heard, is it you that has come from Saskatchewan?» this woman said to me; «Yes», I said to her; «Oh my,» she said, «I am extremely glad when someone comes from over there in Saskatchewan,» she said, «I always have to try to go and meet the person,» she said. «We have been here for a long long time,» she said, «my husband goes around working,» she said, this woman said, «as for us, we are from over there, from *Yêkawiskâwikamâhk*,» this woman said. And evidently it was a little better with that one now, «I will come to visit you, I don't live very far from here,» she said to me.

[10] So it was; of course I was still terribly lonesome, I was so exceedingly lonesome. I truly used to hate it a great deal, finally it was closer to the time now, I so very much wanted to go back home all the time now. Now I did not have much money so that I would have had enough to pay [for the bus home], it was a long

âkâmi-tipahaskân, «tâpiskôt miton êkâ wîhkâc ta-takohtêyân, êkwa,» nititêyihtên, «ita kâ-kî-ohci-sipwêhtêyân.» konita mân êkwa siyîkawîtwâwi, êkwa mân âspin nêtaw-âtoskêtwâwi, êkwa niy ê-pa-pêyakwapiyân, êk ôki kahkiyaw awâsisak ê-kiskinohamâsocik. konita mân êkwa ê-wayawîyân ê-kiyohtêyân wayawîtimihk; nikitahamâkwak mîn êkâ wâhyaw ta-p-~ konita ta-pâh-papâmohtêyân, aniki kinêpikwak k-âyâcik êkotê kâ-misikiticik, 'sîsîkwêwak' k-êtâcik, êkotowahk anihi ê-kostamawicik. wahwâ, kwayask nikî-nitawi-pakwâtên, namôy kakêtihk iyikohk, miton ê-nôhtê-pê-kîwêyân, ê-nôhtê-pê-kîwêyân tahki. kîtahtawê – ômatowihk mâna wâpamonâpiskohk ê-kî-apiyân, ê-asawâpiyân êt-ôtâkosiki, nam âwiyak ê-api-~ ê-pa-pêyakwapiyân; êkotowihk mân ê-kî-apiyân ê-mâtoyân, miton âni kwayask êkospîhk mîna manitow ê-kî-kâh-kiskisiyân mâna. ê-kî-mâtoyân mân ômatowihk ê-apiyân, âpihtâ-kîsikâhk ê-itiskwêpiyân, iyikohk ê-kaskêyihtamân. kîtahtawê, ê-kî-kiskêyimikawiyân ês ôtê, êwako *Saskatchewan* anima, kâ-wîhtamâht ês âwa nikisêyinîm, «matwê-kaskêyihtam awa, nânitaw is âwa, mistahi matwê-kaskêyihtam; êkwa ôma ta-kî-kakwê-nôcihtâyêk êkwa, ta-kî-kakwê-pê-kîwêt, mistah âna kaskêyiht-~ matwê-kaskêyihtam, âpihtâ-kîsikâhk itiskwêpiw, iyikohk ê-~ mistah ê-kaskêyihtahk,» nititikawin ês ânima, îh, tâpwê anim ê-~ ê-kaskêyihtamân mitoni.

[11] êkos êkwa, êkwa mâna, wâwîs cî nika-nipân; kâh-kinwêsêskamik ê-ay-apiyân kâ-tipiskâk, kiyâm âta kâ-nipâcik awâsisak, ê-ay-apiyân mân ê-wa-wani-tipiskapiyân. kîtahtawê, wiy âta wiya kâ-takohtêcik êkotê ê-nâh-nisitawêyimakik, nêhiyawak, ôtê ohc ôtatoskêwak, êkot[ê] ê-pê-tâh-takohtêcik êkwa ôtênâhk, ê-wâh-wâpamihcik, âtiht nipê-nitawâpamikwak ê-pê-kiyokêpayicik, êyiwêhk mân êkota nômanakêsîs ê-cîhkêyihtamân, mâk êkwa mîn êkonik sêpwêhtêtwâwi, êkosi mân ê-pîkiskâtaskasicik, ê-kaskêyihtamân mâna. namôy mîna nikî-ohtaskatâwak ôki, ayisk

way across the border, «It seems as if I will never get back now,» I thought, «there where I have left from.» Every time they all used to desert the place now, every time they used to be off to go to work, then I for my part would simply be all alone and all the children were at school now. I would simply go outside and pace outside now; they also warned me not to go walking around too far, those big snakes, 'rattlers' they called them, that live there, they were afraid of those for me. Oh my, I had come to hate it deeply, so thoroughly, I really wanted to come back home, I wanted to come back home all the time. At one time – I used to sit by this kind, a window, watching for someone every time it was getting to be evening, there was no one, I was all alone; I used to sit by that kind and cry, I also most rightly used to remember God at that time. I used to cry as I sat by this kind, sitting with my face turned to the south, I was so lonesome. At one time, as they evidently knew about me over there in Saskatchewan, evidently my old man was told, «It is obvious that she is lonesome, she is not well, it is obvious that she is terribly lonesome; you should try to make an effort now so that she might try to come home, it is obvious that she is terribly lonesome, she sits with her face turned to the south, she is so terribly lonesome,» that was evidently said about me, look, it was true that I was really lonesome.

[11] So it was now, now least of all could I sleep; I would be sitting up for hours at night, even when the children were sleeping, I would be sitting up, I would be sitting in the dark. At one time at least some people arrived over there that I knew, Crees, they were workers from over here, now they were arriving over there and were being seen in town, some of them came to see me, driving up to come and visit, for a little while there I used to be cheered up despite it all, but every time they left again, their departure would leave me forlorn again, I used to be lonesome. I also could not leave

nikanawêyihtamôhikawin ôk âwâsisak, pîwâpisko-mêskanâhk aw ê-atoskêt nikosis, tahto-kîkisêpâ ê-sipwêpayit. êkwa ani, cîkâht[aw] êkwa [*sic*] kita-pê-kîwêyân, kîtahtawê nikosis ôtênâhk aw ê-kî-~ ê-pê-ohcipayit ê-pônatoskêt [*sic*], «ayi,» k-êtwêt, «miton ôma nisa-sisikotâpisinin, nikâwîs! ôta ê-wâpamak, wîst ôta ê-pê-atoskêt; ôtê ê-pê-itisahoht, ayisk nitâh-âhtitisahokawinân ôma, pîwâpisko-mêskanâhk mâna k-âtoskêyâhk,» itwêw (ôtê ayahk, â, *Rocky Boy* ê-kî-ay-atoskêt ana nisis, tipiyawê nisis, nikâwiy wîtisâna, êwako mîna kinwêsêskamik êkotê ê-kî-ayât, pîhtaw wîwa wiy êkotê ê-wîc-âyâmât otawâsimisa); êwakw ês âwa, êkotê êkwa ê-pê-atoskêt anim ôcênâsihk, êkotê ê-pê-itisahoht êkwa ta-pê-atoskêt. «niwîhtamawâw,» itwêw, «ôta ê-ayâyan, ê-kî-pêsîtân,» itwêw, «pêyak-pîsim isk ôta –~»

[*external break*]

[12] âsay mîn ôta anohc aya ê-wî-pîkiskwêyân, ê-kî-iskosîhtâyân ayi, pêyak anim âcimowin, nôhtaw ê-kî-ayi-mêscipayik, mâk êkwa ôta, êwakw ân[i] ânim ê-wî-kîsîhtâyân ê-wî-kîs-âcimoyân.

[13] â, anima k-âcimoyân, mân-~ ôtê kâ-kî-itohtêyân akâmi-tipahaskânihk, an[a] âna, kîtahtawê kâ-pê-pîhtikwêt nisis, ôta ohci wîsta *Saskatchewan* ê-~, nêtê selpiy ôtênâhk, êkotê ê-ayâyân, 'selpiy' isiyîhkâtêw anim ôtênaw, êkota ê-ayâyân, kâ-pê-wîhtamawit, «ka-kwayâci-wawêyîhkan, nistim! ka-pimi-naskwênitin ici; kinitomikawin ôtê, itê kâ-~ kâ-wîkiyâhk, ê-nitawêyimisk,» itwêw owîkimâkana, êwakw âya, *Rocky Boy*, êkotê wiy â-~ ê-ayât ana nisis, êko-~ êkotê anima t-êsi-kîwêpayit,

the children behind for I had been given responsibility for them, my nephew was working on the railroad, he drove off every morning. Then, when it was close now to the time for me to come back home, at one time my nephew came driving back from town after work, «Ah,» he said, «I had a really surprising encounter, my auntie! I saw someone here, he too has come here to work; he has been posted here, for those of us who work on the railroad sometimes get transferred,» he said (over there, well, at Rocky Boy's, this maternal uncle of mine had been working, my maternal uncle in the narrow sense, my mother's brother, he also had been living over there [*sc.* in the United States] for a long time, in fact he was living over there with his wife and children); it was this one evidently, he was coming to work over there in this little town, he had been posted now to come and work over there. «I told him,» he said, «that you are here, that I had brought you,» he said, «that you were here for one month –~»

[*external break*]

[12] As usual I am going to speak on here [*sc.* on the audio-recorder] again today, I had not finished that one story, it [*sc.* the audio-tape] had run out before I finished, but now I am going to finish it here, I am going to tell the story to the end.

[13] Well, the story I was telling, when I had gone over there to the States, it was that one, at one time my maternal uncle walked in, he is also from here in Saskatchewan, it was over yonder in the town of Shelby, I was staying over there, that town is called Shelby, I was staying there when he came to tell me, «You'll be getting ready beforehand then, my niece! I will swing by and pick you up later; you have been invited over there where we live, she wants you,» he said, referring to his wife, he, my maternal uncle, was living over there at Rocky Boy's, he was driving back

pîwâpisko-mêskanâhk mân ê-kî-papâ-atoskêt. tâpwê êkwa anim êkwa, nikwayâci-wawêyîn sêmâk, sêmâk ohci, miton âyisk nipapâsêyihtên, mîna mistahi nik-~ nikaskêyihtên, tahk âwiyak ê-nôhtê-wâpamak. tâpwê ê-wâpahk, ê-pôn-~ ê-pôyocik otatoskêwak, ê-pôn-âtoskêt [*sic*] pîwâpisko-mêskanâhk, êkota êkwa tâpwê êkwa, nikwayâci-wawêyîn êkwa, mayaw êtikwê ê-pôyot ê-kîsatoskêt [*sic*], êkosi kâ-pê-sipwêp-~ pimi-sipwêpayiw, êkota pê-takopayiw, âsay mâk âyisk nikîsi-wawêyîn.

[14] êkosi, ninaskwênik; «misawâc ayamihêwikîsikâk[i],» îtêw anihi nikosisa, «misawâc ayamihêwikîsikâki, kâwi nika-pê-kîwêhtahânân kikâwîs,» itêw, êkos âni nikîwêhtahik êkwa. êkotê êkwa, ê-itohtêyân êkwa selpiy nêtê – ayahk, nêtê aya prâwinîl [*sic*] – môya, aya, tânis ôma? *Rocky Boy* anim ôcênâs ('ôcênâsihk' ayisk wiyawâw anim îsiyîhkâtamwak nêhiyawak, anim îta otôtên-~, ocôcênâmisiwâw anima); êkos êkotê nititohtânân, â, mitoni nitati-takahkêyihtên âsay êkota wiy âta wiya mîna, ê-sipwêkociniyâhk ê-ati-wâh-wâpahtamân ê-ati-kâh-kiskinohamawit is ôma, itê is ôma mêskanaw ê-at-ây-isinâkwahk, kahkiyaw kîkway ê-ati-kâh-kiskinohamawit ê-ati-pa-pimakociniyâhk, mitoni nipâhpakwatêyihtên. ê-at-îtwahamawit mîna pêyak ispatinâw, «êwako nêma, kâ-têpinâkwahk, êwako 'maskocihciy' k-êsiyîhkâtamihk,» ê-isit ahpô pikw ânim ê-pim-ây-itâpiyâhk, ispatinâw anima. êkosi, nêtê têkopayiyâhk wîkiwâhk, êkotê êkwa, «hâ, atâwêwikamikohk pitamâ ta-kî-ispayiyahk, nawac piko kîkway niwî-nôhtêpayin, t-êsi-miyw-âsamâyahk ot[i] âwa, kistim,» itik owîkimâkana, âsay mîn êkota piyôsi-wîsâmikawiyân êkwa acâwêwikamikosihk êkwa ê-ispayiyâhk. konitênohk pêyak ôcênâs ê-ascêsik ê-apisâsiniyik, cîk êkota kêhciwâk, êkota êkwa ê-ispayiyâhk ê-nitaw-ôcinikêsicik, nipê-kîwânân, êkos êkwa mâci-kîsitêpow êkwa awa, owîkimâkana,

over there, he used to work at various places on the railroad. Now I duly got ready beforehand and made my preparations right away, right away, for I was very impatient and also terribly lonesome and always anxious to see someone. Truly the next day, when the workers stopped, when he stopped his day's work on the railroad, at that time now I had duly got ready beforehand and made my preparations, and as soon as he stopped, I guess, having finished his work, he came driving by, he drove up there, but I had already completed my preparations.

[14] So it was, he picked me up on his way home; «On Sunday, in any case,» he told my nephew, «on Sunday, in any case, I will bring your auntie back home again,» he told him, and with that he now took me home. Over there, now I went to Shelby over yonder – ah, it was over yonder to Browning – no, it wasn't, what was it? It was that little town of Rocky Boy's (*Ôcênâsihk* the Crees for their part call that little town, their little town); so there we went, well, of course I was very happy already going there, as we were charging off I was seeing various things and he was showing me how things looked where the road was going, he was showing me everything as we were speeding along, I was happily distracted. He was also pointing out one particular hill, «That one over yonder, that one which is just visible in the distance, that one is called *Maskocihciy*,» he told me about that particular hill even as we looked about on our way. So, over yonder, as we were arriving over there at their house, «Ho, we have to drive to the store first of all, I am going to be a little short of things, for us to feed your niece well,» his wife said to him, and I was again invited to get in there and come along now and drive to the little store now. It was a little town in an out-of-the-way place, it was right close by there, we drove there now and they went and did a little shopping, then we came back and with that his wife now started to cook and we ate.

nima-mîcisonân. ê-tipiskâk êwakw ân[i] ânima, âsay êkwa êkota ninôhtê-itohtahikwak, kâ-pîhtikwêpayihk mân ôma sîhkêpayîsihk [*sic*] kâ-cikâstêpayihcikêhk, êkotowihk, êkotowihk êkwa nitispayinân tâpwê, ê-nitawi-ka-kitâpahkêyâhk nîpâ-tipisk, êkos îs ê-pa-pôsapiyâhk, ot-~ sîhkêpayîsihk [*sic*]; ê-kîsi-pôy-~, ê-kîsi-pônipayik anima cikâstêpayihcikêwin nipê-kîwêpayinân. nîso-tipiskâw êkota nikî-ayân, êkw ânima wiyâpahk, ôtênâhk êkwa nitispayinân, êyiwêhk mitoni wêhcicawês nipapâm-ôtinikêhikwak, êkwa mîna wîstawâw ê-atâwêstamawicik kîkway, ê-pê-ay-~ ê-pê-itisahahkik ôtê ôma.

[15] êkosi; êhay, êkw êkwa ê-ayamihêwikîsikâk wiyâpahk, ê-ayamihêwikîsikâk êkwa kâ-wawêyî-~ kâ-wawêyîyâhk êkwa, êkw ê-wî-kîwêhtahicik kâwi prâwiniy îsi [*sic*] – mô-~, môy nêtê, 'selpiy' anima k-êsiyîhkâtêk ôtênaw; êkosi nisipwêpayinân. pôt ê-takopayiyâhk êkotê, nikosis awa, wiya pikw ây-apiw, otawâsimisa âta wiy ê-wîtapimât, «ây!» itwêw, masinahikan nipê-miyik, «ôm ôm ê-takopayik,» itwêw, «nôhcâwîs ê-pê-itisahamâsk, miyâmâc êkwa ê-pê-nâtitisahokawiyan ta-kîwêyan,» nititik, «masinahikan ôm», îtwêw; «êkwa mîna ôta awa sôniyâw nikanawêyimâw, nikî-otinâw wiy êwako, mâk ôta nikanawêyimâw. êkoni ê-pê-itisahwât, sôniyâwa ôhi, êwako k-ôh-itêyihtamân, miyâmât ta-kîwêyan êkw ê-nitawêyihtahk,» itwêw. êkosi tâpwê, nimiyik ôhi sôniyâwa, êk ôma masinahikan êkwa, nimiyik mîna, êwako nitayamihtân; pôti tâpwê awa, kâ-pê-masinahamawit ôma, ê-nitawêyihtahk êkwa ta-kakwê-pê-kîwêyân, «mitoni kikôtawêyimikwak awâsisak, ôta ôma êkwa ta-kî-kakwê-pê-kîwêyan êkwa; kîspin namôy kiwî-pê-kîwêhtahikawin, kîspin namôy kikaskihon, êwakw âwa kakwê-pê-âpacih awa sôniyâs ta-pê-kîwêyan! wîpac, nipapâsêyihtênân êkwa, ta-kakwê-takosiniyan,» nipê-it-~ pê-itasinahikêw awa nikisêyinîm. â, miton êkwa nicîhkêyihtên, kêswân ôma mitoni ê-wî-nipahi-kâh-kaskêyihtamân, miton

That same night now they already wanted to take me to a place where you drive in and they show a movie while you are in your car, and in due course we drove to that kind of place and went to watch the movie in the dark of night as we sat in the car; when that movie was finished we drove back home. I stayed there for two nights, and the next morning now we drove to town, they went around and made me buy quite a bit really, and they too were buying things for me which they were sending back over here.

[15] So it was; hey, and now on Sunday morning, it was on Sunday now that we got ready, now they were taking me back to Browning again, no, not over yonder, Shelby that town is called; so we drove off. What was this, when we drove up over there, only my nephew was at home, although he was looking after his children. «Hey!» he said and gave me a letter, «This one arrived,» he said, «my paternal uncle sent it to you, I believe you are being sent for now to go back home,» he said to me, «this is the letter,» he said; «and here I have also been keeping this money, I took that but I have been keeping it here. He sent that, this money, that is why I think that he wants you to go home now, I believe,» he said. And so it was indeed, he gave me the money and he also gave me the letter, and I read it; what was this, he had indeed written to me that he wanted me to try to come back home now, «The children really miss you, you should try to come back home here now; if he is not going to bring you back home, if you do not prevail, try to use this money to come back home! Soon, we are impatient for you to try and arrive,» my old man wrote. Well, now I was very excited, it was the very moment when I was going to be so desperately lone-

êkwa namôy âyiwâk sôskwât ê-nôhtê-kisâtamân, sôskwâc êkwa tahto-kîsikâw miton ê-mâmitonêyihtamân, ê-nôhtê-pê-kîwêyân, mistah âyisk nikî-nitawi-kakwâtakêyihtên. nimiyw-âyân, nimiyo-pamihik, mîcisowinihk isi nikî-miyo-pamihik mistahi nikosis ana. mâk êkwa nikaskêyihtamowinihk, êwakw ânima n-~ kâ-kî-mâyi-tôtâkoyân, osâm mistahi ê-kî-nitawi-pîkiskâtisiyân.

[16] êkos êkwa, tâpwê êkwa, niwawêyîn, ê-wâpahk êkwa, «wâpahki, wî-kîwêyani, môy nânitaw wâpahk[i],» îtwêw, êkosi wiy ôki nisis wâyonipayiwak kâwi, kâw ê-kîwêpayicik êkosi. niy êkwa, kiskê-~ nikiskêyihtamôhâw êkw âna nisis awa, êkosi ta-pê-kîwêyân, hêy, miton êkwa kwayask niwawêyîn, sôskwâc êkwa wiy ê-kî-kîsâc-~ kwayask mân ê-itaskinahcikêyân pôsîwiwata.

[17] wiyâpahk kîkisêpâ, *bus* êkwa êkot[ê] ohti ta-pê-otinak, selpiy anita, iskw ânita tipahaskânihk, êkota isko ê-wî-pê-itoht-~ ta-pê-pôsiyân, êkotê ohci pwas, «â,» itêw otôskinîkîma (pêyak ana côhcôsis êkotê ê-kî-ay-ayât ê-kî-wîc-âyamât ôhi nikosisa, êkoni ôhi kâ-itât (mistahi wiya takahkitâpânêw, tânêhk êtikw âwa kâ-kî-âyimêyihtahk ta-pê-kîwêhtahit?); êkota êkwa pîhtaw ê-mâtatoskêt êkwa anima mitoni kâwi pîwâpisko-mêskanâhk); «â,» itwêw –~ k-êtât ôhi, «niya nîkân kik-êtohtahin, itê k-âtoskêyân; êkos êkwa ka-pê-kîwêhtahâw awa sîhkêpayîs [*sic*], nikâwîs êkwa, kik-êtohtahâw ôta, ôcênâsihk, ta-nitaw-~ ka-nitawi-pôsihâw pwasihk, kwayask ka-wiyihcikêstamawâw, *ticket* mîna kik-âtâwêstamawâw,» itêw ôh âyahk, ôhi côhcôsisa, «ka-wîht-~ ka-wîhtamawâw ana *bus-driver*, 'isko tipahaskânihk awa ê-wî-ati-pôsit, êkota ohci kotaka t-ôtinât pwasa,' êkosi kik-êtâw,» itwêw. tâpwê êkwa, «'niya nîkân kik-êtohtahin, nitâyimêyihtên nikâwîs ta-nôsawâpamak, wiya nîkân t-âti-sipwêhtêt, nawat niya nîkân êkâ –~ niya-~ nawat niya nîkân ta-sipwêhtêyân,» itwêw

some, now I simply did not want to stay any longer, now I was simply agonising about it every day, I wanted to come back home for I had come to suffer dreadfully. My health was good, I was well looked after, when it came to food that nephew of mine had looked after me extremely well. But in my lonesomeness, that is what brought me down, for I had come to be so utterly forlorn.

[16] So it was now, in due course now I got ready, and in the morning now, «Tomorrow, if you are going to go home, it is alright tomorrow,» he said, and with this my maternal uncle and his wife turned around and drove back again, with that they now drove back home again. But as for me, I let my maternal uncle know that I would be going home that way, hey, now I really got ready properly, right away now I made a neat job of packing my suitcases.

[17] Early in the morning I was to take the bus from over there now, from Shelby, up to the border, that was as far as I would ride it, the bus from over there, «Well,» he said to his young man (there was one of the *Côhcôsis* family staying over there, he was staying with my nephew, this is the one he told (he had a very nice car, I wonder why he was so reluctant to take me back home himself?); of course he was starting back to work full-time on the railroad then); «Well,» he said –~ he said to this one, «you will first take me to where I work; then you will bring the car back and then you will take my auntie here to the little town and go and put her on the bus, you will make all the necessary arrangements for her and also buy the ticket for her,» he said to this *Côhcôsis*, «you will tell the bus driver, 'She is going to ride as far as the border, from there she is to take another bus,' you will tell him that,» he said. And truly now, « 'First you will take me, I cannot stand the sight of my auntie leaving, for her to be leaving first, it will be better if I don't –~ it will be better if I leave first,» my nephew said, and

awa nikosis, êkosi kâ-ay-atamiskawak, aspin êkwa ê-sipwêpayicik. wîpac ôma n-~, kâ-takopayit kâw âwa oskinîkiw, têpiyâhk ayisk ôcênâsihk ê-kî-nitawi-nîhtiniht awa, pîwâpisko-mêskanâhk ê-nitaw-âtoskêt, êkos êkwa niy êkwa nipâh-pôsihcikânân, êkos êkwa nititohtahik êkwa pwas-tîpow êkwa, itê ê-ayâk, êkot[ê] êkwa, hâ, nipômêyâpisinin pwas ê-isinâkosit, iyikohk ôtê ôki kiyânaw ê-mâh-miyosicik pwasak, nipômêyâpisinin awa pwas k-ê-~ kâ-wî-pê-pôsiyân awa, kanakêkâ apisîsisiw. êkosi, tâpwê kwayask wiyihcikêw êtikw âwa, êkota isko ta-pê-pôsiyân, tipahaskânihk. êkosi nipê-sipwêkocin-~ nipê-sipwêkocinin, namôy nânitaw nititêyihtên; miton êkospî mêmohci nama kîkway mistahi icwêscamâsowinis ê-ohc-âyâyân, mâk êkwa mîn êkwayâc êkospîhk tâpwê pikw ê-kî-sipwêhtêyân wâhyaw isi.

[18] êkosi; anita kwayask mitoni nitakohtân, â, '*Sweetgrass*' isiyîhkâtêw anima tipahaskân, êkota anim êkwa ta-nîhtakosîyân, êkwa 'wîhkaskwaciya' isiyîhkâtêwa ispatinâwa, êkota ê-ohci-wîhcikâtêk anima tipahaskân. êkota ani namôy nitâhtêyihtên, miton âni wîpac êkota âsay êkota takop-~ nitakohtân, anita, tipahaskânihk. êkota êkwa, miton êkwa êkota niwî-kakwê-iyinîsin, îkamâ iyâkayâsîmoyân; ê-ati-pimitis-~ ê-ati-pimitisahwakik ôki ê-ati-pimi-nîhtâwahitocik, omas-~ nimaskimotinâna ê-at-ô-~-nîhtinamihk, ê-nîhtinamihk êkota ê-ati-sisonêstêki. êkos ê-at-ôtinahkik ôki môniyâskwêwak, ôki môniyâsak, omask-~ opôsîwiwatiwâwa, ê-ati-pîhtikwêcik mân ôma wâskahikan, ê-misâk ôma wâskahikan, êkota ê-ati-pîhtikwêcik, nîsta nitati-~ mitoni nimanâ-nakatâwak ôki môniyâskwêwak tahki ê-askowakik, mihcêtinâniwiw, nîst ôhi *suitcase*a [*sic*] nîsw ê-tahkonamân. êkosi; ê-ati-pakitinahkik mîcisowinâhtik ôma tâpiskôc ê-isinâkwahk, ita ê-ati-nâh-nâwayôstêki; êkota ê-ati-nîhtakosî-~ ê-ati-pakitinahkik ôh ôpôsîwiwatiwâwa, nîst êkota nitahkohtastân ôhi nipôsîwiwata. kiyîsi-tôtamihk êkota, êkwa niy êkwa; niwîhtamâkawin wiya

with that I bid him farewell and off they were. It was not long before the young man came driving back again, for it had just been to go and let this one be dropped off in town to go to his work on the railroad, and so then he and I loaded up the car and with that now he took me to where the bus depot was, and over there then, ho, I was disappointed by the looks of the bus, our own buses over here are so nice, I was disappointed by the looks of the bus that I was going to ride, to top it all off it was small. So it was, he must indeed have made the necessary arrangements, I was to ride the bus up to the border. Thus I sail-~, I sailed off, I did not mind; at that time I did not have any way at all to interpret anything for myself, but then it also was the first time, true enough, at that time that I had ever gone anywhere far away.

[18] So it was; I arrived at that place as planned, well, that border post is called Sweet Grass, there I was to get off the bus now, and the hills are called *Wîhkaskwaciya*, that border post takes its name from there. I did not think it was far, and very soon already I arrived there at the border. There now I was going to try to be really smart since of course I did not speak English; I followed a group of women as they got off the bus, our bags were taken off the bus, they were taken off the bus and put against there. With that these White women, these White people, were taking their suitcases and going into this building, it was a big building, they were going in, and I too made every effort not to let go of these White women and kept right behind them all the time, there were lots of people, and I too was carrying these two suitcases. So it was; they put them on what looked like a table, they were placed there one next to the other; there they put down their suitcases, and I too put my suitcases up on top there. When one was finished there, now it was my turn; I was told that there would be a search

nêtê ta-nitonikêhk, anita nimaskimotihk; «ahpw êtikwê ta-niton-~ ka-nitonikâtikawin,» nititikwak ôki nikosis. tâpwê, êkw âwa kâ-isit aw êkwa, kâ-~ awa kâ-nitawâpênahk ôhi pôsîwiwata, pêyak pik ôma yôhtênam nipôsîwiwat, pâ-~ têpiyâhk ê-kî-wâpahtahk ôhi ê-pâh-pâskinahk kwayask ê-itaskinahcikêyân, «tâniyikohk ohci kîkway kikîwêhtitân ôtê ohci, *States* k-ôhtohtêyan,» nititik. «â, namôy mistahi,» nititâw, «'niyânanosâp tahtwâpisk' k-êtwêhk, êkoyikohk pik ôhci nipimohtatân kîkway *States* ê-ohtohtatâyân,» nititâwak anik êkosi. êkosi ati-masinahikêwak, êkos âni, ati kâw ây-âkwanâpowêham nipôsîwiwat. êkosi nipê-s-~ nitati-~ niwîhtamâk êkwa nêtê t-êtohtatâyân simâkanisak nêtê ê-nîpawicik, êkotê t-êtohtatâyân, nitat-âskowâwak ôki tahki, nikiskinowâpamâwak ayisk. êkos êkot[a] êkwa ka-pakit-~ nitawi-pakitinamawêwak, simâkanisak niwâpahtihâwak ôma nimasinahikanis, masinahikâtêw êtikwê êkota, *Saskatchewan* ê-wî-pê-itohtêyân. êkos êkw êkot[a] êkwa, kâ-tâh-tahkopitahkik ôh âyak, masinahikanis[a] êkwa nipôsîwiwatihk anit[a] ê-wî-tahkopitahkik ôki simâkanisak, «êkosi,» nititikwak, «misawâc ôta wayawîtimihk, t-âstêwa ôhi kahkiyaw, êkosi *Greyhound-bus* ôta ta-takopayiw wîpac, pikw îspihk, êkota ta-mîskoci-pôsihtâniwiw,» nititik. «nêtê ihtakon, *coffee* êkotê ê-ayâk, ê-nitaw-âyâcik ayisiyiniwak, êkotê nitawi-pêho! êkotê mîna pwas-*ticket* k-ôhtinên,» nititikwak ôki, ôki simâkanisak, «êkotê, êkwayâc êkotê t-âtâwêyan, namôy wiy ôta,» nititikwak, «êkotê ka-nitaw-ôhci-otinaman masinahikanis kotak,» nititikwak. êkos ân[i] êkwa nisipwêhtân êkwa, namôy –~ êkot[ê] êkwa mîn êkwa nitati-pimitisahwâwak môniyâskwêwak, aspin ê-nakatamân êkota nipôsîwiwata. êkosi kêsiskâw êkwa nêtê, âsay êkota mistahi nitakahkêyihtên, ôtê ohci cistêmâw ê-nisitawinawak êkotê ê-apit, at-â-~ at-~ mâ-~, ita k-ôhtinamâhk masinahikanisa, nitôtinamâson ta-pîhtwâyân; êkosi mîcisowikamikos êkot[a] ê-ayâk cîki, êkot[a] êkwa

of my bags over yonder; «They may even search your luggage,» my nephew and the others had told me. What he had told me was true, when this one checked the suitcases over, he only opened one of my suitcases, he barely opened it and saw that I had packed it neatly, «For how much are you taking things back home from over there, on your return from the States,» he said to me. «Well, not very much,» I told him, «'fifteen dollars,' as one says, for that much only am I bringing things with me in bringing things back from the States,» I told them that. They proceeded to write that down, and with that he went ahead and closed my suitcase again. So now he told me to take them over yonder, the borderguards were standing over yonder, for me to take them over there, I still followed these women all the time for I guided myself by their example. So they went there and put them down for them, I showed the borderguards this little paper I had, I guess it was written there that I was going to go back to Saskatchewan. So now they were tying them on there, now the borderguards tied the papers on my suitcases. «That's it,» they told me, «they will all be sitting outside here anyway, and soon the Greyhound bus will drive up here, any time now, and they will put them on that bus instead,» he told me. «There is a place over yonder where there is coffee, people are going there, go and wait over there! You will also get the bus ticket over there,» the borderguards told me, «Over there, you can only buy it over there, not here,» they told me, «you will go and get another ticket over there,» they told me. So now I went off, no –~ over there, too, I followed the White women, simply leaving my suitcases there. So I now went over yonder while there was time, I was already really happy there, I recognised the tobacco from over here [*sc.* in Canada] that was sitting over there where we got the tickets, I bought myself tobacco to smoke; with that there was a little restaurant close by there, there we now went and had coffee

ê-nitawi-kwâhpîhkêyâhk ê-mîcisosiyân. ê-pê-wayawîyâhk, awîn âw âsay *Greyhound-bus* kî-apiw. êkos êkota, tâpwê piko âsay mîn êkota nit-~ nitati-pimitisahikân, êkota nimiskamâson pêyak âpihtawikosisâniskwêw, wîst ê-wî-pôsit, mâka wiy ôhpimê ê-wî-itâpôyot, «*Great Falls* isko k-âti-wîtâpôyômitin,» nititik; «êkotê ohci ka-paskêwihitân,» itwêw, «nîst ôhpimê êkwa, kotak pwas t-ôtinak,» itwêw; êkosi, nipê-pôsinân êkwa awa *Greyhound*-pwas, «pitamâ kêhcinâhotân, mahti pôs-~ ta-kwayask-~ ta-pôsihtêki ôta kimaskimotinawa,» nititik. «kiya,» nititâw, «môy ôma niy ê-âkayâsîmoyân,» nititâw. itohtêw êkwa anih êkwa, opamihcikêwa, «êh[a],» îtwêw ana, «nipôsihtân anihi, anihi maskimota, kahkiyaw ôta pôsihtêwa,» itwêw, itâw an-~, êkos ân[i] êkwa, piyê-sipwêkociniyâhk êkwa.

[19] «anita êkwa,» ni-~ niwîhtamâkaw-~ niwîhtamâk êkwa an[a] îskwêw, «anita êkwa ka-paskêwihitân,» itwêw, ayahk, ê-nêhiyawêhk, 'kaskaskisêhkânihk' isiyîhkâtêw anim ôcênâs, êkwa, ê-âkayâsîmohk, '*Lethbridge*' isiyîhkâtêw anim ôtênaw, êkot[a] êkwa isko ta-pê-pôsiyân, êkot[a] êkwa ka-pê-mêskoci-pôsiyân [*sic*], kotak êkwa pwas t-ôtinak, êkoni anihi kahkiyaw kâ-kî-âh-âyimêyihtamân, mitoni mâka nimiyopayin aw âpihtawikosisâniskwêw ê-pê-wîci-pôsîmak. tâpwê nitakohtân anita, â, *Lethbridge* anita nitakwâpôyonân, êkos êkwa êkot[a] êkwa, ninitonawânân êkwa, aw êkwa niya kâ-wî-pê-pôsiyân pwas, *Alberta* is âwa kâ-wî-pê-ispayit pwas ana, êwakw êkwa ta-pê-pôsiyân pwas, misakâmê *Calgary* mîn âti ta-pê-pimâpôyoyân.

[20] êkosi; mitoni nitakahkêyihtên, pôt êkota, «ôki nêhiyawak,» itwêw, «mahti kakwê-kitos! nâ-~» itwêw, «nêhiyawak ôki,» nititik aw âpihtawikosisâniskwêw. tâpwê êkwa ninitawi-kitotâw awa nâpêw, iskwêw mîn âwa, «*Hobbema* ôm ê-oht-~ ohci niyanân,» itwêwak, «êkotê ôma nîstanân ê-isi-kîwêyâhk,

and I had a little something to eat. When we came back out, here the Greyhound bus already sat there! So there I duly followed along as before, there I found myself a Halfbreed woman, she too was going to board the bus but she was going to take it somewhere else, «I will ride together with you to Great Falls,» she told me; «it is from there that I will go off in a different direction from yours,» she said, «as for me, I will go somewhere else then, I am to take another bus,» she said; so it was, and we boarded that Greyhound bus, «First of all let us make sure that our bags are properly put on this bus,» she said to me. «You [*sc.* do it],» I said to her, «as for me, it is the case that I do not speak English,» I said to her. Now she went to that one, the bus driver, «Yes,» that one said, «I put them on, those bags, they are all here on the bus,» he said, she was told, and with that now we were sailing off.

[19] «This is the place now,» that woman now said to me, «this is the place for me to go off in a different direction from yours,» she said, hm, in Cree that little town is called *Kaskaskisêhkânihk* and in English that town is called Lethbridge, this was as far as I was to ride, this was where I was to change buses now, in order to take another bus now, these were all the situations I had dreaded, but I was very fortunate to be riding the bus together with this Halfbreed woman. In due course I arrived at that place, well, we arrived there at Lethbridge on our bus, and there now we looked for the bus that I was going to ride now, the bus that was going to run back to Alberta, this bus I was to ride back now, I was to ride it all the way back to Calgary.

[20] So it was; I was very happy, and there, what was this, «These are Crees,» she said, «go ahead, try to talk to them!» she said, «These are Crees,» this Halfbreed woman said to me. Truly now I went and talked to the man, and also the woman, «We are from Hobbema,» they said, «we are also going back home over

Hobbema [*sic*];» – ês ôk îtowahk kâ-papâm-âtoskêcik ôki, êkotowahk ês ôki, wîstawâw êkw ê-pê-kîwêcik. êkota ani mîna piyê-miyopayiyân, êkonik ê-pê-aspêyimoyân aniki, cîk ê-pê-ay-apicik, êkonik nôh-nâkatôhkân.

[21] êkosi; anit[a] êkwa ê-pê-takohtêyân, êwakw êkwa, â, '*Red Deer*' isiyîhkâtêw ôtênaw, êkwa ê-nêhiyawêhk, 'wâwâskêsîwisîpiy' isiyîhkâtêw anim ôtênaw. êkota âsay mîna, êkot[a] êkwa mîna nipê-~, êkot[a] êkwa kâ-pê-nakipayit mîna pwas êkwayâc, âta wiya nâh-nâway ê-pê-nakît, mâka miton âh-aciyaw, mâk êkwa êkot[a] êkwa wêtinahk, ka-pê-kwâhpîhkêt ahpô awiyak; wahwâ, êkot[a] êkwa mîna nipê-cîhkêyihtên, ninîhci-kwâskohtin; êkot[a] êkwa ninitaw-ôtinamâson kîkway ta-pê-minihkwêyân, êkwa kîkway ta-pê-mîcisiyân, namôy âhpô ninôhtê-apin niya nânitaw ta-mîcisosiyân, iyâyaw nitôcinamâsosin kîkway t-êsi-mîcisoyân. êkosi, kâwi ninitawi-pôsâhtawîn pwasihk, ita kâ-kî-apiyân, kâw êkota nipê-apin. âsay mistahi nipê-~ nipê-takahkêyihtên êkota, cikêmâ âsay êwak ôm ôtênaw wiya nikî-wâh-wâpahtên; «âsay tâpiskôc ôpîm[a] ê-takosiniyân,» nititêyihtên, âsay kahkiyaw êkota ohc îyawis êkwa nipê-kiskêyihtên, isk ôpîma anita. êkos êkwa, piyê-sipwêkocihk pwas, â, mitoni nimiyomahcihon êkwa êkwayâc êkota, ê-pê-ay-itâpiyân ôma wêtinahk mitoni. êkos êkwa, ôpîma êkwa anita, «â, êkota nik-âti-nîhci-kwâskohtin, nik-âti-kiyokân,» nikî-itasiwân wiy ôma. êkosi, tâpwê êkota ê-takwâpôyoyân ôpîma anita, êkota ninîhtakosîn, nâh-nîhtinikâtêwa ôhi nimaskimota. hâ, ninitawi-pîhtikwân êkwa, atâwêwikamikohk êkwa, pôt ôma, âsay mâka wî-ati-tipiskâw êkwa êkota, pôt ôki nêhiyawak êkota kâ-pâh-pimipayicik; ê-na-nîpawiyân ôm êkwa wayawîtimihk, ê-pâh-pimipayicik ôma wâsaskotêw ayisk, «îh, mâniko [*sic*] nâha namôy ôta ohci nâh îskwêw kâ-matwê-nâh-nîpawit, pôsîwiwata an[a] ê-astêyiki ita kâ-nîpawit, kêhtinâc aw âwiyak otakwâpôyow,»

there to Hobbema;» – they evidently were the kind of people who go around working, that kind evidently, and they too were going back home. There too I was fortunate, I felt safe with them, they were sitting close to me and I kept my eyes on them.

[21] So it was; when I arrived at that place, it was that one now, the town is called Red Deer and in Cree that town is called *Wâwâskêsîwisîpiy*. There again, it was there now that the bus stopped for the first time, although it stopped at several places on the way but only for a very short time, but there now for a little while so that one could even have coffee; oh my, there also I was excited now, I jumped down from the bus; there now I went to buy something for myself to drink and something to eat, as for me, I did not even want to sit down anywhere to have a little meal, instead I bought a little something for myself to eat. So I went and climbed back on the bus, where I had been sitting, I returned to my seat. I was really happy there already, for of course I had already seen this town before; «It seems like I have arrived in Hobbema already,» I thought, and now I already knew the entire way from there to Hobbema. So now, as the bus was gaining speed, well, there I really felt good for the first time, I was really at peace as I looked around. So now, there in Hobbema now, «Well, there I will jump down from the bus, I will stop to visit,» I had planned. So truly, as I arrived there in Hobbema, I jumped down from the bus and my bags were taken off the bus. Well, I went inside the store now, what was this, it was already getting dark there, however, what was this, there were Crees who were driving by; as I was standing outside now, for the lights were on as they were driving by, «Look, it appears as if that woman whom you can see standing over yonder is not from here, there are suitcases where she is standing, she is surely someone who has arrived on the bus,»

ê-pim-îtwêcik ês ôki, ês ôk ê-kî-nitawi-pâh-pinikôhkêcik êtikwê ayisiyiniwak.

[22] êkosi; kâ-~ mitoni kâ-pê-o-~-waskakocihkik itê is ôm ê-na-nîpawiyân, cîk ôta, êkota kâ-pê-nakipicikêcik, «tânitê ohci kiya?» k-êsit aw îskwêw, «kêhtinâc ôm ê-kiyôtêhoyan,» k-êsit awa matwê iskwêw. wahwâ, ninipah-âtamimik ê-~ ê-nêhiyawêt awa kwayask, sêhkê mîn ôm ê-kitosit. «êha,» nititâw, «akâmi-tipahaskân mâk ôm ê-ohtâpôyoyân, môy kayâs ôm ê-nîhtakosîyân,» nititâw. «tânitê mâk ôma, nânitaw cî ôm ê-nôhtê-itohtêyan?» nititikwak; «êha,» nititâwak, «ôta ôma pêyak, nicâhkos, tipiyawê mitoni nicâhkos, ê-~ ê-wîkicik, êkotê ôm ê-~ ê-nôhtê-isi-masinahikêhiwêyân t-êtohtahikawiyân,» nititâw. «tânis ê-isiyîhkâsot?» nititikwak, niwîhtamawâwak êkwa, «êkos îsiyîhkâsowak,» nititâwak. «îh, ati-pôs[i]! âstam sôskwât pôsi!» nititikwak; «pôsîhtamaw anihi omaskimota!» itêw okisêyinîma. «êkota anima misawât t-âti-pimipayiyâhk, êkota k-âti-naskwênitinân, môy wâhyaw awasicahîs êkota nîstanân ê-wîkiyâhk,» nititik aw îskwêw, mitoni kâ-wî-ka-kitosiwêcik, itowahk kêswân aw îskwêw, namôy mîna, wiy ât-~ môy ôsk-îskwêw, êwak ôhci êtikwê mistahi kâ-miywêyihtahk ê-~ ê-otôtêmit. êkos êkwa, tâpwê êkwa nipôsin, wahwâ, ninipahi-miywêyihtên, êkonik mîn ôk ê-at-îsi-nakiskamâsoyân! nitati-sipwêpayinân; pôt ôma it[a] ânima k-êtohtêyân nicâhkos, awînik ôki kî-nâh-nîhti-~ mêkwâc kî-kîsi-na-nâh-nîhtakosîwak wîstawâw, êkonik ôki, ôki kâ-wî-~ k-êtohtahikawiyân ôki nicâhkos. «êy,» k-êtât aw îskwêw kâ-têpwâtât, môy cêskwa ninîhtakosîn, mâk êkwa ê-nêh-nêhpêmiyân ôm êkwa ka-nîhtakosîyân, «âstam,» k-êtât, «âstam mâcikôcicân [*sic*],» itêw aw îskwêw. â, âsay awa nicâhkos kî-pêcâstamohtêw, nâway ayisk êkota ê-nakîyâhk, «âstam, mâcikôcican ôta nâway pê-itâpi! kîkway kipêtamâtinân!» itâw awa nicâhkos.

they evidently were saying as they drove by, evidently these people must have gone to play bingo.

[22] So it was; they did a high-speed U-turn and came to where I was standing, close to me, they drove up there and stopped, «Where are you from?» this woman said to me, «Surely you are visiting,» this woman could be heard saying to me. Oh my, she made me extremely grateful by speaking proper Cree, and also by addressing me on her own initiative. «Yes,» I said to her, «but I came on the bus from the States, I got off a little while ago,» I said to her. «But where are you headed, do you want to go somewhere?» they said to me; «Yes,» I said to them, «a cousin of mine, a very close cousin of mine lives here with her family, I want to hire people to take me there,» I said to her. «What is her name?» they said to me, and now I told them, «That is their name,» I said to them. «Look, get in here! Come here and simply get in!» they said to me; «Put her bags in for her,» she told her old man. «We have to go by there anyway, we will swing by there for you, we ourselves live not very far beyond there,» this woman said to me, she was the kind who will talk to anyone, it happened to be this kind of woman, and she was not a young woman, I guess that is why she was glad to be friendly. So I did truly get a ride then, oh my, I was extremely glad that I had met these people! We drove off; what was this, there where I was going, here they were! at that very moment my cousin and her family had just finished getting out of their car too, it was them, the cousin to whom I was being taken. «Hey!» this woman said hollering at her, I had not got out of the car yet but I was just making ready to get out, «Come here,» she said to her, «come here and see,» this woman said to her. Well, already my cousin was coming towards us for we had parked behind them, «Come and see, look in the back here! I have brought you something!» my cousin was told.

[23] hâhêy, kâ-pê-~ âsay mâk êkwa nitati-yôhtêpitên ôm îskwâhtêm, nâway ê-apiyân. «kakwâhyakahkamîk [*sic*], nicâhkos awa! tânitê aw ê-ohtinâyêk nicâhkos,» itwêw sêmak awa; «awas, ê-nîhtakosît aw ôta ôcênâsihk ôpîma, êkota awa ê-pê-naskwênâyâhk,» itwêw, «mitoni nipîtotêyimânân sêmâk ê-pa-pêyakokâpawit, pôsîwiwata it[a] ê-astêyiki, 'miyâmâ [*sic*] awa namôy ôta ohci, awiyak aw ônîhtakosîw,' ê-itwêyân ôma.» – «êkos ân[i] êkota ôma nîstanân ê-pê-pimipayiyâhk ôma, êkâ kâ-pê-nâkatôhkêyâhk niyanân kîkway,» itwêw awa nicâhkos, wîstawâw ês ôm ê-~ pinkow ê-kî-nitawi-mêtawêcik.

[24] êkosi; wahwâ, nimiyopayin êkota âsay mîna. îh, êkota anim êkwa nin-~ nipê-nîso-tipiskwân, ê-wâpahk niwî-pê-pôsin, namôy nitâpwêhtâkwak, kêswân awa nisis êkoca ê-ayâc, môy nipakitinikwak ka-pê-sêmâkohtêyân, ka-pê-pôsiyân sêmâk ê-wâpahk, «ka-kapêsin, ka-~ kêyâpic ôta kik-âyân,» nititikwak. êkosi êkwa tâpwê, «nikakwê-osô-~ nika-kakwê-ayi-~-otinânân sôniyâw ta-miyitâhk,» nititikwak. êkwa mîn âwa nisis, iyikohk ê-osôniyâmisit, êwako mîn êkoyikohk piko nimiyik ât[a] ôm ê-osôniyâmisiyân, mâk ôhtitaw ê-nôhtê-wîcihicik êtikwê sôniyâwa ôhi. êkos âsay mîna nikapêsin; wiyâpahk, wîpac êkwa, âsay mîn êkwa hôpîma [*sic*], kâ-pê-itohtahikawiyân êkwa kâ-pêsiwicik wiy êkota êkwa, êkos ân[i] êkwa, pwas êkwa tâpwê pikw êkwa ê-pimipayit, êkot[a] êkwa nipê-pôsin êkwa.

[25] êkos âni nipê-kî-~ nipê-pa-pimâpôyon, êtimantan âsay mîna nipê-nîhtakosîn, miton ê-wî-kakwê-iyinîsiyân tahki, êkâ ta-kakwê-isi-wanâpôyoyân; nipê-sipwêyâpôyon, êtimantan êk ôhci, kapê-ayi nipê-pimâpôyon, ê-ati-tipiskâk, âsay ôta *North Battleford* ninîhtakosîn, êcik ôm êkwa miton êtikwê ê-pê-~ ê-asawâpamikawiyân êkwa, pikw îspî ta-takohtêyân, tahto-kîsikâw êsa kêkâc ê-itohtêcik ôtênâhk, ê-nitawi-pâh-pêhikawiyân ê-nitawi-nâh-nakiskâkawiyân, nitânis êtikwê –~ nitânis awa mîna;

[23] Oh my gosh, but I had already opened the door now, as I was sitting in the back. «My goodness, it is my cousin! Where did you all get my cousin?» she said right away; «Go away, she got off the bus here in town, in Hobbema, we picked her up there,» she said, «we found her very strange right away when she was standing alone, with her suitcases beside her, 'I do believe she is not from here, this is someone who has got off the bus,' I said.» – «We too drove by there, and it is the case that we, we did not notice anything,» my cousin said, evidently they too had gone to play bingo.

[24] So it was; oh my, I was fortunate there again. Look, I spent two nights there, then the next morning I was going to catch the bus, they did not let me, it so happened my maternal uncle was staying there and they did not let me come back home right away, to come on the bus the next morning, «You will stay the night, you will still stay here,» they said to me. With that indeed, «We will try to get some money to give you,» they now said to me. My maternal uncle now also gave me as much money as he had, although I did have some money of my own, but they still must have wanted to help me with this money. So I stayed for another night again; it was the next morning, soon now, that I was now taken to Hobbema again, that they brought me back there now, and that was it now, in due course now the bus came along without delay, and there I came riding on it now.

[25] So I was now riding along on the bus, in Edmonton I got off again, I was going to try to be really smart all the time so that I would not take the wrong bus; I rode off on the bus, from Edmonton now, I rode along on the bus for a long time, as it was getting dark I got off in North Battleford already, they must have been waiting for me, it appears, expecting me to come any day, they evidently went into town almost every day, they regularly

êkwa mîn ôki kotakak ayisiyiniwak, awîn ôm ê-~, nam âwiyak miton ê-ay-ayât anita pwas-tîpow, iskwêwak nêtê kâ-wâpamakik têhtapiwinihk nîso ê-ay-apicik. «hay, aw îta,» nîso pôsîwiwata ayisk ôhi nitati-pîhtikwatân, «hay, aw îta kâ-pê-pâh-pêhiht, takohtêw an[i] êkwa,» kâ-pê-itwêt awa pêyak iskwêw, êkosi pê-pâh-pasikôwak. «wahwâ, kiyikaw nîstanân ôma mâna ê-pê-pêhitâhk» (ôta ôtênâhk mâka wiy êkonik ê-wîkicik); «nîstanân ôm ê-kî-pê-itwêhiwêcik kikisêyinîm, êyiwêhk ka-pê-pâh-pêhikawiyan, 'pikw îspîhk êkwa ta-takohtêw,' ê-itikawiyan ôma,» nititik aw îskwêw, «êyiwêhk ôma nîstanân mân ê-pê-pêhoyâhk,» itwêw; «mâskôc ôta ayâw kitânis ahpô,» itwêw, «miton ôma tahki kipêh-~ kipêhikawin wiy âta wiy,» îtwêw. êkos ân[i] êkwa, nimaskimota êk ôhi êkw êkota nitastahcikon. tânitê pîtos? – «minihkwêwikamikohk maht îtohtêtân! ohcit[aw] âwiyak [*sic*] nêhiyawak t-âyâcik, êkotê ohci kitaskîwâhk,» nititikwak, «*Sweetgrass*.» tâpwê an[i] êkwa minihkwêwikamikohk (m-~ akâmiskanaw [*sic*] piko, akâmi-mêskanâhkânihk ê-astêk minihkwêwikamik), tâpwê an[i] êkwa, êkotê kâ-nitawi-pîhtikwêyâhk êkwa; hêy, awîn ôma ê-atimastêki ôhi têhtapiwina, ê, pêyak awa nâpêw, mitoni kâ-ciyastâpâpamit [*sic*] ê-ati-pîhtikwêwâyâhk, «hêy, tânitê mâka wiy âw êkwa wêhtohtêt awa, êwako cî awa kâ-kî-sipwêhtêt,» k-êsit awa nâpêw ê-pâhpit ê-pê-kitâpamit, ê-pê-kwêskiskwêyit awîn âwa nitânis ôta kî-atimapiw, «êy, êcik âwa taw-~, nimâmâ êkwa takohtêw,» nititik awa nicânis.

[26] êkosi, êkos ân[i] êkota êkwa, niwawêyapin êkwa niwîtapimâwak nitawîstâkwak, êkot[a] êkwa nitapin êkwa nîsta. «anohc ôma ê-kî-pê-takohtêyân,» itwêw, «ê-pê-pêhitân êyiwêhk,» iti-~, itwêw awa nitânis, êkwa. «'mwêhc ôm êkwa nik-âti-wa-wayawîn, nika-nitawi-sâ-sâkêwê-itâpin,' ê-itêyihtamân, 'pwas-tîpow,'» itwêw. êkos âni êkwa, «nânitaw cî mâk ôma

went to wait for me, they regularly went to meet me, I guess my daughter –~ also my daughter; and also these other people, here there was no one at all at that bus depot, when I saw two women sitting on chairs over yonder. «Ho, there she is,» for I came inside carrying two suitcases, «Ho, there she is, the one they have been waiting for, now she has arrived,» one of these women said, with this they got up and came over. «Oh my, we too have usually been extras coming to wait for you (but they lived here in town); we too came as your old man and the others had sent messages that at least someone should regularly come and wait for you, 'She is to arrive any day now,' was said about you,» this woman said to me, «we for our part at least have come to wait,» she said; «even your daughter is probably here in fact,» she said, «anyway, someone has been waiting for you all the time,» she said. With that now I stored my bags there. Where else? – «Let's go to the bar! There's bound to be some Crees there from your reserve,» they said to me, «from over there at Sweetgrass.» Sure enough to the bar now (the bar was right across the road, across the street), sure enough we now went to go in there; hey, here the chairs were facing the other way! hey, there was a man who noticed me right away as we went in where he was, «Hey, where though is this one now coming from, is she not the one who had left,» this man said about me as he laughed and watched me come towards him, and as another one turned her head around, here it was my daughter sitting here with her back towards me! «Hey, it's her indeed, now my mom has arrived,» my daughter said about me.

[26] So it was, with that now I sat down properly and then I sat with them and they made room for me, now I sat there too. «I came in today,» she said, «to wait for you just in case,» my daughter said now. «'I will go out there this moment, I will go where I have clear lines of sight and take a look,' I thought, 'at the

kâh-kî-isi-kîwânânaw?» nititâw, «t-âti-kîwêyahk.» – «nâh ân[a]!» îtwêw, «ê-ka-~, anohc ê-kakwêcimak, 'kîspin nânitaw isi nikâwiy takohtêci, kâh-kî-kîwêhtahinân cî ici?' ê-itak,» itwêw (pêyak otatoskêw êkota aw ôsîkinikêw ayihk, minihkwêwikamikohk, mâk ê-kî-nakayâskawât mitoni nêhiyawa, êkosi mân ê-kî-itâpatisit ê-kî-mani-kîwêhtahât mâna, ê-kîwêhtahiwêt askîhkânihk is ôm âwiya kâ-wî-micimôhoyit); «'êha,' ê-isit an[a] âta wiy,» itwêw, «pôyoci,» itwêw; «'mâka wîpacês nawat niya nika-kakwê-pôyon,' ê-itwêt aspin, 'nânitaw pêyakosâp,'» itwêw.

[27] êkos ân[i] êkwa, pasikôw êkwa nitawi-wîhtam – kah! namôya, êkotê pê-ay-itoh-~ ê-pimohtêyit, wîhtamawêw, «takohtêw aw êkwa nikâwiy, êwakw âwa k-êtitân, 'takohtêci, kîwêhtahîhkâhk!' k-êtitân,» itêw ôhi môniyâsa, «êha!» itwêw awa môniyâs. êkwa an[i] êkwa, tâpwê, â, êkot[a] êkwa ê-wa-wîtapimakik êkwa ê-ay-apiyân êkwa. â, miton êtikw êkwa pêyakosâp-tipahikan ê-ocihcipayik êkwa, kâ-pê-wîhtamâkoyâhk êkwa ta-nitawi-pêhoyâhk. êkos êkwa ninit-~ ninitawi-~ niwayawînân êkwa, ê-nitawi-pêhâyâhk awa, ê-pê-wayawît êkosi, êkos êkwa *station* êkwa ninitawi-nakînân êkwa nimaskimota êkwa ôhi ê-nitawi-pôsihtâyâhk êkwa.

[28] êkosi, nikîwêhtahikawin. wiy ê-âkwâ-tipiskâk nêtê ê-takohtêyâhk nîkinâhk, ay-ap-~, wiya piko aw ây-apiw nikisêyinîm, mâk âsay ês ê-kî-kawisimocik. â, nipêkohtâso-~, nipêkonânânak. â, mitoni wiy âta wiya cîhkêyihtamwak kahkiyaw, nôsisimisak êkwa mîn âwa nikosis ôta k-âyât, têtiy; miton âni miywêyihtamwak ê-takosiniyân.

[29] êwakw ânima mâna k-êtwêyân, êkospîhk mâmawo-nîkân wâhyaw ê-kî-itohtêyân, namôy kakêtihk ê-kî-~, ê-kî-cacimi-cêpêyimisoy-~-cêpêyimosiyân, wâhyaw ê-wî-itohtêyân, pêyak-pîsim âta piko, mâk êkwa tâpiskôt mitoni misi-kinwêsêskamik ê-kî-itêyihtamân, iyikohk

bus depot,'» she said. With that now, «But is there any way we could go home?» I said to her, «so that we might go home.» – «That one yonder is the one!» she said, «I just asked him, 'If my mother arrives at some time or other, would you take us home afterwards?' I said to him,» she said (for one of the workers there, the one who poured the drinks in the bar, was very much accustomed to the Crees, that is what he used to do, he would make a point of taking them home, he took people home to the reserve when someone was going to be stuck); «'Yes,' he said to me anyway,» she said, «when he quits,» she said; «'But as for me I will try to quit a little early,' is the last he had said, 'about eleven o'clock,'» she said.

[27] So it was now, now she go up and went to tell – not so! no, as he went by over there she told him, «My mother has arrived now; she was the one I told you about, 'When she arrives, then take us home!' I had said to you,» she said to this Whiteman, «Yes!» the Whiteman said. Now then, truly, well, now I sat there with them and now I kept sitting. Well, it must have been eleven o'clock now when he came over to tell us to go and wait. So now we went outside, we went and waited for him, and with that he came out and so we went and stopped at the station now and now we went and put my bags in the car.

[28] So it was, I was taken home. It was late at night when we arrived over yonder at our home, my old man was the only one sitting up, but they had evidently gone to bed already. Well, we woke –~ we shook them awake. Well, of course they were all very excited, my grandchildren and also my son who was there, Teddy; they were very glad that I had arrived.

[29] That is what I have been saying about that time, that it was the very first time I went far away, that I had agreed that I would go far away for a very short time, though only for one month, but that it seemed like such an exceedingly long time to

ê-kî-nitawi-kakwâtakêyihtamân, môya wîhkât kîhtwâm wâhyaw êkos îsi nik-êtohtân ta-pêyakoyân, ê-kî-itêyihta-~ nikî-itêyihtên mân êkospîhk.

[30] êkospîhk nikî-wîhtamâkawin, ês ê-kî-ayihk-~, ê-kiskêyimikawiyân ê-kaskêyihtamân, awîn êtikwê p-~ ê-kî-pawâtikawiyân, âpihtâ-kîsikâhk wâpamonâpisk ê-ihtakohk, tâpwê mîn êkos ê-kî-itôtamân anima, âpihtâ-kîsikâhk ê-ihtakohk wâpamonâpisk, êkota mân ê-kî-apiyân, ê-pêyakwapiyân, ê-wî-nipahêyihtamân, piyisk mân ê-kî-mâtoyân ê-môskwêyihtamân, êkota ê-apiyân. hâw, êwakw êsa nikî-kiskêyimikawin êkospîhk, «matwê-kaskêyihtam awa mistahi, ôta awa kâ-kî-sipwêhtêt, âpihtâ-kîsikâhk ani, êkotê is-ôhtiskawapiw, mistahi matwê-mâmitonêyihtam sôskwâc, kaskêyihtam ani,» ê-kî-itikawiyân ês êkospîhk anima.

[31] êkosi; sêmâk ôki nitâcimo-~, sêmâk awa niwîhtamâk nikiskêyinîm, «kikiskêyimikawin ôm,» îtwêw; «tâpwê anima,» nititâw, «tâpwê êkos ê-ispayik ê-kî-~ tâ-~ ê-tâpwêt anima kâ-itwêt ana,» nititâw, «kâ-kiskiwêhot ana,» nititâw, nititâw awa nikisêyinîm. «êkwa mîn,» îtwêw, «nîst,» îtwêw, «môy kayâs, mistahi nikoskwêyihtên, niwîhtamawâwak ôki ê-waniskâyân, 'hâ, êkwa ani kikâwîwâw, wîpac an[i] êkwa wî-takohtêw,' nititâwak ôk,» îtwêw, «nîsta nimamâhtâwêyihtên, nayêwaci-kîsikanohk ôtê, êkotê iskwêw ê-pê-itwêwitahk, ê-pê-nikamot,» itwêw, «piyisk ôta tâpiskôc capasis ê-pêhtawak ê-pê-nikamot, ôta êk[wa] ôma, êkot[a] êkwa, tâpiskôc êkwa iyinask-~, ôt[a] êkwa kêhciwâk tâpiskôc, askîhk êkw êkot[a] êkwa, êkot[a] êkwa kâ-pê-~, cîk êkwa ê-pê-ayât aw îskwêw ê-itâpiyân, kâ-nisitawinâtân kiya, êkwa ê-pêcâstamohtêyan, êkonik ôki –~ êwako –~ êkoyiw [*sic*] ôki nikî-wîhtamawâwak, anim ê-kî-is-~, anima nîst ê-isi-pawâtitân,» nikî-itik awa niwîkimâkan.

[32] hâw, êwak ôma kâ-wî-âtotamân, môy kakêtihk ê-kî-nayêhtâwêyihtamân êkospîhk, anim ê-isi-papâmâcihoyân

me and that I had come to suffer so dreadfully, I will never again go far away like that, to be alone, I used to think at that time.

[30] At that time I was told that they evidently knew about me that I was lonesome, that I had been dreamt about, I wonder who it was, that there was a window facing south, and it is also true that I did that, that there was a window facing south and that I used to sit there, sitting all alone and getting to be absolutely desperate, that finally I used to be in tears, crying despondently as I sat there. Now then, they evidently knew that about me at that time, «It is obvious that she is terribly lonesome, this one who left over here, she sits with her face turned there to the south, it is obvious that she is thinking terribly troubled thoughts, she is lonesome indeed,» it had evidently been said about me at that time.

[31] So it was; straight away they tol-~, straight away my old man told me about it, «This was known about you,» he said, «That is true,» I said to him, «it is true that this happened, the person who said this speaks the truth,» I said to him, «the one who uttered prophesies about me,» I said to him, I said to my old man. «Now also,» he said, «I too,» he said, «not long ago, I was greatly surprised, I told them when I got up, 'Now then, your mother is soon going to return,' I told them,» he said, «I for my part had the amazing experience that over here midway up in the sky a woman was heard approaching over there, she came singing,» he said, «finally I heard her singing here as if it was down low, now it was here, as if it was over here on earth now, ordinari-~, it was as if it was right here now, here on earth now, now as the woman came close and I looked, I recognised you, you, and you came walking towards me, I told them what I for my part had dreamt about you,» my husband had told me.

[32] Now then, it is this which I was going to tell about, I had found it utterly devastating at that time, when I was travelling

ê-kî-nitawi-misi-mâh-môskwêyihtamân misi-wâhyawêskamik itê ê-kî-itohtêyân. êkoyikohk isko, nikîsîhtân êwakw ânima pêyak âcimowin kâ-kî-nôhtêpayik anim îta, isko ta-kî-âcimoyân, êwak ôm êkwa pitamâ ê-sâkaskinahcâsiyân ôma, âcimowin.

around and had come to cry so despondently in that far away place where I had gone. That is all, I have told it to the end, this one story which had run short [*sc.* of audio-tape], to where I should have told it, and now I have filled up the first part of this little tape with it, with this story.

Sarah Whitecalf at the Linguistics Department's recording studio, University of Manitoba, August 1988.

8

pikw êkwa niya

Now I had to take charge

piko êkwa niya

[1] êkwa, kotak kîkway êkwa, êwako pitamâ nika-pônihtân, nîsta mistahi pîsâkwan nipê-isi-pimâcihowin ôma, tânis ê-kî-pê-is-ôhpikihakik nitawâsimisak. piyisk anima nîst êkota kê-at[i]-ôcihcipayiw [*sic; sc.* kî] ê-kî-pê-at[i]-îsi-ka-kitimahikawiyân; kinwês âta namôy ôhci-minihkwêw niwîkimâkan, mâka kî-ay-ihtakowak (tâpwê mîn ê-ay-ihtakocik ayisk ôki, êkâ kâ-wî-minihkwêhk); piyisk ê-kî-nihtâ-minihkwêt niwîkimâkan, wîc-ôsk-âya ôhi, êkos îsi, ê-kî-nihtâ-min-~ piyisk ê-kî-ati-miywêyihtahk ê-minihkwêt. â, kîtahtawê kâ-wî-mâh-macipêt, ê-macipêt êkwa mâna. îh, nîst ânim êkosi, piyisk ê-kî-~ ê-kî-~ ê-kî-mosci-kostak wiya niya, piyisk nîst ê-kî-minihkwêyân; âta mistahi nikâwiy ê-kî-wî-nipahi-pakwâtahk, môy âyisk nikâwiy ohti-nihtâ-minihkwêw, êkwa mîna, kî-ayamihâw nikâwiy, mitoni k-~ – êkwa niy êkwa ê-môyêyimikawiyân êkwa, ê-mâci-minihkwêmak [*sic; sc.* ê-mâci-wîci-minihkwêmak], ê-mâci-minihkwêyân, niwîkimâkan aw ê-wâh-wîci-minihkwêmak êkwa nîsta, êk ôk âhk îtâp [*sic*] isko – âhk îtâp [*sic*] ôki tâpiskôc owîcêwâkana ôhi, êkos êkwa ês ôk ê-wâh-wîcêwêwiskwêwi-minihkwêcik [*sic*]. piyisk êkotê ê-kî-ohcipayik ê-kî-ohti-nihtâ-minihkwêyâhk nîstanân osk-âyak, ât[a] ê-pê-ayâpisîsisicik [*sic*] ôki nicawâsimisinânak; ê-kî-minihkwêyâhk mâna nîstanân, wâwîs cî wâh-nîmihitohki, êkot[a] ê-kî-kakwâhyaki-cîhkîstamâhk ê-minihkwêyâhk êkwa. îh, êkosi kâ-kî-isi-~, nîsta kahkiyaw k-ôh-at-îsi-~, piyisk êkos ânima

Now I had to take charge

[1] Now something else, I will bring this one to an end for the time being, for me too there is much indeed to be told about the way I made my living all along, how I have been raising my children. For me too [*sc.* as in Rosa Longneck's account] it finally came to pass that I suffered ill-treatment; although for a long time my husband had not been drinking, there were some, on the other hand (for it is true, there are also some where there is not going to be any drinking); finally my husband had become accustomed to drink, the young people he was with, in that way he finally came to like drinking. Well, there came a time when he would get mean when drunk, now he was always mean when drunk. Look, for me too it became that way, finally I too was simply scared of him, finally I too drank; although my mother detested it abjectly, for my mother never took to drink, now my mother also was religious, and now I too gave signs of starting to drink with him, of starting to drink, now I too would drink with my husband, and these false –~ these false, make-believe friends of his, now they were reportedly drinking around with women. Finally it came about as the result that we too had become accustomed to drink with the young people, even though both our children were little; we too always used to drink, especially every time there was going to be a dance, on those occasions we were terribly excited and we drank. Look,

k-êtwêyan, nîsta nikî-ati-kitimahikawin piyisk nayêstaw p-~ minihkwêwin ohci.

[2] nîst êk ôm êkwa, mêtoni tâp-~, miton âni kinwâw, ta-wî-misakâmê-âcimoyân nîst êwak ôma, tânis êkwa nâh-nâway kâ-kî-pê-at[i]-îspayihikoyân aw ôhci nikisêyinîm, tânis ê-pê-isi-pa-pîkopayiyâhk (pimâtisiw ayisk niya nikisêyinîm), êkwa, êkota ohc êkwa piyisk kâ-kî-ati-kakwê-pîkopayiyâ-~, kâ-kî-ati-pa-pîkopayiyâhk ôma, êkwa kâ-kî-pê-sipwêhtêyân; têpakohp-tahtosâp-askiy ôma sâskwatôn êkwa ê-wîkiyân. mâka nikosis awa (nisitawêyimêw awa), êwakw âwa nitawâsimis, êwako nipêpîm – kah êwako kâ-kî-kwêskinit. ôtê êkwa sâskwatôn ê-pê-kiskinohamâsot, nikî-pakwâtên; wiya mîna, namôy ê-ohci-pakitinâyâhk anima, wiya mîn ê-kî-itêyihtahk ôtê ê-wî-pê-kakwê-kiskinohamâsot. âsay nêtê mistahi, *highschool* âsay nêtê ê-mâ-~ ê-wî-mâci-kiskinohamâsot, ôt[ê] êkwa ê-nîpihk êkwa, ôma mâna kâ-mâcîhtâcik kiskinohamawâkanak, êkot[a] êkwa kâ-kî-kakwê-pê-pîhtikwêt nikosis êkwa, ê-kiskinohamâht. môy nânitaw nôh-itânân, âta nikî-âyimêyihtên mistahi, -âyimêyihtênân [*sic*]. êkwa, mâk êcik ân[i] ânohc êkwa êwako niwâpahtên, êcik ân[i] ê-kî-miyo-tôtâsot nikosis; anohc êkwa nama kîkway niwîcihânân, nama kîkway wîcihik ôhtâwiya, namwâc pêyak-pîwâpiskos kîkway wîcihik ôhtâwiya, miton êkwa anohc, misakâ-~ [*sc.* misakâmê], nakânohk [*?sic; sc.* nakanohk] iskohk kî-kîsîhtâw nikosis *highschool*, ôta kî-kîsîhtâw, *university* kî-at[i]-îtohtêw. êkota tânisi kâh-ay-itinikêkwê, âhci piko kî-ati-kâsispowi-kiskinohamâsow, êkota êkwa *Ontario* kâ-kî-itohtêt, *London* isiyîhkâtêw ôtênaw, êkotê êkwa mîna kâ-kî-nitawi-kiskinohamâht, êkot[a] êkwa, miton êkwa êkota kâ-kî-kîsîhtât okiskinohamâsowin, êkot[ê] êkwa kâ-kî-nitawi-wîwit êkwa môniyâskwêwa.

[3] êkos ês âni tâpwê piko (îh, têpakohp-tahtosâp-askiy, anima kâ-kî-minihkwêskiyân kâ-kî-pê-sipwêhtêyân), êkos ânima,

that was how I too, all –~, finally, as I said, finally I too went on to suffer ill-treatment, and only because of drinking.

[2] Now I too, really –~, for me too it is really long to tell my whole story, what happened to me step by step because of my husband, how we came to break up (for in my case my husband is still alive), then, it was for that reason that I finally tried –~, that we gradually broke up, and that I came to leave; for seventeen years now I have been living in Saskatoon. But it was my son (she [*sc.* Freda Ahenakew] knows him), it was that youngest child of mine, my baby – ha, it was he who turned me around. He came to go to school over here in Saskatoon, I had hated it; it also was he, we had not permitted it, it also had been his idea to try to come over here to go to school. He was already very much in over there [*sc.* at Sweetgrass], he was already about to start highschool over there, now it was the time in late summer when the students usually start, now at that time my son came and tried to get in, to be enrolled in school. We did not say anything to him although I dreaded the very thought of it, we dreaded the thought of it. But now, as it turns out, I see today that my son, as it turns out, made the right decision for himself; today we do not support him with anything, his father does not support him with anything, his father does not support him with a single penny, today now really, all along –~ all the way to the end did my son complete highschool, he graduated from it here and went on to university. Whatever must have got into him there, he went on to still further studies, now he went to Ontario, the town is called London, over there he now also went to be educated, and over there now he really completed his education, and it was over there that he went and got married to a White woman.

[3] And thus it was, in due course (look, it has been seventeen years since I had been a confirmed alcoholic and left to come

osâm mistah ê-kî-kitimâkêyimoyân, anima kâ-pê-ay-âcimostâtân; osâm mistah ê-kî-kitimâkêyimoyân, ê-wî-kakwê-ohpikihakik nôsisimak, sâskwatôn êkwa ê-ayâyân; nam âwiyak êkwa nâpêw ta-mamisîyân ta-pamihit. pikw êkwa niya, ta-kakwê-~ ê-kî-kakwê-nihtâwêyihtamân, ê-kî-kakwê-pamihakik nôsisimak. nôsisimak êkwa piko, âsay kî-kâh-kîs-ôhpikiwak nitawâsimisak, nitânis mîna.

[4] êkota êkwa (nipê-ay-itâw aw ânoht, tâpwê, îh, ê-ihkihk nâpêw mîna kâ-maciwê-~ kâ-macêyihcikêt, âta kwayask kâ-tôtamihk, otawâsimisimâwak ohci, kâ-wî-kakwê-ohpikihâyahkik ôma k-êskwêwiyahk; mistahi kipîwêyimikonaw kîhyawêmâ nâpêw, namôy wiya mâmitonêyihtam anima kâ-pê-isi-kakwâtakihikoyâhk ôma otawâsimisiwin, wîst êkâ kîkway ê-âpatêyihtahk, tâpiskôt namôy ê-âyimaniyik, nikî-itêyihtên mâna); êkota êkwa, nôsisimak êkwa, ê-pê-~, namôy ê-mâh-misikiticik, ômayikohk [*gesture*] êtikwê ê-itikitit êkospîhk, anohc simâkanisîhkâniwiw êwako nôsisim; nîso nâpêsisak êk ôskinîkiskwêw, êkosi kâ-kî-pê-isi-sipwêhtêyân, êkot[a] êkwa sâskwatôn kâ-kî-takohtêyân.

[5] êkwa êkot[a] êkwa kâ-kî-pîhtikwahakik êkwa, nistam mâmawocêyask ê-takohtêyân, ôta sôniyâwikimâwiwinihk sâskwatôn, *Indian Affairs*, êkota nîkân kâ-kî-itohtêyân, ê-wî-kakwê-wîcihikosiyân kik ôki nôsisimak. tâpwê mîn êkota nikî-kaskihtân, êkot[a] ê-ohci-wîcihikawiyân. hâw, nikî-asotamâkawin, wâskahikan ê-wî-tipahikêstamâkawiyân, «miskamani wâskahikan – nîkân nitona,» nititikawin, «wâskahikan! êkota ohc êkwa, kî-miskamani wâskahikan, êkot[a] êkwa âpacihcikana ka-miyikawin pîhc-âyihk t-âpacihtâyan,» nikî-itikawin.

[6] nikî-kitimâkisinân, ât[a] êkwa wâskahikan ê-miskamân, ispîhk, ê-kî-mostohtêyâhk, *shopping-bag*[a] ê-tâh-cahkonamâhk [*sic*],

here), thus it was, because I felt so utterly miserable, as I told you [*sc.* Freda Ahenakew] on the way here; it was because I felt so utterly miserable, trying to raise my grandchildren, now I was living in Saskatoon; now there was no man for me to rely on, no man to look after me. Now it had to be me, I had to try to be resourceful, I had to try to look after my grandchildren. It was only my grandchildren now, all my children were already fully grown, including my daughter.

[4] It was then (I already told her [*sc.* Freda Ahenakew] today on the way here, it is true, look, it also happens when a man has no respect for a woman, even when one does things properly for the children when we who are women try to raise them; greatly does the man look down upon us, excessively, he never thinks of how we have been made to suffer in childbirth, as for him, he has no regard for it, as if it were not difficult, I have always thought); it was then, my grandchildren were not big then, my grandson must have been this high [*gesture*] at that time, today he serves in the military reserves; with two little boys and a young woman, that is how I had left to come here, that is when I had arrived here in Saskatoon.

[5] Now it was then that I took them in, as the very first thing as I arrived, here to Indian Affairs in Saskatoon, to Indian Affairs, it was there that I went first, trying to get some welfare for myself and my grandchildren. Indeed, I was successful and was given welfare from there. Well, I was promised that they would pay my rent for a house, «If you find a house – first go and look for a house!» I was told, «Then, after that, once you have found a house, then you will be given household goods for you to use in it,» I was told.

[6] We were poor at the time, even after I found a house, we went about on foot, we each of us carried shopping-bags with

kîkway nicâpacihcikanisinâna; pâh-pêyak kîkwâs, wiyâkanisa, iyikohk ôm ê-nistiyâhk t-ês-âpacihtâyâhk, nimiyo-têpaskinahtânân *shopping-bag*ihk. êkw êkwa ê-mostohtê-pimipiciyâhk, ê-nitawi-pîhtikwêpiciyân ôma *[laughs]*, wâskahikan itê kâ-miskamân. êkwa nicakohpisinâna mîn ê-pimi-câh-cahkonikêsicik ôki, nist ôki nôsisimak, êkwa nîst ôhi nîsw ê-pimi-tahkonamân, otayiwinisiwâwa *suitcase*a [*sic*] wiyawâw tahkonamwak, otayiwinisiwâwa. êkw ânim êkwa, ê-pîhtikwêpiciyâhk, nitânis awa kâ-takohtêt, êkotê nitôtihtikonân, *North Battleford* wiy ê-wîkit, takohtêw. miton êkwa ê-wawiyatêyimikoyâhk, ê-pîhtikwêpiciyâhk wâskahikan, ê-kî-moscihtakapiyâhk, ma kîkway ê-astêk mêmohci [*laughs*].

[7] êkosi, îh, êwakw ânim ê-ispayik; mâka mistahi mîna manitow nikî-mamisîn, ê-~ it[a] ê-pê-p-~ it[a] ê-pê-itohtahakik nôsisimak, «tanênitohk ôm âhci, miyopayiyân; tanênitohk ôm âhci, kwayask isi-pimâcihakik nôsisimak,» nikî-itêyihtên, «â, mîskoc nika-pônihtân kahkiyaw kîkway, mahti! nika-kakwê-kwêski-pimâtisin,» êkosi nikî-itâw awa nikosis ê-wî-sipwêhtêt. êkw êkwa iskwêyâc êkwa *Ontario* kâ-wî-itohtêt, ê-wî-ohpahot; êkosi. êkospîhk mâna nititwân, kikînîhkê [*sic*] ê-kî-mawîhkâtak nikosis, iyikohk ê-ispîhc-âyimêyihtamân, ê-kitimâkêyimak êkwa ê-wî-nakasit, kâ-mâtoyân. êê, nêt[ê] ê-pê-takopayit nakiwacîhk nikosis, ê-pê-nitawi-wâpamit. êkos êkwa, «ê-wî-kîwêyân, nêkâ! kêyâpic ôm ôtê ta-wawêyîyân, pimihâkanihk ê-wî-pôsiyân; ta-wawêyîyân ôma takohtêyâni,» ê-itwêt nikosis.

[8] êkosi; ma [*?record*] nânitaw, êkos êkw ê-ati-wayawît; nitati-wayawîn. êk ôma ê-mênikanihkâtêk wâsakâm niwâskahikaninân, ê-ati-wayawît, iskwâhtêmihk anita pimitapiyiwa êkota osîh-~ osîhkêpayîmisa [*sic*] (âsay kî-otôtâpâniw êkospîhk), êkot[a] êkwa namôy nikî-miciminison, ayisk ôta [*gesture*], tâpiskôc

our measly goods; a little bit each, enough dishes for the three of us to use, we could easily fit them into shopping-bags. We made the move there on foot, I went to move in where I had found the house. And my three grandchildren also carried our little blankets there, and I too carried two of them, they themselves were carrying their clothes, suitcases with their clothes. And it was then, as we were moving in, that my daughter arrived, she turned up over there where we were, she lived in North Battleford, she arrived. She got a big kick out of us moving into the house, we were sitting on the bare floor, there was nothing at all [*laughs*].

[7] So it was, look, that week; but I also greatly relied on God in bringing my grandchildren here, «I wish that I might still be blessed with good fortune; I wish that I might still provide a proper life for my grandchildren,» I thought, «Well, in return I will put an end to all that, let it be! I will try to turn my life around,» that I had told my son as he was about to leave. It was for the last time now, as he was about to go to Ontario, as he was about to fly off; so it was. At that time, I always say, I cried for my living son as one does for the dead, I dreaded it so terribly, I loved him and he was about to leave me, it was then that I cried. Hey, my son had come and driven over there to *Nakiwacîhk* [Sweetgrass], he had come to see me. So it was now, «I am about to go back, mother! I still have to get ready over here [*sc.* in Saskatoon], I am about to travel in an airplane; I have to get ready once I arrive,» my son said.

[8] So it was; not any [*?record*], and with that he went on outside; I too went on outside. Now there was a fence around our house, and as he went on outside, his little car was parked across the gate there (he already had a car at that time), at that point now I could not hold onto myself, for it was here [*gesture*], for it was as

ôt[a] [*gesture of being choked*] ê-itinikawiyân, kâ-mâtoyân êkwa êkot[a] ê-pê-at-~ ê-pê-ocêmit nikosis, nôsisimisak ôki pê-wayawîpahcâwak, ê-âh-atamiskâkoyâhk, êkot[a] êkwa kâ-mâtoyân. â, mitoni nimôskwêyihtên. «â, mâmâ [*sic*]!» k-êtwêt ê-pê-atamiskawit, nitâkwaskitikwênik, «mâmâ [*sic*]!» itwêw, «namôy ôma ê-nitawêyihtamân ta-mawîhkâsiyan,» nititik, «nika-takohtân ôma, ahpô manitowi-kîsikâki nika-takohtân,» itwêw. «ôma kâ-kitahamâtân, êkâ ta-wîti-tôtamômat [*sic*] nôhtâwiy, ê-kakwâtakihtâyan, âsay ôma ê-kakwâtakihtâyan, nimâmâ!» itwêw, «êwak ôhc ôma k-ôh-kitahamâtân, êkâ kiya ta-kakwê-minihkwêyan,» k-êsit. êkosi, «êkosi, mâmâ [*sic*]!» itwêw, mâtow mâka wîsta, ninîswatwêmonân êkwa, wîst êkwa môskomow ôma kâ-kitosit, môskomow wîst ôma. êkosi; â, nikoskwâwâcikâpawin êkwa, «êha!» nititâw, «êha, nikosis! nika-pôyon niya,» nititâw, «nika-pônihtân,» nititâw. êkosi; «êkosi mâka, mâmâ [*sic*]!» itwêw, «nimiywêyihtên,» itwêw, «êkosi, êkây nânitaw itêyiht[a] âyiwâk, mâmâ [*sic*]!» itwêw, «êkây ayiwâk kîkway mokiskâtêyihta! misawât nika-takosinin manitowi-kîsikâki, ka-pê-nitawi-wâpamitinâwâw mîn,» îtwêw. êkosi; êkos âspin nikosis ê-sipwêpayit.

[9] êkos ês ânim êkota ohc êkwa, êkwa wiyîhtamawak[i] êkwa awa niwîkimâkan ta-kakwê-pê-sipwêhtêyâhk, sâskwatôn ta-pê-ispiciyâhk, êkot[ê] ê-nôhtê-pê-ayâyân, wahwâ, nikisîmâw, nikâh-kisiwâhâw! «â, kiya piko sipwêhtê! namôy niya ninôhtê-nakatên ôm ôta. kiya piko nitaw-ây-ayâ êkotê! yîkatêhtê!» piyisk mân ê-wî-ati-kisî-kitosit, «kiya piko yîkatêhtê ôt[a] ôhci, mâka wiya, êkây itêyihta nôsisimak ka-sipwêhtahacik!» nititik; «môy ninitawêyihtên ta-papâ-kakwâtakihacik.» – êkos ânima mwêhc ôm ê-tâpâcimoyân, êkos ânima ê-kî-pê-isi-yîkatêhtêyân. êkwa êkota

if I was being held here [*gesture of being choked*], it was at that point that I cried as my son came to kiss me, and my grandchildren came running outside and he said good-bye to each of us, it was at that point that I cried. Well, I wept in despair. «Well, Mom!» is what he said as he came to say good-bye to me, he embraced me, «Mom!» he said, «I don't want you to cry for me,» he said, «I will be back, I will even be back at Christmas,» he said. «This that I asked you not to do, that you should not join in with my father, you are suffering because of it, you are already suffering because of it, Mom!» he said, «That is why I am asking you not to do it, that you should try not to drink,» is what he said to me. With that he said, «That is it, Mom!» but he too cried, now we both could be heard crying, now he too wept as he spoke to me, he wept too. So it was; well, now I stood still, «Yes!» I told him, «Yes, my son! I will quit, I will,» I told him, «I will put an end to it,» I told him. So it was; «But that is it, Mom!» he said, «I am glad,» he said, «That is it, do not fret anymore, Mom!» he said, «Do not worry anymore about anything! In any case I will come back at Christmas, I will come and see you all again,» he said. So it was; with that my son was gone, driving off.

[9] Thus then, from that point on, every time now I told my husband that we should try to leave and move here to Saskatoon, as I wanted to live over here, oh my, I made him angry by what I said, I got him angry every time! «Well, you leave on your own then! As for me, I do not want to leave this here behind. You go and live over there on your own! Go away!» Finally he would always speak to me in anger, «You go away from here on your own, but do not think of taking my grandchildren away with you!» he told me; «I do not want you to make them suffer as you go about.» – I am telling it exactly in the way it happened, that is how I went away and came here. Now at that point, well, he would

êkwa, â, mitoni nawac piko niwî-kisîmik êkwa, niwî-kâh-kisî-kitotik, êkwa ôs-~, ôsisima ôhi, wiy êkw ê-wî-pa-pamihât, êkwa ê-minihkwêskit, êkwa aw âsay ê-kîs-ôskinîkiskwêwit êwakw âwa omisimâw. wahwâ, matwân cî tâpwê, «tânis êtik ôma k-êtôtamân?» nititêyihtên. mâninakisk êkwa kîmôt [*sic*] nimâmitonêyihtêh êkwa, ohcitaw êkwa ninôhtê-pê-yîkatêhtân, êkos âyisk piko t-êsi-pônihtâyân minihkwêwin, êkâ ta-wî-~ êkâ ta-wîti-tôtamômak [*sic*] ayiwâk. piyisk, kîmôc êkwa niwîhtamawâwak ôki nôsisimak, «tânis ôma kâh-itêyihtên,» nititâw, «kâh-itêyihtênâwâw ta-sipwêhtêyahk, êkotê sâskwatôn kîstanaw t-êspiciyahk» – âsay êkota nikî-pâh-pêhtên ôma kwayask ê-âh-isi-wîcihihcik ôta iskwêwak êkospîhk anima, sâskwatôn, âsay ê-nisitawêyimakik mâna nêtê ê-kî-pê-kâh-kiyokawicik anima, ôt[ê] ê-âh-ohcipayicik. êkosi, «â, niya wiya nika-miywêyihtên,» (kîkwây mân âwâsisak, môy wâhyaw isi-mâmitonêyihtamwak), «â, nika-miywêyihtênân, nika-miywêyihtênân; êkotê nika-kiskinohamâsonân;» wahwâ, cîhkêyihtamwak. «êkâya mâka nânitaw itwêk!» nititâwak, «êkây kîkway kimosômiwâw ta-kiskêyihtam, âhci ka-sipwêhtânâwâw, îh, kipêhtawâwâw; namôy ta-sipwêhtahitakok, niya piko ta-yîkatêhtêwak ê-isi-nitawêyihtahk,» nititâwak ôki nôsisimak. êkosi; êkos ês ân[i] êkwa, kîmôc êkwa ê-wa-wâh-wawêyîsiyâhk êkwa, ôh ôcayiwinisisiwâwa t-êsi-sa-sipwêhtatâcik, êkwa nîsta mîna.

[10] êkos êkwa, nititohtân êkwa, aya, *band-office* êkwa nititohtân êkwa, ê-nitawi-wîhtamân êkwa. (mîna nitati-kîskisokawin, anima pîhtaw niy êkota, namôy nitasamikawin, ôk êkwa piko nôsisimak ê-asamihcik, êkwa awa nikisêyinîm, mitoni niyânanosâp-askiy ê-kî-atoskêt ayi, môniyâsinâhk okistikêwiyiniwa ê-atoskawât.

[FA:] mhm.

îh, êkwa ôma k-âtoskêt okistikêwiyinînâhk, niy êkwa nikîskisokawiwân osâm ohc ê-atoskêt.) wahwâ, nikisiwakocinin

really make me kind of angry now by what he said, he would always speak to me in anger, now he, he would be looking after his grandchildren, and him a confirmed alcoholic and with the oldest sister having already grown into a young woman. Oh my, it was utterly out of the question, «What can I do, I wonder?» I thought. Now I kept on thinking about it in secret, I definitely wanted to go away and come here, for that was the only way to put an end to the drinking, that I would not join in with him anymore. Finally then I told my grandchildren in secret, «What would you think,» I said to her, «What would you all think about us leaving, about us for our part moving over there to Saskatoon» – at that time I had already heard about several cases of women being supported properly here in Saskatoon, some of them I knew had already come to visit me over there, driving out from over here. So it was, «Well, I certainly will like it,» (what is it about children, they don't think far ahead), «Well, we will like it, we will like it; we will go to school over there;» oh my, they were excited. «But do not say anything!» I told them, «Your grandfather is not to know anything about it, you will just leave, look, you have heard him; he does not want me to take you with me, he wants me to go away on my own,» I told my grandchildren. So it was; thus then we secretly got a few of their clothes ready for them to take along, and for me too.

[10] So it was now, now I went there, I went to the Band Office, now I went and gave notice. (I had also been cut off, of course that applied only to me, there had been no welfare for me, only my grandchildren received welfare, now my husband had been working for a solid fifteen years, he had worked amongst the Whites, for a farmer.

[FA:] mhm.

Look, since he worked amongst the farmers, I was cut off on account of him working.) Oh my, I angrily marched over there,

êkwa êkota, nititohtân êkwa *band office*, ninitawi-wîhtên, «ê-wî-piciyân, ê-kîskisoyêk ô-~ kikîskisonâwâw, môy k-â-~ t-âsamikawiyân,» nititâw, «êkosi niwî-sipwêhtân.» – «tânitê kiwî-itohtân?» nititik âw ôtasahkêw. «sâskwatôn ôm ê-wî-ispiciyân,» nititâw, «ê-pê-wîhtamân; ê-wî-piciyân êkotê isi,» nititâw. wahwâ, mitoni nicikâsimâw aw ôcasahkêsis awa, «êha,» nititikwak, «mâka kika-miyitinân masinahikan, t-ômîcisoyêk êkotê kôsisimak k[a]-ôh-asamacik,» itwêw, «ka-miyitin êwakw ân[i] ânima, namôy âyisk sêmâk nânitaw ta-kî-at[i]-âsamikawiyêk, ta-kî-at[i]-ôhci-mîcisoyêk,» nititik. «êkwa mîna, tânis ê-wî-is-îtohtêyan?» nititik, «hâ, nika-~ nika-~ nika-~ nik-ê-~ awiyak êtikwê nika-masinahikêhâw, kit-êtohtahit, k-êspicîhtahikoyâhk êkotê, êkamâ mistahi kîkway,» nititâw. êkosi, «êwako mîna ka-tipahikêstamâtin; awiyak nitonaw t-êspicîhtahisk!» itwêw, «niyânanomitanaw tahtwâpisk awiyak nika-miyâw, awiyak ispicîhtahisk[i] êkotê,» nititik. mitoni kâ-ihkihk nistês awa pêyak ê-môsâpêwit, *truck*a kâkikê ê-kî-ayâwât, êwakw êkwa kîmôc mîna kâ-kakwê-wâpamak. tâpwê nimiskawâw, âta nikostâw nânitaw t-êsit ta-pakwâtamawit ôma ê-wî-pê-piciyân, êkwa mîn âwa nôhtâwiy, mîn êwako mistahi nikostotonâmâw, nânitaw tit-êsit ôma ta-kitahamawit ê-wî-pê-sipwêhtêyân.

[11] êkosi; êy, ê-nahipayik êkwa, «ayi!» nititâw awa nistês, «êkâ atosk-~ êkâ apici kîstâw,» nititâw, «misawâc ôma tahto-kîsikâw ê-sipwêhtêt kîkisêpâ ê-nitaw-âtoskêt,» nititâw, «êkota ka-pê-takopayin, êkota –~ êkos îsi nik-êsi-sipwêhtânân,» nititâw. êkwa anim, «ê-kî-pê-mosci-kîmîyân,» itêyihtâkwan. hâw, kîtahtawê kâ-takopayit nistês, ê-nakipicikêt [*?record*], «êkosi cî? pikw îspîhk cî

now I went to the Band Office, I went and gave notice, «I am about to move, you are cutting me off –~ you have cut me off and I don't get welfare,» I said to him, «so I am going to leave.» – «Where are you going to go?» that welfare officer said to me. «I am going to move to Saskatoon,» I said to him, «I have come to give notice; I am going to move over there,» I said to him. Oh my, I startled that little welfare officer by what I said, «Yes,» they said to me, «But we will give you a cheque so that you all will be able to eat over there and you will be able to get food with that for your grandchildren,» he said, «I will give you that for you will not be able to obtain welfare over there right away, so that you all will be able to eat with that in the meantime,» he said to me. «And also, how are you going to go there?» he said to me, «Well, I will hire somebody, I guess, to take me there, to take our things over there for us, there is not much of it,» I said to him. So it was, «That too I will pay for you; look for someone to take your things there for you!» he said, «I will give fifty dollars to someone if he takes your things over there for you,» he said to me. It actually happened that one of my older brothers, a bachelor, at all times had a truck, now I also secretly tried to see that one. Indeed I found him, though I was afraid that he would speak sternly to me, that he would disapprove of it for me to be moving here, and my father too, I was very much afraid of what he would say, that he would speak sternly to me, that he would caution me against leaving for here.

[11] So it was; hey, now when the time had come, «Well then!» I said to my older brother, «Once your brother-in-law is not at home,» I said to him, «in any case, he leaves every day early in the morning and goes to work,» I said to him, «then you will drive up and that way we will leave,» I said to him. Now one might think, «I simply stole away.» Well, at one time my older brother drove up, and as he came to a stop [*?record*], «Is this it? Could you

ôma kâh-kî-sipwêhtân mâka?» nititik. «âha,» nititâw, «pikw îspîhk ôma êkosi nikâh-kî-isi-~» – êkwa, «pôsihcikêk mâka!» nititikonân. êkw âni piyâh-pôsihcikêsiyâhk êkwa, môy mîna mihcêt nipâkanisa kâ-sipwêhtatâyâhk mîn êkwa, têpiyâhk t-êsi-nipâkêsiyâhk, nânitaw miskamâhk[i] îta t-âyâyâhk. êkosi; êkw ân[i] êkwa kâ-pê-sipwêpayiyâhk êkwa; ôtênâhk, nipê-sipwêhtahikonân êkota. êkwa anita, sôniyâwasinahikan êkwa sôniyâwikamikohk êk ôma, kâ-tipahamâht ôma, êkoni ôhi –~, êwak ôma nimiyâw sôniyâwasinahikan ôma ka-pê-pimohtahit, pitamâ êkwa pimi-nakîw anita sôniyâwikamikohk, êwak ôma sôniyâw-~ sôniyâwasinahikan ê-pimi-mîskotônahk, êkwa mîn ânima niy ôtê t-ôh-mîcisoyâhk. êkosi, niwâ-~, êkos ê-kîsi-mîskotônamâhk êk ôh ê-pê-wayawîyâhk, ê-kîsi-pâh-pôsiyâhk nôhtâwiy êkota kâ-pê-takohtêt,

[FA:] ah!

hây, êwako kâ-kostak. nikî-~ nikî-nihtâ-mâna-mistahi-sôhkê-kitotikonân, konit ê-ay-itâpit ê-pôsihtêyiki ôhi kîkwâs[a] ôhi pit-~ –~, «yaw! tânit[ê] êkwa ê-itohtêyan?» itêw ôhi, '*Johnny*' nititânân mân âwa nistês, «tânitê ê-itohtêyan, *Johnny*?» – «aw âwa ê-itohtaha-~ ê-itohtahakik ôtê,» itwêw; «â, êkotê –~ êkotê –~ êkot[ê] ôma ê-itohtahakik ôki, sâskwatôn ôk ê-itohtahakik,» itwêw, «ê-masinahikêhit awa,» itêw.

[12] âw, mitoni mâk âwa nikiskêyimâw nôhtâwiy ê-pîtotêyihtahk ôhi kîkway ê-is-âsiwatêyiki, môy mâka nânitaw nititik, môy nânitaw itwêw, ayisk nikîsi-pôsinân âsay; êkosi nitisi-sipwêpayinân. îh, êkos ânim ôta kâ-kî-pê-ayâyâhk anima,

[FA:] *Saskatoon.*

êkos ôt[a] ê-kî-isi-takohtahikoyâhk sâskwatôn ôma, âha. pitamâ êkwa awa pêyak iskwêw, ê-nakayâskawak ôta ê-wîkit, êwakw ân[a] êkwa pitamâ nikîwik-~ nikî-wîc-âyâmânân, êkwa niwîcihik

leave at any time then?» he said to me. «Yes,» I said to him, «Yes, I could leave at any time –~» – now, «Load up then!» he said to us. Now we loaded up our few things, there also was not much bedding we took with us as we left, so long as we would have a bit to sleep on once we found some place to stay. So it was; with that now we left to drive here; he left with us for town [*sc.* North Battleford]. At this place now, now it was that cheque at the bank which he was paid with, that one –~, I had given him that cheque to bring me here, on the way he first stopped here at the bank and went to cash that cheque, and I also the one for us to eat with over here. So it was, when we had finished cashing the cheques and came back out and had all got back in the truck, at that moment it was my father who arrived,

[FA:] oh!

oh no, it was he I had been afraid of. He had always been in the habit of speaking to us very harshly, he was just looking at the few things loaded on the truck. «Well now! Where are you going?» he said to him, Johnny we always called my older brother, «Where are you going, Johnny?» – «I am taking this one and her family over here,» he said; «well, I am taking them over there, I am taking them to Saskatoon,» he said, «she has hired me,» he said to him.

[12] Well, I knew very well, however, that my father thought there was something odd about these things that were piled in the truck, but he did not say anything to me, he did not say anything, for we were already all in the truck; and with that we drove off. Look, that is how we came to be here,

[FA:] at Saskatoon.

that is how we were delivered here, it was Saskatoon, yes. For a while now, a certain woman with whom I was acquainted and who lived here, for a while now we stayed with that one, and then

êkwa wâskahikan ê-papâ-nâh-nitonamâhk; êkota êkwa k-âcimoyân êkwa, kâ-mostohtê-pîhtikwêpiciyâhk [*laughs*].

[13] êkos ânima, êkospîhk ohc ôta kâ-kî-ka-kisâtamân êkwa ôma, êkospîhk ôta ohci kâ-mâc-âyâyân. îh, êkos ânima, tâpwê pikw êkos ânima ka-~ ê-kî-pônihtâyân tâpwê niminihkwêwin, mitoni, êkot[a] êkwa mistahi kâ-kî-mâmitonêyihtamân, êkot[a] êkwa manitow kâ-kî-kiskisiyân, mahti ê-wî-kwêski-pimâtisiyân, mîna ê-wî-kakwê-~ ê-nitotamâyân, kwayask nôsisimak ê-wî-kakwê-pamihakik, mîskot mâka ê-wî-kakwê-kaskihtâyân, ê-wî-kakwê-kwêski-pimâtisiyân, nikî-itwân mân êkospîhk anima.

[14] êkosi; êkos ês âni tâpwê piko, ê-ihkihk manitow mistahi kâ-wîsakitêhêyan kîkway, kâ-mawimostawat; ê-ihkihk, kikitimâkihtâk ê-~ manitow, tâpwê ani miton ê-kî-ay-ihkihk, ômis îsi kîkway ê-kî-ati-kisiskâ-kîkway-otinamâsoyân, t-êc-âpacihtâyân [*sic*] kîkway. ahpô mâna sêhkê môniyâsak ê-kî-pê-nitawi-wâpamicik, kîkway kâ-nôhcê-acâwâkêsicik, âsay ê-kî-~ êkot[a] ê-kî-âh-ohtatâwêyân [*sic*] kîkway ê-mâh-miywâsiciki [*sic*], piyisk miton êkos ôm ê-kî-isi-takahkapihisoyân, kîkway ê-âh-atâwêyân âpacihcikana êkos îsi.

[15] êkosi; êkota êkwa kahkiyaw ôki nôsisimak kâ-kî-ka-kîsi-kiskinohamâsocik [*sic*], piyisk ân-~ *highschool* kâ-kî-~-kâh-ki-~-kâh-kiskinohamâsocik, pêyak simâkanisîwiw êwakw âna nipêpîm ta-kî-itwêyân; kâh-kîsîhtâwak okiskinohamâsowiniwâw. aw ôskinîkiskwêw, sêmâk êkota *highschool* kî-pîhtikwahisow wîsta, wîst ê-pimipayihisot, *highschool* kî-itohtêw; êwakw ân[a] ôtê *Lloydminister* êkwa k-âyât, *social worker* k-êtatoskêt. êkosi nîst ê-kî-ay-ispayihikoyân.

[16] êkosi wiy êwako, êkoyikohk isko nikîsîhtân pitamâ âcimowin.

she helped me as we went around looking for a house; it was at that point now what I told about, that we moved into the house on foot [*laughs*].

[13] That was the way, it has been since that time that we have been staying here, it was at that time that I began to live here. Look, that was the way, it is true, I immediately put an end to my drinking, it was at that point, really, that I greatly thought about things, it was at that point that I remembered God, that it would be, that I would turn my life around, that I also would try –~, I prayed for it, that I would try to look after my grandchildren properly, but in return I would try to succeed at it, that I would try to turn my life around, I used to say at that time.

[14] So it was; thus then it happens immediately, when your heart is especially heavy about something and you beseech God; it happens, God listens to you with pity, and in truth it really did happen, in this way I quickly got these things to use in my household. There even were White people always coming to see me, on their own initiative, wanting to sell a few things, already I was buying some nice things from there, in this way finally I was nicely set up, buying various household goods in that way.

[15] So it was; now it was at that point that all my grandchildren completed their schooling, finally they were all in highschool, that one became a soldier, my baby I should say; they all completed their schooling. This young woman right away enrolled herself in highschool on her own, she did things on her own, she went to highschool; she is the one who is now over there at Lloydminster, she is employed as a social worker. As for me, that is what has happened to me.

[16] That is it, I have finished my whole story for the time being.

III

The spiritual life

Sarah Whitecalf, c. 1990.

9

ê-sîkâwîhcikêhk

Observing the mourning ritual

ê-sîkâwîhcikêhk

[1] êy, ôt[a] ôma ê-wî-ay-âcimostawak aw âpisîs niwîcêwâkan, *Freda Greyeyes* [*sc. Ahenakew*], êkwa niya *Mrs Whitecalf*, sâskwatôn ôta ôma kâ-wî-~ k-âcimoyân mâna. êkosi, mitoni ninayêhtâwîn, môy mitoni mistah êkwa kîkway âcimowin nitayân, ta-kî-ât-~ ta-kî-âtotamân ôta, mêkwâc pîhtaw, môy tâpwê nimiyomahcihon êkoyikohk, sôskwâc; mâka niwî-~ niwî-kakwê-tôtên ôma kâ-kî-~ kâ-isi-nitawêyimit awa niwîcêwâkan ôta ti-~ t-âcimostawak, ôta kîkway t-âcimoyân.

[I]

[2] pêyak kîkway nipê-~-nitôs-~-nitôs-~-nitôskamâkawin ôta t-âtotamân, tânêhk ôhci nêhiyawayisiyiniw kâ-sêkipatwât, tânispîhk anim ê-pê-ohci-mâcipayik êwako kâ-kî-pê-sêkipatwât êtikwê ayisiyiniw, mihcêt ê-ta-~, môy ê-tâpwêwakêyihtahkik êwak ôma k-âpihkêcik ayisiyiniwak, nêhiyawak. êkos êkwa, ê-pê-âcimostawit êwakw âwa, tâpiskôc ôtê ê-pêhtawât pêyak ê-kisîmikot ê-mâmawôpihk, êwak ôm ê-~ ê-ohci-nânitaw-itwêyit ôma k-âpihkêcik ôk âyisiyiniwak kâ-sêkipatwâcik, «konit ânima,» ê-itwêcik. mâka namôya, namôy konit ânima, nîs-~ nîstanân kâ-nêhiyawayisiyinîwiyâhk, ê-kî-pê-isi-pakitinikowisiyâhk ôma, cikêmâ niyanân nêhiyawak; êkosi nikî-pakitinikawinân ta-sêk-~

Observing the mourning ritual

[Prologue]

[1] Hey, it is on here [*sc.* on the audio-recorder] I am going to tell my partner Freda Greyeyes [*sc.* Ahenakew] a little story, and as for me, I am Mrs Whitecalf, it is here in Saskatoon that I usually tell my stories. In that way I am really in trouble, I do not really have much in the way of stories now that I could tell on here, at the moment it so happens that I am simply not feeling all that well right now; but I will try to do what my partner wants of me, to tell her stories on here, to tell about something on here.

[**I**] [Cutting One's Hair and other Mourning Rituals]

[2] One subject I have been requested to tell about on here [*sc.* on the audio-recorder] is the reason why Cree people wear braids and when it had started that Indian people must have come to wear braids, since many do not believe that Indians, Crees should braid their hair. And so this one came to tell me that she had apparently heard a certain person in a meeting over there and had been angered by that person's claim that it was pointless when the Indians braid their hair and wear braids, «It is meaningless,» they said. But it is not so, it is not meaningless that we who are Cree Indians were set down here on earth in this way all along by the Powers, for of course we are Crees; this we were set down on

kî-sêk-~ kâ-sê-~ kâ-kî-mâci-sêkipatwâcik ôki, êtikwê pêc[i] [*sic*] ôki kotakak, mê-~ iyin-âyisiyiniwak, kayâs, mêkwâc ê-pê-mâci-iyinîskamikâk ôta, ayisiyiniw, nêhiyawayisiyiniw, ê-pê-pakitinikowisit. êkospîhk ohci sêmâk êtikwê kî-pê-kinwâniskwêw ayisiyiniw, nâpêw, wâwîs cî iskwêwak, mâka nâpêwak ôki, mêcimôhc ohc êkosi ê-kî-pê-~ wîstawâw ê-pê-itâcihocik anima, ê-kî-pê-kinwâniskwêcik, nâpêwak ôki. êkwa, pêyakwan tâpiskôc, êkosi misakâm[ê] êwakw ân[i] ânima êkosi kî-pê-ispayiw.

[3] hâw, êkwa mîna, ôm êkwa kâ-kî-mâci-~ kâ-pê-mâci-paskosikâsocik mihcêt ôki, kî-sêkipatwâwak awâsisak, nâpêsisak kâ-~ ê-~ kî-sa-sêkipacwâsiwak, kiskinohamâtowikamikohk k-êtohtahihcik, kâ-nitawi-pakitinihcik kiskinohamâtowikamikohk. êkot[ê] êkwa, kiskinohamâtowikamikohk k-âyâcik êkonik ôk âwâsisak k-êtohtahihcik k-âti-sêkipatwâcik, kî-ati-kîskisikâtêyiwa osêkipatwâniwâwa, osêkipacwânisiwâwa, ê-kîskisamiyit okiskinohama-~ ôhi kâ-kiskinoham-~ kâ-wî-kiskinohamâhcik ita [*sic*]; êkosi kî-mâci-paskosikâsowak kahkiyaw ôk âwâsisak. êkota ohc ê-kî-iskopayik anima mâci. îh, êkota mîn ôma, môniyâ-~ wâpiski-wiyâs aw ânima, wiy ê-kî-tôtahk anima, kâ-kî-pê-mâci-ati-paskosikâsocik ôk âwâsisak kiskinohamâtowikamikohk êhihtwâwi, âtiht ê-kî-kakânwâniskwêcik awâsisak ê-~ ê-pakitinihcik ê-kî-kîskisikâtêyiki osêkipatwâniwâwa. pêyakwan êkosi iskwêsisak, nikî-~ êwako nikî-pê-ocihci-wâpahtên, ê-sêkipatwâcik kiskinohamâtowikamikohk ê-pakitinihcik, miton êskohtawakêcik, kêkât nawat piko kî-sâkamoniyiwa ohtawakâwâwa, iyikohk ê-kî-isk-~ ê-kî-iskosikâtêyiki wêscakâsiwâwa, kiskinohamâtowikamikohk k-âyâcik mayaw iskwêsisak.

earth to wear –~ when they had begun to wear braids, as these other Indian people must have done all along, since long ago, when the land here had begun to be populated and human beings, Cree Indians, had come to be set down on earth by the Powers. From that very time on the people must have worn their hair long, men and especially women, but the men, they too had forever lived thus and worn their hair long, the men. And it seems it was the same, and so it has been from the beginning.

[3] Well, it was also that many now began to have their hair cut, the children used to wear braids, the little boys used to be wearing braids when they were taken to residential school, when one went and put them in residential school. Now when these children were in residential school and were taken there while wearing braids, at that time their braids were cut off, they cut off their little braids as they were being put in residential school; with that all the children began to have their hair cut. From that point on that was the beginning of the end. Look, that also was the point, the Whit-~, the Whites did that, when these children had begun, one after another, to have their hair cut as they were being placed in residential schools, some had long braids as they were put in and had their braids cut off. It was the same for girls, I have lived long enough to have seen that for myself, that they wore braids when they were put into the residential schools and had them cut off right above their ears, as a matter of fact their ears were almost sticking out, so short had their hair been cut off as soon as the girls were in residential school.

[4] êkwa, êwak ôm ôm êkwa, kâ-kî-pê-is-ô-~-isiyinîhkêcik ôki nêhiyawak ôma kâ-pê-ay-apihkêcik. tânita piko ê-kî-pê-isinâkwahk, ê-kî-pê-itât-~-itwêcik kêhtê-ayak, kê-~ ayisiyiniw, ôk âyisiyiniwak, kâ-mâyipayicik, kâ-mâyipayicik otawâsimisiwâwa ahpô ôsisimiwâwa, mistahi k-ê-~ mistah ê-itêyihtahkik; osâm ê-pakwâtahkik ê-mâyipayicik, êkota êk ôki ayisiyiniwak, nôtikwêw ahpô nâpêw, ê-kî-kîskahamâcik, êkwa, êkota êkwayâc ê-kî-paskososocik, êwakw ânima kayâhtê, mâk êwakw ânima kî-isiyîhkâtêw, 'ê-sîkâwîhcikêhk', kî-itwêwak, ê-pakwâtahkik anima, anim ê-~, ôm ê-mâyipayicik ôma, iyiwê kî-kîs-~ kîs-~ kî-kîskisamwak osêkipatwâniwâwa, ê-kî-tahtâniskwêcik, êwak ôm ôma.

[5] êkwa, m-~ êkota ohc êkwa kahkiyaw, mitoni kî-kitimâkisîhisowak ayisiyiniwak kâ-mâyipayicik, môy tâpiskôc anohc, anohc miywâsin ê-nânapâcihot ayisiyiniw kâ-mâyipayit ciyêkwac. kayâs nama kîkway êwako, kî-kitimâkisiw ayisiyiniw, ê-kî-pê-kwatakihisot [*sic*] mistahi, kâ-mâyipayit otayisiyinîma aw âyisiyiniw. iskwêwak ê-kî-sâsâkihticik êsa mâna, êkâ ê-wî-kikaskisinêcik, nâpêwak mîna, êkâ ê-wî-kikaskisinêcik ê-kî-sâsâkihticik, pikw îtê ê-kî-papâ-mâtocik nâpêwak, âhk îtâp [*sic*] ê-papâ-mâcîcik, mâk êkos ânim ê-kî-isi-papâmatwêmocik êsa mân ôki nâpêwak, iyikohk ê-kî-kitimâkisicik, mistah ê-itêyihtahkik kâ-wan-~ kâ-nakat-~ kâ-wanihâcik owâhkômâkaniwâwa; pêyakwan êkos îskwêwak, konit êsa mâna kâ-kî-sâsâkihticik ôk îskwêwak, oskocâkâsiwâwa ê-îwêkotêyiki ê-îwêpayiniyiki, êkwa ê-kis-~ ê-kîskisahkik osêkipatwâniwâwa.

[6] kîtahtawê, kî-ati-wâh-wîhtamâkowisiwak êkonik ôk ôsîkâwîhcikêwak, osâm mistah ânima ê-pê-kitimahisocik, kîtahtawê pêyak awa nâpêw, ê-mâcît âhk îtâp [*sic*], ê-papâmatwêmot êsa mâna, êkos ôm ôwîkimâkana nâh-napo [*sic*] mitoni ê-kitimâkisîhisocik ê-kitimâkihocik; êkota êkwa, kîtahtawê ê-apit, ê-ma-mâtot ôma;

[4] Now it had all along been the case that the Crees had been living as a people and had been braiding their hair. The only time it had looked like that, the old people used to say, was when people, when people were bereaved, when they suffered the loss of their child or grandchild, they took it very hard; they were grief-stricken by their loss, only then did these people cut off their hair, an old woman or a man, that was the first and only time their hair was cut in the old days but that used to be called 'to observe the mourning ritual', that they used to say, and grief-stricken as they were over their loss, they would deliberately, as if in helpless defiance, cut off their braids and let their hair hang loose on both sides; it was that.

[5] Now from that point on all the people who suffered bereavement would be dressed really miserably, not like today, today it is correct for people who are bereaved to dress up instead. Long ago there was none of that, people used to be so miserable, people made themselves suffer a great deal when they were bereaved of a family member. The women would go barefoot, it is reported, so as not to put their moccasins on, and the men, so as not to put their moccasins on, would also go barefoot, the men would go about hither and thither and cry, going about as if they were setting off to hunt but in reality they would go about wailing, so miserable did these men use to be, they took it so hard when they lost a relative; the same with the women, the women would simply go barefoot, it is reported, their dresses hung in tatters and rags, and they cut off their braids.

[6] After a time those who were in mourning were one by one told by the Powers that they made themselves suffer too much, at one time a certain man reportedly pretended to set off to hunt and went about wailing, and he and his wife both were dressed in rags and suffering great misery; now then, it was as he sat there

kîtahtawê kîkw-~, mâniko [*sic*] kîkway ê-itêyihtahk ê-pêhtahk, kâ-kitotikot ôta awiya, ê-nahikâpawistâkot ôm îta k-âpit, «hâ, nôhtâ, êkosi! êkosi, nôhtâ, pôni-mâto! êkos êkwa, êkoyikohk; mâh-~ mahti pônihtâk ôma kâ-tôtamêk ôma, mistah ôm ê-kitimahiyêk, môy ôma ê-kî-sipwêhtêyân. iyikohk kiyawâw ê-kisâtitakok, ê-kitimâkihtâtakok ôma; mâka namôy nikî-sipwêhtân. êkwa mîna, mâcikôcican nôhtâ, kitâpamin ê-isinâkosiyân! kiyawâw ôma ê-tôtawiyêk ôma k-ôh-isinâkosiyân, nôhtâ!» k-êtikocik ês âwa – okosis[a] âwa awa nâpêw awa k-êtikot. ê-kitâpamât, «mâcikôcican, nôhtâ, pê-kitâpamin!» – «hâ, êkwa konita mâna nikâh-kakwê-cîsihikowisin kîkway, matwân cî tâpwê nikosis, ta-wâpamak ê-kî-nakasit,» itwêw ês âwa kisêyiniw. êkosi, «namôya, nôhtâ, pê-kitâpamin!» tâpwê êtikw êkwa, ê-itâpit, pôt ôh ôta, kî-nîpawiyiwa okosisa. êy, tâniyikohk ês ê-kitimâkinâkosiyit, êkw ê-sâsâkinikâtêyit okosisiwâwa ôhi, mêtoni ê-kicimâkisinâkosiyit [*sic*], ostikwân nisi ês âw ôskinîkiw awa ê-isinâkwaniyik; iyikohk ê-sêhkwêstikwânêt, tâpiskôt môy ôht-~ – namôy êkosi kâ-kî-isîhiht ê-ka-~ kâ-nakataskêt, iyikohk ê-kî-miyonâkosit, ês ê-wawêsîhiht aw ôskinîkiw, nama kîkway êkoni ê-postiskahk awa, namôy kîkway êkosi ê-isinâkosit. kwayask ê-kitâpamât, «mâcikôcican, nôhtâ, pê-kitâpamin kwayask.» ê-kitâpamât, ôta oskîsikoyihk, nâh-nîhtaciwê owaniwâ-~, waniwâhk awa, ê-kitâpamât ôhi, tâpiskôc ê-wî-oy-omikît, tâpiskôc ê-wî-sa-sâkihkowit nîhtaciwê ôta ôma, oskîsikohk, êwako – oskîsikwâpoy an[a] ê-kîsisokot an[a] ôskinîkiw, wîst êkos ânim êtikwê ê-isi-mâtot, ê-mâtot tâpitawi; îh, ôm îyikohk ôtê ê-mawîhkâtiht, wîst êkosi nêtê ê-tôtahk aw ôskinîkiw. hâw, êwakw ânim êkwa, êtikwê wîst êtikw êkwa ê-i-~ ê-i-~ ê-itikowisit nêtê itê k-~ kâ-kî-ohci-nitawêyihtâkosit ta-pê-wîhtahk, ka-pê-wîhtamawât [*sic*] onîkihikwa. «mâcikôcican, nôhtâ, kîwê!

crying, suddenly it seemed to him that he heard something, that someone spoke to him while standing beside where he sat, «Ho, Father, enough! Enough, Father, cease your crying! That is enough now, no more; both of you, please cease of what you are doing, you are causing me great misery and I am unable to leave. I am staying so close to you both and I listen to you with pity; but I am unable to leave. And also, lo, Father, look at me what I look like! It is you two who make me look like this, Father!» is what he and his wife were reportedly told by him – it was this man's son who spoke to him. As he looked at him, «Lo, Father, come and look at me!» – «Ho, now, it is an attempt by the Powers to raise my hopes in vain, could it be in truth that I see my son who has left me,» said this old man. And so it was, «No, Father, come and look at me!» Truly now, as he looked there, I guess, here it was his son standing there. Hey, how miserable he looked, it is reported, and their son's legs were bare, he looked miserable indeed, the young man's head looked so awful; so dishevelled was his hair, as if he had not – that was not how he had been dressed when he had died, the young man had looked so nice, it is reported, he had been well dressed, he had none of those clothes on now, he did not look anything like the way he had looked. As he looked at him closely, «Lo, Father, look at me closely.» As he looked at him, here at his eyes, down on both sides, on his cheeks, as he looked at him, it seemed as if he had scabs, it seemed as if the scabs were almost bleeding down from his eyes – the young man's tears had left his face raw for he too must have been crying in the same way, constantly crying; look, they had been crying for the young man so much over here, and he too had done the same over yonder. Well, it must have been that now he too must have been told by the Powers over there whence he had been summoned that he should come and

kîwêyan[i] ôma, kâsîhkwêhkan!» k-êtât êsa, «sîkahôhkan, kîkway kitayân ta-kikiskaman, mîskotayiwinisêhkan!» ê-~ k-êtikot ês âwa nâpêw ôh ôkosisa, «êkwa nikâwiy, kika-wîhtamawâw; wîst êkosi ta-tôtam, ta-sîkahow; kîkway ê-ayât ta-mîskotiskam, kwayask, ta-mîskotayiwinisêw, ta-nânapâcihisow! êkos ê-isi-~ tahto-kîsikâw êkosi tôtamok, nânapâcihisok! hâw, êkwa nika-miyw-âyân êkota ohci, êwak ôma pônihtâyêko, kîspin kikitimâkêyiminâwâw; ê-kitimâkêyimiyêk ayisk, iyikohk kâ-kitimâ-~ kâ-kitimahisoyêk, pisisik kâ-mâtoyêk, iyikohk ê-mawîhkâsiyek; mâk êkwa, kikitimahinâwâw ôma, mâcikôcican, nânapâcihoyêko, nôhtâ, ômis ôma nik-êsinâkosin,» k-êtikot êsa, «mâcikôcican, kitâpamin!» k-êtikot ês âwa okosis-~, ê-kitâpamât, pôt âwa, êy, oskinîkiw, mitoni mosc-ôy-~ ê-mosci-wâsênâkosit sôskwâc aw ôskinîkiw, iyikohk ê-takahkinâkosit! ôma kâ-kî-isîhot, mwêhc êkos ê-isinâkosit aw ôskinîkiw, ê-isîhot ôma, «îh, êkos ôma nik-êsîhon, pôyoyêko, nânapâcihisoyêko,» k-êtikot êsa, «hâw êkosi, nôhtâ, êwako piko ê-pê-wîhtamâtân! hâ, kîwê, nôhtâ, nitawi-kâsîhkwê! nânapâcihôhkan! sîkahôhkan!» îh, êwakw ânima, êwakw ânima kayâs nêhiyaw-~ nêhiyawi-kîkway, â, tâpwê ês êkwa, ê-kîwêt awa kisê-~ awa nâpêw, ê-takohtêt nêtê, ê-takosihk wîkihk, wîkiwâhk, â, sêmâk ati-kîskwê-kâsîhkwêw awa nâpêw, êkos êkwa ati-sîkahow mîna. «tânis êkwa,» itêyihtamiyiwa owîkimâkana.
kâh-kîsi-kâsîhkwêt [*sic*], kâh-kîsi-sîkahot [*sic*], otinam ôh ôtayiwin-~ otayiwinisa kîkway, yôho [?*sic*], «nah!» k-êtât ês ôwîkimâkana, «kîsta kâsîhkwê! sîkahôhkan! mîskotayiwinisêhkan! hâ, niwâpamâw ani kikosisinaw,» k-êtât ês ôwîkimâkana, «niwâpamâw kikosisinaw; mistah ês ôma ê-kitimahâyahk ôma kâ-tôtamahk, 'â, kîwê, nôhtâ! nitawi-kâsîhkwê! kwayask nitawi-nânapâciho!'

tell, that he should come and tell his parents. «Lo, Father, go home! Once you get home, then wash your face!» is what he reportedly said to him, «Then comb your hair, you have clothes to wear, then change your clothes!» is what this man was told by his son, «And you will tell my mother; let her too do that, let her comb her hair; let her change into clothes she has, let her properly change her clothes, let her tidy herself up! Do this every day, tidy yourselves up! Well, now I will be well from here on in, once you stop this if you take pity on me; for you do take pity on me, having made yourselves suffer and having cried all the time and crying out over me so much; but now you have been causing me misery, lo, once you have tidied up, Father, this is what I will look like,» his son reportedly told him, «Lo, look at me!» his son reportedly told him, and when he looked at him, here was the young man, hey, simpl-~, in an instant the young man simply shone, he looked so beautiful. Just as he had been dressed, exactly that way the young man looked dressed, «Look, thus I will be dressed once you cease of it and tidy yourselves up,» is what he reportedly told him, «Well, enough, Father, that is all I have come to say to you! Ho, go home, Father, go and wash your face! Then tidy up! Then comb your hair!» Look, that is it, that is the Cree way of long ago, well, and truly now, it is reported, this old m-~ this man went home and arrived over yonder, as he got to his place, their place, well, straight away he proceeded to wash his face, without delay, and also to comb his hair. «What now,» his wife thought. When he had finished washing his face and when he had finished combing his hair, he took some clothes, oh, «Here!» he reportedly said to his wife, «You too wash your face! Then comb your hair! Then change your clothes! Ho, I have indeed seen our son,» he reportedly said to his wife, «I have seen our son; we have been causing him great

ê-isit ôma, 'mâcikôcican, ômisi nik-êsinâkosin, kîspin kwayask nânapâcihoyêko,' ê-isit ôma kikosisinaw, kâwi miton ê-miyonâkosit, nistam anima kâ-wâpamak, miton âni kitimâkinâkosiw, ê-îwêpayiniyiki otayiwinisa, iyikohk ê-si-~ ê-ohpwêstikwânêt, tâpiskôc êkâ wîhkâc ê-sîkahot,» ê-~ k-ê-~ ê-itât ês ôwîkimâkana ôhi, «êkosi nitâpwêhtên, ê-pêh-~ ê-wâpamak nikosis, okihciyaw ê-wâpamak, ê-pê-itisahoht ta-pê-wîhtamâkoyahk êwak ôma,» k-êtwêt –~ k-êtât ês âw ôwîkimâkana. îh, êwakw ân[i] ânima, êkos ânima ê-kî-isi-wâh-wîhtamâkowisicik anima, kayâs ôki kêhtê-ayak, iyikohk ê-kî-pê-kitimahisocik; êwak ôma sîkâwîhcikêwin ohci.

[7] mâk êkwa anohc, môy êkwa êwa-~ êwakw âta wiya êkos ê-ispayik. êwak ôhci, mîna niya nitâpwêwakêyihtên, mihcêt ôk ôsk-âyak kinwâniskwêwak, sa-sêkipatwâwak, âtiht nâway ôtê ê-apihkêcik oskinîkiwak. kîtahtawê sisikoc, kâ-kihtimêyihtahkik wêstakâwâwa, kîskisamwak mîn êkonik ôki, kîskisâwâtamwak kâw[i] ôsêkipatwâniwâwa, môy ê-sêkipatwâcik, ê-mosci-~. îh, êwakw ânima mîna, «môy kwayask ê-tôtahk,» itwâniwiw mâna, kîtahtawê sêhkê ayisiyiniw, kâ-kîskisahk osk-âya aw ôsêkipatwâniwâwa ôki kâ-kîskahamâcik; tâpwê êkos ât[i]-îspayiw, mihcêt, tânitahto êkw êkosi nitisi-na-nâkatôhkân ôk ôsk-âyak, mistahi mâyipayiwak ciyêkwac, tâpiskôc kwayâci ê-kîskahamâcik ê-sîkâwîhcikêcik, kâ-kîskisahkik owê-~ wêstakâwâwa, kâ-mêkwâ-ma-miyw-âyâcik, êkonik ôk ôkinwâniskwêwak ôki, kâ-itakik; êkos ê-kî-~, êkosi ê-kî-pê-ispayik anima kayâs, êwak ôma kâ-kî-~ kâ-nôhtê-kiskêyihtahkik ôki. mâk ânohc êkwa miywâsin kâ-isi-wâpahtamân, kâ-wî-nahiniht ayisiyiniw, êkota êkwa, namôy kakêtihk nânapâcihow ayisiyiniw, mîn ômâyipayiw, kâ-mâyipayit, mêtoni kwayask nânapâcihow, kâ-wî-nitawi-nahastamâht owâhkômâkana. êwakw ês ânima ê-miywâsik, kwayask êwako ê-tôtamihk anima, namôy kîkway kakwâtaki-~ kakwâtakihtâwin ôk âyâwak kâ-nakataskêcik.

misery by what we have been doing, 'Well, go home, Father! Go and wash you face! Go and tidy up properly!' he said to me, 'Lo, I will look like this if you tidy up properly,' our son said to me, and he looked really nice again, when I had first seen him he looked really miserable, his clothes all torn and his hair sticking up so much that it seemed as though he had never combed his hair,» he said to his wife, «and so I believe it that I saw my son, that I saw him in person, and that he had been sent here to come to tell us that,» he said –~ he said to his wife. Look, it was that, this is what he had repeatedly been told by the Powers, in the old days the old people used to make themselves suffer so much; this was because of the mourning ritual.

[7] But today now, now at least that does not happen. For this reason, I for one believe that, many of the young people wear their hair long, they wear braids, some of the young men wear a single braid at the back. Sometimes all of a sudden they tire of their hair and cut it off, they cut their braids off again and do not wear braids, simply –~ Look, people also say, «He is not acting properly,» when young people have their hair cut for no apparent reason and they cut off their braids; and it is true that this is beginning to happen, a lot, I have noticed many young people, terrible things befall them instead, it seems as though they had their hair cut in preparation for mourning when they cut their hair while they are still well, these long-haired ones I am talking about; that is what used to happen with respect to this long ago, that is what they wanted to know about. But today now what I see is good, when some person is about to be buried, at that time people get very much dressed up, also the bereaved, they get very properly dressed up when they have a death, when a relative is about to be buried. That is good and it is properly done, in that way the departed do not suffer any torment.

[8] êkwa mîna, kî-kitahamâtonâniwiw, kî-~, mîn ôta, môy kayâs êwako mitoni nikî-pâh-pêhtên, âtiht namôy ê-wî-itohtêcik nânitaw k-êtahkamikahk, mîna, êkosi mîn ê-kî-pê-tôtahkik kayâs ayisiyiniwak, nânitaw k-êsi-mâmawôpayihk, môy ê-kî-wî-itohtêcik, anima –~ nayêstaw êwakw ânim ôhci omâyipayiwiniwâw. nikî-pêhtên mâna mîna, ê-wîhtamâht awa, nîst ât-~, nîst êkota pêyak kîkway pawâtamowin nikî-ayân, ê-~ ê-pê-wîhtamâht ês âwa, ê-papâ-~ ê-kî-papâ-mâtot mâna kâh-kapê-ayi, «hâ, maht êkwa! ta-pônihtâw kôhtâwînaw ôma kâ-tôtahk, mistahi nikitimâkisin. êkos ôma, môy wîhkâc ôma pîhtêyask ê-kî-itohtêyân, ita kâ-mihcêtihk,» ê-itwêt –~ ê-itiht awa kâ-pawâtiht awa, êkos ôma mâna, wayawîtim-âyihk êsa mân ê-papâ-ay-ayât awa; ita ôma kâ-mihcêtiwiht, môy pîhtêyask ê-kî-itohtêt, nayêstaw tahki wayawîtim-âyihk ê-papâ-ay-ayât, ê-akâwâtahk pîhtêyask kit-êtohtêt, ê-kitimâkinawât ôhi, onîkihikwa, iyikohk ê-kitimâkisiyit. êwakw ânima nikî-pêhtên nîsta, mîn êkwa môy kayâs êwakw ânima êkosi k-êspayik. tâpwê mîn êwakw ânima miyâmâc, êkosi namôy ê-isi-miywâsik, t-êsi-ka-~-kakwâtakihiht êtikwê onîkânohtêw.

[9] êkoni ôhi kâ-kî-~ kâ-nôhtê-âcimostawak awa. tâpwê âta wiya mistahi ê-âyimahk ôma, êkos îsi k-êspayihikohk [*sic*], mistahi kîkway osâm, k-êspayi-~ k-êspayihikocik ayisiyiniwak. êwakw ân[i] ânim âwa ê-nôhtê-âcimoyân, kayâs nêhiyawi-kîkway tânis ê-kî-pê-ispayik, nêhiyaw-âya ôhi kîkway, kâ-kî-pê-ma-mâyipayihk nanâtohk isi.

[II]

[10] êkwa, kotak kîkway nik-âtotên. â, miywâsin êkwa mitoni, mîna ê-wî-ati-kîs-~-kwêskinâkwahk kitaskînaw, tânôtân[i] êtikwê, êtikwê âyimâtahkamik, mihcêt, môy kiwâpamânawak

[8] Now also people used to warn one another, here also not long ago I heard this on several occasions that some people [*sc.* in mourning] would not go to some event or other and that the people of old had also done that, when there was some kind of gathering or other, that they would not be able to go there and that this was due solely to the the fact that they were in mourning. I have also heard it told about this person, and I too have had one kind of dream about it, that it was told about this person that he had gone about crying all day long, «Ho, please now! Let our father cease of what he is doing, I am so very miserable. It is thus that I can never go into the inner circle where the many are gathered,» he said –~, it was said of the one who figured in the dream, and it is in this way that this dead person stays around on the outside; wherever the many are gathered with respect to him, he cannot go into the inner circle, he merely hangs around on the outside at all times although he longs to be in the inner circle, looking upon his parents with pity since they are so miserable. I too have heard that, and that also happened not long ago. And that is true, I do believe, and it is not good for those who precede us in death to be made to suffer like that.

[9] These are the things I wanted to tell her. It is very difficult, that is true, when one has something like this happen, when something bad happens to people. That I wanted to tell about for her, what happened in the Cree way long ago, all the various Cree things that have to do with bereavement.

[**II**] [The Two Religions]

[10] Now I will tell about another thing. Well, now it is very beautiful and our earth is about to change into spring colours again, how beautiful it must be when it has fully come to pass,

kitayisiyinîminawak, namôy âhpô ê-otisâpahtahkik, ta-kîsi-kwêskinâkwaniyik askiy, ê-at-ôtisâpahtahkik nôhtaw ê-~ ê-~ ê-~ ê-wanâpamâyahkik, ê-nakataskêcik, ê-sipwêhtêcik, âta wiy âyisk êtikwê wîstawâw, it[a] ê-kî-iskwâhtâyit manitowa opimâtisiwiniwâw, êkoyikohk kâ-~ kâ-sipwêhtêcik êkonik ôki ayisiyiniwak, êkosi mâna mîna nititêyihtên niya.

[11] mâka êyiwêhk, namôy kakêtihk iyikohk ta-kâkîsimohk, ôma k-âti-kwêskinâkwahk askiy, niya mân êkosi ê-tôtamân, âta wiya namôy niya piko, pikw îtê omawimoscikêw, onêhiyawi-kâkîsimow, êwak ôma pêyak ê-aspi-kâkîsimot ôma, ê-nitotamât ta-kakwê-otisâpahtamihk ta-kwêskinâkwahk askiy; nanâtohk is ôma, kîkway ta-miyonâkwahk, kitaskînâhk ôta, t-ât[i]-îsi-kwêskinâkwahk, sakâwa ôhi, mîn ôma kitaskînaw ôma, k-êtwêcik nêhiyawak, 'kikâwînaw,' itwêwak ôma, askiy ôma. êwako mîna, iyikohk t-âci-askihtakwaskamikâk misiwê ê-isi-tahkoskâtamahk askiy ôma, misiwê ê-isi-têpâpiyahk. êwakw ân[i] ânima misakâmê okâkîsimowak, tânôtân[i] êsa êtikwê ê-ispîhcâk, iyikohk okâkîsimowak ê-pê-nitotamâcik, êwak ôma ta-kakwê-otisâpahtamihk, otawâsimisimâwak oyôsisimiwâ-~ oyôsisimiwâwa, ê-nitotamâkêstamawâcik, êwak ôma ta-kakwê-otisâpahtamihk ôma kahkiyaw, wâwîs cî wiy ôma, ôk ômawimoscikêwak, okâkîsimowak, onipâkwêsimowinihkêwak, êkota namôy kakêtihk pêhtâkwan, iyikohk kâkîsimowin êwak ôm ôma, ê-nitotamâhk ta-kakwê-otisâpahtamihk, 'kâ-misâk mîkiwâhp' ê-isiyîhkâtahkik, êwako kahkiyaw kâ-pimi-nitotahkik ayisiyiniwak, mâka mihcêt, nôhtêsimikowak [*sic*], êwakw ân[i] ânima ta-kî-otisâpahtahk ayisiyiniw, ê-âyimahk; êkwa mîna, kiyâm, ê-nêhiyâwiyâhk ôma niyanân, êwakw ânima kâ-misâk mîkiwâhp ka-tâp-~ ta-tâpwêwakêyihtamihk, tâpwê anima, êwakw âyisk kiyânaw kâ-nêhiyâwiyahk, ê-kî-pê-miyikawiyahk ês ôta, êwako t-ôtayamihâwiniyahk, êwak ôma kâ-misâk mîkiwâhp.

many of our family members we do not see since they did not even live to see the earth having completed the change into spring colours, before they might have lived to see it we no longer saw them since they departed this earth, they departed, although they too, to be sure, departed at the point that God had allotted to their lives, and as for myself, that is also what I always think.

[11] But at least one should pray a great deal when the earth is changing into spring colours, I always do that, although I am not the only one, there are worshippers everywhere, chanters of Cree prayers, adding this one thing to their chanted prayers and asking that one might be granted to live to see the earth change into spring colours; for things to look beautiful in their various ways here on our earth and for the change into spring colours to proceed in this way, the woods, and also our earth, as the Crees say, 'our mother' the Crees say of the earth. This also, that the land should be so verdant everywhere we step on this earth, everywhere our eyes reach. This the chanters of prayers have been asking for all along, however far the land stretches, so far have the chanters of prayers been asking that one might try to live to see this, the children, and praying for their grandchildren, that one might try to live to see this, all of us, especially this, these worshippers, these chanters of prayers, the ones who hold the Sundance, you hear a great deal of praying there, so much chanting of prayers, as one asks that one might try to live to see the day of the 'Sundance Lodge' [*lit.* 'Big Lodge'] as they call it, this is what they all seek as they go along, all the people, but many are worn out by it, for it is difficult for a person to be able to live to see that; now also, as for us who are Crees [*sc.* not including the audience], let it be that one should believe in that Sundance Lodge, for it is true for all of us who are Crees [*sc.* including the audience] that this Sundance Lodge has been granted to us here to have as our religion.

[12] hâ, êkwa ôma mîna, môy mâna n-~, môy mâna nita-~ nipa-pâhpîwakêyihtên, ôma mîn-~ âyamihâwin, êwako piko, nîsw êkoni, niy ôti wiya, êkoni nîso nipimitisahên, nipâhkw-âyamihân. êkosi, ê-wî-nipiyân, nikî-asocikân, kâwi kwayask nitayamihâwin ê-wî-otinamân, «pimâtisiyâni, kwayask nik-âyamihân kâwi,» nikî-itwân, pâhkw-âyamihâwin ôma, âta ê-wîcêhtamân mîn ôma, nêhiyawi-mawimoscikêwin, mâka namôya wiya ê-asênamân. êkoni nîso piko niya, kâkîsimowina ôhi ê-pimitisahamân. tâpwê ê-pimâtisiyân, êkospîhk ohti tahto-nîpin niwî-kakwê-kaskihtân kâ-mâmaw-âyamihâhk, êkotê ê-isi-pimitisahikêyân, êwakw ânima nitasocikêwin kêyâpic ê-pimitisahamân, namôy nitasênên ayamihêwi-saskamowin, kâ-wî-pê-miyit ayamihêwiyiniw, mistahi nitâpacihtân êkotowahk, âhkosîwikamikohk, nêtawi-~ êtâmoyâni, nêtawi-pîhtikwêyâni, êwak ôhc êtikwê mâna, êyiwêhk, âstamihk k-ês-âyâyân, k-âstêwêpahokawiyân wîpac; wêsâmihk ôta nistam k-âyâyân, miton êtikwê ê-kî-nêsow-âyâyân, ayamihêwiyiniw kî-pê-itohtêw, ê-pê-ayamihêstamawit, ayamihêwi-saskamowin ê-pê-miyit. êkwa, iskwêyâc ayisiyiniw kâ-wî-nakataskêt, kâ-kî-tôminiht ayisiyiniw, êkotowahk nik-~ ê-kî-pê-miyit mask-~ ayamihêwiyiniw. «hâ, tânis êtik ôma?» k-êtêyihtamân; êkosi ê-kî-pê-kiskêyihtamân êwakw ânima onêsowisiw, kâ-tôminiht oskahtikohk ocihcîhk, êkos ê-pê-isîhcikâsit ayamihêwiyiniw, «tânis ôma, matwân cî ôm ê-wî-nipiyân.» âta wiya mân ê-kî-isi-pêhtamân, «ta-nakataskêt ayisiyiniw, ta-miyo-nakataskêt, awêkâ cî mîna, êkota t-ôh-pimâtisit, êkoni nîso-kîkway,» êkosi mân êwakw ânima ê-kî-isi-pêhtamân ê-itakihtêk êwakw ânim âyamihâwin, êkoni nikî-mâmitonêyihtên, tâpwê. tâpwê nikî-pê-wayawîn êkospîhk, namôy kayâs êwako, môy êtikwê nîso-pîsim. anohc âsay mîna wîpac ôma, âsay mîna nikî-nayêhtâw-âyân, nikî-nitawi-pîhtikwân mîn âhkosîwikamik. mâka, êkos ânima pêskis ê-isi-mamisîyân anima, mân êkotê k-êtâmoyân, mistah âyamihêwiyiniw – âsay

[12] Well, now also, I do not laugh at the Christian religion, this only, these two, for me in any case, I practise both of these, I am a Roman Catholic. Thus, as I was about to die, I made a promise that I would take up my religious practice properly again, «If I live, I will again practise the Christian religion properly,» I had said, it is the Roman Catholic religion, although I also follow the Cree way of worship, it is not that I am rejecting that. For me these two are the only ways of chanting prayers I practise. Truly I did live, and since that time I try to take part in the pilgrimage every summer, I follow along over there and I still keep my promise, I do not reject the Catholic communion when the priest comes to give it to me, I make great use of that kind in the hospital each time I take refuge there, each time I go in there, that must be the reason I get at least somewhat better, why they get me better fast; even more, when I was in there for the first time and must have been really close to death, the priest came in to pray for me and gave me communion. Now, when a person is about to depart this earth, when a person is given the extreme unction, the priest had come to give me that kind. «Well, I wonder what is happening?» I thought; in that way I came to know that, when a person who is close to death has oil put on the forehead and on the hands, as the priest came and performed this ritual for me, «What is happening, I wonder if I am about to die?» Although I had often heard, «For a person to depart this earth, for a person to depart this earth in peace, or else also to live from this moment on, these are the two alternatives,» that I had often heard is the value of that sacrament, and I did think of these two, it is true. And it is true, I did get out of the hospital at that time, that was not long ago, not two months ago, I guess. Today, as usual in short order, again as usual I am not well and I went back into the hospital. But in this way I rely on that [*sc.* Christianity] at the same time, I take refuge there, and the

ê-kiskêyihtâkosiyân êkota âhkosîwikamikohk, ayamihâwin ôm ôhci, sêmâk ê-pê-itohtêcik ayamihêwiskwêwak, âsay ê-pê-miyicik ayamihêwi-saskamowin; kiyikaw ê-nitomicik ê-pê-nâtitâpâsicik cêhcapiwinisihk, ayamihêwikamikohk ê-isi-nitawi-pîhtikwêyâhkinicik, êkotê ê-nitawi-wîcihiwêyân, ot-~ otâhkosiwak kahkiyaw mân êkotê ê-nitawi-pîhtikwêcik, ê-nitaw-âyamihâcik k-ôtâkosik. êkon ânihi nîso-kîkway mîna niya nitâpwêwakêyihtên, êwak ôma mawimoscikêwin ôma.

[13] êkosi, namôy âyiwâk kîkway nika-kî-tasihtên, mâka, tanênitohk ôma, êkosi k-~ ôki kîc-âyisiyinînawak kâ-wî-kakwê-nêhiyawi-mawimoscikêcik, ta-kî-wîcihihcik anima êyiwêhk, wê-~, iyikohk wiy êkâ awiyak ta-tâpwêwakêyihtahk kîkway êyiwêhk, ê-nitotamâkêstamâkêcik, namôy âni piko wiyawâw ê-nitotamâkêstamâsocik ôki kâ-wî-kakwâtakihisocik kâ-wî-mânokêcik, êyiwêhk, ta-wîcihihcik, êkos îs ôma kâ-kâkîsimostamâkêcik, pikw îs âwiya, kâ-nitawi-miyihcik wêpinâsona, ê-kâkîsimostamâkêcik, oyôsisimimâwa otawâsimisiwâwa, êkos ê-isi-pîkiskwêstamâhcik êkotowihk anima.

priest very much – they already know me at the hospital, because of this religion, and the nuns came right away and they already came to give me communion; they further invited me and came to fetch me in a wheelchair and went and pushed me to the chapel, and I go there to participate, all the sick people go in there and pray in the evening. As for me, I believe in these two religions, it is this way of worship.

[13] That is it, I will not be able to discuss anything further but I wish that, when they are about to try to worship in the Cree way, it should at least be possible for our fellow people to be helped, instead of someone not believing in anything; since they plead for others, since those who make themselves suffer [*sc.* by fasting] and set up a lodge [*sc.* the Sundance Lodge] do not only plead for themselves, at least they should be helped when they are in this way chanting their prayers for others, for anyone, when people go and give them pieces of cloth and they chant their prayers for others, for their grandchildren and their children, in this way speaking for others in that place [*sc.* the Sundance Lodge].

Manitow kâ-matwêhikêt, viewed from the east, 2019.

10

manitow kâ-matwêhikêt

Where the spirits drum (I)

manitow kâ-matwêhikêt

[FA:] êkwa ê-kî-nitawêyihtaman êwako kâ-~ ka-pêhtâkwahk, anima kêhcinâc.

[SW:] êkwa pêyak, anoht nipêhtên, êwako mâna mistahi ê-kî-pakosêyimoyân, ômatowihk [*points to audio-recorder*] ta-kî-astêk, êwakw ân[i] ânima, kayâs âcimowin, kayâs ê-kî-pê-ispayik; wanipayiw êwakw ânima nipîkiskwêwininân tânitê êtikwê, êwakw ânim ôsâm kâ-kî-nitawêyihtamân mâna, ta-kî-êwakw-ânima-kâhcitinahk [*sic*] awa niwâhkômâkan awa pîkiskwêwin anima, niwîcêwâkanis, mâka, ahpô êtikwê kîtahtawê wêtinahk apiyâhko, kêyâpic êwako nikâh-kî-osîhtânân anima, ta-tâpâtotamân anima, mitoni nimicimêyihtên êwakw ân[i] ânima misawâc, ta-kî-tâpâtotamân tânis ê-kî-pê-ispayik, mîn êkwa ohc [*?record*] an[a] ân[a] ôskinîkiskwêw, nitaskînâhk ohc ânima, êkwa mîn êkota ohci ê-wîhcikaniwik anim îta anima kâ-kî-ispayik anima. êwakw ân[i] ânima nimihtâtên mitoni.

Where the spirits drum (I)

[FA:] And you definitely wanted that one to be [*sc.* recorded and] heard.

[SW:] Now one more, I heard about it [*sc.* the loss of an earlier recording of this text] today, I have always wished for that one to have been recorded on this kind [*points to audio-recorder*], that one in particular, that story of long ago, it happened long ago; but our recording of that got lost [*sc.* through a technical accident], I do not know where it has gone, I had especially wanted that my relative [*sc.* Freda Ahenakew] should manage to preserve that text on audio-tape, my dear partner, but perhaps at some time when we are sitting quietly we would still be able to accomplish that, for me to tell it exactly, at any rate I have it very much in my mind so that I will be able to tell it exactly as it had happened, –~ also about [*?record*] that young woman, it happened on our reserve, and because of that also, that place where it happened is called after it, I am very sorry about that [*sc.* the fact that it has so far remained unrecorded].

[1] ôtê ayi – â, âsay mîna niy ôta ôma kâ-wî-âcimoyân, *Mrs Whitecalf* kâ-wî-pîkiskwêt. ôtê, nitaskînâhk ôm ê-wî-âtotamân, pêyak, môy wîhkâc ê-pêhtâkwahk êtikwê nânitaw ta-pê-pêhtamân ôma, êwako ôma, misî-~ [*?sic*] âcimowin ôma. nôhkom mân ê-kî-âtotahk, êkwa, êkota êwako nikî-tasihtênân ê-kî-âh-apiyâhk ôtê sâskwatôn, êwak ôm ê-wî-tasihtamân, pêyak iskwêw êkota, kî-pîkiskwêw, «tâpwêwin anima,» wîst êsa mân ê-kî-pêhtahk êwak ôm ôma âcimowin ôma, wîsta kî-nâh-nômakê-âtotam êkota, tânisi mâna wîst ê-kî-itihtahk, anim êkos ê-kî-isi-pa-pêhtahk.

[2] êwak ôm ôma nitaskînân, 'nakiwacîhk' k-êsiyîhkâtêk, êkota, pêyak anima misi-tahtakwaskamikâw, wâwâki ê-pimi-wîkihk ôm ê-~ ê-isihtik sîpîsis, êkwa êkota, kayâs êsa mân êkota ayisiyiniwak ê-misi-~, nîswayak anima miton ê-mâh-misi-wîhkwê-paskwâk ê-mâh-misi-paskwâk, êkot[a] ês ê-kî-wîkihk mâna. ê-kî-mâh-mitêwicik êkota ayisiyiniwak, êkos ês ânima mêkwâc êkot[a] ê-itahkamikahk ê-mâh-mitêwihk anima.

[3] kîtahtawê, kâ-wanipayit êkota ohc ôskinîkiskwêw, ê-wanihiht. êkwa êtikwê, ê-mac-îtêyihcikâtêw [*sic*] oskinîkiskwêw awa, êk ôskinîkiwak êkwa ôki, ê-~ ê-nâh-nâkatôhkêhk êk ôk ôskinîkiwak ê-nâh-~, nam âwiyak –~, kahkiyaw ihtakowak oskinîkiwak, nam âwiyak wanipayiw oskinîkiw, ta-kî-sipwêhtahiht aw ôskinîkiskwêw nânitaw isi. kahkiyaw oskinîkiwak ôki, m[a] âwiyak, m[a] âwiyak wanipayiw, nam âwiyak kôtawêyimâw. hâ, êkwa oskinîkiskwêw êkwa aw âspin kâ-wanihiht, â, êkwa âta ê-nâh-nitonikêhk êkwa, aw ôskinîkiskwêw awa, ê-nâh-nitonât –~ ê-nâh-nitonâht êkwa tânitê, nama nânitaw miskawâw, nama nânitaw miskikâtêyiw ita ta-kî-misiwanâcihot aw ôskinîkiskwêw. piyisk aniyê nêwo-tipiskâw; âsay êkwa êkota pakwâtamiyiwa onîkihikwa.

[1] Over there – well, as usual it is I who is about to tell a story on here [*sc.* on the audio-recorder], it is Mrs Whitecalf who is about to speak. Over there, I am going to tell a story about our reserve, a certain story, it is never heard, I suppose, for me to have heard it elsewhere, this story. My grandmother used to tell it, then we had discussed it when we were all sitting together over there at Saskatoon, and as I was going to discuss it a certain woman over there had spoken, «It is a true story,» she too, it is said, used to hear this story, she too had told early parts of it there, how it had sounded to her, the way she had been hearing it.

[2] At our reserve, at *Nakiwacîhk* [Sweetgrass] as it is called, there it is a large area of level ground, with people living along this creek as it winds its way back and forth, now there long ago, it is said, people used to live in two places, on big arc-shaped meadows, on big meadows, it is said. There the people used to hold the Medicine Rite, it was in the midst of that being held, it is said, they were holding the Medicine Rite.

[3] It was all of a sudden that a young woman disappeared from there, she was lost. Now they must have suspected that something evil had happened to this young woman, and now, as they took note of the young men, none of the young men –~, the young men were all present, none of the young men had disappeared so that the young woman might have been taken off to some place or other. Of all the young men, not one, not one had disappeared, none of them caused concern by being absent. Well, now the young woman was simply gone, she was lost, well, now they sent out search parties, to be sure, for this young woman, searching for her –~ now they searched for her where she might have gone, but they did not find her anywhere, no place was found anywhere where this young woman might have met her death.

[4] êkw êkwa, mwêhc ê-nêwo-~ ê-kî-nêwo-tipiskâk, mitoni kîkisêpâ, kîtahtawê ôm ê-ispatinâk – 'manitow kâ-matwêhikêt' isiyîhkâtêw êwakw ân[i] ânim îspatinâw, ê-pê-misi-nêtinâk, mêton ê-misi-pôsiskatinâk, âh-âyîtaw ê-nêtinâk, êkota ôma sîpîsis ê-pê-wa-wâwâkihtik, ê-pê-pinasiwêhtik, êkwa êwak ôma 'manitow kâ-matwêhikêt' k-êsiyîhkâtêk. kayâs êsa mâna kêhtê-ayak ê-kî-pêhtahkik êkota êt[i]-ôtâkosiki ê-kî-matwê-matwêhoht êkota, 'wîhpihtakahikan' kî-isiyîhkâtêwak mâna, êkoni ê-kî-pêhtawâcik êsa mâna, ê-matwê-matwêhoht êkota wîhpihtakahikan, êwakw ân[i] ânima, anima kâ-pê-nêtinâk ispatinâw. êwak ôhci kî-kiskêyihtamwak awîna ta-nitawi-matwêhwât êkotê mistikwaskihkwa, nam âwiyak; êwak ôhci kâ-kî-isiyîhkâtahkik anima, 'manitow kâ-matwêhikêt' kî-isiyîhkâtamwak, êwakw ânim îspatinâw.

[5] êkwa mân êkota, nikî-ocih-~ nikî-wâpamâw êwakw âna, an[a] âsiniy ana, mwêhci tâpwê iskwâhtêm êtikwê iyikohk, iyikohk ê-kî-~, êkosi pâskac ê-kî-isi-kinosit ana, an[a] âsiniy, nayawatatâwâhk mân ê-kî-â-~ tâpiskôc ê-kî-âswapit ana êkota an[a] âsiniy, kî-wâpiskisiw mân ân[a] âsiniy. «êwakw ânim ôtiskwâhtêmiwâw,» ê-kî-itwêcik êsa mâna kêhtê-ayak, «anik êkota pîhc-âyihk manitowak k-âyâcik, êwakw ân[i] ânim ôtiskwâhtêmiwâw,» ê-kî-itwêcik êsa mâna.

[6] hâw, ôm êkwa, kîkisêpâ ê-waniskâcik ôk âyisiyiniwak, kîtahtawê êsa kâ-wâpamâcik, êkotê tahkohtâmatin ês ê-matwê-apiyit awiya, ispatinâhk, mitoni kîkisêpâ; hâ, sêmâk pîtotêyimêwak, sêmâk awa kisêyiniw pêyak kâ-nitawi-wîhtamâht ta-têpwêt, ta-wîhtahk, aw –~, ôt[ê] ê-matwê-wâpamiht, awiyak êkotê ê-matwê-ay-apit, mamâhtâwêyihtamwak sêmâk mitoni, awîna –~ awîn îtê wîpac t-êtohtêt ta-nitawi-sâkêwêt êkotê. wâsakâmêw

Finally it had been four nights; already now at this point her parents were grief-stricken.

[4] Now then, when exactly four nights had passed, early in the morning, it was all of a sudden on this hill – that hill is called *Manitow kâ-matwêhikêt*, it projects sharply high above, it is a really steep gully with sharply projecting hills on either side, there this creek comes flowing down, winding its way back and forth, now that is called *Manitow kâ-matwêhikêt*. Long ago the old people, it is said, used to hear there, in the early evenings, the distinct sound of a medicine drum being beaten there, they used to call it a *wîhpihtakahikan* [*lit.* hollowed-out drum], they used to hear that, it is said, one could distinctly hear a hollowed-out drum being beaten there, it came from that sharply projecting hill. For that reason they knew who would go and beat the medicine drum over there, nobody; for that reason is why they gave that place its name, *Manitow kâ-matwêhikêt* they used to call that hill.

[5] There now I used to see that one, that rock, it truly must have stood exactly as high as a door, as it happens that rock used to be that high, at the mid-point of the steep bank that rock used to stand as if leaning, and that rock was white. «That is their door,» the old people used to say, it is said, «of those spirits that dwell inside, that is their door,» they used to say, it is said.

[6] Well, now as these people got up in the morning, it was all of a sudden, it is said, that they saw a figure, it is said, over there on the hilltop someone was recognisably sitting, it is said, on the hill, early in the morning; well, right away they thought the figure odd, right away they went and told a certain old man about it so that he would call out and tell about it that someone could distinctly be seen there, that someone was recognisably sitting over there, and right away they found it very strange, who –~ who might have gone there so early on to go and come into view over

awa kisêyiniw, ê-pimi-sâkitot, ê-pimi-pîkiskwêt, «kitâpamihk nâha! mâcikôcican itâpik nêtê, nêma ê-kâp-~ ispatinâw, kâ-nêtinâk, nâha kâ-matwê-cîpatapit matwê, ta-kî-ay-ihkin êwakw âwa oskinîkiskwêw ôta kâ-wanihiht,» k-êtât –~ [kâ]-pim-îtwêt [*?sic*] ês âwa kisêyiniw. ê-nâspici-pêyakohtât êkos ê-pim-îtwêt, ôh âyisiyiniwa ê-pimi-wa-wîhtamawât, «mahti, oskinîkiwak, otêmiwâwa kit-ôtinêwak, maht êkotê kit-êspayiwak ka-nitawâpênikêwak êkoni ôhi, êwakw âw âwa kâ-wâpamiht itê kâ-matwê-apit,» itwêwak –~ pim-îtwêw awa kisêyiniw. êkwa ani tâpwê êkwa, oskinîkiwak êk ôki, wêtinastimwêcik êsa, otê-~ otêmiwâwa êkwa ê-otinâcik, êkwa, êkotê êkwa ê-ispayicik êkwa. ê-ati-takopayicik êkotê, tâpwê nîhc-âyihk ê-ayâcik ê-itâpicik, tâpwê kî-matwê-apiyiwa êkota tahkohtâmatin, kîsi-tahkohc-âyihk [*sic*]. «hâ, êwako miyâmâc awa tâpwê,» itwêwak, êkwa êsa k-âm-~ k-âmaciwê-têhtapicik, ôta nahiyikohk ê-ihtâcik, namôy pakitinikwak tit-ôtihtâcik êkota ôh ôskinîkiskwêwa, êkosi kâ-kitotikocik: «â, niy âni, nipimâtisin ani,» k-êtikocik êsa, «niy âni, nipimâtisin; êkoyikohk isko, êkâ ayiwâk pê-itohtêk!» k-êtikocik êsa, «kiyâm wâwonîk! nitawi-wîhtamok! ninîkihikwak nitawi-wîhtamâhkok, kanâtanohk mîkiwâhp ta-cimatâwak, êkota nik-êsi-kîwân, êkwa wî-pîhtikwêyâni, êkota ta-miyâhkasikâniwiw, êkota nika-pîhtikwân; êkwa nikâwiy, â, kanakê pêyakwêskihk kîsitêw t-ôsîhtâw, êkot[a] êkwa t-âcimoyân tânis ôma ê-kî-isi-pîhtikwêyân ôta,» itwêw êsa. êkosi; «êkos âni, niyâk, kîwêpayik! misawâc ani, kîsahkamikisiyêko, mîna ka-pê-sipwêpayinâwâw, ka-pê-wîhtamawinâwâw, êkây mâk ôta ta-pê-isk-ôtisiyêk kisiwâk. êkosi nika-nîhtaciwân, êkos êkwa nika-kîwân,» itikwak êsa.

[7] êy, êkos ês êkwa ê-kîwêpayicik êkwa, ê-nitawi-wîhtahkik, «tâpwê ês ân[a] êwako,» itwêwak ês ôk

there. The old man made his round, announcing it and speaking as he went along, «Look at that figure yonder! Behold, look over yonder, to the hill over yonder, the steep hill, that figure yonder who is recognisably sitting upright, recognisably, it may be the case that this is the young woman who has been lost here,» he said to them –~ said this old man, it is said, as he went along. He kept saying this one thing over and over as he went along, telling the people about it as he went along. «Well then, let the young men take their horses, well then, let them ride over there to make certain about that one, that one who is recognisable as a sitting figure,» they said –~ the old man said as he went along. Now then truly the young men, taking their horses, it is said, took their horses now and now rode over there. As they rode up to the place over there, truly still being beneath and looking there, truly she was recognisably sitting on top of that hill there, fully on top of the hill. «Well, assuredly it is truly her,» they said, and now they rode up the hill, it is said, and when they were here at the right distance, that young woman did not let them come close to that place, addressing them thus: «Well, it is me indeed, and I am indeed alive,» is what she said to them, it is said, «it is me indeed, and I am alive; only this far, do not come any closer!» is what she said to them, it is said, «Well then, turn around! Go and tell about it! Go and tell my parents, let them set up a tipi in a clean place, to that I shall return home, and once I am about to enter, let them burn incense there, then I shall enter; now my mother, well, let her prepare at least one kettle of cooked food, for me to tell my story there of how I had entered in here,» she said, it is said. Thus; «Thus, indeed, you all go, you all ride back home! At any rate, once you have completed your preparations, you will ride off again and come and tell me, but you should not come close to me here. In that way shall I go

ôskinîkiwak nêtê ê-takopayicik. «hâ, mâk êkos ê-itwêt, 'kîwêpayik!' (namôy âni nipakitinikonân cîki t-êtohtêyâhk) 'kîwêpayik, nitawi-wîhtamok! nikâwiy nôhtâwiy, mahti kanâtanohk patotê-ayihk ta-cimatâwak mîkiwâhp, â, êkota ôma kê-pîhtikwêyân. êkwa nikâwiy pêyakwêskihk kîsitêw t-ôsîhtâw,' itwêw ês âw ôskinîkiskwêw.»

[8] êkos êtikwê êkwa tâpwê; êy, êk ôk –~ êk ônîkihikomâwak mistahi miywêyihtamwak, cikêmô ê-wî-mâh-môskwêyihtahkik otânisiwâwa, tânitê êtikwê piko ê-itêyihtahkik, miton êkwa miywêyihtamwak, êkwa an[i] ês êkwa, kâ-papâsinikêhk ês êkwa ê-mâmawi-wîcihihcik ôki mîkiwâhp ê-~ kanâtanohk ê-nitawi-cimatâwiht êkwa. kâh-kîsi-tôtahkik [*sic*] êkwa êwak ôma, mêton îyikohk ê-kaskihtâcik mâmawôhkamâtowak, ê-wî-kakwê-kanâcihtâcik ôma mîkiwâhp, kwayask ê-wî-kakwê-isîhcikêcik. êkwa kâh-kîsi-tôtahkik [*sic*], êkwa aw îskwêw êkwa mîn êkwa, kîsitêw êkwa ê-osîhtâcik êkwa, wîcihik mîn êwako wîc-îskwêwa; kîsitêw êkwa ê-osîhtâcik ôm êkwa, pêyakwêskihk. kâh-kîsi-tôtahkik [*sic*] êkos êkwa, êkos êkwa, miton êkwa kîsi-waw-~-wawêyîwak êkwa. êkwa êtikw êkot[a] êkwa, oskinîkiwak kâ-sipwêtisahohcik êkwa, ê-nitawi-nitomâcik êk ôh â-~ ôh âyi, oskinîkiskwêwa. êkosi pê-isi-wâwonipicikêwak ê-pê-kîwêpayicik. êkos êkwa, ê-takopayicik anit[a] êkwa, êkos êkwa na-nîhtaciwêw aw âspin aw ôskinîkiskwêw awa, aw êkwa ê-kîwêt êkwa.

[9] êkwa, namôy nôh-pêhtên kîkway mistahi-kîkway ta-kî-miyikot, ôhi, ôhi kâ-kî-otinikot. tâpwê ayisk êkota ê-kî-pîhtikwêt anima, ôm îspatinâw. êkwa nêtê ê-takohtêt, tâpwê

down the hill, in that way then shall I return home,» she said to them, it is said.

[7] Hey, thus now they rode back home, it is said, and went and told about it, «It is truly her, it is said,» the young men said, it is said, as they arrived over yonder on their horses. «Well, but she said this, 'Ride back home!' (she would not let us get close at all), 'Ride back home, go and tell about it! My mother and father, well then, let them set up a tipi in a clean place apart from the camp, well, it is there that I will enter. And let my mother prepare one kettle of cooked food,' this young woman said, it is said.»

[8] That is the way it must truly have been now; hey, now the parents were very glad, of course they had been about to lament the loss of their daughter and wondering where of all places she might have gone, now they were very glad and it was then, it is said, that they all made haste now, it is said, and all worked together to help them in setting up a tipi for her in a clean place. When they had completed that, they worked together as much as they could in trying to clean up this tipi, trying to do things properly. Then when they had completed that task, now that woman and her household also prepared cooked food now, and her fellow-women also helped her; now they prepared cooked food, one kettle of it. Now when they had completed that task in that way, now they really made ready. Now it must have been at this point that the young men were sent off, now they went to summon that young woman. With that they turned their horses around and rode back home. Thus now, as they arrived there on their horses, this young woman now was gone, she was walking down the hill, and then she returned home.

[9] Now, I have not heard of anything, of anything important, that they would have given her, those who had abducted her. For truly she had entered this hill there. Now when she came

ê-miyâhkasikêwiht, ê-wî-pîhtikwêt ita êkwa; êkos êkwa ê-pîhtikwêt êkwa. nêwo-tipiskâw ôma kâ-wanihot, ôma k-ôtiniht; tâpiskôc êsa, namôy kakêtihk ê-kîhkâmâkosit ayisiyiniw, iyin-âyisiyiniw, âsay êkos ê-isimâ-~ ê-isimâhcikêt ôma, ôh âyisiyiniwa, ê-kîhkâyâpasot, osâm anim îtê nêwo-tipiskâw ê-ayât. êkota ês êkwa, ê-kî-ma-miyâhkasikêwiht ês êkwa, kâ-mâci-pîkiskwêt awa, aw îskwêw, ê-kî-~, tâpiskôc mîkiwâhp ê-isinahk, ôhi kâ-pê-nâtikot; ê-nipât, ê-pê-nâtikot ôhi, okihciyaw sôskwâc ê-wanihot. êkosi; kayâhtê piko nêtê pîhc-âyihk ê-ayât mîkiwâhp ôma, «âyiman ani, ita kâ-pê-ohci-wayawîyân, miton ân[i] êtataw nipakitinikwak ôki, mistah âyimisiwak,» itwêw êsa, «âtiht âsônê âyimisiwak, miton âni ê-têtipêwêpicik ôki ayis-~ ôki kisêyiniwak, âtiht osk-âyak, êkwa nêtê iskwâhtêmihk, êkâ ta-kî-wayawîyân, âh-âyîtaw-iskwâht ê-apicik, êkotê, êkonik tahk êkwa ê-nitohtahkik tânisi ta-tôtâkawiyân, ta-nipahikawiyân tahki, êkos ê-isi-nitawêyihtahkik ôk âtiht, tahki 'kiposkâhk! kiposkâhk!' ê-itwêcik ês ôki» (cikêmô mîna ê-astâhiwêcik ôki iyinito-ayisiyiniwak, nânitaw isi ta-sâkôcihtwâcik, ta-pê-nâtâcik ôhi, ôh ôskinîkiskwêwa, êwak ôhc ânima miton ê-kanawêyimiht awa, êkâ nânitaw ta-kakwê-isi-otiniht ta-wayawît); «'kiposkâhk! kiposkâhk!' tahk ê-itikawiyân,» ê-itwêt ês âwa oskinîkiskwêw.

[10] nêwo-tipiskâw êkw êkota, ê-wâh-wâpani-nikamoyit ôhi kisêyiniwa, ê-wâh-wâpani-nikamototâkot; âtiht ê-kiskinohamâkot miyo-kîkway, âtiht ta-m-~ ta-macîhkwasit –~ ta-maci-pawâmit, êkos âtiht ê-isi-kiskinohamâkot osâm piko. êkosi, tahk âta ê-âyimêyihtahk, ê-âyimêyihtahk sôskwâc, êkâ ê-tâpwêhtawât maci-pawâmiwin kit-âyât. â, mâk êkwa, piyisk ês êkwa mitoni asotamâk, êkwa ês ôk âta kâ-miywâtisicik ôki kisêyiniwak, ê-kakêtahamâcik, ê-kakêtahamâcik, kiyâm êkâ ka-misiwanâcihimiht, «mistahi kôtawêyimik okêhtê-ayima,» ê-itwêcik.

up to the place over yonder [*sc.* the lodge prepared for her], truly they burnt incense for her where she was about to enter; and thus now she entered. It was for four nights that she had been lost, that she had been abducted; it was as if, it is said, terribly strong was the smell of humans, of human beings, already it smelled to her like that, she smelled the strong odour of these humans, because of where she had been for four nights. It was at this point, then, it is said, now when they had been burning incense for her, it is said, that this woman began to speak, it seemed to her as if it was a tipi, the place to which they brought her; in her sleep they brought her, and right away she was lost, bodily. Thus it was; before she knew it she was over yonder inside that tipi, «It was difficult indeed there from where I have come outside, they just barely let me go, they are severe in the extreme,» she said, it was said, «some are especially severe, these old men really sat in a full circle, some young ones now over yonder by the entrance, so that I could not go outside, they sat on either side of the entrance, over there, and they were listening all the time to what was to be done to me, to how I was to be killed, all the time, some of them wanted that, 'Block her way! Block her way!' they said all the time, it is said» (of course the human beings also had them worried, that they might in some way overpower them, that they might come and fetch the young woman back, that is why she was closely guarded so that no attempt would be made to take her in some way, so that she would go outside). «'Block her way! Block her way!' was said about me all the time,» the young woman said, it is said.

[10] At that point now for four nights these old men kept singing ritual songs until dawn each night, singing ritual songs for her until dawn each night; some teaching her good things, some to have evil dreams –~ to have an evil dream guardian, some teaching her mostly that. Thus it was, although she resisted that all the time,

[11] êkos êkwa êkota êkwa, piyisk êkwa, ê-kî-nêwo-tipiskâk êkwa, êkot[a] ês êkwa, «hâ,» k-êtikot êsa, «êkwa kika-kîwân, mistahi kakwâtakêyihtamwak kinîkihikwak, â, ôm ê-wanihikawiyan,» itikwak –~ itik ês ôhi kisêyiniwa, «mâk êkwa kika-kîwân,» itikow [*sic*] – «'êkây mâka êkos îsi pakitinihk, piko kîkway ta-wî-~ ta-tôtahk!' âhci piko ê-isicik ôki kotakak ê-itwêcik, êkây êkosi t-êsi-pakitinikawiwak,» itwêw ês âw ôskinîkiskwêw, êkota ês êkwa kâ-itiht, «otawâsimisici, nistam kê-otawâsimisit, êkoni ta-mêkit,» êkos êsa k-êtiht êkwa, «êkosi ta-wayawît, otawâsimisici, êkota ta-wayawît; êkwa, nistam kiy-ônâpêmit, êkoni mîna, êkoni mîna, êkon êkwa tâpiskôc ê-asahkêt (kinwês ês âni, kî-micimêyimow nâpêwa ta-wîcêwât, ê-âyimêyihtahk otawâsimisici, kit-~ kita-mêkit, aspin ê-mêkit otawâsimisici; kinwês êsa kî-pêyakow), piyisk, piyisk êkos ês êkwa kâ-pakitiniht êkwa ê-pê-wayawît, êkoni êkwa ôhi naskomow ês êkwa, nistam otawâsimisici, êkwa onâpêmici mîna, êkos êkoni êkwa, êkot[a] ês êkwa kâ-pakitiniht êkwa; êkoni anih êkwa nanâtohk kîkway ê-kî-kiskinohamâkot, kîkway wiy âta wiya, tânisi t-êsi-kakwê-isi-~ t-êsi-nanâtawihiwêt ôma. êkwa, miyâmâ êsa, nayêstaw miyâhkasikana kî-miyâw, êkoni anih êsa piko kâ-pê-kikît anihi, ê-pê-kiki-wayawît, kî-itwêw –~ kî-itwêw mâna nôhkom.

[12] êkosi, kiyîs-âtotahk, m-~ ê-kîs-âcimot êkw âw âw îskwêw êkwa, êkwa ê-mîcisowiht êkwa. êkos ês âni, kî-itâw êsa mitoni tita-nôtikwêwit, isko êwak ôm ôma, ta-nôtikwê-~ ta-nôtikwêwit mîskot mitoni, t-ôtisâpahtahk wâpistikwânêwin, êkos êsa kâ-itikot anihi kâ-kî-otinikot êkota manitowa. êwakw ân[i] ânima 'manitow kâ-matwêhikêt', kî-sêsêskêyihtâkwan, «cikêmâ êkota ê-kî-wa-wîkicik ôki, êkâ kâ-miyohkwastimiwêcik ôki kâ-wî-kakwê-wayêsîhkwastimiwêcik,» ê-kî-itwêcik mân êkota

she resisted that right away, she did not agree to their demand that she have an evil dream guardian. Well, but now, it is said, finally they threatened her greatly now, it is said, even though now the old men who were good cautioned against it, cautioning against it, that she should not be put to death, «Her parents are in great anguish about her,» they said.

[11] Thus then at that point, finally now, when it had been four nights, at that point now, it is said, «Well,» is what they said to her, «now you shall return home, your parents are suffering greatly, well, that you have been lost,» they said to her, these old men, it is said, said to her, «but now you shall return home,» they said to her – «'But do not let her go like this, she has to do something!' these others still said about me, lest I simply be released from their power like that,» this young woman said, it is said, that is what she had been told at that point now, it is said, «When she has a child, when she will have her first child, for her to give that one up,» was what she was told now, it is said, «in that way for her to go outside, if she has a child, on that condition for her to go outside; then, when she will have her first husband, that one also, that one also, as if she were now feeding him to the spirits» (for a long time indeed, it is said, she held back from taking a husband, she dreaded the thought of having to give up her child when she had one, as she left giving up her child when she had one; for a long time she did stay unmarried, it is said), finally, finally it was in this way now that she was let go and came outside, now she had made her response, it is said, that she would in this way give up her first child and her husband also, it was only at this point now, it is said, that she was let go; now they had taught her various things, things to be sure with which she would try to heal people. Now I do believe that she was only given sage-brush to be burnt as incense, it is said, that was the only thing she carried with her as she came, it

ayisiyiniwak êwakw ân[i] ânima. kîspin awiyak êkota, êkota ê-pawâmit kîkway, êwakw ân[a] ê-~ ê-wayêsîhkwasit, êkwa êkota awa nôto-~, êwakw âw ôskinîkiskwêw k-âcimak, kî-yi-~ nôhkom mâna kî-wîhêw, 'picwêkan' kî-isiyîhkâsow aw-~ aw îskwêw, êwakw âwa kâ-kî-wanihiht ês ôskinîkiskwêw, 'picwêkan' êsa kî-isiyîhkâsow.

[13] êkosi, kîhtwâm êkwa, ê-otawâsimisit êtikwê, êkon êkwa kî-ohpikihêw êkwa êkoni awa otawâsimisa êkwa, êkota ohci nikiskisin mâna, ê-nâh-nipâkwêsimohk, ita kâ-kî-ohc-âtotahk nôhkom awa, êkota awa kisêyiniw ôta, nâtakâm ôtê isi, kî-wîhcikaniwiw êwako, miyâmâ ani, 'câhcâhkayow' kâ-kî-itiht ana kisêyiniw, awêkâ cî mîn 'ôcastoyiw', nîkân êwako, êkoni nîso-wîhowina nikotwâw, êkonik ôki kâ-kî-wîcêwâcik anihi, êkoni ê-kî-otânisit awa picwêkan anihi, êkoni ê-kî-ohpikiyit anihi, otânisa anihi. êkota mâna, êkos ânih ê-kî-isiyîhkâtât nôhkom anihi, 'picwêkan' ê-kî-isiyîhkâtât, êwakw âw êsa kâ-kî-wanihot anita anima, êwakw ânim âskîhkân anima, nakiwaciy ôma, 'manitow kâ-matwêhikêt' k-êsiyîhkâtêk. êkosi, êkoyikohk isko mîn êwako kâ-isko-pêhtamân; mêkwâc anim ê-mâh-mitêwihk anim êwako.

[14] êkosi, kî-nôtikwêwiw ês âna tâpwê ana, êwakw ân[a] âna 'picwêkan' kâ-kî-itiht. îh, êwakw ânima pêyak, êwakw ânim ê-mamâhtâwahk âcimowin. êwako namôy wîhkâc awiyak nipê-pêhtawâw êkota kayâsi-kêhtê-ayak ôki, êwako ta-kî-âtotahkik; nayêstaw piko mân êkos ê-kî-isi-pêhtawakik ôki ohc ê-pê-awâsisîwiyân, 'manitow kâ-matwêhikêt', 'manitow kâ-matwêhikêt' ê-kî-isiyîhkâtahkik, to-~ tânêhk ôhci k-ôh-isiyîhkâtêk? wîhpihtakahikan mân êkota êt-ôtâkosik[i] ês ê-kî-pêhtâht, êkosi piko mân ê-kî-isi-pêhtawakik ê-kî-itwêcik,

is said, carrying it with her as she came out, she used to say –~ my grandmother used to say.

[12] Thus, when she had completed telling about it, when that woman now had completed telling her story, now they held a ritual meal with respect to her. Thus indeed, it is said, she had been told, it is said, that she would live until she was a very old woman, to that point, that in return she would live to be a very old woman and that she would live to see her hair turn white, thus, it is said, the spirits who had abducted her had told her at that point. It used to be feared indeed, that place, *Manitow kâ-matwêhikêt*, «Of course it is the case that those who used to be dwelling there were giving people bad dreams in their sleep and would try to deceive people in their sleep,» people there used to say about that place. If someone there has a dream spirit, that one is being deceived in his sleep, and that is where that old –~ that young woman of whom I have been telling, my grandmother used to identify her by name, this woman was called *Picwêkan*, that young woman who had been lost, it is said, she was called *Picwêkan*, it is said.

[13] Thus, the next time now she had a child, I suppose, that child of hers she now did raise, and from that I remember at various Sundances, where my grandmother used to tell me this, on that occasion this old man here, towards the north, he used to be talked about a great deal, I believe that old man's name was *Câhcâhkayow*, or else also *Ocastoyiw*, it was that first one or either of these two names, they used to live with that one, the one whom this *Picwêkan* had as her daughter, that one lived to grow up, that daughter of hers. On that occasion my grandmother had called her that, she had called her *Picwêkan*, she was the one who had been lost, it is said, at that place, on that reserve, this *Nakiwaciy*, at

ê-kî-matwêhoht, êwak ôhc ôma k-ôh-isiyîhkâtêk, ê-kî-itwêcik mân ôki kêhtê-ayak kayâs.

[15] êkwa, nikiskisin mâna wiya, matwân cî wiya piko êkos ê-kî-isîhcikêt nôhkominân pêyak, ê-kî-tahkohtaciwêt mân êkota ispatinâhk ôma, wêpinâsona mân ê-kî-wîcêwak –~ ê-kî-tahkonahk, ê-kî-wîcêwâyâhk mân ê-iskwêsisiwiyâhk, wêpinâsona ê-tahkonahk, êkotê ê-kî-~ mân ê-nitâ-~-ayamihtâkosit; ê-kî-ma-miywâwacikêt mân êkotê tahkohtâmatin, êkwa niyanân mâna, ohpimê ê-ay-apiyâhk, pêyak iskwêsis ê-wîc-~ ê-wîcêwât awa nôhkom, ôsisimisa wîsta; ê-kî-na-nitohtawâyâhk mâna, ê-ati-pa-pâh-pîkiskwêt ê-kâkîsimot, êkoni ôhi.

[16] pêyakwâw mîna nikî-wâpamâw, wêpinâsona, êkwa pâskisikan; êkota ê-kî-nitawi-wêpinâsot êkoni ôhi, êkos âspin iskwayât, nîswâw ê-kiskisiyân mân êkota ê-kî-tahkohtaciwê-wîcêwâyâhk. êwakw ânim êkoyikohk isko nitâtotên, êwakw ân[i] ânima mistahi ê-nôhtê-kiskêyihtamôhakik ôk âyisiyiniwak ôtê kê-nîkâniwik, tânêhki –~, tânêhk ânima k-ôh-isiyîhkâtêk êwako, nitaskînâhk ispatinâw.

Manitow kâ-matwêhikêt as it is called. That is it, also, this is all I have heard of that; that happened while they were holding the Medicine Rite.

[14] That is it, that one did truly live to be an old woman, it is said, that one who used to be called *Picwêkan*. Look, this is one, this is a strange story. I have never heard that of anyone, that the really old people there would be able to tell that story; that was the only name I heard them use since I was a child, *Manitow kâ-matwêhikêt,* they used to call it *Manitow kâ-matwêhikêt*, why is it called this? A hollowed-out drum used to be heard there in the early evenings, it is said, that is all I used to hear them say, that a medicine drum used to be beaten there, that is why it is called that, the old people used to say long ago.

[15] Now I always remember about one of our grandmothers, and I wonder if she was the only to have performed this ritual, that she used to go up there on top of this hill carrying cloths and I used to go with her –~ we used to go with her when we were little girls, she used to carry cloths and she could be heard praying over there; she used to be hauling worthwhile things over there to the top of the hill, and as for us, we used to sit off to the side, one little girl this grandmother of mine took along, she was her own grandchild; we used to hear her go along reciting her prayers and chanting prayers, to those [*sc.* the spirits].

[16] Once I also saw her, with flags and a gun; she had gone and placed them there as an offering to those [*sc.* the spirits], thus she left for the last time, twice I remember us going up to the top of the hill there with her. I have told all of that, I greatly want the people there in the future to know about that indeed, why the hill on our reserve is called that.

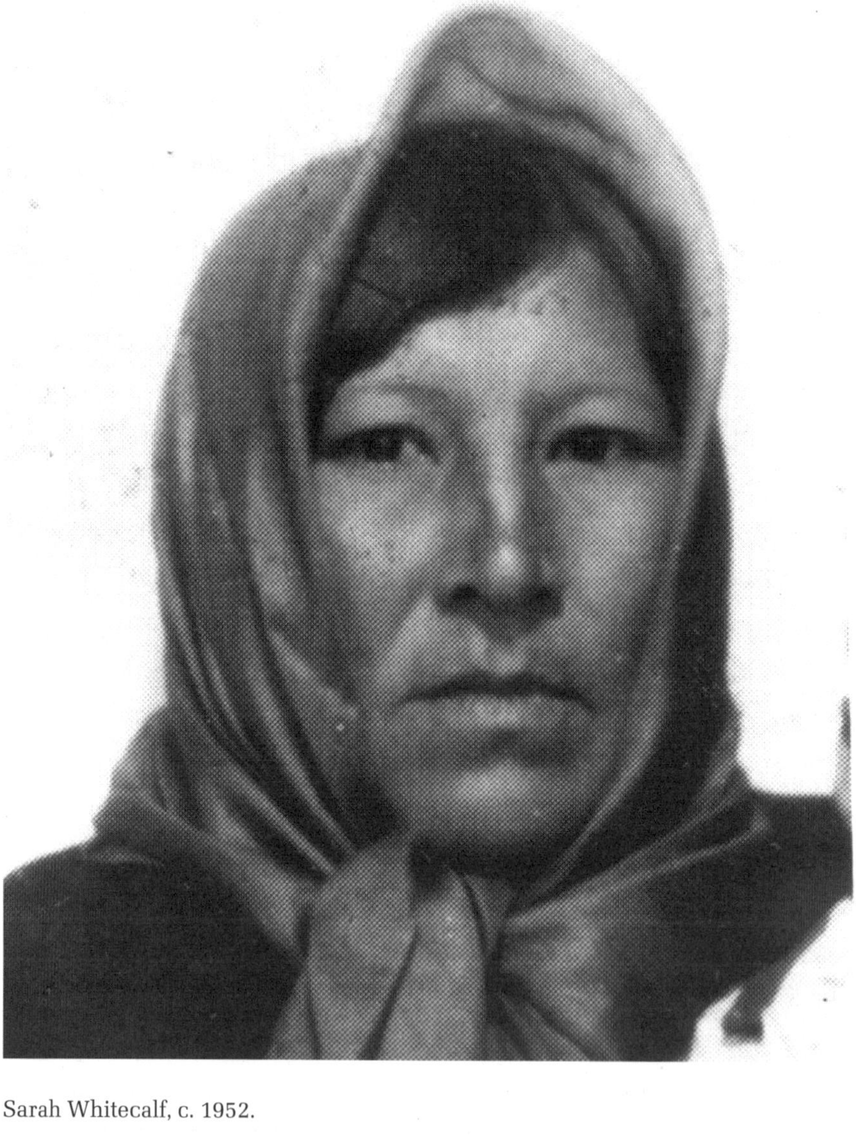

Sarah Whitecalf, c. 1952.

11

manitow kâ-matwêhikêt

Where the spirits drum (II)

manitow kâ-matwêhikêt

[SW:] ôm êkwa *Sweetgrass* êkwa kâ-nitawêyihtahk âcimowin awa t-âstâwak ôta.

[1] â, âsay mîna niya, ôma kâ-~ ôta kâ-wî-âcimoyân, *Mrs Whitecalf*, ôta sâskwatôn, êkos êkwa, kotak mîna nika-mâcîhtân âcimowin, ôta nik-âstân. awa ê-nitawêyihtahk niwîcêwâkanis, kîkway ta-mâh-mâmiskôtamwak ôta.

[2] ôtê nitaskînâhk, *Sweetgrass*, êkwa ê-nêhiyawiyîhkâtêk, 'nakiwaciy' isiyîhkâtêw êwak ôma nitaskînân ôma, ôtê, êkwa, êkota pêyak ôma kâ-nitawêyihtahk niwîcêwâkanis kêyâpit t-âtotamân; ayahk, pêyak êkotê ispatinâw, ê-mamâhtâwinâkwahk, 'manitow kâ-matwêhikêt' ê-isiyîhkâtahkik mân âyisiyiniwak; kayâs ohc êkosi ê-pê-isiyîhkâtêk anima askîhk-~ anim îspatinâw, ê-mamâhtâwinâkwahk. êkota pohci-~ pohci-pasahcâhk ê-pê-pimihtik sîpîsis, wâwâki, wâhyawêskamik ê-ohc-îhtik anima sîpîsis. êkwa mân ê-itwêhk êwakw ânima sîpîsis, âsay anita ayisiyiniwak ita kâ-wîkicik ôki, askîhkâniwiyiniwak, «nâh-nâway, môhkiciwanipêkwa ê-pim-âyâki,» ê-itwêhk mâna, «iskw êwakw ân[i] ânima manitow kâ-matwêhikêt, misakâmê êwakw ân[i] ânima môhkiciwanipêkwa, mitoni ê-mihcêtiki,» ê-itwê-~ ê-itwêcik mâna, ôk êkotê ayisiyiniwak. êkwa, êwak ôma -~ ôma -~ manitow kâ-matwêhikêt ôma kâ-wî-âyimôtamân.

Where the spirits drum (II)

[SW:] Now she wants me to put that story about Sweetgrass on here [*sc.* on the audio-recorder] for her.

[1] Well, as usual it is I who is about to tell a story on here, it is Mrs Whitecalf here in Saskatoon, thus now I will also begin another story, and I will put it on here. It is my dear partner's wish that I should discourse about things for her on here.

[2] It is there at our reserve, at Sweetgrass, and in Cree this reserve of ours is called *Nakiwaciy*, there, now it is one story about that place which it is my dear partner's wish that I should still tell, ah well, a certain hill over there looks strange, the people usually call it *Manitow kâ-matwêhikêt*, ever since the old days that res-~, that hill has been called by that name, it looks strange. Through a deep gully a creek comes running down there, winding its way back and forth, that creek comes down a great distance. Now it is usually said about this creek, already by the people who live there, people belonging to the reserve, «There are springs along it, all the way back,» they usually say, «right up to that *Manitow kâ-matwêhikêt*, there are springs in great number all the way,» the people over there usually say. Now, it is this, this *Manitow kâ-matwêhikêt*, that is what I am going to discuss.

[3] kayâs êsa, êkota, êkota mâna ê-kî-pimokêcik ôk âyisiyiniwak, nakiwacîwiyiniwak ôki, êkwa êkota âpihtâ-kîsikâhk isi, êkota ê-misi-tahtakwaskamikâk, êkota mâna nîstanân nikî-wîkinân kêhciwâk cîki, sisonê sîpîsisihk ôma ê-pimi-wâwâkastêki ôhi wâskahikana ê-isi-wa-wîkihk. êwak ôm ôma, ita ôma ê-misi-tahtakwaskamikâk, namôy ôhci-pa-pîkopicikâtêw ôma tahtakwahcâw ôma, «êkota êsa kayâs ayisiyiniwak ê-wîkicik, ê-mâh-mitêwihk,» kî-itwêwak mâna nôhkom, ê-mâh-mitêwicik ês êkota ayisiyiniwak; m-~ êwakw ân[i] ânima 'mitêwikamik' k-êsiyîhkâtêk, ê-kî-maskihkîhkêcik anima kisêyiniwak ôki kayâs, anima 'mitêwikamik' kâ-kî-isiyîhkâtêk, mâka wâh-wîhkâc, namôya wiya wâh-wîpac êkos ê-ohc-îtahkamikisicik, êtikwê pêyakwâw pêyak-askiy, tahto-nîpin wiy âta wiya ê-kî-osîhtâcik maskihkiya, ê-kî-maskihkîhkêcik; êwakw ân[i] ânima 'mitêwikamik' anima k-êsiyîhkâtêk, «ê-kî-mitêwicik» kî-itwâniwiw mâna. êkos ês ânim êkospîhk êkota mêkwâc ê-âh-itahkamikahk, ê-mihcêtokamikahk, ê-wîhkwêstêki mîkiwâhpa, mêkwâc ê-mâh-mitêwihk ês ôma.

[4] kîtahtawê, kâ-wanihiht êsa pêyak iskwêw, oskinîkiskwêw; kâ-wanihiht ês âwa oskinîkiskwêw. êêy, êkwa êsa mitoni ê-nitonikêhk kwayask êsa, ê-nitonikêhk êsa misiwê, kiyikaw oskinîkiwak ê-atâmêyimihcik ta-sipwêhtahâcik ôh ôskinîkiskwêwa, mâka namôya, kahkiyaw ôk ôskinîkiwak ê-~ ê-m-~-nitonâhcik, kahkiyaw, nam âwiyak kôtawêyimâw, oskinîkiwak ôki, tahtw êkota ê-ayâcik; nam âwiyak kôtawêyihtâkosiw oskinîkiw, mîna wîhtamwak môy ê-~ kîkway nânitaw isi, oskinîkiskwêwa êkoni ôhi, ta-kî-mikoskâcihâcik nânitaw isi.

[5] êkosi; miton êsa pakwâtamwak ôki, onîkihikomâwak, misiwê ê-nâh-nitonikêhk, ê-papâmipayicik oskinîkiwak ê-têhtapicik,

[3] Long ago, it is said, the people there used to dwell in a row, the *Nakiwaciy* people, now there towards the south it is a large level area there, and we too used to live nearby, close to this place, the houses were placed along the creek winding back and forth and people were living that way. Where it is a large level area, the land had not been broken for planting, the ground was level, «There, it is said, people lived long ago when one held the Medicine Rite,» my grandmother and those in her household used to say, the people used to hold the Medicine Rite there, it is said, that *mitêwikamik* [*lit.* Medicine Lodge] as it is called, the old men of long ago used to make medicines with it, it was that *mitêwikamik* as it used to be called, but only once in awhile, they did not hold that rite very often, perhaps once a year, but every summer at least they used to prepare medicines, they used to make medicines; that was the *mitêwikamik* as it is called, *ê-kî-mitêwicik* [*lit.* they held the Medicine Rite] one used to say. At that time that rite was in the midst of being conducted there, the lodges were many, the tipis were set up in an arc while they were holding the Medicine Rite, it is said.

[4] It was all of a sudden that a certain woman was lost, it is said, a young woman; that this young woman was lost, it is said. Hey, now, it is said, they searched properly, it is said, they searched all over, it is said, they further blamed the young men for abducting the young woman, but nothing, they looked for all the young men, all of them, none of them caused concern by being absent, as many of the young men as were there; none of the young men caused concern by being reported absent, and they also declared that they had not in any way, that they had in no way been bothering that young woman.

[5] That was it; the parents were grief-stricken, it is said, searches were undertaken all over, the young men riding about on horseback, the searches were carried on in all directions and every-

pikw îtê ê-papâ-nitonikêhk ê-nitonikêwahkamikahk, ê-nitonâht aw îskwêw –~ aw ôskinîkiskwêw, tânitê?

[6] kîtahtawê, piyisk nêwo-tipiskâw ê-ispayik, awa oskinîkiskwêw ê-wanihiht, piyisk ê-nêwo-tipiskâk, kîtahtawê kîkisêpâ, mitoni kîkisêpâ, kîtahtawê êsa, êkos ânim ê-tôtahk awa pêyak kisêyiniw, ê-wa-wayawîcik êtikwê, kâ-têpâpamâcik, êwak ôm ôm îspatinâw ôma, 'manitow k-ê-~ kâ-matwêhikêt' k-êsiyîhkâtamihk – pitamâ êkota nika-pacâcimosin, êwakw ân[i] ânim îspatinâw ôma 'manitow kâ-matwêhikêt' k-êsiyîhkâtamihk, kâkikê êsa mân êkota ê-kî-pêhtâht, 'wîhpihtakahikan' kî-isiyîhkâtêwak mistikwaskihkwa, anohc kiyânaw 'mistikwaskihk' isiyîhkâtam-~ isiyîhkâtâw ana, mâka pîtos-âya, ê-kî-ispaskisot êsa ana kîkway, matwân cî mistik kîkwâyak êtikwê, êkota pahkêkin anima ê-kî-wêwêkahpitahkik, êwakw ân[i] ânima wîhpihtakahikan, êkoni, êkotowahk êsa mân ê-kî-pêhtawâcik, ê-kî-kakwâhyaki-kisîwêyit êsa mâna, k-âti-wawâninâkwahk êsa mâna, ê-kî-pêhtâht êkota êwakw âna, ê-matwê-matwêhoht êkota anima, êwak ôm îspatinâw ôma; êwak ôhc ânima 'manitow kâ-matwêhikêt' k-ôh-isiyîhkâtêk anim îspatinâw.

[7] êkwa, êkwa ôm âspin k-âcimoyân, ê-kîkisêpâyâk, kâ-wâpamiht ês âwiyak ê-cîpatapit êkotê ispatinâhk, anima (nîsta mâna nikî-âh-âmaciwân kayâs, êwakw ânim îspatinâw), ê-mamâhtâwinâkwahk, mêton ê-kakwâhyak-îspahcâk, -kakwâhyaki-ispâmatinâk [*sic*], namôy mîn âsiskiy ta-kîskatâwahkâk, namôya, mâka mwêhc ê-kîskatâwahkâk, tâpiskôc ê-pimi-kîskahtisikâtêk, mâk êkos îsi maskosiya ê-âmaciwêkihki anim îspatinâw anima, anima kâ-kîs-~ anima kâ-kîskatâwahkâk tâpiskôc, môy tâpiskôt mâna wiy ôhi sîpîhk kâ-kâh-kîskatâwahkâki mostatâwahkâwa, nama kîkway mâs-~ maskosiy; mitoni mân ê-kî-mamâhtâwinâkwahk anim îspatinâw. êkwa, êkota îpêhcâhk,

body took part in the search, looking for this woman –~ this young woman, where might she have gone?

[6] It was all of a sudden, when finally four nights had passed since this young woman had been lost, when finally it had been four nights, it was all of a sudden in the morning, early in the morning, it was all of a sudden, it is said, as a certain old man did that [*sc.* the morning call to prayer] and they must have gone outside, that they clearly saw someone, it was on the hill which one calls *Manitow kâ-matwêhikêt* – here I will digress a little from my story, for a little while, on that very hill which one calls *Manitow kâ-matwêhikêt*, it is said, one used to hear it there all the time, *wîhpihtakahikan* [*lit.* hollowed-out drum] they used to call the medicine drum, amongst ourselves today it is called *mistikwaskihk* [*lit.* tree drum], but it used to stand a different height off the ground, it is said, I wonder about the tree trunk they must have been, over that they used to stretch hide, that was the hollowed-out drum, that kind they used to hear, it is said, it used to have a terribly loud voice, it is said, at dusk one used to hear that one, it is said, one could distinctly hear it being beaten there on this hill; that is why that hill is called *Manitow kâ-matwêhikêt*.

[7] Now, as I was telling the story when I left off, it was in the morning that someone could be seen, it is said, sitting upright on the hill over there, that hill (I too used to go up that hill in the old days), it looks strange, the land really is terribly high, it is a terribly high hill, so that its steep banks are not of earth, no, but they are cut exactly, as if they had been cut along with a tool, but such that there is grass growing up the side of that hill, as if it were a cutbank, but not like the usual cutbanks of a river, the bare cutbanks which have no grass on them; that hill really used to look

asiniy mâna ê-kî-apit, ê-kîs-kîskisit ê-wâpiskisit an[a] âsiniy, îpêtinâhk êkota ê-kî-apit mân ân[a] âsiniy. êkwa mân êkoni ê-kî-itwêcik, «êkon-~ êkoni anihi otiskwâhtêmiwâw, aniki manitowak êkota k-âyâcik,» ê-kî-itwêcik mân ês âyisiyiniwak.

[8] êkwa, ayahk –~, hâw, êkwa aw êkwa, ê-têpâpamiht ê-matwê-cîpatapit, êkotê ayisiyiniw matwê, «hâw!» kâ-pimi-têpwêcik êsa, kisêyiniw ês âwa pêyak kâ-pimi-têpwêt, «mâcikôcican! itâpik nêm îspatinâw! ôma, êwako manitow kâ-matwêhikêt, awiyak an[i] êkotê matwê-ayâw, ê-matwê-~, ispatinâhk êkotê tahkohtâmatin, ê-matwê-ayât êkotê awiyak; maht ês ôskinîkiwak, ta-têhtapiwak, kit-êspayiwak êkotê, pêyâhtik t-âswêyihtamwak,» itwêwak ês ôki –~, pim-îtwêw awa nâpêw, awa kisêyiniw awa; «ahpô êtikwê ta-kî-ay-ihkin, aw ôskinîkiskwêw kâ-wanihiht, ahpô êtikw ân[a] êwako,» itwêwak ês ôk âyak –~, pim-îtwêw awa kisêyiniw, tâpwê ês êkwa oskinîkiwak ês ôki ê-sîhkimihcik, otêmiwâwa ê-otinâcik têhtapîwatimwa; nêwo ê-ispayicik ês êkwa êkotê ispatinâhk, ta-nitawi-kêhcinâhowak ta-nitawâpênikêwak.

[9] êkwa êtikwê tâpwê, tahkohtaciwê-~ ê-at-îspayicik ôm êkotê, mayaw êkot-~, môy cêskwa t-âmaciwêcik, âsay kâ-têpâpamâcik, tâpwê awiya êkotê ispatinâhk ê-matwê-apiyit, tahkohtâmatin, âmaciwê-têhtapiwak sôskwâc. nahiyikohk ê-ayâcik, kâ-matwê-kitotikocik: «êkoyikohk, êkây ayiwâk, êkây cîki miton ôta pê-takohtêk!» kâ-matwê-itikocik êsa; «niy ôma,» k-êtikocik êsa, «niy ôma; êtikwê nikôtawêyimikawin,» itwêw –~ itwêwak ê-~ itwêw ês âwa oskinîkiskwêw awa, «nitawi-wîhtamok! nikâwiy nôhtâwiy, nitawi-wîhtamâhk! mîkiwâhp kanâtanohk

strange. Now there on its slope a rock used to sit, that rock was white and sharply cut on both sides, and that rock used to sit there on the slope of the hill. Now about this they used to say, «That is their door, of those spirits who dwell there,» the people used to say, it is said.

[8] Now, now then –~, well, now one could see the figure clearly, recognisably sitting upright, recognisably a human being over there, «Well!» they called out as they went along, it is said, this certain old man called out as he went along, «Behold! Look to that hill over yonder! This one, that *Manitow kâ-matwêhikêt*, somebody is recognisably over there, recogn-~ on top of the hill over there, somebody is recognisably over there; let the young men mount their horses and ride over there, let them be gentle and take care,» they said, it is said –~, said this man as he went along, this old man; «it may even be the case, I suppose, that it is the young woman who has been lost, it may just be her,» they said, it is said –~, said this old man as he went along, and now truly, it is said, as the young men, it is said, were being urged they took their horses, their steeds; four of them now riding over there, it is said, to that hill, they were to go and make sure, they were to make certain of it.

[9] Now it must truly have been, as they rode up to the top –~ as they approached that place over there, as soon as –~, they were not yet going up the hill when they already clearly saw a figure, it was true that someone was recognisably sitting over there on the hill, it was the top of the hill and they straight away rode up the hill. As they were at the right distance, she could distinctly be heard speaking to them: «Only this far, no closer, do not come up really close to here!» was what she could distinctly be heard saying to them, it is said, «It is me,» is what she said to them, «it is me; there must be anguish over my disappearance,» she said –~ they said –~ this young woman, it is said, said to them, «Go and tell

ta-nitawi-cimatâwak, ita ê-kanâtahcâk, êkota ta-nitawi-cimatâwak mîkiwâhp nikâwiy; êkwa, êkota nika-nîhtaciwân, nika-pê-wîhtamâkawin –~ ka-pê-wîhtamawinâwâw nikotwâw, kîsahkamikahki; êkwa, ta-kîsicêposiw nikâwiy pêyakwêskihk, kîsitêw t-ôsîhtâw. êkota êkwa nika-~, êkota nika-nîhtaciwân, nika-pîhtikwân; êkota anima ta-pîhtikwêyân, anima mîkiwâhp ita cimatêki, mâka, ta-miyâhkasikêwak ici, wî-pîhtikwêyâni, ita wî-pimohtêyâni. miton âni, ka-~ nika-~ ka-nât-~ ka-n-~ ê-kanâtahk ôma,» itwêw êsa, «ôma kâ-w-~ kâ-wî-kîwêyân,» itwêw; «misawâc êkotê nik-âcimon, êkota anim êkwa pîhtikwêyâni nik-âcimon,» itwêw ês âw îskwêw.

[10] êkosi, kîwêpayiwak ôki. nêtê têkopayicik mîkiwâhpihk wîhtamwak, «tâpwê an[a] êwako,» itwêwak, «êwakw âw âwa, tâpwê aw ôskinîkiskwêw ana kâ-wanihiht,» itwêwak. «mâka, 'kîwêk! nitawi-wîhtamok! kanâtanohk, patotê-ayihk, êkota ta-cimatâwak mîkiwâhp nikâwiy nôhtâwiy,' it-~ nititikonân; 'êkwa pêyakwêskihk kanakê kîsitêw, ta-kîsisam nikâwiy, êkwa ta-miyâhkasikâniwiw, ta-pimi-miyâhkasikêwak,' it-~ nititikonân, 'êkosi ka-pê-wîhtamawinâwâw kîsahk-~ kîsi-tôtahkwâwi kahkiyaw,' nititikonân ani,» itwêwak ês ôk ôskinîkiwak.

[11] êkosi tâpwê, êha, mistah ês êkwa miywêyihtamwak ôk ônîkihikomâwak. êkwa êsa mîkiwâhp ê-nitonahkik êkwa ê-miywâsiniyik, êkwa ê-kanâtahcâk êkwa (wîcôhkamawâwak, môy pêyakôhkamâtowak, cîhkîstamawâwak mistahi), ê-nitawi-mânokêhk kanâtanohk êkwa. ê-kîsi-tôtamihk, kwayask ê-kanâcihtâcik pîhc-âyihk, t-êsi-miyonâkwahk; êkwa kîsitêw êkwa ê-kîsisahkik iskwêwak, pêyakwêskihk ê-osîhtâcik mîciwin. kiyîsi-tôtahkik, êkwa êkot[a] êkwa, sipwêpayiwak êk ôk ôskinîkiwak âsay mîna, êkwa ê-nitawi-wîhtamawâcik. hâ, têkopayicik, «âsay êkwa,» itêwak,

about it! Go and tell my mother and father about it! Let them go and set up a tipi in a clean place, where the ground is clean, there let my mother and her household set up a tipi; then I shall go down the hill there, someone will come and tell me about it –~ one or the other of you will come and tell me about it when the preparations have been completed; then let my mother do some cooking, let her prepare one kettle of cooked food. At that point then I shall come down the hill and enter; I will enter that tipi there where it is set up, but later let them burn incense when I am about to enter, where I am about to go. It really has to be clean,» she said, it is said, «where I am about to return home,» she said; «at any rate, I shall tell my story over there, once I have entered that lodge, then I shall tell my story,» said that woman, it is said.

[10] Thus they rode back home. As they rode up to the tipis, they told about it, «It is truly her,» they said, «she is that one, she is truly the young woman who has been lost,» they said. «But, 'Return home, go and tell about it! In a clean place, apart, there let my mother and father set up a tipi,' she told us; 'now, as long as there is one kettle of cooked food, let my mother cook it done, and let there be burning of incense, let them go along and burn incense,' she told us, 'then you shall come and tell me once they have completed it all,' she did tell us,» the young men said.

[11] Thus truly, yes, now the parents were very glad, it is said. Now they looked for a good tipi, it is said, and a clean site (everyone helped them, they did not do it alone, people were eagerly joining in with them), now they went and prepared the lodge on a clean site. When they had finished setting it up, they properly cleaned it inside so that it would look good; then the women cooked the food done, they prepared one kettle of food. As they finished their tasks, at that point then the young men rode off as before, now they went to tell her about it. Well, as they were

«â, ka-pê-~ ka-pê-nîhtaciwêyan êkwa,» itêwak. êkosi, «êhaq!» itwê-~ itwêw ês âw îskwêw. êkos ânim êkwa, tâpwê kîwêpayiwak ôki. êkos êkwa aw îskwêw êkwa, na-nîhtaciwêw êkwa, ê-kîwêt êkwa, wiyê [*sic*], ê-têpinâkwahk êkota ohc ânima tahtakwaskamikâw, wâwîs êtikwê mihcêt mîkiwâhpa anim êkotê ê-cimatêki, miton êtikwê wâhyaw kî-ohci-têpinâkwan.

[12] êkosi; têkohtêt nêtê mîkiwâhpihk, kî-itwêw êsa mâna, «mân[i] âwêsk[a] âw îyin-âyisiyiniw, mistahi okîhkâspakosih, ê-itêyihtamân,» kî-itwêw êsa mân ân[a] îskwêw, ispîhk êkw ê-otihtât ayisiyiniwa, wiya nêwo-tipiskâw ê-kanawêyimikot ôhi kîk̦way ôhi, âtayôhkana. êkwa ês êkota êkwa ê-pim-~ ê-miyâhkasikêwiht, ita ê-pimohtêt, êkos ê-isi-pîhtikwêt.

[13] êkosi; êkwa ês êkot[a] êkwa, wîhtam êsa, «â, niwîhtamâkawin, ê-wîhtamâkawiyân ôma, 'â, êkwa ka-pakitinitinân êkwa ta-wayawîyan, êkwa kika-kîwân,' nititikawin, 'mistahi kinîkihikwak matwê-kaskêyihtamwak, ôma, ôt[a] ê-kisâtinitâhk,' itiko-~ it-~ nititik-~ nititikwak, ôki kâ-kanawêyimicik êkota,» itwêw êsa, «êkota anim îta k-âpiyân ispatinâhk, êkota anima, pîhc-âyihk ê-kî-kanawêyimikawiyân, mîkiwâhp êkota pîh-~ ê-cimatêk, êkot[a] ê-pîhtikwêyân ê-itêyihtamân ê-pîhtikwêyân, mîkiwâhp tâpiskôc, êkot[a] ê-tasi-kanawêyimicik,» itwêw êsa. «miton ân[i] âkwâc, wêskwâhtêmihk, êkotê ê-wîtapimakik ôki,» itwêw êsa, «êkwa nêtê iskwâhtêmihk, âh-âyîtaw-iskwâht êkotê ê-apicik, tahk êkonik ê-kisiwâsicik, 'kanawêyim-~ kanawêyimihkok –~ kanawêyihtamok êwako iskot-~ êwakw îskwâhtêm, êkâyi [*sic*] nânitaw t-êsi-pihkohot ta-wayawît,' ê-itwêcik ôki kisêyiniwak; kisêyiniwak ê-isinawakik ê-wâsakâmêpicik, miton ê-wâh-wâpistikwânêcik,» ê-kî-itwêt êsa mân âna, an[a] îskwêw (tâpwê ôm âcimowin êwak ôm ôm ôma [*sic*], môya wiy âtayôhkêwin, mosci-âcimowin ôma k-âtotamân). êkwa êtikwê, «êkwa, piyisk êkwa, ê-nikam-~ ê-nikamohi-~ ê-nikamohicik

riding up, «Now it is time already,» they said to her, «well, for you to come down the hill now,» they said to her. This was it; «Yes!» said this woman, it is said. Thus now they truly rode back home. And thus this woman was going down the hill now, returning home now, for that level area was fully visible from there, especially since there must have been many tipis standing over there, it must have been highly visible from afar.

[12] This was it; as she was arriving at the tipi over yonder, she did say, it is said, «In my dreams it always appears as if human beings had a strong taste [*sic*], it seems to me,» that woman did say, it is said, at the time she now came up to the people, for these things had kept her for four nights, these dream spirits. There now, it is said, they burned incense for her where she went, in this way she entered.

[13] Thus, there now she told about it, it is said, «Well, I was told this, as I was told this, 'Well, now we will let you go, to go outside, now you shall return home,' I was told, 'your parents are greatly distressed, it is obvious, that we are holding you back here,' they said to me, those who kept me there,» she said, it is said, «at that place where I sat on the hill, at that place I had been kept inside, a lodge stands there, I entered there, it seemed to me, entering it as if it were a lodge, there I was being kept the whole time,» she said, it is said. «It was very much in the back, opposite the entrance, there I sat with them,» she said, it is said, «now over yonder, at the entrance, on either side of the entrance over there, there they sat, and they were angry all the time, 'Keep her! Keep them –~ you all guard that entrance lest she escape in some way and go outside,' these old men said; they looked like old men to me and they sat in the round, they all had really white hair,» that woman had said, it is said (this story is true, that is the case, it is not a myth, what I am relating is a factual account). It must have been then,

mân ôki kisêyiniwak nêwo-tipiskâw ôma, ê-nikamohicik, êkwa âtiht ê-wî-nipahicik, tahk êkosi ê-is-âsotamawicik âtiht ôki, ê-wî-nipahicik; êkwa âtiht ôki kisêyiniwak, mistah ê-pîkiskwêcik ê-nitotamâkêstamawicik, ê-~ kiyâm êkâ ta-misiwanâcihikawiyân, kiyâm ta-pimâtisiyân,» ê-itwêt ês âw îskwêw. «êkwa êkota, 'â mâka, ôma t-êsi-nitawêyihtamahk ôma, êkosi tôtahki ka-pakitinânaw, êkwa ta-wayawîw êkwa, wâpaniyik[i] êkwa ôma ta-wayawîw êkwa, ta-kîwêw,' k-êtwêcik ôki kisêyiniwak kotakak,» itwêw ês âwa. «'ôma, ôma nistam kê-wîcêwât nâpêwa, tita-wanihêw anihi nâpêwa, êkoni k-âsamikonaw; otawâsimisici, êkota, êkoni mîna k-âsamikonaw ôhi, otawâsimisa; êkoni asotamâkoyahko, êkosi wî-tôtahki, êkosi ka-pakitinânaw ta-wayawîw, mâka mîskoc kinwês kita-pimâtisiw, ta-nôtikwêwiw awa, mîskoc êwakw ân[i] ânima; êkwa mîna, namôy konita ta-kisâtinâyahk ôta iyikohk, ômayikohk kâ-nikamohâyahk kahkiyaw êkoni, êkwa mîn êkot[a] ôhci kîkway ta-kiskêyihtamâsow, ôm ôta ê-tasi-kanawêyimâyahk,' itwêw êsa –~ itwêwak ês ôki kisêyiniwak ôki, 'ka-kiskinohamawâyahk kîkway, t-êsi-âpatisit kîkway, ta-mamisîwâtiht,' ê-isicik aniki kisêyiniwak,» itwêw êsa. «êkota êkwa, 'êhak' [*sic*]!' k-êtwêyân, ê-nôhtê-pê-wayawîyân tâpwê,» itwêw ês âw îskwêw; «'êhaq! nika-tôtên,' k-êtakik,» itwêw ês âw îskwêw. «hâw, êkota êkwa, ê-kîkisêpâyâk êcik ôm êkwa, anim êtikwê êkwa, kâ-pakitinicik êkwa, tâpiskôc ê-wayawîyân mîkiwâhpihk ohci, êkos ê-itêyihtamân, êkos ê-isinamân,» ê-kî-itwêt êsa mân ân[a] îskwêw – êkos ôma mâna n-~ ê-kî-itâcimot kâ-kî-oyôhkomiyân ê-kî-âtotahk, êkota anima wîstawâw ês ê-wîkicik ôki nôhkom anima.

«Finally, now these old men made me sing ritual songs, for four nights they made me sing ritual songs, now some of them were going to kill me, some of them constantly threatening me with that, that they were going to kill me; now some of the old men were speaking a great deal and pleading on my behalf that I should not be put to death, that I should be allowed to live,» this woman said, it is said. «At that point now, 'Well, on the other hand, if she does what we want, we will let her go, then she will go outside, then, once dawn breaks, she will go outside and return home,' said these other old men,» this one said, it is said. «'It is this, when she will first take a husband, let her lose that man, let her feed him to us; when she has a child, at that point let her also feed that one to us, her child; if she promises us these, if she is going to do that, on that condition we will let her go and she is to go outside, but in return let her have a long life, let her live to be an old woman, she is to have that in return; and it is also not for nothing that we would hold her back here so long, making her sing all these ritual songs so thoroughly, from that also let her have mystical knowledge of things, from us having kept her here the whole time,' he said, it is said –~ the old men said, it is said, 'for us to teach her things so that she will be of use in some way and that people will rely on her for them,' these old men said to me,» she said. «It was at this point now that I said 'Yes!', I truly wanted to come back outside,» this woman said, it is said, «'Yes! I will do it,' is what I told them,» this woman said, it is said. «Well, at this point now, as morning broke, what was this, it must have been then that they now let me go, it was as if I went outside from the lodge, it seemed to me that way, it looked to me that way,» that woman did say, it is said – that is how my late grandmother used to tell the story when she told it, they too lived right there, my grandmother and her household.

[14] êkosi tâpwê; kâh-kîs-âcimot [*sic*] ês êwako aw îskwêw, êkos êkwa êkot[a] êkwa kîsitêw êkwa ôma, ê-pîkiskwâtamoht êkwa. êkot[a] êkw ê-mîcisot êkwa awa, ê-asamiht aw îskwêw, ê-wîcihiwêt ôma ê-kîsitêpowiht ôm ê-~ ê-asamiht; êkosi mân ê-kî-itâcimot nôhkom.

[15] êkos ânima tâpwê; êwakw âw âw îskwêw, 'picwêkan' kî-isiyîhkâsow êsa, êwakw âw âw îskwêw kâ-kî-otinikot kîkway mac-âya, môy piko nôhkom ê-ohci-kiskêyihtahk, mihcêt ês ânim ê-kî-kiskêyihtahkik; pêyak nikî-pêhtawâw, wîst êsa mân ôhkoma êkos ê-kî-itâtotamiyit anima êwak ôm ôma.

[16] êkwa, êwakw âw âw îskwêw, tâpwê, nikî-wâpamimâwa êkoni ôh ôtânisa, kî-ka-kêhtê-~ âsay ê-nôtikwêwit an[a] îskwêw kâ-kî-wâpamak, êcik êkoni ôh ôh, â, êtikw âwa, otânisa anih âwa, picwêkan awa, manitowa êwako kâ-kî-otinikot. îh, êkoni wiy âta wiy ôtânis[a] ê-kî-pimâtisiyit, môy mâka wîhkâc nipêh-~ nôh-pêhtên wiya, taht-~ tânitahto k-ây-ihtasiyikwêni [*sic*] otawâsimis[a] ê-pimâtisiyit, êkoyikohk isko mâna nikî-pa-pêhtên nôhkom aw êkosi ê-kî-ay-itâcimot. ê-mamâhtâwahk anim îspatinâw; nitak[a] êtikwê, êkâ kîkway êkwa ê-ay-ispayik êwakw ân[i] ânima, êkâ kîkway êkota mistahi kâ-sa-sêkihikohk [*sic*] êwakw ânima, êkos îsi kîkway kita-ispayik, êkonik aniki. mâka wiya mân ôma, mihcêcis ê-pâh-pêhtawakik ôk êkotê, êkota anima kîkway, ê-câh-cikahciwihikocik kâ-nipâcik ôma, ê-kâ-~ ê-pawâtahkik tâpiskôc, ê-pawâtahkik kîkway êkota, kîkway wîstawâw, mâk êkwa itâwak êkonik ôki, tâpiskôc ê-maci-pawâmit, «êkota kîkway, ê-wayêsîhkwastimikot,» ê-itâcik mân âtiht ôk êkota ôk âyisiyiniwak.

[17] êkwa, anoht-~ êkos êkwa anim îyikohk êkotê kâ-kî-ay-ayâyân, nama wîhkâc matwân cî anim ôsâm ayisiyiniwak

[14] Truly this was it; when that woman had finished telling her story, it is said, now then, at that point they recited prayers over the cooked food with respect to her. At that point this one now ate, this woman was ritually fed, she took part as they cooked the food done with respect to her and she was ritually fed; in this way my grandmother used to tell the story.

[15] That was the way it truly was, it was that woman, her name was *Picwêkan*, it is said, she was the woman who had been abducted by some evil beings, not only my grandmother used to know about it, many used to know about that, it is said; I have heard one woman say that, her grandmother too, it is said, used to tell that story the same way.

[16] Now, it was this woman [*sc. Picwêkan*], it is true, I did see her daughter, she was an old –~ that woman was already an old woman when I saw her, what was that, it was her, well, it must have been her daughter, the daughter of this *Picwêkan* whom the spirits had abducted. Look, this daughter of hers at least had lived, but I have never heard how many of her children they may have been that lived, that is all of the story I used to hear the way my grandmother had been telling it. That hill is strange; it is a lucky thing, I suppose, that these things are not happening now at that place, that there is nothing at that place greatly to frighten anyone, for things like that to happen, with those [*sc.* the spirits]. But I do hear a few talking from time to time about that place there, of something startling them sometimes in their sleep, as if they were dreaming of something, that they too dream about something there, something, but it is said about those, as if someone had an evil dream spirit, «Something is there that is deceiving them in their sleep,» some of the people there say about them.

êkw êkot[a] ê-ayâcik, êkos ês ânim êkwa, namôy wîhkâc kîkway ê-ohci-pêhtâht êkota mistikwaskihk, kîhtwâm wîhkâc tita-pa-pêhtâkosit, kayâs êtikw ânima mêkwâc ê-kanâtahk êkâ tâpwê ê-ayisiyinîskâk kâ-kî-pêhtâht ês âna mân êkota, mistikwaskihk ê-matwê-matwêhoht ana wîhpihtakahikan, êwak ôhc ânima 'manitow kâ-matwêhikêt' k-êsiyîhkâtêk.

[18] êkwa, ê-kiskisiyân mân ê-awâsisîwiyân, nîswâw wiya kêhtinâc ê-kî-wîcêwâyâhk mâna nôhkominân, matwân cî anima wîsta kîkway êkotê ê-kî-kiskêyihtamâsot ana nôhkominân, miton ê-kî-nôtikwêwit nôcikwêsiw, ê-kî-âmaciwêt mâna nôhkominân an[a] ê-kî-pimitisahwâyâhk. môy wîhkât konit âwiyak êkos îsi mistahi ta-sa-sâ-sâkêwêt êkotê anima ta-nitaw-~ ispatinâhk ôma, ahpô mân-~, mitoni mân ê-kî-akâwâtamâhk kîtahtawê, ê-nôhtê-nitawi-sa-sâkêwêyâhk êwakw ânima mis-îspatinâw, êkot[a] ânim ê-kî-kiskêyihtamân nîswâw awa nôhkom, ê-kî-wîcêwâyâhk mâna; wêpinâson mân ê-kî-tahkon-~ ê-kî-tahkonahk, êkwa ayi, pâskisikan; îh, kayâs ôh îyinito-pâskisikana, êkotowahk mân ê-kî-sipwêhtatât ana nôhkominân, êkwa mân êkotê ê-kî-tahkohtaciwêyâhk. êkotê mân êkwa ê-kî-nitaw-âyamihtâkosit ana nôhkominân, ê-kâkîsimot ê-pâh-pîkiskwêt ôm êkos îsi, êkwa mân ê-kî-mâtot mâna, ispimihk ê-isisowiniskêyit; ohpimê mâna niyanân nikî-ay-apinân ê-~, konit îtê, têpiyâhk mân ê-kî-na-nitohtawâyâhk ôma kâ-~, êkos ânima mân êkotê ê-kî-ohtaskatahk anima wêpinâson êkw ânima pâskisikan. êkon ânihi mân ê-kî-nitawi-wêpinâsot êkotê, êwakw 'ê-wêpinâsohk' k-êsiyîhkâtêk. êkos ê-kî-isîhcikêt ana mâna nôhkominân ê-kî-ka-kiskêyimak; êwakw ân[i] ânim ôhci, 'manitow kâ-matwêhikêt' k-êsiyîhkâtêk anima. âstamispîhk iyikohk ayisiyiniwak kâ-kî-ayâcik, nama wîhkâc kîkway

[17] Now, today –~, thus, so long as I have lived over there, there has never been anything like this, perhaps because people now live over there, this is the way it is now, it is said, and never has there been an instance of the medicine drum being heard over here, that it should ever be heard again, in the old days that place must have been clean during the time and truly without people when that medicine drum was heard there, when one could distinctly hear the hollowed-out drum being beaten, that is why that hill was called *Manitow kâ-matwêhikêt*.

[18] Now I remember, when I was a child, twice certainly I did go along with our grandmother, I wonder if she too, that grandmother of ours, had some mystical knowledge about that place over there, she was very old, a little old woman, that grandmother of ours used to go up that hill and we used to follow along with her. There was never much of anyone appearing in view gratuitously on that hill over there, or –~ we used to be very keen to go up there sometime, we wanted to go and come into view on that big hill, I do know that I went up there with this grandmother of ours twice; she carried cloth and, ah, a gun; look, a single-shot gun of long ago, that kind that grandmother of ours took with her, now we went up on top of the hill over there. Over there now that grandmother of ours went and could be heard praying, chanting and reciting her prayers like that, and she used to cry in her praying, with her arms stretched up high; as for us, we would stay to the side somewhere, we just listened to her as she –~ in this way she left that cloth and that gun behind over there. She went and left these as offerings over there to those [*sc.* the spirits], that was called *ê-wêpinâsot* [*sc.* she makes an offering]. That is the ritual that grandmother of ours used to perform, and I knew that of her; and that was why that place was called *Manitow kâ-matwêhikêt*. When

ohci-môyêyihtâkwan êkota anima êkos îsi, kîkway kîhtwâm kit-ây-ispayik ta-pa-pêhtamihk kîkway êkota, nama kîkway.

[19] êkoyikohk iskohk êwak ôm ê-kî-pêhtamân mîna, âcimowin k-âtotamân.

people later came to live there in such numbers, never was anything like that felt there, for something like that to happen again, for them to hear something there, nothing.

[19] That is all of that story I also used to hear, the story I have told.

Sarah Whitecalf at Sweetgrass Sundance, 1974.

12

manitow kâ-matwêhikêt

Where the spirits drum (III)

manitow kâ-matwêhikêt

[SW:] â, ayihk, âsay mîn ôta, anohc niwî-âcimosinân apisîs, môy êkwa kinwês, êkos êkwa, iskwayâc anohc, ta-kîsîhtâyâhk. nimiywêyihtên ê-wî-kîsi-tôtamâhk ôma, ôta kâ-pê-itohtêyâhk kâ-pê-apiyâhk; kâ-pê-wîtapimâyâhk awa nitôkimâminân, niwîcêwâkaninân [*laughs*].

[1] êkos êkwa, pêyak kîkway niwî-âcimoscawâsiwak ôta, tâpwêwin ê-kî-ispayik, ê-kî-pê-isi-~-isi-pa-pêhtamân mâna. ôm ôtê, pêyak mâna (nôhkom ê-kî-pêhtawak, mw-~ – nôhkom ê-kî-ohpikihit) kayâs, êkotê ôtê nakiwacîhk, tâpwê êkos ê-kî-ispayik, ê-kî-pê-wâpahtahk wiya nôhkom, ôma 'nakiwacîhk' ôtê k-êsiyîhkâtêk, kayâs êsa nistam ayisiyiniwak êkotê ê-papâ-wâh-wîkicik, namôy cêskwa askîhkân ê-otinikâtêk anima nakiwaciy. êkospîhk êsa, êwakw ân[i] ânima 'nakiwaciy' k-êsiyîhkâtêk, ê-tâpwê-wîyîhkâtêk [*sic; sc.* -wîhyîhkâtêk] anima, êwak ôm ôma k-êsiyîhkâtêk êwakw âskîhkân, ê-pimi-misi-wacîwik anima ômis îsi [*gesture*], êkwa mitoni nak-âyihk, êkota piko nîhc-âyihk ayisiyiniwak mân ê-kî-ayâcik; êkwa, ê-misi-tahtakwaskamikâk êkota mitoni, êkota ês ê-wîkicik kayâs

Where the spirits drum (III)

[SW:] Well, now then, here as usual we are going to do a little story-telling today, not a long session now in order for us to finish it, today being the last day. I am glad that we are going to finish this task, having travelled here and having come to sit here; having come to sit here with this boss of ours [*sc.* Chris Wolfart], with our partner [*laughs*].

[1] Thus now I am going to tell them [*sc.* Freda Ahenakew and Chris Wolfart] a little story about one thing on here [*sc.* on the audio-recorder], it is a true account of what took place as I have always heard it. It was over there, one of them used to (I used to hear my grandmother, my grandmother raised me), it truly happened over there, there at *Nakiwacîhk* [Sweetgrass] long ago, my grandmother had witnessed it herself, it was there at *Nakiwacîhk*, long ago people at first lived here and there at various sites over there, it is said, that *Nakiwaciy* had not yet been taken as a reserve. At that time, it is said, that place that is called *nakiwaciy* [*lit.* the hill's edge] was truly given that name, it is this reserve that bears that name, the hill is big all along like this [*gesture*], and the people used to live right up against the edge, only there beneath

nêhiyawak, ê-~ ê-mâh-~ ê-kî-mâh-mâmaw-âyâcik êsa mâna, ê-kî-mâh-mâmawi-wîkicik nêhiyawak. nikî-wâpaht-~ nikî-~, êkota mwêhc ânim ê-kî-wîkiyâhk mâna, êkwa mân ômis îsi [*gesture*] âpihtâ-kîsikâhk is ânima, êkota ê-misi-wîhkwê-paskwâk ê-misi-paskwâk. êkota anim ê-kî-wîkiyâhk, êkota mâna nôhkom ê-kî-itwahikêt, «êkot[a] ê-wîkicik ayisiyiniwak kayâs; êkota ê-wîkihk,» itwêw, «êkota ôm ê-wîkihk,» itwêw; êkwa nêtê, ôma waciy ôma k-êtwêyân, êkota, mêton ômis îsi [*gesture*] ê-pis-~ ê-pôsiski-pasahcâk, êkota sîpîsis ê-pê-pinasiwêhtik, ômis îs [*gesture*] ôma ê-pis-~ ê-pôsiski-pasahcâk, namôy mîna asiskiy ê-nôkwahk anima kâ-kîskatâwahkâk anima tâpiskôt, sôskwât tâpiskôc ê-âmaciwê-maskosiya-ohpikihki ôhi misakâmê. miton ê-mamâhtâwinâkwahk êwakw ânim îspatinâw, 'manitow kâ-matwêhikêt' isiyîhkâtamwak nêhiyawak êkota nakiwacîhk, êwako ispatinâw.

[2] «êwako,» mâna kî-itwêw nôhkom, «kayâs êsa mân êkota nêhiyawak, 'manitow ê-matwêhikêt' ê-kî-itwêcik kayâs, mistikwaskihk tâpiskôc» (mâka 'wîhpihtakahikan' kî-isiyîhkâtêwak êsa, kîkwây êtikwê, ê-wîhpahwâcik misi-mistikwa, êkwa êkota pahkêkin, tâpiskôc mistikwaskihk), êkotowahk êsa mâna k-ôtâkosik êkota ê-kî-pêhtawâcik êkotê anim îspatinâhk, ê-pêhtâkosit ana. nam âwiyak ayisiyiniw êkotê ê-ayât, nam âwiyak ê-wâpamiht, nayêstaw ana mistikwaskihk êsa mân ê-kî-matwêhoht êkotê. êkwa, êwak ôhci kâ-kî-isiyîhkâtahkik anima 'manitow kâ-matwêhikêt', kî-isiyîhkâtamwak anim îspatinâw. êwakw ân[i] ânima, ê-kî-~ «ê-mamâhtâwahk,» ê-kî-itwêcik mân ânim îspatinâw.

the edge; now, it is a very large level area there, and there, it is said, the Crees used to live long ago, usually staying together in groups, it is said, the Crees dwelling together in groups. I have seen it myself, we used to live right there, and this way [*gesture*] towards the south side there is a large arc-shaped meadow, a large meadow. There we used to live, and there my grandmother used to point, «There the people used to live long ago; there people lived,» she said, «there people lived,» she said; and over yonder the hill that I spoke about, there it is cleft like this [*gesture*] by a really steep gully, a creek comes running down there, the hill is cleft like this [*gesture*] by a deep gully, and no earth can be seen on that cutbank and it seems as if grass were growing right away, all the way up the slope. That hill looks very strange, and the people there at *Nakiwacîhk* call that hill *Manitow kâ-matwêhikêt*.

[2] «This place,» my grandmother used to say, «long ago the Crees used to call this place *Manitow kâ-matwêhikêt*, it is said, long ago, as if it was a medicine drum» (but they used to call it a *wîhpihtakahikan*, it is said, I am not sure what that was, they hollowed out big trees, and then hide over it, as if it was a medicine drum), that kind, it is said, they used to hear it in the evenings over there at that hill, that one could be heard. No human being at all was over there, nobody could be seen, only that medicine drum used to be beaten over there, it is said. Now, it was for this reason that they used to call it *Manitow kâ-matwêhikêt*, that was their name for that hill. That one, «It is strange,» they used to say about that hill.

[3] êwako, «êkota ôm ê-mâmawi-wîkihk,» itwêw nôhkom, «kîtahtawê oskinîkiskwêw pêyak,» itwêw, «môy cêskw ê-onâpêmit, kâ-wanihiht,» itwêw, «wanihâw, êy, êkwa ê-nitonikêhk,» itwêw, «misiwê,» itwêw; «namôy â-~ oskinîkiwak ê-nitonâhcik, nam âwiyak wanihâw, nam âwiyak kôtawêyimâw oskinîkiw,» itwêw, «ta-kî-sipwêhtahikot oskinîkiwa,» itwêw. «êkosi, misiwê êkwa ê-nitonâht, nêwo-tipiskâw ê-wanihiht aw ôskinîkiskwêw,» itwêw, «nêwo-tipiskâw, misiwê ê-nitonâht,» itwêw, «kîtahtawê, ê-kî-nêwo-tipiskâk, kâ-wâpamiht êkotê ispatinâhk awiyak ê-cîpatapit,» itwêw.

[4] «hâ, wiya kîkisêpâ ôma tahk ôskinîkiwak ê-papâmi-têhtapicik, âhci piko ê-nitonikêtisahohcik,» itwêw. «kîtahtawê awiyak ê-~ nâpêw ê-wa-wayawît êtikwê, kâ-têh-têpwêhk,» itwêw, «'mâcikôcican, itâpik! nêtê itâpik ispatinâhk! namôy cî aw êwako oskinîkiskwêw kâ-wanihot, nâh âwiyak ispatinâhk kâ-cîpatapit. mahti, oskinîkîtik, niton-~ kitêmiwâwak otinihkok! nitawâpênikêk nâha, awiyak k-ôtihtikonaw! ahpô êtikw âwiyak ê-otihtikoyahk; nitawâpênikêk! aswêyihtamok, pêyâhtik ispayik! awêkâ cî êwakw âw îskwêw awa kâ-wanihiht!' isi-têh-têpwêwak kisêyiniwak,» itwêw, «ê-têpwêhk,» itwêw.

[5] «êkosi tâpwê,» itwêw; «tâpwê oskinîkiwak ôk,» îtwêw, «têhtapiwak ê-ispayicik êkotê,» itwêw. «cîki ê-at-âmat-~ mitoni (iyikohk ê-ispâk anima ispatinâw, êtataw mân ê-kî-nôkosit awiyak, wâwîs cî tita-pêyakot ômis îsi, otêhtapiwak êtataw mâna ê-kî-nôkosicik, iyikohk ê-ispâk anima ispatinâw, manitow

[3] At that place, «While people were staying there in a group,» my grandmother said, «it was all of a sudden that a certain young woman,» she said, «she was not yet married, that she was lost,» she said, «she was lost, hey, now they undertook a search,» she said, «everywhere,» she said; «none –~ they looked for the young men, none of them was missing, none of the young men caused concern by being absent,» she said, «that a young man might have taken her off with him,» she said. «Thus they now looked for her everywhere, the young woman was lost for four nights,» she said, «for four nights they looked for her everywhere,» she said, «it was all of a sudden, after the fourth night, that they saw someone sitting upright on the hill over there,» she said.

[4] «Well, it was morning and the young men were riding about all the time, they were still being sent out to search,» she said. «It was all of a sudden, as someone, a man, must have been going outside, that everyone was calling out,» she said, «'Behold, look! Look on the hill over yonder! Might it not be that young woman who was lost, that somebody over yonder who sits upright on the hill. Well then, you young men, take then your horses! Make certain about that figure over yonder, someone has come to visit us! Either someone must have come to visit us; make certain! Take care, ride up gently! or else it is that woman who has been lost!' thus all the old men were calling out,» she said, «people were calling out,» she said.

[5] «Thus it truly was;» she said; «truly these young men,» she said, «mounted their horses and rode over there,» she said. «Riding uphill –~ close, very (that hill is so high that a person used to be barely visible, especially when alone like that, the horsemen themselves used to be barely visible, so high is that hill, that

kâ-matwêhikêt êwako); îh, êkotê, tâpwê êkwa k-âmaciwê-têhtapicik ôk ôskinîkiwak, pôti – cîk ê-at-âyâcik, ê-at-âmaciwêcik, pôt ôh êkota oskinîkiskwêwa, êkoni ôhi kâ-wanihimiht ôhi, kâ-nisitawinawâcik êkota ê-ay-apiyit tahkohc ispatinâhk,» itwêw. «êkosi, tako-têhtapiwak êkotê nîhcipayihowak, 'hâ, tânisi? kiy ôma kâ-wanihikawiyan, tâpitaw ôm ê-nitonikêhk, ê-nitonâkawiyan; mistahi pakwâtamwak kikâwiy kôhtâwiy ê-wanihikawiyan,' k-êtâcik, itêwak ôk ôskinîkiwak,» itwêw. «êkosi, 'â, â, ê-kî-otinikawiyân ôma, êkwayâc ôm ê-pê-wayawîyân,' k-êtwêt ês âw ôskinîkiskwêw,» itwêw – «mâka, êkos ôma kîwêk! nitawi-wîhtamok! ôm îta kâ-wîkihk, êkotê takohtêyêko nikâwiy nôhtâwiy, ê-kan-~ mîkiwâhp, mîkiwâhp patotê-ayihk, wayawîtim-âyihk, itê êkâ ê-wîkihk, itê ê-kanâtahcâk, êkota ta-nitawi-mânokêwak mîkiwâhp; êkota, êkota nika-takohtân, êkotê kê-nitawi-pîhtikwêyân nîkân, mâka ta-miyâhkasikâniwiw êkota takohtêyâni wî-pîhtikwêyâni. êkwa mîna, apisîs ta-kîsicêposiwak; êkota t-âcimoyân êkwa, ê-wî-âcimoyân tânis ôm ê-~ ê-~ ê-isi-pakit-~ ê-isi-pimâtisiyân,» ê-itwêt ês âwa oskinîkiskwêw, «êkwa êkota nika-mîcisosinân nika-wîci-mîcisômâwak êkota, ninîkihikwak, mîna tahto kê-pê-nitohtahkik. êkosi ka-nitaw-îsi-wîhtênâwâw, niyâk êkosi! kîwêpayik, nitawi-wîhtamok! êkosi, êkos âni, nik-âti-sa-sipwêhtân itâp, wîhkâcês! nêma kîs-âyâyêk-~-twâwi [*sc.* kîs-âyâyêko, kîs-âyâtwâwi], kîsi-mânokêhki,» itwêw ês âw îskwêw. êkosi isi-sipwêpayiwak ôk ôskinîkiwak, ê-kîwêpayicik.

Manitow kâ-matwêhikêt); look, it was over there that these young men now truly were riding up the hill, behold – as they came close, as they were coming up the hill, behold here it was this young woman, the one who had been lost, whom they recognised as she sat there on top of the hill,» she said. «Thus they rode up to her and jumped off their horses over there, 'Well, how are you? It is you that has been lost, there has been a search going on all along, a search for you; your mother and father are grief-stricken that you have been lost,' is what they said to her, these young men said to her,» she said. «Thus, 'Well, well, it is that I was abducted and that I have only just come outside,' is what that young woman said, it is said,» she said – «But you return home like this! Go and tell about it! Here where the people live, when you arrive over there at my mother's and my father's place, let them go and set up a tipi, a tipi apart, at a place outside the camp, where nobody lives, where the ground is clean, there let them go and prepare a lodge; there, there I shall arrive, for me to go and first enter over there, but let there be burning of incense once I arrive there and am about to enter. Now let them also cook a little food; there for me to tell my story, as I am about to tell my story, how I was releas-~ how I came to live through it,» the young woman said, it is said, «There then we shall eat a little, I shall eat there with my parents, and also with as many as may come to listen. In this way you will go and tell about it, go then! Ride back home, go and tell about it! Thus, thus indeed I shall set off on foot later, in a little while! Once they have finished their tasks over yonder, once the preparation of the lodge has been completed,» this woman said, it is said. With that the young men rode off, riding back home. As they were coming up to the tipis over yonder, now they told about this, «Truly it is her, that young

nêtê têkopayicik mîkiwâhpihk, êwak ôm êkwa wîhtamwak, «tâpwê an[a] êwako, êwako kâ-kî-wanihot oskinîkiskwêw. mâka, nipê-kîwêtisahokonân, ta-pê-wîhtamâhk, 'hâw, nikâwiy nôhtâwiy, mîkiwâhp pêyak ta-nitawi-cimatâwak ohpimê, ê-kanâtahcâk ita, êkota ta-cimatâwak mîkiwâhp, êkota nik-~ êkota kîwêyâni, êkota nika-pîhtikwân, mâka ta-miyâhkasikêwak wî-pîhtikwêyâni; êkwa mîna, kîsitêw apisîs t-ôsîhtâwak, kîsicês, êkota nika-wîci-mîcisômâwak nikêhtê-ayimak, mîna kotakak ayisiyiniwak. êkota ê-wî-âcimoyân tânêhk ôma kâ-wanihi-~ kâ-kî-wanihikawiyân,' itwêw ês âw ôskinîk-~, itwêw an[a]·âspin,» itwêwak ês ôk ôskinîkiwak.

[6] êkosi; êkos êkwa, êy, iyikohk êk ôk ê-miywêyihtahkik ôki kêhtê-ayak, ê-papâsinikêcik êkwa pêyak osk-âyi mîkiwâhp ê-ihtakoniyik êtikwê êkota, êwakw ânim êkwa kâ-mâmawôhkamâtocik ôk âyisiyiniwak, êkw êkwa patotê, itê ê-kanâtahcâyik, êkotê ê-nitawi-mânokêhk ôma mîkiwâhp êkwa. êk ôma k-êsi-kiskinohamâhcik, ê-papâsîcik ôk îskwêwak ê-kîsitêpocik, kîkway kîsicêw, ê-wî-asamiht êkwa awa kâ-~, awa kâ-~, awa kâ-wî-takohtêt.

[7] êkosi; ê-kîsipayik êwako, ê-kîsi-tôtahkik, êkos êkwa, âsay mîn âwa pêyak êkwa nômakê-~, «nômakê-sipwêpayi! wâh-wâstahamâhk! ka-pâh-pimicipayinâwâw! ka-wâh-wâstahikêyêk, êkos êkwa nâha ka-pê-sipwêhtêt.» êkos êkwa ê-pê-kîs-âyâcik ôki, êkos êkwa ê-sipwêpayit awa pêyak ê-têhtapit, âstamita pê-nîhc-âyihk tahtakwaskamikâw, mân êkota isko ê-ispayit aw ôskinîkiw. êkot[a] êkwa, ê-pâh-pimi-têhtapit, ê-pâh-pimicipayit, ê-wâh-wâstahamawât ôh ôskinîkiskwêwa, êkos êkwa aw ôskinîkiskwêw êkwa pê-pinasiwêw êkwa pê-sa-sipwêhtêw. êkosi, pê-kîwêpayiw aw ôskinîkiw, pê-tata-~ pê-sa-sipwêpayiw.

woman who had been lost. But she has sent us back home to come and tell about it, 'Well, let my mother and father go and set up a tipi by itself off to the side, where the ground is clean, there let them set up a tipi and there, once I return home, there I shall enter, but let them burn incense once I am about to enter; let them also prepare a small amount of cooked food, a little cooked food, there I shall eat with my parents and also with other people. There I am going to tell my story of why I had been lost,' the young wom-~ it is said, that one said as we rode off,» the young men said, it is said.

[6] Thus it was; thus now, hey, the old people were so glad now, now they made haste, and there must have been one new tipi available there, that was the one which all the people together now set up, apart now, where the ground was clean, over there they now went to prepare this lodge. And as they had been instructed, the women hastened and did the cooking, a little cooked food, now the one who was about to arrive would be ritually fed.

[7] Thus it was; when that was finished, when they had finished their tasks, now then as usual one of the young men [*sc.* was instructed] to proceed part of the way –~, «Ride off but only part of the way! All of you wave your arms at her! Let all of you ride back and forth from side to side [*sc.* in order to attract her attention]! for you to wave your arms so that she over yonder will set off to come here.» Thus now, when these [*sc.* the women] were finished with their tasks, thus now one of the young men set off on horseback, on this side beneath the edge of the hill towards the hither side there is a level area, up to there that young man rode. There now he rode back and forth, riding back and forth from side to side, waving his arms at the young woman, and thus now the young woman came down the hill and came walking towards them. Thus the young man came riding back home, he set off and came towards them on horseback.

[8] êkos êkwa aw ôskinîkiskwêw êkwa, anita piyê-takohtêt mîkiwâhpihk, tâpwê miyâhkasikêwân, atamiskâk ôhtâwiya okâwiya, atamiskâk. êkosi pîhtikwêw; êkosi wîhtam ta-pîhtikwêyit ayisiyiniwa, ê-wî-âcimot êkwa.

[9] «â,» kî-itwêw êsa, «nêwo-tipiskâw, nêwo-tipiskâw anima, êkâ ayisiyinînâhk ê-ayâyân; mistah âni kîhkâmâkosiw ayisiyiniw, âsay ê-pasoyân,» ê-itwêt êsa, ê-kî-itwêt ês ân[a] îskwêw; «ayisiyiniw âsay nipason; tâpiskôc ê-kîhkâmâkosit osâm nêwo-tipiskâw ohpimê ê-ayâyân,» ê-itwêt ês ân[a] îskwêw.

[10] êkosi; êkwa êkota ês êwakw ânim êkwa kâ-mâtâcimot; «ê-kî-otinicik, ê-pê-nâsicik kîkway, ayisiyiniw ê-itêyim-~ ê-itêy-~ ê-itâpisiniyân, êkosi ê-tâpwêhtawakik,» itwêw êsa, tâpiskôt nâpêwa ê-itêyihtahk, êkoni ê-sipwêhtahikot. «êkos êkwa, êkota anima, êwakw ân[i] ânim îspatinâw, êkota anim ê-kî-itohtahicik anima, êkota ê-pîhtikwahicik; mîkiwâhp ê-isinamân, êkot[a] ê-pîhtikwê-~, aspin pikw êkota ê-pîhtikwêyâhk, mîkiwâhp ê-isinamân, êkotê ê-pîhtikwêyâhk; ê-pîhtikwêyâhk ôma mîkiwâhp, âyîtaw-iskwâht anita ê-apicik nâpêwak, êkota ohc ômis [*gesture*] ê-itapicik, ê-wâsakâmêpicik ôma mîkiwâhp, tâpiskôt kisêyiniwak kahkiyaw ê-têtipêwêpicik, nam âwiyak iskwêw,» ê-itwêt êsa.

[11] êkwa, «êkota êkwa, nêwo-tipiskâw ê-wâh-wâpani-nikamocik ôki kisêyiniwak, ê-kiskinohamawicik ôhi kîkway, êkos îsi ê-wî-kitimâkêyimicik ât[a] ê-kiskinohamawicik. êkwa, ita tita-wayawîyân êspayiki wâh-pakitinitwâw[i] ôki, êkonik ê-miywâtisicik ôki kisêyiniwak ôki wâh-pakitinitwâwi, nêk[i] êkwa nêtê, 'asonihk!' âtiht ôk ê-pîkiskwêcik, 'asonihk, asonihk! êkây

[8] Thus now, as the young woman was coming up to that tipi now, truly there was burning of incense for her and her father and mother greeted her, they greeted her. Thus she entered; thus she declared that the people should enter and that now she was about to tell her story.

[9] «Well,» she had said, it is said, «for four nights, it has been four nights that I have not been amongst humans; very strong indeed is the smell of humans, I already smell them,» she said, it is said, that woman had said, it is said. «I already smell humans; it seems as if their odour is strong for I have been away for four nights,» that woman said, it is said.

[10] Thus it was; it was at this point now, it is said, that she began to tell her story of what had happened; «They had abducted me, something coming and taking me away, I thought –~ they looked like humans to me, thus I gave in to them,» she said, it is said, as if they were men, she thought, those that took her away. «Thus then, it was there, that very hill, there they had taken me and there they took me inside; it looked like a lodge to me, as we went inside there, the moment we went inside there, it looked like a lodge to me, there we went inside; as we went inside that lodge, there were men sitting on either side of the entrance, there they sat like this [*gesture*], sitting in the round in that lodge, sitting in a full circle as if they were all old men, not a single woman,» she said, it is said.

[11] Now, "There then, for four nights these old men were singing ritual songs until dawn each night, teaching me these things, in this way they were going to take pity upon me, to be sure, by teaching them to me. Then, at the point where the time came for me to go outside, every time they were about to let me go, every time these good old men were about to let me go, some of those over yonder spoke, 'Take care to hold her!' said some of

pakitinihk, êkây pakitinihk êkos îsi ta-wayawîw! nipahihk, nipahihk!' ês ôk âyak, êkonik mâna kâ-itwêhk ê-macisicik nêhiyânâhk isi ê-wayêsîhkwastimiwêcik» ('mistahkêsiwak' k-êtihcik ôki, kâ-âkayâsîmohk *lion* [*?sic*], itowahk aniki mistahkêsiwak; kinwâyowêwak mân ânik ôtê [*gesture*], mis-~ misâyiwa ostikwâniwâwa, êkwa ôtê [*gesture*] wâhyaw isi osowâwa mâna piskwacâyiwa ôta [*gesture*], kikiskêyihtên, êkotowahk ôki, mâka ayisiyiniw[a] ê-isinawât awa nâ-~ aw îskwêw awa, kikiskêyihtên, ayisiyiniwak ê-itêyihtahkik [*sic*], ôma mîna, konit ê-isinamôhikot anima mîkiwâhp, môy tâpwê êkotowahk pîhc-âyihk êkota ê-ihtakohk anima.)

[12] êkos êkwa, «mwêhc êkwa ê-nêwo-tipiskâk, tahk[i] êkwa ê-wî-nipahicik ôki kotakak,» itwêw êsa, êkwa, «mwêhc êkwa ê-nêwo-tipiskâk, 'hâ, anohc êkwa, iskwayâc êkwa, êkwa kika-pakitinitinân ta-kîwêyan, ka-wayawîn êkwa. kikaskêyihtamihtâson tâpwê, itê ôma kâ-kî-pê-ohci-sipwêhtahitâhk,'» k-êtikot ôhi kisêyiniwa.

[13] êkwa, «êkota êkwa, mâk êkwa, ôma wî-wayawîyani, tânisi kiy-êsi-kîwêyan, hâw, nistam onâpêmiyani, kika-miyinân; tita-nipiw, nistam onâpêmiyani, awêkâ cî ocawâsimisiyani, tita-~ nistam ayâwaci ocawâsimisiyani, tita-nipiw; hâw, tân ânih êkoni nîso wâh-tôtaman? awa kicawâsimis cî kiwî-miyinân tita-nipit, awêkâ cî awa kinâpêm, nistam onâpêmiyani, tita-nipiw cî êwako?» – «êhaq,» k-êtwêt êsa, «môy wiya nitawâsimis,» k-êtwêt êsa, «ninâpêm, nistam onâpêmiyâni, êwako kimiyitinâwâw,» k-êtwêt ês âw îskwêw – «iyikohk ê-sêkisiyân, êkos êkwa ê-wî-nipahikawiyân, êkây êkoni wîh-mêkiyâni,» ê-itwêt ês ân[a] ôskinîkiskwêw.

[14] êkosi; «êkot[a] êkwa, êkota kâ-pakitinikawiyân ka-pê-wayawîyân,» kî-itwêw ês ân[a] ôskinîkiskwêw; «ê-mêkiyân

them, 'Take care to hold her! Take care to hold her! Do not let her go, do not let her go outside like this! Kill her, kill her!» said these ones, it is said, the ones of whom one says amongst the Crees that they are evil and deceive people in their sleep» (they are called *mistahkêsiwak*, in English the term is *lion* [*?sic*], these lions are of this kind; they have long tails over here [*gesture*], their heads are big, and then there [*gesture*] at the far end their tails end in a tuft here [*gesture*], you know, they are of that kind, but they looked like humans to this woman, you know, humans think that, and also this, they deceived her into perceiving it as that lodge, that place there was not in fact inside that kind).

[12] Now then, «Now when it was exactly the fourth night, all the time now these others were going to kill me,» she said, now, «exactly in the fourth night now, 'Ha, tonight is the last one, now we will let you go to return home, now you shall go outside. You truly have caused distress about you, over there whence we had taken you away to come here,'» is what these old men said to her.

[13] Then, «Now then, however, once you are about to go outside, how you might return home, well, when you first take a husband you shall give him to us; he is to die, when you first take a husband, or else when you have a child, when you first have a child, it is to die; well, which of these two are you going to surrender? Are you going to give us your first-born child for it to die or your husband, when you first take a husband, shall that one die?» – «Yes,» is what she said, it is said, «not my child,» is what she said, it is said, «my husband when I first take a husband, that one I give to you,» is what this woman said, it is said – «I was so frightened that I was now about to be killed unless I gave that one up,» this young woman said, it is said.

[14] Thus it was; «It was at that point now, it was at that point that I was let go to come outside there,» that young woman

nistam onâpêmiyâni, êkota, êkâ t-âyisiyinîwit, tita-nipit onâpêmiyâni. mâk âwa nitawâsimis, êwako nisâkihâw, môy êwako êkosi ninôhtê-tôtên, ta-mêkiyân; t-âsahkêyân anima, aniki nipit-~ nipitwâwi,» kî-itwêw ês ân[a] ôskinîkiskwêw. êkos ês ânim[a] êkotê ê-kî-itâcimot ana, an[a] ôskinîkiskwêw – îh, êwak ôhc ânima, ê-kî-mamâht-~ tâh-tâ-~, tâpwêwin êwak ôma k-âcimoyân, nôhkom ê-kî-pêhtawak mân êkos ê-kî-itâcimot.

[15] âstamispîhk ôtê nâtakâm, tânitê êtikwê mân ê-kî-ohci-picicik an[a] îskwêw, nôtikwêw ana, êkon ânihi mâna nôhkom ê-kî-nisitawêyimât anihi, «êwakw âw âw îskwêw, okâwiya kâ-kî-wanihimiht êkotê nakiwacîhk, kâ-kî-otinikoyit manitowa, êwakw âw âw ê-kî-oyôkâwît, 'picwêkan' kî-isiyîhkâsow an[a] ôskinîkiskwêw ana, kâ-kî-wanihiht êkotê nakiwacîhk,» ê-kî-itwêt mâna nôhkom.

[16] «êkosi mîna, nititikwak an[i] âta wiya ôki kâ-kî-otinicik,» itwêw ês âwa oskinîkiskwêw, «'kika-wâpistikwânân ani, kika-kêhtê-ayiwin,' nikî-itikwak,» kî-itwêw ês ân[a] ôskinîkiskwêw – êwako tâh-tâpwê mîn âcimowin, êkoyikohk iskohk kâ-pêhtawak nimos-~ nôhkom ê-kî-âcimot mâna, êwako nakiwacîhk anima. êwako mitoni mis-îspatinâw, 'manitow kâ-matwêhiket' isiyîhkâtêw ê-nêhiyawêhk. mâka êwakw ân[i] ânima, êkonik – mân ânihi kisêyiniwa k-êtihtawât, anihi k-êsinawât an[a] îskwêw, êkonik êtikw âniki mân êkota anihi ê-kî-matwêhwâcik, ê-kî-pêhtâht êsa mâna k-ât-ôtâ-~ k-ât[i]-ôtâkosik êkotê ana, ê-matwêhoht ana kîkway êkotê. êwak ôhc ânima kâ-isiyîhkâtêk ispatinâw, 'manitow kâ-matwêhikêt'; mâk âstamispîhk êkwa êkotê ê-mihcêticik ayisiyiniwak, wâskahikana ê-astêki, môy wîhkâc kîkway ohci-pêhtâkwan.

had said, it is said; «I gave up my first husband, at that point, that he would not live, that he would die when I married him. But my child, that one I do treasure, I did not want to do that to that one, that I would give it up; that I would yield it up to be eaten once one or the other of them dies,» that young woman did say, it is said.. Thus, it is said, she had told her story over there, that young woman – look, that is why this was strange –~ it is a true story that I have been telling, in this way I used to hear my grandmother tell it.

[15] Later on over there up north, I do not know from where that woman used to travel with her household, that old woman, my grandmother did recognise her, «That is the woman whose mother had been lost over there at *Nakiwacîhk*, whom the spirits had abducted, this one used to have her as her mother, *Picwêkan* had been the name of that young woman who had been lost over there at *Nakiwacîhk*,» my grandmother used to say.

[16] «Thus also they had said to me, however, those who had abducted me,» the young woman said, it is said, «'You shall indeed live to see your hair turn white, you shall grow to be an old woman,' they had said to me,» that young woman had said, it is said – and this, too, is a true story through and through, that is all I had usually heard my grandfa-~ my grandmother tell of that story about *Nakiwacîhk*. That really big hill is called *Manitow kâ-matwêhikêt* in Cree. But it is that place, the ones – she thought they sounded like old men, the ones that woman thought looked like old men, they must have been the ones who used to beat that medicine drum there, when it used to be heard, it is said, in the early evening over there, when that thing was being beaten over there. That is why the hill is called *Manitow kâ-matwêhikêt*; but more recently now many people live over there, there are houses standing there, and never has anything been heard.

[17] mâk êkwa mîskot mîna, anima waciy, nakiwaciy, kâ-tip-~ kâ-tipiskâk ôma, ê-kî-pêhtâkwahk mân ânima waciy, 'hoššš' tâpiskôc ê-itwêhk, tâpiskôc ê-yôtik, êkosi mân ê-kî-isi-pêhtahkik; kâ-wa-wayawîhk ôma kâ-tipiskâk, êkosi mâna ê-kî-itihtâkwahk anima. êkwa wiyawâw kî-itwêwak mân âyisiyiniwak, «ê-wî-yôtik anima, êwako k-ôh-itihtâkwahk ôma waciy,» kî-itwêwak mâna. kî-nakayâskikâtêw, êwakw ânim ê-kî-pêhtamihk mâna, «ê-wî-yôtik, êwak ôhc ôma k-ôh-pêhtâkwahk waciy,» kî-itwêwak mâna.

[18] âstamispîhk ôta, êkos ânim êkwa kî-sîkawîwak ayisiyiniwak, pêc[i] êkwa tahkohtâmatin, misiwê âstamitê, êkot[ê] êkwa mêkwâc ayisiyiniwak kâ-mihcêticik ôma kâ-wîkicik. âstamispîhk pêyakw-âyi (nama kîkway wâskahikan sôskwâc êkw êkota kî-astêw nîhc-âyihk nêtê, itê ayisiyiniwak kâ-kî-wîkicik), âstamispîhk pêyakw-âyi, wâskahikanis êkotê kî-nitaw-ôsîhtâwak, konita pikinik [*sic*] mâna tâpiskôc, êkos îsi êkotê ê-nitaw-âyâcik, k-âyamihêwikîsikâk. êwakw ân[a] âna nâpêw êkota pêyak êsa kî-pa-pêyakow nîpinohk, êwakw âna nikî-pêhtawâw, «kêyâpic anima mâna waciy ês ânim ê-pêhtâkwahk, anima mâna kâ-kî-itihtâkwahk, kêyâpic nipêhtên têpiskâki, kîtahtawê ê-pêhtâkwahk êwakw ânima waciy,» nititâcimostâk êwakw ân[a] âna nâpêw êkota kâ-kî-ay-ayât. êkosi wiy êwakw ânim êkoyikohk iskohk nikîsîhtân.

[17] But then again, in return, that hill, that *nakiwaciy*, at night that hill used to be heard as if one said *hošš̌š̌*, as if there were a wind gust, that is what they used to hear; when one went outside at night, that is the noise one used to hear. And the people themselves used to say, «It is going to be windy, that is why this hill is heard to make that noise,» they used to say. People used to get accustomed to it, as they used to hear that, «It is going to be windy, that is why this hill is heard,» they used to say.

[18] More recently here, in this way the people now deserted that place [*sc.* the river flats], coming to the top of the hill, all over this side, over there is where people nowadays live in great numbers. More recently one couple (now there are practically no houses at all standing down over yonder, where the people used to live), more recently one couple had gone and built a little house over there, more or less like a picnic-shelter, and in this way they simply went to stay there on a Sunday. That man lived there alone, it is said, last summer, and I have heard that one say, «That hill can still be heard, it is said, as its sound used to be heard, I still hear it at night, sometimes that hill can be heard,» the man who had stayed there told me. Thus I have finished it, all of that story.

Sarah Whitecalf and Freda Ahenakew in Winnipeg, August 1988.

FREDA AHENAKEW, founding Director of the Saskatchewan Indian Languages Institute, earned her MA in Cree linguistics at the University of Manitoba. In 1997 she was awarded an honorary doctorate by the University of Saskatchewan. She was made a member of the Order of Canada in 1998.

SARAH WHITECALF is the author of an earlier volume of Cree texts:

kinêhiyâwiwininaw nêhiyawêwin / The Cree Language is Our Identity: The La Ronge Lectures of Sarah Whitecalf, edited, translated and with a glossary by H.C. Wolfart and Freda Ahenakew. Publications of the Algonquian Text Society / Collection de la Société d'édition de textes algonquiens. Winnipeg: University of Manitoba Press, 1993.

TED WHITECALF is the author's son and a professional photographer. As the founder of Sweet Grass Records / Productions in Saskatoon he has created a substantial catalogue of indigenous music and many collections of portraits accompanied by brief autobiographies.

H.C. WOLFART has been committed to the analysis of the Cree language since his student days, always with a focus on grammatical structures and the literary tradition. He is University Distinguished Professor Emeritus of Linguistics at the University of Manitoba.

FURTHER PLAINS CREE TEXT EDITIONS BY F. AHENAKEW AND H.C. WOLFART

Alice Ahenakew

âh-âyitaw isi ê-kî-kiskêyihtahkik maskihkiy / They Knew Both Sides of Medicine: Cree Tales of Curing and Cursing Told by Alice Ahenakew, edited, translated and with a glossary by H.C. Wolfart and Freda Ahenakew. Publications of the Algonquian Text Society / Collection de la Société d'édition de textes algonquiens. Winnipeg: University of Manitoba Press, 2000.

Glecia Bear, Irene Calliou, Janet Feitz, Minnie Fraser, Alpha Lafond, Rosa Longneck and Mary Wells

kôhkominawak otâcimowiniwâwa / Our Grandmothers' Lives as Told in Their Own Words, told by Glecia Bear *et al.*, edited and translated by Freda Ahenakew and H.C. Wolfart. Saskatoon: Fifth House Publishers, 1992. [reprinted with a new preface, Canadian Plains Resarch Center, Regina, 1998]

Kâ-mimikwatowêt / William Greyeyes
'The Travelling Companion, told by *Kâ-mimikwatowêt* / William Greyeyes,' edited and translated by H.C. Wolfart and Freda Ahenakew. *in:* H.C. Wolfart, 'Two Plains Cree Performances of a pre-Victorian *Kunstmärchen*,' Appendix, pp. 177-215, *Anthropological Linguistics* 56(2):159-218, 2014.

Kâ-pimwêwêhahk / Jim Kâ-Nîpitêhtêw
ana kâ-pimwêwêhahk okakêskihkêmowina / The Counselling Speeches of Jim Kâ-Nîpitêhtêw, edited, translated and with a glossary by Freda Ahenakew and H.C. Wolfart. Publications of the Algonquian Text Society / Collection de la Société d'édition de textes algonquiens. Winnipeg: University of Manitoba Press, 1998.

Kêkêk / Cecilia Masuskapoe
piko kîkway ê-nakacihtât: kêkêk otâcimowina ê-nêhiyawastêki, mitoni ê-âh-itwêt mâna Cecilia Masuskapoe, itasinahamiyiwa ôhi nîso, H.C. Wolfart êkwa Freda Ahenakew [There's Nothing She Can't Do: Kêkêk's Autobiography Published in Cree, exactly as told by Cecilia Masuskapoe, in a critical edition by H.C. Wolfart and Freda Ahenakew]. Algonquian and Iroquoian Linguistics Memoir 21. Winnipeg, 2010.

Emma Minde
kwayask ê-kî-pê-kiskinowâpahtihicik / Their Example Showed Me the Way: A Cree Woman's Life Shaped by Two Cultures, told by Emma Minde, edited, translated and with a glossary by F. Ahenakew and H.C. Wolfart. Edmonton: University of Alberta Press, 1997.

Joseph Tootoosis
'John Beaverbone's Story as Retold by Joseph Tootoosis,' edited and translated by Freda Ahenakew & H.C. Wolfart. *in:* H.C. Wolfart, ed., *Linguistic Studies Presented to John L. Finlay*, pp. 1-12, Algonquian and Iroquoian Linguistics Memoir 8. Winnipeg, 1991.

Peter Vandall and Joe Douquette
wâskahikaniwiyiniw-âcimowina / Stories of the House People, told by Peter Vandall and Joe Douquette, edited, translated and with a glossary by Freda Ahenakew. Publications of the Algonquian Text Society / Collection de la Société d'édition de textes algonquiens. Winnipeg: University of Manitoba Press, 1987.